T0350259

Data Warehouses and OLAP: Concepts, Architectures and Solutions

Robert Wrembel
Poznań University of Technology, Poland

Christian Koncilia
Panoratio GmbH, Germany

IRM Press

Publisher of innovative scholarly and professional infor-
mation technology titles in the cyberage

Hershey • London • Melbourne • Singapore

Acquisitions Editor:	Kristin Klinger
Development Editor:	Kristin Roth
Senior Managing Editor:	Jennifer Neidig
Managing Editor:	Sara Reed
Assistant Managing Editor:	Sharon Berger
Copy Editor:	April Schmidt
Typesetter:	Diane Huskinson
Cover Design:	Lisa Tosheff
Printed at:	Integrated Book Technology

Published in the United States of America by
IRM Press (an imprint of Idea Group Inc.)
701 E. Chocolate Avenue, Suite 200
Hershey PA 17033-1240
Tel: 717-533-8845
Fax: 717-533-8661
E-mail: cust@idea-group.com
Web site: http://www.irm-press.com

and in the United Kingdom by
IRM Press (an imprint of Idea Group Inc.)
3 Henrietta Street
Covent Garden
London WC2E 8LU
Tel: 44 20 7240 0856
Fax: 44 20 7379 0609
Web site: http://www.eurospanonline.com

Copyright © 2007 by Idea Group Inc. All rights reserved. No part of this book may be reproduced, stored or distributed in any form or by any means, electronic or mechanical, including photocopying, without written permission from the publisher.

Product or company names used in this book are for identification purposes only. Inclusion of the names of the products or companies does not indicate a claim of ownership by IGI of the trademark or registered trademark.

Library of Congress Cataloging-in-Publication Data

Data warehouses and OLAP : concepts, architectures, and solutions / Robert Wrembel and Christian Koncilia, editors.
    p. cm.
  Summary: "This book provides an insight into important research and technological problems, solutions, and development trends in the field of data warehousing and OLAP. It also serves as an up-to-date bibliography of published works for anyone interested in cutting-edge DW and OLAP issues"--Provided by publisher.
  Includes bibliographical references and index.
  ISBN 1-59904-364-5 (hardcover) -- ISBN 1-59904-365-3 (softcover) -- ISBN 1-59904-366-1 (ebook)
  1. Data warehousing. 2. OLAP technology. I. Wrembel, Robert. II. Koncilia, Christian, 1969-
  QA76.9.D37D392 2007
  005.74--dc22
                        2006027721British Cataloguing in Publication Data

A Cataloguing in Publication record for this book is available from the British Library.

All work contributed to this book is new, previously-unpublished material. The views expressed in this book are those of the authors, but not necessarily of the publisher.

Data Warehouses and OLAP: Concepts, Architectures and Solutions

Table of Contents

Foreword

Data warehouse systems have become a key component of the corporate information system architecture, in which they play a crucial role in building business decision support systems. By collecting and consolidating data from a variety of enterprise internal and external sources, data warehouses try to provide a homogeneous information basis for enterprise planning and decision making. We have recently witnessed a rapid growth both in the number of data warehousing products and services offered as well as in the acceptance of these technologies by industry. Within recent years, data warehouses have faced a tremendous shift from simple centralized repositories used to store cash-register transactions to a platform for data integration, federation, and sophisticated data analysis. Nowadays, data warehousing technologies are successfully used in many industries including retail, manufacturing, financial services, banking, telecommunication, healthcare, and so forth.

Data warehousing technology is currently a very active field of research. Research problems associated with creating, maintaining, and using data warehouse technology are partially similar to those specific for database systems. In fact, a data warehouse can be considered as "large" database system with additional functionality. However, the well-known problems of index selection, data partitioning, materialized view maintenance, data integration, query optimization, have received renewed attention in warehousing research. Some research problems are specific to data warehousing: data acquisition and data cleaning, data warehouse refreshment, evolution of data warehouse schema, multidimensional and parallel query optimization, conceptual modeling for the data warehouses, data quality management, and so forth. This book addresses all the above mentioned issues in the area of data warehousing from multiple perspectives, in the form of individual contributions written by prominent data warehouse technology researchers, and it also outlines new trends and future challenges in the context of next generation data warehouse systems.

In reading the book, I was impressed by how much the field of data warehousing has advanced and matured. The book describes different aspects of data warehousing technology and gives an insight into important research, technological, and practical problems and solutions related to the data warehousing technology. The content of the book covers fundamental aspects of data warehousing technology such as the conceptual modeling and design of data warehouse systems, data warehouse refreshment, query optimization, indexes, integration of the data warehouse technology with data mining techniques, and, finally, new trends in data warehousing such as temporal semistructured data models and spatial online analytical processing.

I am pleased to recommend this book to the readers. If you are a researcher, a data warehouse developer, or just a keen reader wishing to understand important aspects of data warehouses and their potential, you will find that this book provides both a solid technical background and state-of-the-art knowledge on this interesting and important topic. The book is a valuable source of information for academics and practitioners who are interested in learning the key ideas in the field of data warehousing. This book is likely to become a standard reference in the field of data warehousing for many years.

Tadeusz Morzy
Poznań University of Technology, Poland
June 2006

Preface

Nowadays the economy is characterized by fast and continuously changing markets and business opportunities. Therefore, in order to be successful, it is essential for an enterprise to make right business decisions and to make them fast. Business decisions are taken on the basis of analyses of the past and current condition of an enterprise as well as market analysis and predictions for the future. To this end, various business operational data collected during the lifetime of an enterprise are analyzed. Typically, operational data are stored within an enterprise in multiple data storage systems (subsystems) that are geographically distributed, are heterogeneous and autonomous.

The heterogeneity of data storage systems means that they come from different software vendors; they are implemented in different technologies (e.g., C, C++, .Net, Java, 4th generation programming languages); they offer different functionality (e.g., fully-functional databases, ODBC data sources, spreadsheets, Web pages, text files); they use different data models (e.g., relational, object-relational, object-oriented, semistructured) and different storage techniques; they are installed on different operating systems and use different communication protocols.

The autonomy of data storage systems implies that they are often independent from each other and remain under separate, independent control; that is, a local system's administrator can decide which local data are to be accessible from the outside of the system.

The management of an enterprise requires a comprehensive view of all aspects of a company, thus it requires access to all possible data of interest stored in multiple subsystems. However, an analysis of data stored in distributed, heterogeneous, and autonomous subsystems is likely to be difficult, slow, and inefficient. Therefore, the ability to integrate information from multiple data sources is crucial for today's business.

Data Warehouse and OLAP

One of the most important approaches to the integration of data sources is based on a *data warehouse* architecture. In this architecture, data coming from multiple external data sources (EDSs) are extracted, filtered, merged, and stored in a central repository, called a data warehouse (DW). Data are also enriched by historical and summary information. From a technological point of view, a data warehouse is a huge database from several hundred GB to several dozens of TB. Thanks to this architecture, users operate on a local, homogeneous, and centralized data repository that reduces access time to data. Moreover, a data warehouse is independent of EDSs that may be temporarily unavailable. However, a data warehouse has to be kept up to date with respect to the content of EDSs, by being periodically refreshed.

The content of a DW is analyzed by the so called online analytical processing (OLAP) applications for the purpose of discovering trends, patterns of behavior, and anomalies as well as for finding hidden dependencies between data. The outcomes of these analyses are then the basis for making various business decisions. The market analysis of demand and supply is one of important steps in taking strategic decisions in a company. Likewise, an analysis of the development and course of diseases as well as the impact of different medications on the course of illnesses is indispensable in order to choose the most efficient methods of treatment. Many other applications include, among others: stock market, banking, insurance, energy management, and science. Data warehouses and OLAP applications are core components of decision support systems.

Since the late 1980s, when the data warehouse technology developed, most of large and midsize companies worldwide have been building their own DWs into their information system infrastructures and have been successfully applying this technology in business. Major commercially available database management systems (e.g., Oracle9i/10g, IBM DB2 UDB, Sybase IQ, Computer Associates CleverPath OLAP, NCR Teradata Database, Hyperion Essbase OLAP Server, MS SQL Server, SAP Business Warehouse, SAS Enterprise BI Server) include the DW and OLAP technologies in their database engines. However, despite some substantial achievements in this technology, it still is and will be a very active research and technological field. The OLAPReport (2004) estimates that the total worldwide OLAP market constantly grew from less than $1 billion in 1994 to less than $5 billion in 2005, and it will grow up to $6 billion in 2007. The META Group's (currently Gartner) survey estimates that the OLAP market will be worth almost $10 billion in 2008 (EDWMarket, 2004). For these reasons, it is important to understand the core technological issues and challenges in the field of DW and OLAP.

Technological and Research Challenges

The size of a DW, high complexity of OLAP queries as well as the heterogeneous nature of integrated data pose serious research and technological challenges. Intensive research is conducted in several fields, that include, among others: schema design methodology and implementation models, data loading and DW refreshing techniques, efficient query processing, metadata management, and data quality issues (cf. Nguyen, Tjoa, & Trujillo, 2005).

A DW is designed for quick data retrieval by ad-hoc queries. These queries often compute aggregates based on other aggregates by rolling them up or they analyze details by drilling the aggregates down. Moreover, data are analyzed in the context of other data, for example, the monthly sales of products by particular shops. In order to support such kinds of analytical queries, a DW typically uses a multidimensional data model (Gyssens & Lakshmanan, 1997). In this model, facts representing elementary data being the subject of analysis are organized in n-dimensional spaces, called data cubes.

An n-dimensional data cube can be implemented either in MOLAP servers or in ROLAP servers. In the former case, a cube is stored either in a multidimensional array or in a hash table (e.g., SQL Server) or as the value of a binary large object (e.g., Oracle) or as another specialized data structure like Quad tree or K-D tree. In the latter case, a cube is implemented as the set of relational tables, some of them represent dimensions, and are called dimension tables, while others store values of measures, and are called fact tables. Two basic types of ROLAP schemas are used for an implementation of a cube, that is, a star schema and a snowflake schema (Chaudhuri & Dayal, 1997). The efficiency of executing OLAP queries strongly depends on an implementation data model and the type of the ROLAP schema used. Therefore, a lot of work is being spent on developing DW design methods (e.g., Adamson & Venerable, 1998; Kimball, Reeves, Ross, & Thornthwaite, 1998; Luján-Mora & Trujillo, 2004) and on modeling dimensions (e.g., Hurtado & Mendelzon, 2002; Letz, Henn & Vossen, 2002).

Having designed and implemented a DW one has to load it with data. The process of loading data into a DW is organized into several steps that include: (1) reading data from data sources, (2) transforming data into a common data model, (3) cleansing data in order to remove inconsistencies, duplicates, and null values, (4) integrating cleansed data into one set, (5) computing summaries, and (6) loading data into a DW. This process, called ETL (Extraction, Translation/Transformation, Loading), is executed by a software layer located between data sources and a DW (Kimball & Caserta, 2004; Simitsis, Vassiliadis, Terrovitis, & Skiadopoulos, 2005). The software includes: monitors that are responsible for detecting and reading changes in data sources, wrappers that are responsible for transforming a source data model into a common DW model as well as an integrator that is responsible for integrating data, cleansing them and loading them into a DW (Widom, 1995).

The initial loading into an empty DW reads all data of interest from EDSs and stores them in a DW. As the data sources are operational systems that are used everyday, their content changes frequently. As a consequence, the content of a DW becomes obsolete and has to be refreshed. A data warehouse is often implemented as the collection of materialized views, thus the problem of a DW refreshing transforms to the problem of maintaining and refreshing materialized views. This problem has been extensively investigated by the research community (Gupta & Mumick, 1999; Roussopoulos, 1998) and has resulted in multiple algorithms for refreshing materialized views. Typically, refreshing a materialized view is a costly task. In order to optimize it, multiple incremental refreshing techniques have been proposed. They can be categorized as refreshing with accessing data sources (e.g., Ceri & Widom, 1991) as well as self-maintainable refreshing (e.g., Samtani, Kumar, & Mohania, 1999). In the latter case, additional data structures are stored in a DW along with materialized views in order to eliminate the need of accessing data sources.

The process of refreshing a materialized view is usually executed concurrently with transactions on data sources and with user analytical queries. Such concurrent executions may result in inconsistent data stored in materialized views and erroneous results of analytical queries. Multiple solutions for avoiding these problems have been developed, that is, recomputing a view from scratch, applying compensation algorithms, maintaining versions of views, using additional data structures and transactions (e.g., Gupta & Mumick, 1999; Quass & Widom, 1997; Zhuge, Garcia-Molina & Wiener, 1996). Yet another problem is related to maintaining consistency of multiple dependent views during the process of their refreshment (e.g., Colby, Kawaguchi, Lieuwen, Mumick, & Ross, 1997; Zhuge, Wiener, & Garcia-Molina, 1997).

OLAP applications analyze data by means of complex queries ranging from a few to dozens operations of joining, filtering, grouping, and aggregating. Since these queries are very complex and they often read terabytes of data, their execution may take dozens of minutes, hours, or even days. Therefore, a key issue is the data warehouse efficiency. Well developed solutions to this problem are based on materialized views and query rewriting as well as on advanced index structures.

A challenging issue within the first solution concerns the selection of such a set of materialized views that: (1) will be used for optimizing the greatest possible number of the most expensive queries and (2) whose maintenance will not be costly. Several research works have addressed this problem and they have proposed multiple algorithms for selecting optimal sets of materialized views for a given query workload (e.g., de Sousa & Sampaio, 1999; Gupta, 1997; Theodoratos & Xu, 2004).

A specific characteristic of OLAP queries that typically join fact tables with multiple dimension tables as well as a specific distribution of values in fact tables requires different indexing schemes. Three kinds of indexes have been developed in order to optimize OLAP queries, namely, join indexes, bitmap indexes, and bitmap join indexes (e.g., Aouiche, Darmont, & Boussaïd, 2005; O'Neil & Graefe, 1995; Valduriez, 1987; Wu, Otoo, & Shoshani, 2004). The efficiency of executing OLAP queries can also be increased by parallel processing and data partitioning techniques (e.g., Furtado, 2004; Rao, Zhang, Magiddo, & Lohman, 2002; Stöhr & Rahm, 2001).

The ETL and refreshing processes may insert erroneous or inconsistent data into a DW. As a consequence, user analyses will produce confusing or wrong results. That, in turn, may result in disastrous business decisions made by decision makers. For these reasons, research focused also on measuring and assuring data quality (e.g., Jarke, Jeusfeld, Quix, & Vassiliadis, 1998; Vassiliadis, Bouzeghoub, & Quix, 1999).

For a long period of time, the existing DW technologies have tacitly assumed that a DW is time invariant; that is, its schema and the structure of dimensions do not change during a DW lifetime. In practice, however, a DW structure changes as the result of the evolution of EDSs (Rundensteiner, Koeller, & Zhang, 2000), changes of the real world represented by a DW, new user requirements, as well as the creation of simulation environments, to list the most common cases. Several approaches to handling changes in DWs have been developed. They are categorized as supporting DW evolution (e.g., Blaschka, Sapia, & Höfling, 1999), temporal extensions (e.g., Hurtado, Mendelson, & Vaisman, 1999; Eder, Koncilia, & Morzy, 2002), simulation (e.g., Balmin, Papadimitriou, & Papakonstanitnou, 2000) as well as versioning (e.g., Body, Miquel, Bédard, & Tchounikine, 2002; Golfarelli, Lechtenbörger, Rizzi, & Vossen, 2004; Morzy & Wrembel, 2004).

In order to work properly and efficiently, all the above mentioned issues and techniques need to use metadata. Managing various types of metadata in DWs also has received a lot of attention resulting in widely accepted industry standard CWM (OMG, 2003; Vetterli, Vaduva, & Staudt, 2000), supported by major DW software vendors.

Despite the continuous development in the data warehousing technology that has lasted fore more than 20 years, it is still a very active area of research. Although most of the discussed research and technological achievements have been incorporated into various commercial database/data warehouse management systems, the discussed issues are still being investigated and the already implemented technologies are being further improved.

Further Development Directions

The already mature technologies discussed in the previous section are continuously being developed but new areas of research and new challenges appear on the scene. These new issues come from various novel information technologies applied to real business.

Nowadays, huge amounts of data are stored in various Web systems, typically in the XML format. These data are crucial for business and, therefore, there is a need to analyze them in a similar way as in traditional DWs. This requirement led to several attempts to build data warehouses from Web data sources (e.g., Golfarelli, Rizzi, & Vrdoljak, 2001) and to provide OLAP functionality for XML documents (e.g., Nassis, Rajugan, Dillon, & Rahayu, 2005; Park, Han, & Song, 2005).

Advanced image processing technologies make the use of images and maps easier and more common, for example, Google Maps and NASA Earth Observing System Data and Information System (EOSDIS). In order to use information hidden in this kind of data a user needs a technology that combines the functionality of Geographical Information Systems with the functionality of data warehouses and OLAP. To this end, the so called Spatial OLAP systems are being developed (e.g., Stefanovic, Han, & Koperski, 2000).

Last but not least, our environment is becoming gradually filled with different kinds of sensors, for example, monitoring the intensity of traffic, controlling physical parameters of technological processes, and monitoring patients' vital signs. Sensors produce streams of data that have to be analyzed, often online. Stream data arrive also from other sources, for example, a click-stream form on the Internet, shares from a stock market, and transmission signals in telecommunications. Stream data are characterized by a continuous flow, requiring huge storage space. In order to reduce the space, historical data are stored as summaries or samples. Typically, incoming stream data need to be continuously analyzed. This leads to challenges in (1) querying streams online, (2) querying both historical summarized/sampled data and just incoming data, as well as (3) quickly accessing data, that is, indexing. Some substantial achievements have already been done in this area and some attempts have been made towards implementing DWs for stream data (Stream, 2006).

As it can be clearly observed, there are multiple kinds of data warehouses (relational, XML, spatial, stream) storing data of different formats and offering different functionality. Users of these technologies are often interested in combining data coming from multiple DWs. This requirement leads to the problem of integrating heterogeneous DWs (Torlone & Panella, 2005).

Book Objectives

The goal of this book is to provide an insight into important research and technological problems, solutions, and development trends in the field of data warehousing and OLAP. The content of the book encompasses important aspects of these technologies, from a DW designing and implementing, via data integration, loading, and DW refreshing, advanced query optimization techniques, to new areas of DW application. As such, the book:

- Provides the current state of the research and technology in the aforementioned domains,

- Constitutes a resource of possible solutions and technologies that can be applied when designing, implementing, and deploying a DW, and

- Serves as an up-to-date bibliography of published works for anyone interested in cutting-edge DW and OLAP issues.

Since the book covers a wide range of technical, technological, and research issues concerning DW and OLAP technologies, it is intended for data warehouse designers, administrators, programmers, and project managers. It offers them a better understanding of challenges, possible solutions, and advanced applications of these technologies. Moreover, technical aspects covered in the book will suit the contents of many DW courses offered at universities both in Europe and in the U.S. For this reason, the book can be a useful resource for students as well.

Structure of the Book

The body of the book consists of 13 chapters divided into four sections. Each of the sections addresses a particular research and technological area, namely:

- Modeling and designing,
- Loading and refreshing,
- Efficiency of analytical processing, and
- Advanced technologies and applications.

Section I addresses issues concerning one of the initial steps in the whole life cycle of a data warehouse, namely, requirements analysis, conceptual modeling, and designing. This section consists of three chapters.

Chapter I, *Conceptual Modeling Solutions for the Data Warehouse*, by Stefano Rizzi, focuses on a conceptual modeling that provides abstract representations of warehousing process, data structures, and architectures. The aim of conceptual modeling is to assure that a model is independent of an implementation. The author concentrates on a conceptual graphical model called the *dimensional fact model* (DFM) that was developed to support multidimensional modeling. The representation of the reality constructed using the DFM consists of the set of *fact schemata*. The basic concepts of the model include facts, measures, dimensions, and hierarchies. The DFM suits the variety of modeling situations that may be encountered in real projects of small to large complexity. The chapter provides a comprehensive set of solutions for conceptual modeling according to the DFM and serves a DW designer as a practical guide for applying different modeling solutions. The chapter provides also a foundation for the rest of the book as it discusses fundamental concepts used in the DW technology, among others: multidimensional modeling; dimensions and their attributes; and shared, incomplete, recursive, and dynamic hierarchies.

Chapter II, *Handling Structural Heterogeneity in OLAP*, by Carlos A. Hurtado and Claudio Gutierrez, goes beyond the DFM model and it focuses on modeling dimensions that may have different structures; that is, they are heterogeneous. Such dimensions are created as the result of mixing multiple dimensions with different structures into a single dimension. In the chapter, the authors show how to incorporate structural heterogeneity in the design of OLAP models, explain why structural heterogeneity weakens aggregate navigation, survey different techniques to deal with heterogeneity, present a class of dimension integrity constraints to model structural heterogeneity, and demonstrate the practical application of dimension constraints to support aggregate navigation.

Chapter III, *Data Quality-Based Requirements Elicitation for Decision Support Systems*, by Alejandro Vaisman, presents a DW design method that supports complete and consistent elicitation of functional and nonfunctional requirements. Functional requirements take into consideration queries issued in applications, whereas nonfunctional requirements comprise data structures and data quality. The author argues that traditional design methods for requirements elicitation are inappropriate in the field of decision support systems, and presents the so called DSS-METRIQ method. The outcomes of the method are the set of requirement documents and the specification of the operational data sources that can satisfy user requirements. The chapter contains also the state-of-the-art in the field of requirements elicitation and design methods.

Section II addresses the problems related to loading data into a data warehouse and keeping the content of a DW up to date. This section is composed of two chapters.

Chapter IV, *Extraction, Transformation, and Loading Processes*, by Jovanka Adzic, Valter Fiore, and Luisella Sisto, is an experience report on the application of the ETL process to real world cases. The main focus of this chapter is on designing ETL processes for high data loading frequency, for large volumes of loaded data, and for complex data processing/transformations. In this context, the authors identify the most common critical issues and constraints that have an impact on designing the ETL processes. As the ETL design solution, the authors propose to apply a layered infrastructure. The infrastructure is composed of typically used functionalities and services in the ETL scenario and it is a basis for building various applications. The infrastructure includes, among others: DBMS access modules, file access modules, parallel read/write modules, and data processing modules. The authors also discuss and give practical suggestions on implementation issues including database partitioning options, parallel processing, and pipelining in the context of ETL.

Chapter V, *Data Warehouse Refreshment*, by Alkis Simitsis, Panos Vassiliadis, Spiros Skiadopoulos, and Timos Sellis, focuses on methods for designing efficient workflows of tasks within ETL processes. The features that make ETL challenging include, among others: huge data volumes, assuring the quality of data, assuring high performance, adapting workflows after changes in data sources, and changes in a data warehouse itself. As a response to these challenges, the authors propose a modeling approach/framework and its examplary application for the construction of ETL workflows. This approach is based on the life cycle of the ETL processes. The life cycle consists of four phases: reverse engineering and requirements collection; logical design; tuning and physical design; and software construction. The aim of the presented framework is to facilitate, manage, and optimize the design and implementation of the ETL workflows in order to create an optimal workflow. The framework supports all the phases of ETL design, from the initial design to a deployment stage and utilization, under continuous evolution of a data warehouse. The chapter contains also a comprehensive state of the art on commercially available tools and research achievements in the field of ETL.

Section III describes challenges and solutions to the problem of assuring the efficiency of analytical processing. Fundamental research and technological solutions to this problem include optimization techniques of star queries, indexing, partitioning, and clustering.

Chapter VI, *Advanced Ad Hoc Star Query Processing*, by Nikos Karayannidis, Aris Tsois, and Timos Sellis, focuses on efficient processing of OLAP queries. OLAP applications rely heavily on the so called star queries that join fact tables with multiple dimension tables. Reducing execution time of such joins is crucial for a DW performance. To this end, a new approach to fact table organization has been developed, called a hierarchical clustering. The hierarchical clustering allows clustering of fact data according to paths in dimension hierarchies. This clustering technique exploits path-based surrogate keys. In the context of hierarchical clustering, star query processing changes radically. In this chapter, the authors present a complete abstract processing plan that captures all the necessary steps in evaluating star queries over hierarchically clustered fact tables. Furthermore, the authors discuss issues on optimizing star queries within the context of the abstract processing plan and they define the abstract operations in terms of physical operations over the CUBE File data structure.

Chapter VII, *Bitmap Indices for Data Warehouses*, by Kurt Stockinger and Kesheng Wu, overviews the issues related to a special kind of index used for optimizing OLAP queries, namely, the bitmap index. Typically, bitmap indexes work well for attributes of low cardinality since the indexes are small for such atrributes. The higher cardinality of an indexed attribute, the larger size of a bitmap index. In order to reduce the sizes of bitmap indexes various techniques are used. This chapter overviews such techniques, namely, encoding, compression, and binning and it focuses on a particular compression technique called a word-aligned-hybrid compression.

Moreover, the authors present multiple experimental results comparing different encoding techniques and showing the characteristics of the word-aligned-hybrid compression. The results indicate that for high cardinality attributes compressed bitmap indexes also offer good index characteristics with respect to their sizes and query response times.

Chapter VIII, *Indexing in Data Warehouses: Bitmaps and Beyond*, by Karen C. Davis and Ashima Gupta, elaborates further on the issues presented in Chapter VII. In this chapter the authors focus on an alternative encoding technique that is based not only on values of indexed attributes but also on an additional knowledge derived from queries. This knowledge is used for constructing the so called property maps, each of which describes properties of indexed attributes. The characteristics of property maps with respect to query processing is the main contribution of this chapter. Additionally, the chapter contains a concise overview of different kinds of bitmap indexes.

Chapter IX, *Efficient and Robust Node-Partitioned Data Warehouses*, by Pedro Furtado, addresses the problem of running large data warehouses efficiently on low cost platforms. In order to achieve this goal, the author proposes to partition a data warehouse over multiple servers (nodes) in a network. Such a partitioning may cause other challenges in assuring data availability as well as distributed analytical query optimization. In this chapter the author shows how to use replicas for the purpose of designing a robust data warehouse partitioning strategy that guarantees efficient OLAP processing and data availability. The author also concentrates on data partitioning strategies as well as on efficient parallel join processing and query transformations.

Chapter X, *OLAP with a Database Cluster*, by Uwe Röhm, presents clustered data warehouse architecture as an alternative to the approach discussed in Chapter IX. The clustered architecture is based on a cluster of commercial off-the-shelf computers as hardware infrastructure that run off-the-shelf database management systems as transactional storage managers. In this architecture, the same data may be distributed over several nodes by using replication mechanisms. As a consequence, some replicas may be out of date. In order to handle queries on outdated data, the author proposes an approach to replication management, called freshness-aware scheduling, that introduces a new quality-of-service parameter. This parameter allows the specification of an explicit freshness limit in queries having an impact on replicas used in these queries. Based on the value of quality-of-service a query may be routed to the most appropriate node. Multiple query routing strategies and physical data design alternatives are also discussed in this chapter.

Section IV focuses on new domains for applying the data warehouse and OLAP technologies. These novel domains pose new challenges, among others in data modeling techniques, assuring analytical processing efficiency as well as in data storage/organization techniques.

Chapter XI, *Towards Integrating Data Warehousing with Data Mining Techniques*, by Rokia Missaoui, Ganaël Jatteau, Ameur Boujenoui, and Sami Naouali, addresses problems and presents solutions for coupling data warehousing and data mining technologies. The work aims at developing an approach for flexible and efficient answer to data mining queries addressed either to a relational or a multidimensional database. The authors investigate the two following techniques. The first one exploits lattice based mining algorithms for generating frequent closed itemsets from multidimensional data. The second technique uses new operators, similar in spirit to the OLAP ones, in order to support data mining on demand. These new operators working on concept lattices include projection, selection, and assembly.

Chapter XII, *Temporal Semistructured Data Models and Data Warehouses*, by Carlo Combi and Barbara Oliboni, extends the application of the DW technology to semistructured data that may evolve in time. In order to store and analyze data of this kind, the authors propose a graph-based temporal semistructured data model. In this model, semistructured data are represented as a labeled graph with complex nodes representing abstract entities, simple nodes representing primitive values as well as with edges connecting nodes. Labels are associated with nodes and edges. Temporal aspects of data are handled by including valid time intervals in labels. In order to assure the consistency of this model, the authors propose two kinds of integrity constraints, namely, basic and domain-dependent ones. Basic constraints have to be satisfied by every graph, whereas domain-dependent constraints can be defined either for some specific nodes and edges or for the whole graph for a specific application domain.

Chapter XIII, *Spatial Online Analytical Processing (SOLAP): Concepts, Architectures, and Solutions from a Geomatics Engineering Perspective*, by Yvan Bédard, Sonia Rivest, and Marie-Josée Proulx, makes the reader familiar with challenges related to analyzing spatial data within the so called framework of spatial OLAP. The chapter outlines the particularities of spatial data and presents the state of the art of spatial OLAP applications. The main part of the chapter discusses the concepts, issues, challenges, and solutions related to spatial OLAP. This valuable discussion results from the experience of the authors with building a commercially available spatial OLAP system.

Robert Wrembel
Poznań, Poland

Christian Koncilia
Munich, Germany

June 2006

References

Adamson, C., & Venerable, M. (1998). *Data warehouse design solutions*. John Wiley & Sons.

Aouiche, K., Darmont, J., & Boussaïd, O. (2005). Automatic selection of bitmap join indexes in data warehouse. In A. Min Tjoa & J. Trujillo (Eds.), *International Conference on Data Warehousing and Knowledge Discovery* (LNCS 3589, pp. 64-73). Springer Verlag.

Balmin, A., Papadimitriou, T., & Papakonstanitnou, Y. (2000). Hypothetical queries in an OLAP environment. In A. El Abbadi, et al. (Eds.), *International Conference on Very Large Data Bases* (pp. 220-231). Morgan Kaufmann.

Blaschka, M., Sapia, C., & Höfling, G. (1999). On schema evolution in multidimensional databases. In M. K. Mohania & A. Min Tjoa (Eds.), *Data warehousing and knowledge discovery* (LNCS 1676, pp. 153-164). Springer-Verlag.

Body, M., Miquel, M., Bédard, Y., & Tchounikine, A. (2002). A multidimensional and multiversion structure for OLAP applications. In D. Theodoratos (Ed.), *ACM International Workshop on Data Warehousing and OLAP* (pp. 1-6). ACM Press.

Ceri, S., & Widom, J. (1991). Deriving production rules for incremental view maintenance. In G. M. Lohman et al. (Eds.), *International Conference on Very Large Data Bases* (pp. 577-589). Morgan Kaufmann.

Chaudhuri, S., & Dayal, U. (1997). An overview of data warehousing and OLAP technology. *SIGMOD Record, 26*(1), 65-74.

Colby, L. S., Kawaguchi, A., Lieuwen, D. F., Mumick, I. S., & Ross, K. A. (1997). Supporting multiple view maintenance policies. In J. Peckham (Ed.), *ACM SIGMOD International Conference on Management of Data* (pp. 405-416). ACM Press.

de Sousa, M. F., & Sampaio, M. C. (1999). Efficient materialization and use of views in data warehouses. *SIGMOD Record, 28*(1), 78-83.

Eder, J., Koncilia, C., & Morzy, T. (2002). The COMET metamodel for temporal data warehouses. In A. Banks Pidduck, et al. (Eds.), *International Conference CAiSE* (LNCS 2348, pp. 83-99). Springer-Verlag.

EDWMarket. (2004). *The evolving enterprise data warehouse market: Part 1*. Retrieved June 15, 2006, from http://www.teradata.com/t/pdf.aspx?a=83673&b=118524

Furtado, P. (2004). Workload-based placement and join processing in node-partitioned data warehouses. In Y. Kambayashi, et al. (Eds.), *International Conference on Data Warehousing and Knowledge Discovery* (LNCS 3181, pp. 38-47). Springer-Verlag.

Golfarelli, M., Lechtenbörger, J., Rizzi, S., & Vossen, G. (2004). Schema versioning in data warehouses. In S. Wang, et al. (Eds.), *Conceptual Modeling for Advanced Application Domains, ER 2004 Workshops* (LNCS 3289, pp. 415-428). Springer-Verlag.

Golfarelli, M., Rizzi, S., & Vrdoljak, B. (2001). Data warehouse design from XML sources. In J. Hammer (Ed.), *ACM International Workshop on Data Warehousing and OLAP* (pp. 40-47). ACM Press.

Gupta, H. (1997). Selection of views to materialise in a data warehouse. In F. N. Afrati & P. G. Kolaitis (Eds.), *Database theory: ICDT* (LNCS 1186, pp. 98-112). Springer-Verlag.

Gupta, A., & Mumick, I. S. (Eds.). (1999). *Materialized views: Techniques, implementations, and applications.* MIT Press.

Gyssens, M., & Lakshmanan, L. V. S. (1997). A foundation for multi-dimensional databases. In M. Jarke, et al. (Eds.), *International Conference on Very Large Data Bases* (pp. 106-115). Morgan Kaufmann Publishers.

Hurtado, C., & Mendelzon, A. (2002). OLAP dimension constraints. In L. Popa (Ed.), *ACM SIGACT-SIGMOD-SIGART Symposium on Principles of Database Systems* (pp. 169-179). ACM Press.

Hurtado, C. A., Mendelzon, A. O., & Vaisman, A. A. (1999). Maintaining data cubes under dimension updates. In *Proceedings of the International Conference on Data Engineering* (pp. 346-355). IEEE Computer Society Press.

Jarke, M., Jeusfeld, M. A., Quix, C., & Vassiliadis, P. (1998). Architecture and quality in data warehouses. In B. Pernici & C. Thanos (Eds.), *International Conference on Advanced Information Systems Engineering* (LNCS 1413, pp. 93-113). Springer-Verlag.

Kimball, R., & Caserta, J. (2004). *The data warehouse ETL tookit.* John Wiley & Sons.

Kimball, R., Reeves, L., Ross, M., & Thornthwaite, W. (1998). *The data warehouse lifecycle toolkit.* John Wiley & Sons.

Letz, C., Henn, E. T., & Vossen, G. (2002). Consistency in data warehouse dimensions. In M. A. Nascimento, et al. (Eds.), *International Database Engineering & Applications Symposium* (pp. 224-232). IEEE Computer Society Press.

Luján-Mora, S., & Trujillo, J. (2004). Physical modeling of data warehouses using UML. In K. Davis & M. Ronthaler (Eds.), *ACM International Workshop on Data Warehousing and OLAP* (pp. 48-57). ACM Press.

Morzy, T., & Wrembel, R. (2004). On querying versions of multiversion data warehouse. In K. Davis & M. Ronthaler (Eds.), *ACM International Workshop on Data Warehousing and OLAP* (pp. 92-101). ACM Press.

Nassis, V., Rajugan, R., Dillon, T. S., & Rahayu, J. W. (2005). A requirement engineering approach for designing XML-view driven, XML document warehouses. In *Proceedings of the International Computer Software and Applications Conference (COMPSAC)* (pp. 388-395). IEEE Computer Society Press.

Nguyen, T. M., Min Tjoa, A., & Trujillo, J. (2005). Data warehousing and knowledge discovery: A chronological view of research challenges. In A. Min Tjoa & J. Trujillo (Eds.), *Data warehousing and knowledge discovery* (LNCS 3589, pp. 530-535). Springer-Verlag.

OLAPReport. (2004). *Market share analysis.* Retrieved June 15, 2006, from http://www.olapreport.com/Market.htm

OMG (Object Management Group). (2003). *Common warehouse metamodel specification, v1.1.* Retrieved June 15, 2006, from http://www.omg.org/cgi-bin/doc?formal/03-03-02

O'Neil, P., & Graefe, G. (1995). Multi-table joins through bitmapped join indices. *SIGMOD Record, 24*(3), 8-11.

Park, B. K., Han, H., & Song I. Y. (2005). XML-OLAP: A multidimensional analysis framework for XML warehouses. In A. Min Tjoa & J. Trujillo (Eds.), *Data warehousing and knowledge discovery* (LNCS 3589, pp. 32-42). Springer-Verlag.

Quass, D., & Widom, J. (1997). On-line warehouse view maintenance. In J. Peckham (Ed.), *ACM SIGMOD International Conference on Management of Data* (pp. 393-404). ACM Press.

Rao, J., Zhang, C., Megiddo, N., & Lohman, G. (2002). Automating physical database design in a parallel database. In M. J. Franklin et al. (Eds.), *ACM SIGMOD International Conference on Management of Data* (pp. 558-569). ACM Press.

Roussopoulos, N. (1998). Materialized views and data warehouses. *SIGMOD Record, 27*(1), 21-26.

Rundensteiner, E., Koeller, A., & Zhang, X. (2000). Maintaining data warehouses over changing information sources. *Communications of the ACM, 43*(6), 57-62.

Samtani, S., Kumar, V., & Mohania, M. (1999). Self maintenance of multiple views in data warehousing. In *Proceedings of the ACM CIKM International Conference on Information and Knowledge Management* (pp. 292-299). ACM Press.

Simitsis, A., Vassiliadis, P., Terrovitis, M., & Skiadopoulos, S. (2005). Graph-based modeling of ETL activities with multi-level transformations and updates. In A. Min Tjoa & J. Trujillo (Eds.), *International Conference on Data Warehousing and Knowledge Discovery* (LNCS 3589, pp. 43-52). Springer-Verlag.

Stefanovic, N., Han, J., & Koperski, K. (2000). Object-based selective materialization for efficient implementation of spatial data cubes. *IEEE Transactions on Knowledge and Data Engineering, 12*(6), 938-958.

Stöhr, T., & Rahm, E. (2001). WARLOCK: A data allocation tool for parallel warehouses. In P. M. G. Apers et al. (Eds.), *International Conference on Very Large Data Bases* (pp. 721-722). Morgan Kaufmann.

Stream. (2006). *Stanford Stream Data Manager.* Retrieved June 15, 2006, from http://hake.stanford.edu/stream/

Torlone, T., & Panella, I. (2006). Design and development of a tool for integrating heterogeneous data warehouses. In A. Min Tjoa & J. Trujillo (Eds.), Data warehousing and knowledge discovery (LNCS 3589, pp. 105-114). Springer-Verlag.

Theodoratos, D., & Xu, W. (2004). Constructing search space for materialized view selection. In K. Davis & M. Ronthaler (Eds.), *ACM International Workshop on Data Warehousing and OLAP* (pp. 48-57). ACM Press.

Valduriez, P. (1987). Join indices. *ACM Transactions on Database Systems (TODS), 12*(2), 218-246.

Vassiliadis, P., Bouzeghoub, M., & Quix, C. (1999). Towards quality-oriented data warehouse usage and evolution. In M. Jarke & A. Oberweis (Eds.), *International Conference CAiSE* (LNCS 1626, pp. 164-179). Springer-Verlag.

Vetterli, T., Vaduva, A., & Staudt, M. (2000). Metadata standards for data warehousing: Open information model vs. common warehouse metadata. *SIGMOD Record, 29*(3), 68-75.

Widom, J. (1995). Research problems in data warehousing. In *Proceedings of the Fourth International Conference on Information and Knowledge Management* (pp. 25-30). ACM Press.

Wu, K., Otoo, E. J., & Shoshani, A. (2004). On the performance of bitmap indices for high cardinality attributes. In M. A. Nascimento et al. (Eds.), *International Conference on Very Large Data Bases* (pp. 24-35). Morgan Kaufmann.

Zhuge, Y., Garcia-Molina, H., & Wiener, J. L. (1996). The strobe algorithms for multi-source warehouse consistency. In *Proceedings of the Conference on Parallel and Distributed Information Systems* (pp. 146-157). IEEE Computer Society Press.

Zhuge, Y., Wiener J., Garcia-Molina, H. (1997): Multiple view consistency for data warehousing. In W. A. Gray & P. A. Larson (Eds.), *International Conference on Data Engineering* (pp. 289-300). IEEE Computer Society Press.

Acknowledgments

The editors would like to acknowledge the help of all involved in the review process of the book. The reviewers provided comprehensive, critical, and constructive comments. Without their support the project could not have been satisfactorily completed.

List of Reviewers

Bartosz Bębel, Poznań University of Technology, Poland

Mauricio Minuto Espil, Pontificia Universidad Católica, Argentina

Pedro Furtado, University of Coimbra, Spain

Matteo Golfarelli, University of Bologna, Italy

Carlos Hurtado, Universidad de Chile, Chile

Stanisław Kozielski, Silesian University of Technology, Poland

Jens Lechtenbörger, University of Münster, Germany

Sergio Luján Mora, University of Alicante, Spain

Christoph Mayer, OFFIS, Germany

Dieter Mitsche, ETH Zurich, Switzerland

Stefano Rizzi, University of Bologna, Italy

Kurt Stockinger, University of California, USA

David Taniar, Monash University, Australia

Alejandro Vaisman, Universidad de Buenos Aires, Argentina

Marek Wojciechowski, Poznań University of Technology, Poland

Special thanks also go to the published team at Idea Group Inc. In particular, to Jan Travers and Mehdi Khosrow-Pour who gave us the opportunity to publish the book. Thank you also to our development editor, Kristin Roth, who assisted us through the process of editing the book.

Robert Wrembel
Poznań, Poland

Christian Koncilia
Munich, Germany

June 2006

Section I

Modeling and Designing

Chapter I

Conceptual Modeling Solutions for the Data Warehouse

Stefano Rizzi
DEIS-University of Bologna, Italy

Abstract

In the context of data warehouse design, a basic role is played by conceptual modeling, that provides a higher level of abstraction in describing the warehousing process and architecture in all its aspects, aimed at achieving independence of implementation issues. This chapter focuses on a conceptual model called the DFM that suits the variety of modeling situations that may be encountered in real projects of small to large complexity. The aim of the chapter is to propose a comprehensive set of solutions for conceptual modeling according to the DFM and to give the designer a practical guide for applying them in the context of a design methodology. Besides the basic concepts of multidimensional modeling, the other issues discussed are descriptive and cross-dimension attributes; convergences; shared, incomplete, recursive, and dynamic hierarchies; multiple and optional arcs; and additivity.

Copyright © 2007, Idea Group Inc. Copying or distributing in print or electronic forms without written permission of Idea Group Inc. is prohibited.

Figure 1. The cube metaphor for multidimensional modeling

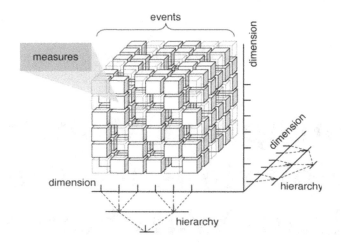

Introduction

Operational databases are focused on recording transactions, thus they are prevalently characterized by an OLTP (online transaction processing) workload. Conversely, data warehouses (DWs) allow complex analysis of data aimed at decision support; the workload they support has completely different characteristics, and is widely known as OLAP (online analytical processing). Traditionally, OLAP applications are based on *multidimensional modeling* that intuitively represents data under the metaphor of a cube whose cells correspond to events that occurred in the business domain (Figure 1). Each event is quantified by a set of measures; each edge of the cube corresponds to a relevant dimension for analysis, typically associated to a hierarchy of attributes that further describe it. The multidimensional model has a twofold benefit. On the one hand, it is close to the way of thinking of data analyzers, who are used to the spreadsheet metaphor; therefore it helps users understand data. On the other hand, it supports performance improvement as its simple structure allows designers to predict the user intentions.

Multidimensional modeling and OLAP workloads require specialized design techniques. In the context of design, a basic role is played by *conceptual modeling* that provides a higher level of abstraction in describing the warehousing process and architecture in all its aspects, aimed at achieving independence of implementation issues. Conceptual modeling is widely recognized to be the necessary foundation for building a database that is well-documented and fully satisfies the user require-

Copyright © 2007, Idea Group Inc. Copying or distributing in print or electronic forms without written permission of Idea Group Inc. is prohibited.

ments; usually, it relies on a graphical notation that facilitates writing, understanding, and managing conceptual schemata by both designers and users.

Unfortunately, in the field of data warehousing there still is no consensus about a formalism for conceptual modeling (Sen & Sinha, 2005). The entity/relationship (E/R) model is widespread in the enterprises as a conceptual formalism to provide standard documentation for relational information systems, and a great deal of effort has been made to use E/R schemata as the input for designing nonrelational databases as well (Fahrner & Vossen, 1995); nevertheless, as E/R is oriented to support queries that navigate associations between data rather than synthesize them, it is not well suited for data warehousing (Kimball, 1996). Actually, the E/R model has enough expressivity to represent most concepts necessary for modeling a DW; on the other hand, in its basic form, it is not able to properly emphasize the key aspects of the multidimensional model, so that its usage for DWs is expensive from the point of view of the graphical notation and not intuitive (Golfarelli, Maio, & Rizzi, 1998).

Some designers claim to use star schemata for conceptual modeling. A *star schema* is the standard implementation of the multidimensional model on relational platforms; it is just a (denormalized) relational schema, so it merely defines a set of relations and integrity constraints. Using the star schema for conceptual modeling is like starting to build a complex software by writing the code, without the support of and static, functional, or dynamic model, which typically leads to very poor results from the points of view of adherence to user requirements, of maintenance, and of reuse.

For all these reasons, in the last few years the research literature has proposed several original approaches for modeling a DW, some based on extensions of E/R, some on extensions of UML. This chapter focuses on an ad hoc conceptual model, the *dimensional fact model* (DFM), that was first proposed in Golfarelli et al. (1998) and continuously enriched and refined during the following years in order to optimally suit the variety of modeling situations that may be encountered in real projects of small to large complexity. The aim of the chapter is to propose a comprehensive set of solutions for conceptual modeling according to the DFM and to give a practical guide for applying them in the context of a design methodology. Besides the basic concepts of multidimensional modeling, namely facts, dimensions, measures, and hierarchies, the other issues discussed are descriptive and cross-dimension attributes; convergences; shared, incomplete, recursive, and dynamic hierarchies; multiple and optional arcs; and additivity.

After reviewing the related literature in the next section, in the third and fourth sections, we introduce the constructs of DFM for basic and advanced modeling, respectively. Then, in the fifth section we briefly discuss the different methodological approaches to conceptual design. Finally, in the sixth section we outline the open issues in conceptual modeling, and in the last section we draw the conclusions.

Copyright © 2007, Idea Group Inc. Copying or distributing in print or electronic forms without written permission of Idea Group Inc. is prohibited.

Related Literature

In the context of data warehousing, the literature proposed several approaches to multidimensional modeling. Some of them have no graphical support and are aimed at establishing a formal foundation for representing cubes and hierarchies as well as an algebra for querying them (Agrawal, Gupta, & Sarawagi, 1995; Cabibbo & Torlone, 1998; Datta & Thomas, 1997; Franconi & Kamble, 2004a; Gyssens & Lakshmanan, 1997; Li & Wang, 1996; Pedersen & Jensen, 1999; Vassiliadis, 1998); since we believe that a distinguishing feature of conceptual models is that of providing a graphical support to be easily understood by both designers and users when discussing and validating requirements, we will not discuss them.

The approaches to "strict" conceptual modeling for DWs devised so far are summarized in Table 1. For each model, the table shows if it is associated to some method for conceptual design and if it is based on E/R, is object-oriented, or is an ad hoc model.

The discussion about whether E/R-based, object-oriented, or ad hoc models are preferable is controversial. Some claim that E/R extensions should be adopted since (1) E/R has been tested for years; (2) designers are familiar with E/R; (3) E/R has proven flexible and powerful enough to adapt to a variety of application domains; and (4) several important research results were obtained for the E/R (Sapia, Blaschka, Hofling, & Dinter, 1998; Tryfona, Busborg, & Borch Christiansen, 1999). On the other hand, advocates of object-oriented models argue that (1) they are more expressive and better represent static and dynamic properties of information systems; (2) they provide powerful mechanisms for expressing requirements and constraints; (3) object-orientation is currently the dominant trend in data modeling; and (4) UML, in particular, is a standard and is naturally extensible (Abelló, Samos, & Saltor, 2002; Luján-Mora, Trujillo, & Song, 2002). Finally, we believe that ad hoc models compensate for the lack of familiarity from designers with the fact that (1) they achieve better notational economy; (2) they give proper emphasis to the peculiarities of the multidimensional model, thus (3) they are more intuitive and

Table 1. Approaches to conceptual modeling

	E/R extension	object-oriented	ad hoc
no method	Franconi and Kamble (2004b); Sapia et al. (1998); Tryfona et al. (1999)	Abelló et al. (2002); Nguyen, Tjoa, and Wagner (2000)	Tsois et al. (2001)
method		Luján-Mora et al. (2002)	Golfarelli et al. (1998); Hüsemann et al. (2000)

Copyright © 2007, Idea Group Inc. Copying or distributing in print or electronic forms without written permission of Idea Group Inc. is prohibited.

Figure 2. The SALE fact modeled through a starER (Sapia et al., 1998), a UML class diagram (Luján-Mora et al., 2002), and a fact schema (Hüsemann, Lechtenbörger, & Vossen, 2000)

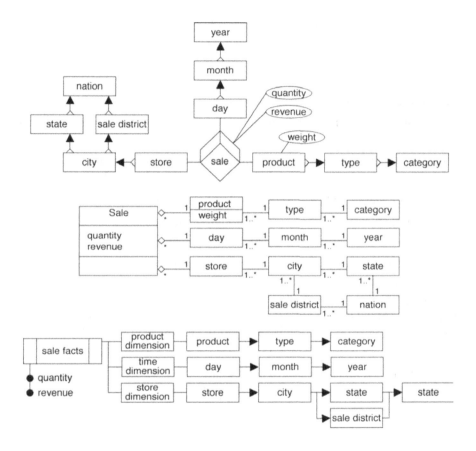

readable by nonexpert users. In particular, they can model some constraints related to functional dependencies (e.g., convergences and cross-dimensional attributes) in a simpler way than UML, that requires the use of formal expressions written, for instance, in OCL.

A comparison of the different models done by Tsois, Karayannidis, and Sellis (2001) pointed out that, abstracting from their graphical form, the core expressivity is similar. In confirmation of this, we show in Figure 2 how the same simple fact could be modeled through an E/R based, an object-oriented, and an ad hoc approach.

Copyright © 2007, Idea Group Inc. Copying or distributing in print or electronic forms without written permission of Idea Group Inc. is prohibited.

The Dimensional Fact Model:
Basic Modeling

In this chapter we focus on an ad hoc model called the dimensional fact model. The DFM is a graphical conceptual model, specifically devised for multidimensional modeling, aimed at:

- Effectively supporting conceptual design
- Providing an environment on which user queries can be intuitively expressed
- Supporting the dialogue between the designer and the end users to refine the specification of requirements
- Creating a stable platform to ground logical design
- Providing an expressive and non-ambiguous design documentation

The representation of reality built using the DFM consists of a set of *fact schemata*. The basic concepts modeled are facts, measures, dimensions, and hierarchies. In the following we intuitively define these concepts, referring the reader to Figure 3 that depicts a simple fact schema for modeling invoices at line granularity; a formal definition of the same concepts can be found in Golfarelli et al. (1998).

> **Definition 1:** A *fact* is a focus of interest for the decision-making process; typically, it models a set of events occurring in the enterprise world. A

Figure 3. A basic fact schema for the INVOICE LINE fact

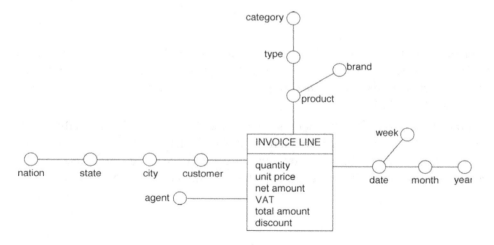

Copyright © 2007, Idea Group Inc. Copying or distributing in print or electronic forms without written permission of Idea Group Inc. is prohibited.

fact is graphically represented by a box with two sections, one for the fact name and one for the measures.

Examples of facts in the trade domain are sales, shipments, purchases, claims; in the financial domain: stock exchange transactions, contracts for insurance policies, granting of loans, bank statements, credit cards purchases. It is essential for a fact to have some *dynamic* aspects, that is, to evolve somehow across time.

> **Guideline 1:** The concepts represented in the data source by frequently-updated archives are good candidates for facts; those represented by almost-static archives are not.

As a matter of fact, very few things are completely static; even the relationship between cities and regions might change, if some border were revised. Thus, the choice of facts should be based either on the average periodicity of changes, or on the specific interests of analysis. For instance, assigning a new sales manager to a sales department occurs less frequently than coupling a promotion to a product; thus, while the relationship between promotions and products is a good candidate to be modeled as a fact, that between sales managers and departments is not—except for the personnel manager, who is interested in analyzing the turnover!

> **Definition 2:** A *measure* is a numerical property of a fact, and describes one of its quantitative aspects of interests for analysis. Measures are included in the bottom section of the fact.

For instance, each invoice line is measured by the number of units sold, the price per unit, the net amount, and so forth. The reason why measures should be numerical is that they are used for computations. A fact may also have no measures, if the only interesting thing to be recorded is the occurrence of events; in this case the fact scheme is said to be *empty* and is typically queried to count the events that occurred.

> **Definition 3:** A *dimension* is a fact property with a finite domain and describes one of its analysis coordinates. The set of dimensions of a fact determines its finest representation granularity. Graphically, dimensions are represented as circles attached to the fact by straight lines.

Typical dimensions for the invoice fact are product, customer, agent, and date.

Copyright © 2007, Idea Group Inc. Copying or distributing in print or electronic forms without written permission of Idea Group Inc. is prohibited.

Guideline 2: At least one of the dimensions of the fact should represent time, at any granularity.

The relationship between measures and dimensions is expressed, at the instance level, by the concept of event.

Definition 4: A *primary event* is an occurrence of a fact, and is identified by a tuple of values, one for each dimension. Each primary event is described by one value for each measure.

Primary events are the elemental information which can be represented (in the cube metaphor, they correspond to the cube cells). In the invoice example they model the invoicing of one product to one customer made by one agent on one day; it is not possible to distinguish between invoices possibly made with different types (e.g., active, passive, returned, etc.) or in different hours of the day.

Guideline 3: If the granularity of primary events as determined by the set of dimensions is coarser than the granularity of tuples in the data source, measures should be defined as either aggregations of numerical attributes in the data source, or as counts of tuples.

Remarkably, some multidimensional models in the literature focus on treating dimensions and measures symmetrically (Agrawal et al., 1995; Gyssens & Lakshmanan, 1997). This is an important achievement from both the point of view of the uniformity of the logical model and that of the flexibility of OLAP operators. Nevertheless we claim that, at a conceptual level, distinguishing between measures and dimensions is important since it allows logical design to be more specifically aimed at the efficiency required by data warehousing applications.

Aggregation is the basic OLAP operation, since it allows significant information useful for decision support to be summarized from large amounts of data. From a conceptual point of view, aggregation is carried out on primary events thanks to the definition of dimension attributes and hierarchies.

Definition 5: A *dimension attribute* is a property, with a finite domain, of a dimension. Like dimensions, it is represented by a circle.

For instance, a product is described by its type, category, and brand; a customer, by its city and its nation. The relationships between dimension attributes are expressed by hierarchies.

Copyright © 2007, Idea Group Inc. Copying or distributing in print or electronic forms without written permission of Idea Group Inc. is prohibited.

Definition 6: A *hierarchy* is a directed tree, rooted in a dimension, whose nodes are all the dimension attributes that describe that dimension, and whose arcs model many-to-one associations between pairs of dimension attributes. Arcs are graphically represented by straight lines.

Guideline 4: Hierarchies should reproduce the pattern of interattribute functional dependencies expressed by the data source.

Hierarchies determine how primary events can be aggregated into secondary events and selected significantly for the decision-making process. The dimension in which a hierarchy is rooted defines its finest aggregation granularity, while the other dimension attributes define progressively coarser granularities. For instance, thanks to the existence of a many-to-one association between products and their categories, the invoicing events may be grouped according to the category of the products.

Definition 7: Given a set of dimension attributes, each tuple of their values identifies a *secondary event* that aggregates all the corresponding primary events. Each secondary event is described by a value for each measure that summarizes the values taken by the same measure in the corresponding primary events.

We close this section by surveying some alternative terminology used either in the literature or in the commercial tools. There is substantial agreement on using the term *dimensions* to designate the "entry points" to classify and identify events; while we refer in particular to the attribute determining the minimum fact granularity, sometimes the whole hierarchies are named as dimensions (for instance, the term "time dimension" often refers to the whole hierarchy built on dimension date). Measures are sometimes called *variables* or *metrics*. Finally, in some data warehousing tools, the term *hierarchy* denotes each single branch of the tree rooted in a dimension.

The Dimensional Fact Model: Advanced Modeling

The constructs we introduce in this section, with the support of Figure 4, are descriptive and cross-dimension attributes; convergences; shared, incomplete, recursive,

Copyright © 2007, Idea Group Inc. Copying or distributing in print or electronic forms without written permission of Idea Group Inc. is prohibited.

and dynamic hierarchies; multiple and optional arcs; and additivity. Though some of them are not necessary in the simplest and most common modeling situations, they are quite useful in order to better express the multitude of conceptual shades that characterize real-world scenarios. In particular we will see how, following the introduction of some of this constructs, hierarchies will no longer be defined as trees to become, in the general case, directed graphs.

Descriptive Attributes

In several cases it is useful to represent additional information about a dimension attribute, though it is not interesting to use such information for aggregation. For instance, the user may ask for knowing the address of each store, but the user will hardly be interested in aggregating sales according to the address of the store.

> **Definition 8:** A *descriptive attribute* specifies a property of a dimension attribute, to which is related by an *x*-to-one association. Descriptive attributes are not used for aggregation; they are always leaves of their hierarchy and are graphically represented by horizontal lines.

There are two main reasons why a descriptive attribute should not be used for aggregation:

> **Guideline 5:** A descriptive attribute either has a continuously-valued domain (for instance, the weight of a product), or is related to a dimension attribute by a one-to-one association (for instance, the address of a customer).

Cross-Dimension Attributes

> **Definition 9:** A *cross-dimension attribute* is a (either dimension or descriptive) attribute whose value is determined by the combination of two or more dimension attributes, possibly belonging to different hierarchies. It is denoted by connecting through a curve line the arcs that determine it.

For instance, if the VAT on a product depends on both the product category and the state where the product is sold, it can be represented by a cross-dimension attribute as shown in Figure 4.

Copyright © 2007, Idea Group Inc. Copying or distributing in print or electronic forms without written permission of Idea Group Inc. is prohibited.

Figure 4. The complete fact schema for the INVOICE LINE fact

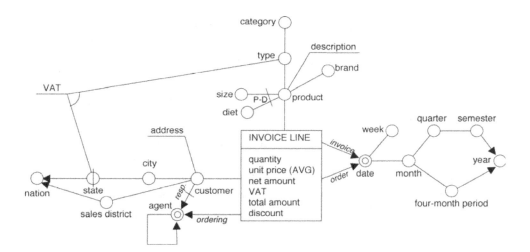

Convergence

Consider the geographic hierarchy on dimension *customer* (Figure 4): customers live in cities, which are grouped into states belonging to nations. Suppose that customers are grouped into sales districts as well, and that no inclusion relationships exist between districts and cities/states; on the other hand, sales districts never cross the nation boundaries. In this case, each customer belongs to exactly one nation whichever of the two paths is followed (customer → city → state → nation or customer → sales district → nation).

> **Definition 10:** A *convergence* takes place when two dimension attributes within a hierarchy are connected by two or more alternative paths of many-to-one associations. Convergences are represented by letting two or more arcs converge on the same dimension attribute.

The existence of apparently equal attributes does not always determine a convergence. If in the invoice fact we had a brand city attribute on the product hierarchy, representing the city where a brand is manufactured, there would be no convergence with attribute (customer) city, since a product manufactured in a city can obviously be sold to customers of other cities as well.

Copyright © 2007, Idea Group Inc. Copying or distributing in print or electronic forms without written permission of Idea Group Inc. is prohibited.

Optional Arcs

Definition 11: An *optional arc* models the fact that an association represented within the fact scheme is undefined for a subset of the events. An
optional arc is graphically denoted by marking it with a dash.

For instance, attribute diet takes a value only for food products; for the other products, it is undefined.

In the presence of a set of optional arcs exiting from the same dimension attribute,
their *coverage* can be denoted in order to pose a constraint on the optionalities involved. Like for IS-A hierarchies in the E/R model, the coverage of a set of optional
arcs is characterized by two independent coordinates. Let a be a dimension attribute,
and $b_1,..., b_m$ be its children attributes connected by optional arcs:

- The coverage is *total* if each value of a always corresponds to a value for at
  least one of its children; conversely, if some values of a exist for which all of
  its children are undefined, the coverage is said to be *partial*.
- The coverage is *disjoint* if each value of a corresponds to a value for, at most,
  one of its children; conversely, if some values of a exist that correspond to
  values for two or more children, the coverage is said to be *overlapped*.

Thus, overall, there are four possible coverages, denoted by T-D, T-O, P-D, and P-O.
Figure 4 shows an example of optionality annotated with its coverage. We assume
that products can have three types: food, clothing, and household, since expiration
date and size are defined only for, respectively, food and clothing, the coverage is
partial and disjoint.

Multiple Arcs

In most cases, as already said, hierarchies include attributes related by many-to-one
associations. On the other hand, in some situations it is necessary to include also attributes that, for a single value taken by their father attribute, take several values.

Definition 12: A *multiple arc* is an arc, within a hierarchy, modeling a
many-to-many association between the two dimension attributes it connects.
Graphically, it is denoted by doubling the line that represents the arc.

Copyright © 2007, Idea Group Inc. Copying or distributing in print or electronic forms without written permission of
Idea Group Inc. is prohibited.

Figure 5. The fact schema for the SALES fact

Consider the fact schema modeling the sales of books in a library, represented in Figure 5, whose dimensions are *date* and book. Users will probably be interested in analyzing sales for each book author; on the other hand, since some books have two or more authors, the relationship between book and author must be modeled as a multiple arc.

> **Guideline 6:** In presence of many-to-many associations, summarizability is no longer guaranteed, unless the multiple arc is properly *weighted*. Multiple arcs should be used sparingly since, in ROLAP logical design, they require complex solutions.

Summarizability is the property of correcting summarizing measures along hierarchies (Lenz & Shoshani, 1997). Weights restore summarizability, but their introduction is artificial in several cases; for instance, in the book sales fact, each author of a multiauthored book should be assigned a normalized weight expressing her "contribution" to the book.

Shared Hierarchies

Sometimes, large portions of hierarchies are replicated twice or more in the same fact schema. A typical example is the temporal hierarchy: a fact frequently has more than one dimension of type date, with different semantics, and it may be useful to define on each of them a temporal hierarchy month-week-year. Another example are geographic hierarchies, that may be defined starting from any location attribute in the fact schema. To avoid redundancy, the DFM provides a graphical shorthand for denoting hierarchy sharing. Figure 4 shows two examples of shared hierarchies. Fact INVOICE LINE has two date dimensions, with semantics invoice date and order date,

Copyright © 2007, Idea Group Inc. Copying or distributing in print or electronic forms without written permission of Idea Group Inc. is prohibited.

respectively. This is denoted by doubling the circle that represents attribute date and specifying two *roles* invoice and order on the entering arcs. The second shared hierarchy is the one on agent, that may have two roles: the ordering agent, that is a dimension, and the agent who is responsible for a customer (optional).

> **Guideline 8:** Explicitly representing shared hierarchies on the fact schema is important since, during ROLAP logical design, it enables ad hoc solutions aimed at avoiding replication of data in dimension tables.

Ragged Hierarchies

Let $a_1,..., a_n$ be a sequence of dimension attributes that define a path within a hierarchy (such as city, state, nation). Up to now we assumed that, for each value of a_1, exactly one value for every other attribute on the path exists. In the previous case, this is actually true for each city in the U.S., while it is false for most European countries where no decomposition in states is defined (see Figure 6).

Definition 13: A *ragged* (or *incomplete*) *hierarchy* is a hierarchy where, for some instances, the values of one or more attributes are missing (since undefined or unknown). A ragged hierarchy is graphically denoted by marking with a dash the attributes whose values may be missing.

As stated by Niemi (2001), within a ragged hierarchy each aggregation level has precise and consistent semantics, but the different hierarchy instances may have different length since one or more levels are missing, making the interlevel relationships not uniform (the father of "San Francisco" belongs to level state, the father of "Rome" to level nation).

There is a noticeable difference between a ragged hierarchy and an optional arc. In the first case we model the fact that, for some hierarchy instances, there is no value for one or more attributes *in any position of the hierarchy*. Conversely, through an

Figure 6. Ragged geographic hierarchies

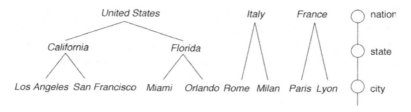

Copyright © 2007, Idea Group Inc. Copying or distributing in print or electronic forms without written permission of Idea Group Inc. is prohibited.

optional arc we model the fact that there is no value for an attribute *and for all of its descendents*.

> **Guideline 9:** Ragged hierarchies may lead to summarizability problems. A way for avoiding them is to fragment a fact into two or more facts, each including a subset of the hierarchies characterized by uniform interlevel relationships.

Thus, in the invoice example, fragmenting INVOICE LINE into U.S. INVOICE LINE and E.U. INVOICE LINE (the first with the state attribute, the second without state) restores the completeness of the geographic hierarchy.

Unbalanced Hierarchies

> **Definition 14:** An *unbalanced* (or *recursive*) *hierarchy* is a hierarchy where, though interattribute relationships are consistent, the instances may have different length. Graphically, it is represented by introducing a cycle within the hierarchy.

A typical example of unbalanced hierarchy is the one that models the dependence interrelationships between working persons. Figure 4 includes an unbalanced hierarchy on sale agents: there are no fixed roles for the different agents, and the different "leaf" agents have a variable number of supervisor agents above them.

> **Guideline 10:** Recursive hierarchies lead to complex solutions during ROLAP logical design and to poor querying performance. A way for avoiding them is to "unroll" them for a given number of times.

For instance, in the agent example, if the user states that two is the maximum number of interesting levels for the dependence relationship, the customer hierarchy could be transformed as in Figure 7.

Dynamic Hierarchies

Time is a key factor in data warehousing systems, since the decision process is often based on the evaluation of historical series and on the comparison between snapshots of the enterprise taken at different moments. The multidimensional models implicitly assume that the only dynamic components described in a cube are the events that

Copyright © 2007, Idea Group Inc. Copying or distributing in print or electronic forms without written permission of Idea Group Inc. is prohibited.

Figure 7. Unrolling the agent hierarchy

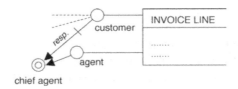

instantiate it; hierarchies are traditionally considered to be static. Of course this is not correct: sales manager alternate, though slowly, on different departments; new products are added every week to those already being sold; the product categories change, and their relationship with products change; sales districts can be modified, and a customer may be moved from one district to another.[1]

The conceptual representation of hierarchy dynamicity is strictly related to its impact on user queries. In fact, in presence of a dynamic hierarchy we may picture three different temporal scenarios for analyzing events (SAP, 1998):

- **Today for yesterday:** All events are referred to the current configuration of hierarchies. Thus, assuming on January 1, 2005 the responsible agent for customer Smith has changed from Mr. Black to Mr. White, and that a new customer O'Hara has been acquired and assigned to Mr. Black, when computing the agent commissions all invoices for Smith are attributed to Mr. White, while only invoices for O'Hara are attributed to Mr. Black.

- **Yesterday for today:** All events are referred to some past configuration of hierarchies. In the previous example, all invoices for Smith are attributed to Mr. Black, while invoices for O'Hara are not considered.

- **Today or yesterday (or historical truth):** Each event is referred to the configuration hierarchies had at the time the event occurred. Thus, the invoices for Smith up to 2004 and those for O'Hara are attributed to Mr. Black, while invoices for Smith from 2005 are attributed to Mr. White.

While in the agent example, dynamicity concerns an arc of a hierarchy, the one expressing the many-to-one association between customer and agent, in some cases it may as well concern a dimension attribute: for instance, the name of a product category may change. Even in this case, the different scenarios are defined in much the same way as before.

On the conceptual schema, it is useful to denote which scenarios the user is interested for each arc and attribute, since this heavily impacts on the specific solutions to be adopted during logical design. By default, we will assume that the only interesting scenario is today for yesterday—it is the most common one, and the one whose

Copyright © 2007, Idea Group Inc. Copying or distributing in print or electronic forms without written permission of Idea Group Inc. is prohibited.

Table 2. Temporal scenarios for the INVOICE fact

arc/attribute	today for yesterday	yesterday for today	today or yesterday
customer-resp. agent	YES	YES	YES
customer-city	YES		YES
sale district			YES

Table 3. Valid aggregation operators for the three types of measures (Lenz, 1997)

	temporal hierarchies	nontemporal hierarchies
flow measures	SUM, AVG, MIN, MAX	SUM, AVG, MIN, MAX
stock measures	AVG, MIN, MAX	SUM, AVG, MIN, MAX
unit measures	AVG, MIN, MAX	AVG, MIN, MAX

implementation on the star schema is simplest. If some attributes or arcs require different scenarios, the designer should specify them on a table like Table 2.

Additivity

Aggregation requires defining a proper operator to compose the measure values characterizing primary events into measure values characterizing each secondary event. From this point of view, we may distinguish three types of measures (Lenz & Shoshani, 1997):

- **Flow measures:** They refer to a time period, and are cumulatively evaluated at the end of that period. Examples are the number of products sold in a day, the monthly revenue, the number of those born in a year.

- **Stock measures:** They are evaluated at particular moments in time. Examples are the number of products in a warehouse, the number of inhabitants of a city, the temperature measured by a gauge.

- **Unit measures:** They are evaluated at particular moments in time, but they are expressed in relative terms. Examples are the unit price of a product, the discount percentage, the exchange rate of a currency.

The aggregation operators that can be used on the three types of measures are summarized in Table 3.

Copyright © 2007, Idea Group Inc. Copying or distributing in print or electronic forms without written permission of Idea Group Inc. is prohibited.

Definition 15: A measure is said to be *additive* along a dimension if its values can be aggregated along the corresponding hierarchy by the sum operator, otherwise it is called *nonadditive*. A nonadditive measure is *nonaggregable* if no other aggregation operator can be used on it.

Table 3 shows that, in general, flow measures are additive along all dimensions, stock measures are nonadditive along temporal hierarchies, and unit measures are nonadditive along all dimensions.

On the invoice scheme, most measures are additive. For instance, quantity has flow type: the total quantity invoiced in a month is the sum of the quantities invoiced in the single days of that month. Measure unit price has unit type and is nonadditive along all dimensions. Though it cannot be summed up, it can still be aggregated by using operators such as average, maximum, and minimum.

Since additivity is the most frequent case, in order to simplify the graphic notation in the DFM, only the exceptions are represented explicitly. In particular, a measure is connected to the dimensions along which it is nonadditive by a dashed line labeled with the other aggregation operators (if any) which can be used instead. If a measure is aggregated through the same operator along all dimensions, that operator can be simply reported on its side (see for instance unit price in Figure 4).

Approaches to Conceptual Design

In this section we discuss how conceptual design can be framed within a methodology for DW design. The approaches to DW design are usually classified in two categories (Winter & Strauch, 2003):

- Data-driven (or supply-driven) approaches that design the DW starting from a detailed analysis of the data sources; user requirements impact on design by allowing the designer to select which chunks of data are relevant for decision making and by determining their structure according to the multidimensional model (Golfarelli et al., 1998; Hüsemann et al., 2000).

- Requirement-driven (or demand-driven) approaches start from determining the information requirements of end users, and how to map these requirements onto the available data sources is investigated only *a posteriori* (Prakash & Gosain, 2003; Schiefer, List & Bruckner, 2002).

While data-driven approaches somehow simplify the design of ETL (extraction, transformation, and loading), since each data in the DW is rooted in one or more attributes

Copyright © 2007, Idea Group Inc. Copying or distributing in print or electronic forms without written permission of Idea Group Inc. is prohibited.

of the sources, they give user requirements a secondary role in determining the information contents for analysis, and give the designer little support in identifying facts, dimensions, and measures. Conversely, requirement-driven approaches bring user requirements to the foreground, but require a larger effort when designing ETL.

Data-Driven Approaches

Data-driven approaches are feasible when all of the following are true: (1) detailed knowledge of data sources is available *a priori* or easily achievable; (2) the source schemata exhibit a good degree of normalization; (3) the complexity of source schemata is not high. In practice, when the chosen architecture for the DW relies on a *reconciled level* (or *operational data store*) these requirements are largely satisfied: in fact, normalization and detailed knowledge are guaranteed by the source integration process. The same holds, thanks to a careful source recognition activity, in the frequent case when the source is a single relational database, well-designed and not very large.

In a data-driven approach, requirement analysis is typically carried out informally, based on simple requirement glossaries (Lechtenbörger, 2001) rather than on formal diagrams. Conceptual design is then heavily rooted on source schemata and can be largely automated. In particular, the designer is actively supported in identifying dimensions and measures, in building hierarchies, in detecting convergences and shared hierarchies. For instance, the approach proposed by Golfarelli et al. (1998) consists of five steps that, starting from the source schema expressed either by an E/R schema or a relational schema, create the conceptual schema for the DW:

1.   Choose facts of interest on the source schema

2.   For each fact, build an *attribute tree* that captures the functional dependencies expressed by the source schema

3.   Edit the attribute trees by adding/deleting attributes and functional dependencies

4.   Choose dimensions and measures

5.   Create the fact schemata

While step 2 is completely automated, some advanced constructs of the DFM are manually applied by the designer during step 5.

On-the-field experience shows that, when applicable, the data-driven approach is preferable since it reduces the overall time necessary for design. In fact, not only conceptual design can be partially automated, but even ETL design is made easier since the mapping between the data sources and the DW is derived at no additional cost during conceptual design.

Copyright © 2007, Idea Group Inc. Copying or distributing in print or electronic forms without written permission of Idea Group Inc. is prohibited.

Requirement-Driven Approaches

Conversely, within a requirement-driven framework, in the absence of knowledge of the source schema, the building of hierarchies cannot be automated; the main assurance of a satisfactory result is the skill and experience of the designer, and the designer's ability to interact with the domain experts. In this case it may be worth adopting formal techniques for specifying requirements in order to more accurately capture users' needs; for instance, the goal-oriented approach proposed by Giorgini, Rizzi, and Garzetti (2005) is based on an extension of the Tropos formalism and includes the following steps:

1.   Create, in the Tropos formalism, an *organizational model* that represents the stakeholders, their relationships, their goals as well as the relevant facts for the organization and the attributes that describe them.

2.   Create, in the Tropos formalism, a *decisional model* that expresses the analysis goals of decision makers and their information needs.

3.   Create preliminary fact schemata from the decisional model.

4.   Edit the fact schemata, for instance, by detecting functional dependencies between dimensions, recognizing optional dimensions, and unifying measures that only differ for the aggregation operator.

This approach is, in our view, more difficult to pursue than the previous one. Nevertheless, it is the only alternative when a detailed analysis of data sources cannot be made (for instance, when the DW is fed from an ERP system), or when the sources come from legacy systems whose complexity discourages recognition and normalization.

Mixed Approaches

Finally, also a few *mixed* approaches to design have been devised, aimed at joining the facilities of data-driven approaches with the guarantees of requirement-driven ones (Bonifati, Cattaneo, Ceri, Fuggetta, & Paraboschi, 2001; Giorgini et al., 2005). Here the user requirements, captured by means of a goal-oriented formalism, are matched with the schema of the source database to drive the algorithm that generates the conceptual schema for the DW. For instance, the approach proposed by Giorgini et al. (2005) encompasses three phases:

1.   Create, in the Tropos formalism, an *organizational model* that represents the stakeholders, their relationships, their goals, as well as the relevant facts for the organization and the attributes that describe them.

Copyright © 2007, Idea Group Inc. Copying or distributing in print or electronic forms without written permission of Idea Group Inc. is prohibited.

2. Create, in the Tropos formalism, a *decisional model* that expresses the analysis goals of decision makers and their information needs.

3. Map facts, dimensions, and measures identified during requirement analysis onto entities in the source schema.

4. Generate a preliminary conceptual schema by navigating the functional dependencies expressed by the source schema.

5. Edit the fact schemata to fully meet the user expectations.

Note that, though step 4 may be based on the same algorithm employed in step 2 of the data-driven approach, here navigation is not "blind" but rather it is actively biased by the user requirements. Thus, the preliminary fact schemata generated here may be considerably simpler and smaller than those obtained in the data-driven approach. Besides, while in that approach the analyst is asked for identifying facts, dimensions, and measures directly on the source schema, here such identification is driven by the diagrams developed during requirement analysis.

Overall, the mixed framework is recommendable when source schemata are well-known but their size and complexity are substantial. In fact, the cost for a more careful and formal analysis of requirement is balanced by the quickening of conceptual design.

Open Issues

A lot of work has been done in the field of conceptual modeling for DWs; nevertheless some very important issues still remain open. We report some of them in this section, as they emerged during joint discussion at the *Perspective Seminar on "Data Warehousing at the Crossroads"* that took place at Dagstuhl, Germany on August 2004.

- **Lack of a standard:** Though several conceptual models have been proposed, none of them has been accepted as a standard so far, and all vendors propose their own proprietary design methods. We see two main reasons for this: (1) though the conceptual models devised are semantically rich, some of the modeled properties cannot be expressed in the target logical models, so the translation from conceptual to logical is incomplete; and (2) commercial CASE tools currently enable designers to directly draw logical schemata, thus no industrial push is given to any of the models. On the other hand, a unified conceptual model for DWs, implemented by sophisticated CASE tools, would be a valuable support for both the research and industrial communities.

Copyright © 2007, Idea Group Inc. Copying or distributing in print or electronic forms without written permission of Idea Group Inc. is prohibited.

- **Design patterns:** In software engineering, design patterns are a precious support for designers since they propose standard solutions to address common modeling problems. Recently, some preliminary attempts have been made to identify relevant patterns for multidimensional design, aimed at assisting DW designers during their modeling tasks by providing an approach for recognizing dimensions in a systematic and usable way (Jones & Song, 2005). Though we agree that DW design would undoubtedly benefit from adopting a pattern-based approach, and we also recognize the utility of patterns in increasing the effectiveness of teaching how to design, we believe that further research is necessary in order to achieve a more comprehensive characterization of multidimensional patterns for both conceptual and logical design.

- **Modeling security:** Information security is a serious requirement that must be carefully considered in software engineering, not in isolation but as an issue underlying all stages of the development life cycle, from requirement analysis to implementation and maintenance. The problem of information security is even bigger in DWs, as these systems are used to discover crucial business information in strategic decision making. Some approaches to security in DWs, focused, for instance, on access control and multilevel security, can be found in the literature (see, for instance, Priebe & Pernul, 2000), but neither of them treats security as comprising all stages of the DW development cycle. Besides, the classical security model used in transactional databases, centered on tables, rows, and attributes, is unsuitable for DW and should be replaced by an ad hoc model centered on the main concepts of multidimensional modeling—such as facts, dimensions, and measures.

- **Modeling ETL:** ETL is a cornerstone of the data warehousing process, and its design and implementation may easily take 50% of the total time for setting up a DW. In the literature some approaches were devised for conceptual modeling of the ETL process from either the functional (Vassiliadis, Simitsis, & Skiadopoulos, 2002), the dynamic (Bouzeghoub, Fabret, & Matulovic, 1999), or the static (Calvanese, De Giacomo, Lenzerini, Nardi, & Rosati, 1998) points of view. Recently, also some interesting work on translating conceptual into logical ETL schemata has been done (Simitsis, 2005). Nevertheless, issues such as the optimization of ETL logical schemata are not very well understood. Besides, there is a need for techniques that automatically propagate changes occurred in the source schemas to the ETL process.

Conclusion

In this chapter we have proposed a set of solutions for conceptual modeling of a DW according to the DFM. Since 1998, the DFM has been successfully adopted, in real

Copyright © 2007, Idea Group Inc. Copying or distributing in print or electronic forms without written permission of Idea Group Inc. is prohibited.

Figure 8. Editing a fact schema in WAND

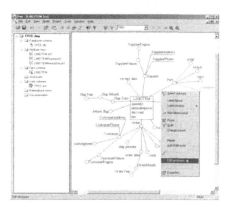

DW projects mainly in the fields of retail, large distribution, telecommunications, health, justice, and instruction, where it has proved expressive enough to capture a wide variety of modeling situations. Remarkably, in most projects the DFM was also used to directly support dialogue with end users aimed at validating requirements, and to express the expected workload for the DW to be used for logical and physical design. This was made possible by the adoption of a CASE tool named WAND (warehouse integrated designer), entirely developed at the University of Bologna, that assists the designer in structuring a DW. WAND carries out data-driven conceptual design in a semiautomatic fashion starting from the logical scheme of the source database (see Figure 8), allows for a core workload to be defined on the conceptual scheme, and carries out workload-based logical design to produce an optimized relational scheme for the DW (Golfarelli & Rizzi, 2001).

Overall, our on-the-field experience confirmed that adopting conceptual modeling within a DW project brings great advantages since:

- Conceptual schemata are the best support for discussing, verifying, and refining user specifications since they achieve the optimal trade-off between expressivity and clarity. Star schemata could hardly be used to this purpose.

- For the same reason, conceptual schemata are an irreplaceable component of the documentation for the DW project.

- They provide a solid and platform-independent foundation for logical and physical design.

- They are an effective support for maintaining and extending the DW.

- They make turn-over of designers and administrators on a DW project quicker and simpler.

Copyright © 2007, Idea Group Inc. Copying or distributing in print or electronic forms without written permission of Idea Group Inc. is prohibited.

References

Abelló, A., Samos, J., & Saltor, F. (2002, July 17-19). YAM2 (Yet another multidimensional model): An extension of UML. In *Proceedings of the International Database Engineering & Applications Symposium* (pp. 172-181). Edmonton, Canada.

Agrawal, R., Gupta, A., & Sarawagi, S. (1995). *Modeling multidimensional databases* (IBM Research Report). IBM Almaden Research Center, San Jose, CA.

Bonifati, A., Cattaneo, F., Ceri, S., Fuggetta, A., & Paraboschi, S. (2001). Designing data marts for data warehouses. *ACM Transactions on Software Engineering and Methodology, 10*(4), 452-483.

Bouzeghoub, M., Fabret, F., & Matulovic, M. (1999). Modeling data warehouse refreshment process as a workflow application. In *Proceedings of the International Workshop on Design and Management of Data Warehouses*, Heidelberg, Germany.

Cabibbo, L., & Torlone, R. (1998, March 23-27). A logical approach to multidimensional databases. In *Proceedings of the International Conference on Extending Database Technology* (pp. 183-197). Valencia, Spain.

Calvanese, D., De Giacomo, G., Lenzerini, M., Nardi, D., & Rosati, R. (1998, August 20-22). Information integration: Conceptual modeling and reasoning support. In *Proceedings of the International Conference on Cooperative Information Systems* (pp. 280-291). New York.

Datta, A., & Thomas, H. (1997). A conceptual model and algebra for on-line analytical processing in data warehouses. In *Proceedings of the Workshop for Information Technology and Systems* (pp. 91-100).

Fahrner, C., & Vossen, G. (1995). A survey of database transformations based on the entity-relationship model. *Data & Knowledge Engineering, 15*(3), 213-250.

Franconi, E., & Kamble, A. (2004a, June 7-11). The GMD data model and algebra for multidimensional information. In *Proceedings of the Conference on Advanced Information Systems Engineering* (pp. 446-462). Riga, Latvia.

Franconi, E., & Kamble, A. (2004b). A data warehouse conceptual data model. In *Proceedings of the International Conference on Statistical and Scientific Database Management* (pp. 435-436).

Giorgini, P., Rizzi, S., & Garzetti, M. (2005, November 4-5). Goal-oriented requirement analysis for data warehouse design. In *Proceedings of the ACM International Workshop on Data Warehousing and OLAP* (pp. 47-56). Bremen, Germany.

Golfarelli, M., Maio, D., & Rizzi, S. (1998). The dimensional fact model: A conceptual model for data warehouses. *International Journal of Cooperative Information Systems, 7*(2-3), 215-247.

Copyright © 2007, Idea Group Inc. Copying or distributing in print or electronic forms without written permission of Idea Group Inc. is prohibited.

Golfarelli, M., & Rizzi, S. (2001, April 2-6). WAND: A CASE tool for data warehouse design. In *Demo Proceedings of the International Conference on Data Engineering* (pp. 7-9). Heidelberg, Germany.

Gyssens, M., & Lakshmanan, L. V. S. (1997). A foundation for multi-dimensional databases. In *Proceedings of the International Conference on Very Large Data Bases* (pp. 106-115), Athens, Greece.

Hüsemann, B., Lechtenbörger, J., & Vossen, G. (2000). Conceptual data warehouse design. In *Proceedings of the International Workshop on Design and Management of Data Warehouses*, Stockholm, Sweden.

Jones, M. E., & Song, I. Y. (2005). Dimensional modeling: Identifying, classifying & applying patterns. In *Proceedings of the ACM International Workshop on Data Warehousing and OLAP* (pp. 29-38). Bremen, Germany.

Kimball, R. (1996). *The data warehouse toolkit*. New York: John Wiley & Sons.

Lechtenbörger , J. (2001). *Data warehouse schema design* (Tech. Rep. No. 79). DISDBIS Akademische Verlagsgesellschaft Aka GmbH, Germany.

Lenz, H. J., & Shoshani, A. (1997). Summarizability in OLAP and statistical databases. In *Proceedings of the 9th International Conference on Statistical and Scientific Database Management* (pp. 132-143). Washington, DC.

Li, C., & Wang, X. S. (1996). A data model for supporting on-line analytical processing. In *Proceedings of the International Conference on Information and Knowledge Management* (pp. 81-88). Rockville, Maryland.

Luján-Mora, S., Trujillo, J., & Song, I. Y. (2002). Extending the UML for multidimensional modeling. In *Proceedings of the International Conference on the Unified Modeling Language* (pp. 290-304). Dresden, Germany.

Niemi, T., Nummenmaa, J., & Thanisch, P. (2001, June 4). Logical multidimensional database design for ragged and unbalanced aggregation. *Proceedings of the 3rd International Workshop on Design and Management of Data Warehouses,* Interlaken, Switzerland (p. 7).

Nguyen, T. B., Tjoa, A. M., & Wagner, R. (2000). An object-oriented multidimensional data model for OLAP. In *Proceedings of the International Conference on Web-Age Information Management* (pp. 69-82). Shanghai, China.

Pedersen, T. B., & Jensen, C. (1999). Multidimensional data modeling for complex data. In *Proceedings of the International Conference on Data Engineering* (pp. 336-345). Sydney, Austrialia.

Prakash, N., & Gosain, A. (2003). Requirements driven data warehouse development. In *Proceedings of the Conference on Advanced Information Systems Engineering—Short Papers*, Klagenfurt/Velden, Austria.

Priebe, T., & Pernul, G. (2000). Towards OLAP security design: Survey and research issues. In *Proceedings of the ACM International Workshop on Data Warehousing and OLAP* (pp. 33-40). Washington, DC.

Copyright © 2007, Idea Group Inc. Copying or distributing in print or electronic forms without written permission of Idea Group Inc. is prohibited.

SAP. (1998). *Data modeling with BW*. SAP America Inc. and SAP AG, Rockville, MD.

Sapia, C., Blaschka, M., Hofling, G., & Dinter, B. (1998). Extending the E/R model for the multidimensional paradigm. In *Proceedings of the International Conference on Conceptual Modeling*, Singapore.

Schiefer, J., List, B., & Bruckner, R. (2002). A holistic approach for managing requirements of data warehouse systems. In *Proceedings of the Americas Conference on Information Systems*.

Sen, A., & Sinha, A. P. (2005). A comparison of data warehousing methodologies. *Communications of the ACM, 48*(3), 79-84.

Simitsis, A. (2005). Mapping conceptual to logical models for ETL processes. In *Proceedings of the ACM International Workshop on Data Warehousing and OLAP* (pp. 67-76). Bremen, Germany.

Tryfona, N., Busborg, F., & Borch Christiansen, J. G. (1999). starER: A conceptual model for data warehouse design. In *Proceedings of the ACM International Workshop on Data Warehousing and OLAP*, Kansas City, Kansas (pp. 3-8).

Tsois, A., Karayannidis, N., & Sellis, T. (2001). MAC: Conceptual data modeling for OLAP. In *Proceedings of the International Workshop on Design and Management of Data Warehouses* (pp. 5.1-5.11). Interlaken, Switzerland.

Vassiliadis, P. (1998). Modeling multidimensional databases, cubes and cube operations. In *Proceedings of the 10th International Conference on Statistical and Scientific Database Management*, Capri, Italy.

Vassiliadis, P., Simitsis, A., & Skiadopoulos, S. (2002, November 8). Conceptual modeling for ETL processes. In *Proceedings of the ACM International Workshop on Data Warehousing and OLAP* (pp. 14-21). McLean, VA.

Winter, R., & Strauch, B. (2003). A method for demand-driven information requirements analysis in data warehousing projects. In *Proceedings of the Hawaii International Conference on System Sciences*, Kona (pp. 1359-1365).

Endnote

[1]   In this chapter we will only consider dynamicity at the *instance* level. Dynamicity at the *schema* level is related to the problem of evolution of DWs and is outside the scope of this chapter.

Copyright © 2007, Idea Group Inc. Copying or distributing in print or electronic forms without written permission of Idea Group Inc. is prohibited.

Chapter II

Handling Structural Heterogeneity in OLAP

Carlos A. Hurtado
Universidad de Chile, Chile

Claudio Gutierrez
Universidad de Chile, Chile

Abstract

Structural heterogeneous OLAP data arise when several OLAP dimensions with different structures are mixed into a single OLAP dimension. In this chapter, we examine the problems encountered when handling structural heterogeneity in OLAP and survey techniques that have been proposed to solve them. We show how to incorporate structural heterogeneity in the design of OLAP models. We explain why structural heterogeneity weakens aggregate navigation, the framework that guides users to formulate correct OLAP operations and systems to efficiently process them. We survey different techniques to deal with heterogeneity, including the modeling of heterogeneity by unbalanced dimensions, the solution proposed by Kimball, and the use of null elements to fix heterogeneity. Finally, we present a class of integrity constraints to model structural heterogeneity, called dimension constraints, introduced in previous work of the authors. We show the practical application of dimension constraints to support aggregate navigation and some of the aforementioned techniques for dealing with the problem.

Copyright © 2007, Idea Group Inc. Copying or distributing in print or electronic forms without written permission of Idea Group Inc. is prohibited.

Introduction

Much of the success of OLAP can be attributed to the intuitive approach to data visualization provided by the multidimensional data model. Nowadays, the notions of facts and dimensions have been largely disseminated among database practitioners and researchers and have been proved to be useful metaphors to support querying data for decision support. The simplicity of the multidimensional model, however, stands on some assumptions about the regularity of data which are unnatural in many applications. In this chapter, we study the implications of relaxing one of the cores of such assumptions, namely the *homogeneity* of the structure of OLAP dimensions. Structurally heterogeneous OLAP data have been reported in the OLAP literature almost since the origins of the term OLAP itself and have concentrated significant research work since then (Hurtado, Gutierrez, & Mendelzon, 2005; Huseman, Lechtenborger, & Vossen, 2000; Jagadish, Lakshmanan, & Srivastava, 1999; Kimball, 1996; Lehner, Albrecht, & Wedekind, 1998; Malinowski & Zimanyi, 2004; Pedersen, Jensen, & Dyreson, 2001).

Motivation

In the multidimensional data model, dimensions represent the perspectives upon which data is viewed, and facts represent events that associate points of such dimensions to measures. For example, a sale of a particular product in a particular store of a retail chain can be viewed as a fact, which may be represented as a point in a space whose dimensions are products, stores, and time, and can be associated with one or more measures such as price or profit.

The phenomenon we study in this chapter is related to OLAP dimensions and, more precisely, to their structure. The structure of a dimension is modeled as a hierarchy of categories. Each category represents a level of abstraction upon which facts are aggregated. For example, in a dimension that models the products of a retailer, shown in Figure 1, we have a category *Product* which rolls up to a *Brand* category, which in turn rolls up to the top category *All*. The elements of the dimensions are grouped into the categories and connected by a child/parent relationship, which yields a hierarchy of elements which parallels the hierarchy of categories. Following terminology from Jagadish et al. (1999) and from Hurtado et al. (2005), we refer to the hierarchies of categories and elements respectively as hierarchy schema and hierarchy domain.

Each element of a dimension can be viewed as having a structure on its own. This structure of an element is the subgraph of the hierarchy schema induced by the ancestors of that element and their child/parent relationship. In our example of Figure 1, the Product element p_1 has the entire hierarchy schema as structure, and

Copyright © 2007, Idea Group Inc. Copying or distributing in print or electronic forms without written permission of Idea Group Inc. is prohibited.

Figure 1. A homogeneous product dimension; (a) hierarchy schema; (b) hierarchy domain

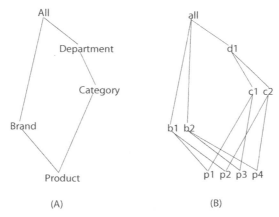

(A)   (B)

Note: To each category node in (a) correspond a set of element nodes in (b). This dimension is homogeneous; that is, each element node has the same structure; their ancestors induce the same subgraph.

the Brand element b_2 only has the substructure composed by the categories Brand and All. Nevertheless, all the elements in the same category have the same structure in this dimension. In this sense the dimension can be regarded as structurally homogeneous.

In several situations, the structure of the elements in a category may not be the same. Dimensions may require mixing in a single category elements representing the same conceptual entity, but having different structure. These dimensions, which are the focus of this chapter, have been called *non-covering* (Malinowsky & Zimanyi, 2004; Pedersen et al., 2001), structurally heterogeneous (Hurtado & Mendelzon, 2002; Hurtado et al., 2005), or *ragged* in the OLAP industry.

Kimball (1996), modeling products of retailers, coined the term *heterogeneous products* to refer to product elements that exhibit irregularities in their dimension structure. As an example, he stated that virtually every financial services database has products with different structures. A bank could easily have a dozen or more product types such as savings account, time deposit, or credit card, and each of them may have its own set of categories and measures. Similar situations arise in other application domains such as retail, insurance, subscription, and voyages business. As an example, consider the product dimension for a retail warehouse given in Figure 2, which has product elements with different structures. Products may be musical (e.g., CDs) or electrical products (e.g., speakers, audio systems). The electrical products have brands, but the musical do not. Similarly, not all the products are sold on shelves of physical stores, since the retailer has an e-commerce site

Copyright © 2007, Idea Group Inc. Copying or distributing in print or electronic forms without written permission of Idea Group Inc. is prohibited.

Figure 2. A heterogeneous product dimension; (a) hierarchy schema; (b) hierarchy domain

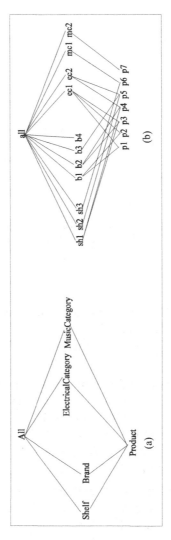

Note: This dimension is heterogeneous; that is, there are element nodes with different structures. For example, the element p_1 and p_6 belong to the same category but have different structures.

where some products are offered. Figure 3 shows the different structures mixed in this heterogeneous version of a product dimension. The example could be turned much more complex if we consider different categories and attributes associated to electric products such as speakers, video systems, and so on.

In a relational database setting, an OLAP dimension can be viewed as a set of tuples, whose attributes are the categories of the hierarchy schema. In particular, if the

Copyright © 2007, Idea Group Inc. Copying or distributing in print or electronic forms without written permission of Idea Group Inc. is prohibited.

Figure 3. Different structures mixed in the heterogeneous dimension of Figure 2

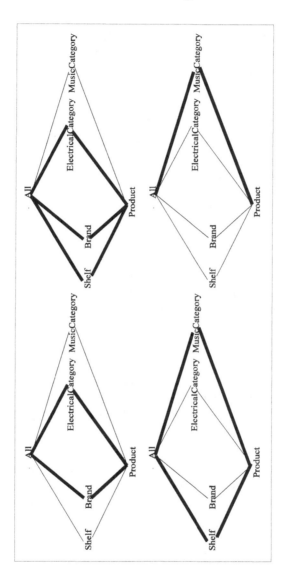

data are modeled using a star schema (Kimball, 1996), the dimension would be a single table having a tuple for each leaf element in its hierarchy domain. One may generalize this idea and think of an element as a tuple composed of the ancestor's elements and their attributes. As an example, the element p_1 in the dimension of Figure 1 produces the tuple:

Copyright © 2007, Idea Group Inc. Copying or distributing in print or electronic forms without written permission of Idea Group Inc. is prohibited.

[*Product*: p_1, *Brand*: b_1, *Category*: c_1, *Department*: d_1, *All*: *all*].

By viewing a dimension as a set of relational tuples, it is not difficult to realize practical situations that cause structural heterogeneity. As an example, the problem may arise when the OLAP server extracts tuples from more than one table having different attributes. In addition, a table itself may have nonapplicable attributes or missing values, which translate into non-applicable attributes for the corresponding elements in the dimension. As an example, the following two structurally different tuples arise for the product elements p_1 and p_6 in the dimension of Figure 2:

[*Product*: p_1, *Brand*: b_1, *ElectricalCategory*: ec_1, *All*: *all*],

[*Product*: p_6, *Shelf*: sh_1, *MusicalCategory*: mc_1, *All*: *all*].

The nonapplicability of categories is not the only situation that causes structural heterogeneity. A difference in the hierarchical arrangement of the categories of two elements may cause heterogeneity. As an example, consider the product dimension of Figure 4. The two different structures mixed in the top category of this dimension are shown in Figure 5. The elements p_1, p_2, p_3, p_4 have the structure shown in the left-hand side of Figure 5, and the element p_5 has the structure of the right-hand side. Notice that the elements have the same set of categories in their structures.

A homogeneous model for this dimension can be obtained simply by abstracting away the child/parent relation from *Brand* to *Category*. However, the heterogeneous version models an underlying hierarchy path from some products via some brands to some categories, which can be of interest to be navigated by users via standard OLAP operations. As we will illustrate in further sections, the artificial flattening of the hierarchy is not in general the best approach to handle structural irregularities. It is central to OLAP systems to take advantage of the hierarchical arrangement of data in dimensions at the query formulation and query processing stages.

In OLAP, queries are essentially views that aggregate raw facts to a granularity specified by a list of categories, called granularities, selected from a list of dimensions. The central technique for speeding up OLAP query processing is to materialize (precompute) some aggregate views and use them for the derivation of other aggregate views, using operations called roll-up operations. Aggregate navigation, a central technique in OLAP, is the process of finding and testing correct derivations of aggregate views from other precomputed aggregate views at lower granularities. Since the cost of computing a cube view is essentially linear in the number of facts accessed in the computation, this technique can speed up this processing by a factor which can be up to several orders of magnitude in real scenarios (Kimball, 1995). The central problem caused by heterogeneity is the obsolescence of the framework

Copyright © 2007, Idea Group Inc. Copying or distributing in print or electronic forms without written permission of Idea Group Inc. is prohibited.

Figure 4. A heterogeneous version of a product dimension; (a) hierarchy schema; (b) hierarchy domain

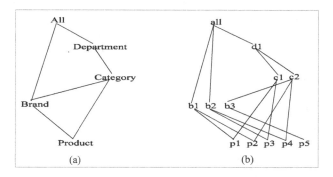

(a)   (b)

Figure 5. Different structures mixed in a heterogeneous dimension of Figure 4

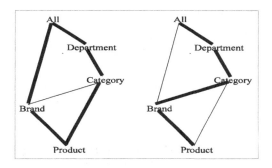

of OLAP aggregate navigation that underlies OLAP systems, which yields the inefficiency of computing the aggregate views always from the raw facts.

Content

In this chapter, we show how to incorporate structural heterogeneity in OLAP data models. We explain the central concepts of the graph model proposed in previous work (Hurtado et al., 2005), and study structural heterogeneity in this framework. We explain why structural heterogeneity weakens the role of the hierarchy schemas in supporting aggregate navigation, and in helping users to formulate correct OLAP operations. We also explain the implication of heterogeneity to star and snowflake models.

Copyright © 2007, Idea Group Inc. Copying or distributing in print or electronic forms without written permission of Idea Group Inc. is prohibited.

We study different solutions proposed to keep the ability of OLAP systems to perform aggregate navigation when the dimensions are structurally heterogeneous. We overview the modeling of heterogeneity by the unbalanced dimensions of Jagadish et al. (1999) and the solution proposed by Kimball (1996). We also explain how the irregularity of heterogeneous dimensions can be fixed with null elements, which is the approach of Pedersen, Jensen, and Dyreson (1999).

The solutions have in common that heterogeneous data are transformed into homogeneous data; thus any commercial OLAP system may be used to handle the data. In these frameworks, getting rid of heterogeneity becomes a problem that appears in the design and preprocessing stage of OLAP data. We explain a different strategy to approach the problem, which is the model heterogeneity at the schema level of the dimensions by enriching it with a class of integrity constraints called dimension constraints introduced in previous work (Hurtado & Mendelzon, 2002; Hurtado et al., 2005). Dimension constraints are Boolean expressions over categories and paths of them, which allow stating restrictions on the structure of the dimension elements. We explain two major applications of dimension constrains. We show the role dimension constraints play in supporting transformations of heterogeneous dimensions to the structural adaptations. We also explain how standard OLAP aggregate navigation can be extended to heterogeneous schemas by performing inference over dimension constraints.

Finally, we present the conclusions and outline open problems.

Structural Heterogeneity

We will start this section by studying dimensions, facts, cube views, and data cubes, which are the main notions in the multidimensional data model. We also define structural heterogeneity. Then we will explain the notion of aggregate navigation and the problems caused by heterogeneity.

Dimension Modeling

In this section we introduce a model of OLAP dimensions presented in previous work (Hurtado et al., 2005), which considers notions from previous dimension models (Cabibbo & Torlone, 1998; Hurtado, Mendelzon & Vaisman, 1999; Jagadish et al., 1999) and formalizes them in terms of basic notions of graph theory. Basic notions of graph theory used can be consulted in any standard graph theory book (West, 1996). The model allows heterogeneity, among other features not encountered in traditional dimension models. By "traditional" we refer to the most common type

Copyright © 2007, Idea Group Inc. Copying or distributing in print or electronic forms without written permission of Idea Group Inc. is prohibited.

of dimensions that appear in textbooks, white papers, and early research papers on OLAP, first formalized by Cabbibo and Torleone (1998).

Hierarchy Schema

The hierarchy schema is the standard structure for representing the semantics of OLAP dimensions. This structure is common to different models. The hierarchy schema is modeled as a directed acyclic graph (DAG) $(C, \prec)$ whose set of nodes C contains categories, and $\prec$ represents the incidence relation, that is, $c_1 \prec c_2$ indicates that the category c_1 is connected to the category c_2 in the hierarchy schema. We will draw the direction of the edges always upward. The DAG has a distinguished category All reachable by a path from every other category (top category). There may be several nodes with no ancestors (bottom categories). A *hierarchy path* is a path of categories from a bottom category to the top category. As an example, the graphs in the left-hand sides of Figures 1, 2, and 4 are hierarchy schemas.

The notion of hierarchy schema presented has two differences with the traditional notion for homogeneous dimensions. First, we allow more than one bottom category. This is important in order for the model to allow unbalanced dimensions, a structural adaptation of dimension models, which will be explained in what follows. Second, the model allows *shortcuts* in the hierarchy schema. A *shortcut* is a path of length greater than one between a pair of adjacent categories. As an example, the path *Brand* $\prec$ *Category* $\prec$ *Department* $\prec$ *All* in Figure 4a is a shortcut. Shortcuts are important in heterogeneous data because they allow the modeling of the situation where an element skips a parent category when going to a higher category. As an example, the city of Washington may skip the category *State* and go directly to the category *Country* in a dimension representing locations.

Hierarchy Domain

The hierarchy domain is the graph that models the hierarchical arrangement of the elements of the dimension. It is also formalized with a DAG, where the nodes represent the elements of the dimension. Formally, the hierarchy domain is a pair $(M, <)$, where M is the set of elements of the dimension and $<$ represents the child/parent relationship between elements. The DAG has a distinguished top node *all*. As an example, in the dimension of Figure 4, we have $p_5 < b_3 < c_2 < d_1 < all$. The descendant/ancestor relationship, denoted $<$, is the transitive closure of the relation $<$. As an example, in the dimension of Figure 4, from the existence of a child/parent path from 5 to *all*, it follows $p_5 < all$. The hierarchy domain may have many bottom elements, but it is not allowed to have shortcuts. The reason for this is that a shortcut from an element e_1 to an element e_2 is redundant information. As examples, the graphs in the right-hand sides of Figures 1, 2, and 4 are hierarchy domains.

Copyright © 2007, Idea Group Inc. Copying or distributing in print or electronic forms without written permission of Idea Group Inc. is prohibited.

Dimension

A dimension comprises a hierarchy schema $(C, \prec)$, a hierarchy domain $(M, <)$, and a function $\delta : M \to C$ that defines the category to which each element belongs. In particular, the element *all* is mapped to the category *All*, that is, $\delta(all) = All$. The fundamental property of the function δ is that whenever two elements satisfy $e_1 < e_2$ in the hierarchy domain, the corresponding categories to which they belong satisfy $\delta(e_1) \prec \delta(e_2)$. In other words, an edge in the hierarchy domain implies an edge between the corresponding categories in the hierarchy schema. In more technical words, the function δ is a *graph morphism* (West, 1996) that relates the two graphs of a dimension. As an example, consider the dimension of Figure 4. Here, because $b_3 < c_2$, there must exist an edge from *Brand* to *Category* (i.e., *Brand* $\prec$ *Category*) in the hierarchy schema.

A central restriction in OLAP data models (Cabibbo & Torlone, 1998; Hurtado & Mendelzon, 2001, 2002; Hurtado et al., 2005; Lehner et al., 1998) is that each element of a category c should go (directly or indirectly) to no more than one element in each category above the category c. This restriction is called strictness. Formally, if $x < y$ and $x < z$ for two different elements y, z, then $\delta(y) \neq (z)$. The handling of nonstrict dimensions in OLAP has been studied by Pedersen et al. (1999) and by Malinowski and Zymanyi (2004). This issue is orthogonal to the topics treated in this chapter.

Defining Heterogeneity

Heterogeneity can be characterized in the graph model in a simple way. A dimension is homogeneous if for every pairs of connected categories c_1, c_2 (i.e., $c_1 \prec c_2$), each element of c_1 has a parent in c_2. A dimension is heterogeneous if it is not homogeneous. As an example, the dimension of Figure 1 is homogeneous. In contrast, the dimensions of Figures 2 and 4 are heterogeneous.

Rollup Relation

There could be different approaches to query OLAP data over graph models of dimensions like the model explained here. Jagadish et al. (1999) propose SQL(H), a query language that includes the descendant/ancestor relationship as a built-in predicate which allows for succinctly expressing many useful queries in an SQL style. The rollup relation between two categories allows expressing relational queries over the graph model of the dimension (e.g., using SQL). Let c_1, c_2 be two categories of a fixed dimension such that c_1 reaches c_2 in the hierarchy schema (i.e., $c_1 \prec$

Copyright © 2007, Idea Group Inc. Copying or distributing in print or electronic forms without written permission of Idea Group Inc. is prohibited.

c_2). The rollup relation from c_1 to c_2 in a dimension δ, denoted $\Gamma[c_1, c_2]$ is defined as the relational table having attributes c_1, c_2, and containing the set of tuples $[c_1 : e_1 : c_2 : e_2]$ such that $\delta(e_1) = c_1$, $\delta(e_2) = c_2$, and $e_1 < e_2$. Notice that the rollup relation is defined for pairs of categories that are (directly or indirectly) connected in the hierarchy schema. Note also that the notions of strictness and homogeneity can be defined in terms of the rollup relation. A dimension is strict if and only it has functional (i.e., single valued) rollup relations. A dimension is homogeneous if and only if each rollup relation $\Gamma[c_1, c_2]$ is total over the elements in c_1.

Facts and Data Cubes

A fact is a data entity that relates a list of elements, taken from a list of dimensions, to measures of interest. Facts may be represented as tuples in fact tables. A multi-dimensional database comprises a set of dimensions, along with a base fact table, that is, a fact table whose attributes are the bottom categories of the dimensions. If the dimension has many bottom categories, we may define a new unique category, containing all the bottom elements, to address the base facts.

Cube Views, Data Cube

OLAP users need to analyze facts aggregated at multiple levels of abstraction. The basic query that aggregates base facts at a granularity given by a list of categories, one per dimension, is called a cube view. As an example, consider that the list of dimensions has only the dimension of Figure 1. In this case, a granularity also can be specified with a single category. The base fact table is the table *SalesAtProduct* which has as attributes *Product* and *Amount* (this last attribute is the measure). A cube view that sums the amounts sold at the category *Department* can be defined by the following aggregate query:

SELECT *Department*, SUM(*Amount*)

FROM *SalesAtProduct*,Γ[*Product,Department*]

WHERE *SalesAtProduct.Product*=Γ[*Product,Department*].*Product*

GROUP BY *Department*.

A data cube is the set of all possible cube views defined over a list of dimensions, a base table, and aggregated measures. In the context of a fixed data cube, we may denote a cube view simply as *CV*[*G*] where *G* is a granularity (list of categories). As an example, the previous cube view can be denoted simply as *CV*[*Department*].

Copyright © 2007, Idea Group Inc. Copying or distributing in print or electronic forms without written permission of Idea Group Inc. is prohibited.

OLAP Aggregate Navigation

Rollup and Drilldown Operations

There are two main operators to move among the different cube views in a data cube, namely the rollup and drilldown operators (Jarke, Lenzerini, Vassiliou, & Vassiliadis, 1997). Given two granularities G and G', a rollup operation aggregates the cube view $CV[G]$ to the granularity G'. As an example, a rollup from a single-category granularity *Category* to the granularity *Department* in a data cube for the dimension of Figure 1 can be defined using the following aggregate query:

SELECT *Department*, SUM(*Amount*)

FROM *CV[Category]*,Γ[*Category,Department*]

WHERE *CV[Category].Category*=Γ[*Category,Department*].*Category*

GROUP BY *Department*.

This rollup operation, applied to the cube view $CV[Category]$ aggregates the facts in it to the granularity of aggregation specified by the category *Department*. In the context of a fixed data cube we abbreviate this rollup operation as ROLLUP *Category* TO *Department*. Rollup operations have also been called *summarizations* (Lenz & Shoshani, 1997) or *consolidations* (Harinarayan, Rajaraman, & Ullman, 1996). The drill down operation has the inverse effect of the rollup operation and allows users to move to a cube view at a lower granularity.

Dependence

The possible roll-up and drill-down operations can be represented by a structure called cube dependence graph, which is defined as the direct product of the list of hierarchy schemas involved. That is, a granularity G' is connected to a granularity G if their corresponding categories are pairwise connected in the corresponding dimension.

The cube dependence graph is a useful representation for the system and user to navigate throughout aggregates at different granularities (Harinarayan et al., 1996). The cube dependence graph also generalizes structures to visualize aggregate views proposed for statistical databases, such as in the statistical object representation model by Rafanelli and Shoshani (1990). As an example, Figure 6 shows a cube dependence graph for the product dimension of Figure 1 and a time dimension with categories *Day*, *Year*, and *All*.

Copyright © 2007, Idea Group Inc. Copying or distributing in print or electronic forms without written permission of Idea Group Inc. is prohibited.

A fundamental property of a cube dependence graph in traditional OLAP models (homogeneous dimensions) is that the rollup operations are correct in the following sense: if a granularity *G* reaches *G'*, then the following holds: *CV*[*G'*]= ROLLUP *G* TO *G'*. That is, the cube view at *G'* can be correctly computed by a rollup operation from *G* to *G'*. In the terminology of Harinarayan et al. (1996), *G' depends* on *G*. Thus dependency between granularities corresponds to reachability in the cube dependence graph. Of course, in order for this to happen the aggregate function involved should be *distributive*. A distributive aggregate function can be computed on a set of measures by partitioning the set into disjoint subsets, aggregating each separately, and then computing the aggregation of these partial results with another aggregate function (which in many cases is the same function). Among the SQL aggregate functions, COUNT, SUM, MIN, and MAX are distributive. As we will see later, in this setting, the correctness of the rollup operations requires the dimensions to be homogeneous.

Summarizability

The notion of summarizability was proposed to study aggregate navigation for statistical objects and OLAP dimensions (Hurtado & Mendelzon, 2001, 2002; Hurtado et al., 2005; Lehner et al., 1998; Lenz & Shoshani, 1997). Summarizability refers to the conditions upon which a rollup operation defined over a single dimension is correct; that is, summarizability corresponds to dependence for single categories taken from a fixed dimension. For the one-dimensional case, the cube dependence graph is just

Figure 6. A cube dependence graph

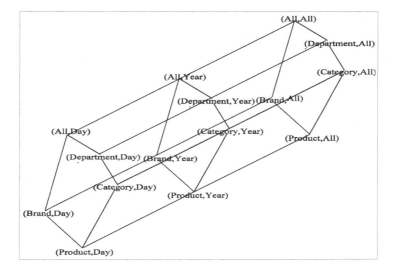

Copyright © 2007, Idea Group Inc. Copying or distributing in print or electronic forms without written permission of Idea Group Inc. is prohibited.

the hierarchy schema, and consequently in traditional OLAP models (homogeneous dimensions) summarizability is equivalent to reachability in the hierarchy schema.

Anomalies Caused by Heterogeneity

The main role of the schema of a dimension is to guide users in the application of OLAP operations and to prevent users from formulating erroneous operations. Heterogeneity may turn hierarchy schemas into entangled structures for visualizing OLAP data and formulating correct aggregate operations.

Complexity of Heterogeneous Dimensions

In the presence of heterogeneity the hierarchy schema may become awkward. A heterogeneous dimension comprising a dozen product types may carry more than 100 categories, and some of them would be empty for almost every element of the dimension (Kimball, 1996). The problem is not only that some categories are not valid for some elements, but that different combinations of categories and paths may not be valid, and the hierarchy schema does not provide enough semantics to understand this. Consequently, it may be difficult for users to understand the hierarchy domain by visualizing the hierarchy schema, as can be observed in the dimension of Figure 7. This dimension is a more complex heterogeneous version that models electronic products and CDs of a retailer.

Implications for Summarizability

In a heterogeneous dimension the rollup operations are not necessarily correct. Stated in OLAP terminology, in heterogeneous dimensions summarizability does not necessarily correspond to reachability in the hierarchy schema. That is, we cannot infer the correctness of rollup operations just by viewing the hierarchy schema. As an example, the rollup operation

ROLLUP *Brand* TO *Category*

is not correct in the dimension of Figure 4, since some products would not be counted in the derivation. In general, under heterogeneity, hierarchy schemas may have inconsistent paths, that is, paths $c_1 \prec c_2 \prec c_3 \prec ... c_n$ in the hierarchy schema for which some category $i+1$ is not summarizable from its preceding category i in the path. As an example, the following hierarchy path is inconsistent in the dimension of Figure 7:

Copyright © 2007, Idea Group Inc. Copying or distributing in print or electronic forms without written permission of Idea Group Inc. is prohibited.

Figure 7. A heterogeneous dimension: (a) hierarchy schema; (b) hierarchy domain

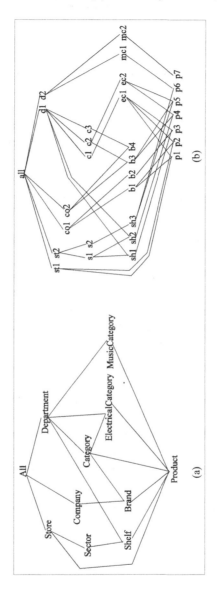

Product ≺ ElectricalCategory ≺ Category ≺ Department ≺ All.

In contrast, the path *Product ≺ Brand ≺ Company ≺ All* is consistent for the same dimension.

Copyright © 2007, Idea Group Inc. Copying or distributing in print or electronic forms without written permission of Idea Group Inc. is prohibited.

Implications for the Cube Dependence Graph

When the homogeneity condition is dropped, the correctness of a rollup operation does not follow from the cube dependence graph. The problem can be easily realized by noting that the cube dependence graph of a single dimension corresponds to its hierarchy schema. The anomalous behavior of the cube dependence graph has deep implications for OLAP query processing, since the cube dependence graph is used in algorithms to compute and maintain data cubes (Mumick, Quass, & Mumick, 1997), and to speed up OLAP query processing (Harinarayan et al., 1996).

Implications for Relational OLAP Models

Kimball (1996) argues that the best logical model to place OLAP queries is the star schema. In the star schema the dimension consists of a single table where the categories are arranged as attributes. We will refer to this table as a star dimension. The table organizes the dimension elements as tuples, and allows simple tuple browsing to place filters in OLAP queries. A star dimension requires the hierarchy schema to have a single bottom category, which is the key attribute of the table. The edges in the hierarchy schema are regarded as functional dependencies over the table.

Another relational realization of OLAP data is the snowflake schema, which yields snowflake dimensions. A snowflake dimension has one table per category c, which stores together all the rollup relations to the parent categories of c. The tables are normalized avoiding redundant data. However, in contrast to the star dimension, the snowflake dimension requires to process join operations over its tables, in order to assemble tuples for browsing and aggregate query processing.

Relationship among Graph, Star, and Snowflake Dimensions

Dimensions in the graph model we presented (we will refer to them simply as dimensions, in contrast to star and snowflake dimensions) can be easily translated to a star dimension (Hurtado et al., 1999), provided the dimension is homogeneous and has a single bottom category. The table has as attributes the categories of the dimension. For each bottom element m of the graph dimension, there is a tuple in the table composed of the ancestors of m. As an example, Table 1 shows the star dimension corresponding to the dimension of Figure 4.

The translation of a star dimension to a graph dimension requires capturing the rollup relations from the table. It is simply obtained by projecting the table over

Copyright © 2007, Idea Group Inc. Copying or distributing in print or electronic forms without written permission of Idea Group Inc. is prohibited.

Table 1.

Product	Brand	Category	Department
p_1	b_1	c_1	d_1
p_2	b_1	c_2	d_1
p_3	b_2	c_1	d_1
p_4	b_2	c_2	d_1
p_5	b_3	c_2	d_1

the categories involved in the rollup relation. As an example, the rollup relation $\Gamma[Brand,Category]$ can be obtained by the following query:

SELECT *Brand,Category* FROM Table_Product.

The translation between graph and snowflake dimensions is straightforward.

The problems reported in this chapter also appear in star and snowflake dimensions. We next explain further implications of heterogeneity for them.

Allowing Heterogeneity

In a relational table each element of dimension table needs one entry for each attribute. Thus in order to allow structural heterogeneity in star and snowflake schemas, null values should be allowed in the tables. It is not easy to do this since functional dependencies should be interpreted in presence of null values. In order to allow nulls, Lehner et al. (1998) propose weak functional dependencies, that is, functional dependencies $A \rightarrow B$ that do not constrain tuples when they have null values in the attribute B. The attributes that participate in the right sides of weak functional dependencies are treated outside the hierarchy schema as descriptive attributes for the categories. Weak functional dependencies can be used in snowflake dimensions. However, in star dimensions we may also need to interpret functional dependencies when nulls appear in the left side of the functional dependence. An additional problem is that due to the denormalized nature of star dimensions, heterogeneity may lead to a proliferation of null values in the table. Due to these problems, some researchers have stated that the star schema does not allow structural heterogeneity (Jagadish et al., 1999).

Copyright © 2007, Idea Group Inc. Copying or distributing in print or electronic forms without written permission of Idea Group Inc. is prohibited.

Table 2.

Brand	Category
b_1	c_1
b_1	c_2
b_2	c_1
b_2	c_2
b_3	c_2

Implications to the Representation of the Hierarchy Domain

In the presence of heterogeneity there is no precise correspondence between dimensions and star dimensions. The hierarchy domain (i.e., the hierarchical arrangement of elements) of a heterogeneous dimension may not be correctly captured by the star dimension. As an example, if we represent the heterogeneous dimension of Figure 4 as a star dimension, we cannot recover the original child/parent relation back. Indeed, if we try to recover the rollup relation $\Gamma[Brand,Category]$, we obtain the relation with a single pair $[Brand: b_3,Category:c_2]$. The original rollup relation is show in Table 2.

Among other problems, this implies that the standard semantics of drilldown and rollup operations differ for both models. Notice also that in this case, although the dimension is heterogeneous, its star representation does not have null values. This situation illustrates that, as explained in the introductory section, heterogeneity is not only caused by the nonapplicability of attributes (e.g., dimension of Figure 2) but also by the mixture of hierarchies in the dimension (e.g., dimension of Figure 4).

Adapting Heterogenous Dimensions

The general approach to handle structural heterogeneity in OLAP is to adapt or transform the dimensions in order to obtain homogeneous data. In this section we examine two approaches along this idea. First, we explain the use of null elements, and then we explore structural adjustments of heterogeneous dimension necessary to obtain homogeneous dimensions. In the latter case, the hierarchy schemas of the original dimensions are modified.

Copyright © 2007, Idea Group Inc. Copying or distributing in print or electronic forms without written permission of Idea Group Inc. is prohibited.

Null Elements

At first sight, as heterogeneity is nothing more than having elements without parents in some categories, the problem could be solved straightforwardly by adding null elements. In this form a heterogeneous dimension would be turned homogeneous without any modification of its structure. However, it is not easy to add null elements to get a homogeneous dimension whose rollup relations are strict, that is, without violating the fundamental property of dimensions explained. Using a single null element *null*, as in the relational database setting, does not prevent this problem. Pedersen et al. (1999) propose a method for adding null elements which overcomes this drawback. The central idea is to allow adding different nulls, which may be the result of breaking up some of the original elements of the dimension. The nulls are interpreted as regular elements and the resulting dimension is homogeneous, so the framework of aggregate navigation can be applied.

The transformation has low and practical complexity and can be applied to OLAP data in a preprocessing stage before loading the data cube. An algorithm, called *MakeCovering,* performs the transformation. The algorithm has polynomial time complexity on the size of the dimension. More precisely, the algorithm takes $O(k^2 n \log n)$, where k is the number of categories, and n is the size of the largest rollup relation.

In many situations the null elements have a low interference with the original data; and therefore handling heterogeneity with null elements has practical applicability in many cases. Intuitively, in such cases, the null elements play the role of the *other* or the *unknown* class. However, in worst-case scenarios, the transformation may lead to dimensions with many new null elements per category. In these cases, the number of rows of the data cube and cube views may be considerably increased due to the null elements. As some original elements of the dimension may be broken up into different nulls, the semantics of the original dimension may be altered. As an example, Figure 8 shows a homogeneous version of the dimension of Figure 4 with null elements. Notice that in order for the dimension to be strict, the elements b_1 and b_2 have been broken up into the null elements b_{11} , b_{12} and b_{21} , b_{22}, respectively. Also notice that the edges *Brand* ≺ *Category* and *Product* ≺ *Category* are not required in this dimension. Now, the hierarchy schema only models the hierarchy path *Product* ≺ *Brand* ≺ *Category* ≺ *Department* ≺ *All*.

Although the addition of nulls turns hierarchy paths consistent, null elements may cause meaningless aggregations inside rollup operations. As an example, consider the dimension of Figure 4, and the fact table *SalesAtProduct* representing the sales of the retailer. We may compute the sales and break them down by brands using the following rollup operation:

ROLLUP *Product* TO *Brand.*

Copyright © 2007, Idea Group Inc. Copying or distributing in print or electronic forms without written permission of Idea Group Inc. is prohibited.

Figure 8. A version of the dimension of Figure 4 with null elements: (a) hierarchy schema; (b) hierarchy domain

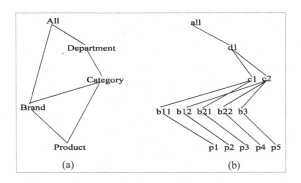

Nothing will prevent the OLAP system from scanning the entire set of base facts to compute the answer. However, not all of the base facts have brands; thus they are not needed in the aggregation.

Null values may also interfere with the result of more complex aggregate queries placed over facts at the data cube. An example is a class of queries that involves multiple dependent aggregates called *multifeature aggregates* (Chatziantoniou & Ross, 1996). Consider the following query that computes the maximum amount over all the total amounts sold for each brand:

SELECT *Brand*, MAX(*Amount*)

FROM *CV*[*Brand*].

The result would be incorrect if the total sales at some null element surpass the sales of each brand. This can happen in the dimension at hand if the sales of musical products surpass the sales for each electrical product. Lehner et al. (1998) report additional anomalies in actual OLAP scenarios due to contradictory queries that arise when handling heterogeneity with nulls.

Structural Adaptations

Another adaptation of standard dimension models to overcome the problems posed by structural heterogeneity is proposed by Jagadish et al. (1999). The main property of this model is to allow hierarchy paths starting from different bottom categories. In this setting the hierarchy paths look unbalanced, from where comes the motivation for calling so dimensions having this property. This model is subsumed by

Copyright © 2007, Idea Group Inc. Copying or distributing in print or electronic forms without written permission of Idea Group Inc. is prohibited.

Figure 9. An unbalanced dimension that models the Product dimension of Figure 2: (a) hierarchy schema; (b) hierarchy domain

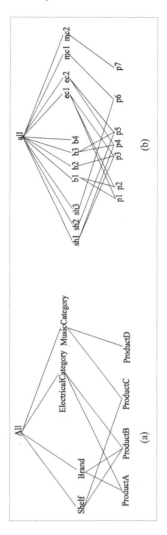

the graph model described in this chapter. The term unbalanced dimension is also used to refer to dimensions which handle child/parent relationships that cannot be modeled with fixed length paths in the dimension hierarchy (a good example is the relation boss/employee in a company). This use of the term slightly differs from the use given in this chapter.

The unbalancedness of the hierarchy schema is not allowed in traditional models, as in the early model of Cabbibo and Torleone (1998), along with the snowflake and the star schemas. The restriction of having a bottom category in these models is due

Copyright © 2007, Idea Group Inc. Copying or distributing in print or electronic forms without written permission of Idea Group Inc. is prohibited.

Figure 10. An unbalanced dimension that models the Product dimension of Figure 4: (a) hierarchy schema; (b) hierarchy domain

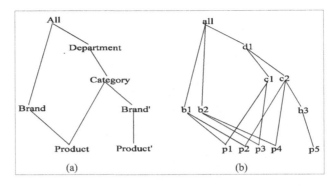

to the simplicity of having a unique bottom granularity at which the base facts are addressed (the attribute associated to such category participates in the composed key of the fact table in star and snowflake schemas). By allowing many bottom categories, the heterogeneous dimension can be broken up into the different structures that are mixed in the original dimension. In this form a homogeneous dimension having consistent paths for aggregate navigation is obtained.

Several commercial OLAP systems allow storing this sort of structure. Basically the user should enter separately each hierarchy path in a dimension set to allow multiple hierarchies.

As an example, Figure 9 shows an unbalanced homogeneous dimension that models the product dimension of Figure 2. Notice that the two dimensions have the same hierarchy domain. However, in the new dimension the products are broken up and stored in different categories for each of the four structures of Figure 3. Figure 10 shows an unbalanced homogeneous version for the heterogeneous dimension of Figure 4.

The model provides flexibility to define a different base fact table for each bottom category, a single base fact table for all the categories, or both. If we consider different fact tables, the hierarchy paths of the former are consistent. Now the cube view *CV[Department]* can be correctly computed by the rollup:

ROLLUP *Category* TO *Department*

If we consider cube views defined over a single base fact table that contains all the elements, the hierarchy paths are not consistent. In this case we need ROLLUP operations that combine categories, as we will see in the next section.

Kimball (1996) proposes a similar solution to deal with heterogeneity, but in his approach the homogeneous structures mixed are placed in separate dimensions.

Copyright © 2007, Idea Group Inc. Copying or distributing in print or electronic forms without written permission of Idea Group Inc. is prohibited.

Although the problem to solve is the nonapplicability of attributes, that is, the form of heterogeneity illustrated in the dimension of Figure 4, the solution works for the general case. The approach involves partitioning the original data cube into one data cube for each dimension. A dimension that contains the structure shared by all the resulting homogeneous dimensions, called the core dimension, is kept with a data cube, called core data cube, which aggregate facts at all the bottom elements of the original dimension.

Dimension Constraints

In this section we describe the approach of modeling heterogeneity with integrity constraints. We explain the framework of dimension constraints (Hurtado & Mendelzon, 2001; Hurtado et al., 2005), a class of integrity constraints for OLAP data that provide semantics to the hierarchy schema so that it is turned into a better abstraction to capture heterogeneity.

We first motivate dimension constraints. Then we explain how the homogeneous structures mixed in the dimension, called frozen dimensions, can be computed from the constraints, and explain inference of dimension constraints in this framework. Finally, we show the application of dimension constraints to support the structural adaptations explained in the previous section, and to reason about the correctness of OLAP aggregate operators in heterogeneous dimensions.

Examples

Dimension constraints are statements that specify categories and paths allowed in the structures of the elements of a dimension. We will illustrate the flavor of dimension constraints using the dimension of Figure 4. Observe that every product element of this dimension has the categories *Brand* and *ElectricalCategory* appearing together or not appearing at all. This can be expressed with the following constraint:

$\langle Product, Brand \rangle \Leftrightarrow \langle Product, ElectricalCategory \rangle.$

This constraint is a statement that holds for all elements at the category *Product*, which is the *root category* of the constraint. As an example, if we take the element p_1 and replace it in the constraint we obtain the expression:

$\langle p_1, Brand \rangle \Leftrightarrow \langle p_1, ElectricalCategory \rangle,$

Copyright © 2007, Idea Group Inc. Copying or distributing in print or electronic forms without written permission of Idea Group Inc. is prohibited.

which means that p_1 has an ancestor in *Brand* if and only if p_1 has an ancestor in *ElectricalCategory*. So the constraint allows to discard the structures in which *Brand* and *MusicCategory* do not appear together. This is important, since if we generalize the dimension of Figure 4 to have n different categories instead of just four, there might be $2^n - 1$ possible structures (one for each nonempty subset of categories). The hierarchy schema does not provide semantics to discard any of such structures.

Dimension constraints are Boolean combinations of atomic statements called *atoms*. We use the standard Boolean connectives ($\wedge, \vee, \neg, \Leftrightarrow, \Rightarrow$). Atoms are the expressions in brackets. As an example, the constraint:

$$\neg \langle Product, ElectricalCategory \rangle \vee \neg \langle Product, MusicCategory \rangle$$

states that the products have parents in either *ElectricalCategory* or *MusicCategory* but not in both of them.

We need negation, conjunction, and disjunction, to restrict structures and to reason about summarizability (Hurtado et al., 2005). This motivated us to incorporate the entire expressiveness of the Boolean connectives into dimension constraints. Dimension constraints also incorporate atoms of the form $\langle Product, Brand= b_3 \rangle$ called *equality atom* which make it possible to place restrictions conditioned on particular elements. As an additional example, we may write that the products that belong to brand b_3 are sold on shelves, using the following constraint:

$$\langle Product, Brand=b_3 \rangle \Rightarrow \langle Product, Shelf \rangle.$$

The constraints we have already showed are statements about the applicability of categories. We may also need to place restrictions about the applicability of hierarchy paths. We use *paths atoms* for this purpose. As an example, in the dimension of Figure 7, we may state that the products that belong to the electrical category ec_2 have the path $Brand \prec Category \prec Department \prec All$ in their structure, using the following constraint:

$$\langle Product, ElectricalCategory=ec_2 \rangle \Rightarrow \langle Product, Brand, Category, Department, All \rangle.$$

There are also atoms that restrict categories that may be indirectly reached by the root category. As an example, the dimension of Figure 4 may be modeled with just the following constraint:

$$\langle Product, Brand \rangle \vee \langle Product, .., Category \rangle.$$

Copyright © 2007, Idea Group Inc. Copying or distributing in print or electronic forms without written permission of Idea Group Inc. is prohibited.

With this constraint we discard structures that do not contain *Brand* or *Category*. However, the product elements may reach both directly or indirectly the elements at *Category*. In particular, the edge *BrandCategory* allows some elements to reach *Category* indirectly passing through *Brand*.

In previous work (Hurtado et al., 2005), dimension constraints are compared with other classes of constraints proposed to capture different forms of heterogeneity for OLAP (Huseman et al., 2000; Lehner et al., 1998), relational (Goldstein, 1981), and semistructured (Abiteboul & Vianu, 1999; Buneman, Fan & Weinstein, 1998) data. Among them, the constraints of Husemann et al. (2000) are closely related to dimension constraints in that they address a form of structural heterogeneity study in this chapter. These constraints are subsumed by dimension constraints. They allow expressing that two paths in the hierarchy schema that start from a single category are mandatory or alternative

Extracting Homogeneous Structures

In general, a hierarchy schema allows an exponential number of homogeneous structures and we may express them succinctly with dimension constraints. The situation is analogous to using propositional formulas to specify the truth values of a set of propositions. In the framework of dimension constraints the propositions are the atoms that state which parts of the homogeneous structure allowed. Such structures, called frozen dimensions, are themselves important to support visualization and to transform heterogeneous dimensions to structural adaptations previously explained. In addition, they are the basis for an inference algorithm for dimension constraints.

In previous work (Hurtado et al., 2005), we propose an algorithm to compute the frozen dimensions that arise in a dimension schema. A dimension schema is a hierarchy schema along with a set of dimension constraints. The algorithm explores subgraphs of the hierarchy schema, and tests whether they satisfy the constraints. The subgraphs are built by traversing the hierarchy schema from the bottom categories, and using dimension constraints for pruning. The algorithm runs in exponential time in the size of the schema. An experimental evaluation provided shows that the set frozen dimensions can be computed in the order of the few seconds for dimension schemas of around 25 categories and 120.000 frozen dimensions, that is, for schemas of much more complexity than the ones found in practical scenarios.

Inference

In the framework of dimension constraints the hierarchy schema is augmented with constraints yielding the notion of dimension schema. A dimension schema is a pair

Copyright © 2007, Idea Group Inc. Copying or distributing in print or electronic forms without written permission of Idea Group Inc. is prohibited.

$D = (H, \Sigma)$, where H is a hierarchy schema, and Σ is a set of dimension constraints. A dimension schema specifies a set of possible dimensions, that is, the dimensions that have the hierarchy schema H and satisfy the set of constraints Σ. Those dimensions are the possible instances of the schema.

A dimension schema D *logically implies* a dimension constraint α, if every dimension d over the schema D satisfies α. The *implication problem* for dimension constraints is the problem of determining, given a dimension schema D and a dimension constraint α, whether D implies α. Although the implication problem for dimension constraints is CoNP-complete in the size of the schema, due to the sizes of schemas occurring in practice, it is treatable. The problem reduces to computing the frozen dimensions of the schema. An algorithm to test implication based on the computation of frozen dimensions, called *Dimsat*, is presented in Hurtado et al. (2005). Here, experiments show that *Dimsat* takes few seconds to test the implication of a dimension constraint from a highly heterogeneous schema of 25 categories.

Supporting Structural Adaptations

The framework of dimension constraints and frozen dimensions can be used to automate the construction of the structural adaptations explained in previous sections. In this form we may use the semantics of the schema to transform heterogeneous dimensions, a task that could be difficult to do manually when handling complex dimensions. As an example, it is not easy to obtain the unbalanced dimension of Figure 11 from the entangled product dimension of Figure 7.

Frozen dimensions correspond to the homogeneous dimensions in the decomposition proposed by Kimball (1996), so the decomposition can be obtained by the algorithm that computes frozen dimensions, explained before. In Hurtado and Gutierrez (2004), we propose an algorithm that transforms heterogeneous dimension schemas into the unbalanced homogeneous schemas of Jagadish et al. (1999), we called canonical schemas. The algorithm first computes the set of frozen dimensions of the original schema and then iteratively splits the categories that cause heterogeneity. In each split operation the hierarchy schema is transformed so that the resulting hierarchy schema has a single category for each different frozen dimension over the category. The algorithm outputs a dimension schema having the constraints that state the homogeneity condition. If the set of frozen dimensions are precomputed, the algorithm runs in time $O(f n^3)$, where n is the size of the hierarchy schema, and f is the number of frozen dimensions.

The transformation described has an important property. The resulting schema is equivalent to the original schema in that they both model the same set of hierarchy domains (Hurtado & Gutierrez, 2004). This proves that heterogeneous schemas can be transformed into canonical schemas without losing information capacity in the schemas, and without breaking down the hierarchy arrangement of elements.

Copyright © 2007, Idea Group Inc. Copying or distributing in print or electronic forms without written permission of Idea Group Inc. is prohibited.

Figure 11. An unbalanced dimension: (a) hierarchy schema; (b) rollup relation

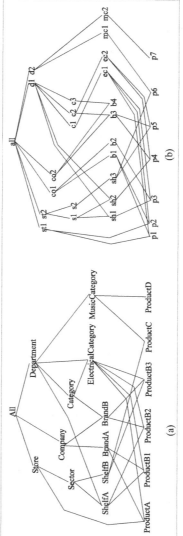

Supporting Aggregate Navigation

Integrity constraints can be also used to support aggregate navigation. Hierarchy schemas enriched with dimension constraints become an adequate abstract model to infer the correctness of rollup operations if one may want to keep the heterogeneous structure of the dimension. In some situations it can be useful to keep the heterogeneous structure, since it allows fewer categories and to more naturally

Copyright © 2007, Idea Group Inc. Copying or distributing in print or electronic forms without written permission of Idea Group Inc. is prohibited.

group elements into categories. A smaller number of categories might exponentially decrease the number of cube views we may need to handle and store in star and snowflake realizations.

We next show that the problem of testing the correctness of a rollup operation (that is, summarizability) reduces to an inference problem over dimension constraints. Rollup operations can be generalized rollup operations to allow the combination of several granularities (Hurtado & Mendelzon, 2001, 2002; Hurtado et al., 2005). This is needed since one may obtain a cube view by combining other cube views in heterogeneous dimensions. As an example in the dimension of Figure 4 the cube view *CV[All]* can be computed by the following rollup operator, that combines the cube views *CV[MusicCategory]* and *CV[ElectricalCategory]*:

ROLLUP *MusicCategory,ElectricalCategory* TO *All*.

In order to check the correctness of this operation, two constraints about (a) disjointness and (b) completeness of the categories combined should be inferred from a dimension schema *D* that models the dimension. Therefore the problem reduces to testing the following constraints:

(a) $\neg \langle Product,MusicCat,All\rangle \vee \neg \langle Product,ElectricalCat,All\rangle$

(b) $\langle Product,MusicCat,All\rangle \vee \langle Product,ElectricalCat,All\rangle$.

Here the atom $\langle Product,MusicCat,All\rangle$ expresses that the product element go the element *all* in *All* passing through an element in *MusicCat*. The other atom is interpreted similarly.

In previous work (Hurtado & Gutierrez, 2003), we provide an algorithm to compute the set of correct rollup operations from the dimension schema. As the dimension schema is fixed, the correct operations can be computed once before the data cube is queried. In addition, dimension constraints allow identifying consistent paths of aggregation in the hierarchy schema. As an example, from a schema *D* that models the dimension of Figure 7, one may want to check whether the path *Product≺Brand≺Company≺All* is consistent, which reduces to testing the implication of following constraint $\langle Product,Brand,Company,All\rangle$ from the schema *D*.

Conclusion

When the homogeneity condition is dropped the framework for aggregate navigation that underlies OLAP systems cannot be applied. In this chapter we have surveyed

Copyright © 2007, Idea Group Inc. Copying or distributing in print or electronic forms without written permission of Idea Group Inc. is prohibited.

different methods to deal with this problem. The situation can be handled by adding null elements in a way such that we obtain homogeneous dimensions with all the standard properties. This seems to be a practical solution in many situations, in particular when heterogeneity arises as an exception due to incomplete information, or when the structure of the dimension is simple. In other cases, it seems better to repair the structure so it can serve to guide users in query formulation. Using these techniques we can transform heterogeneous into homogeneous data so that the standard framework of OLAP aggregate navigation applies. We have also explained the framework of dimension constraints, which allow to capture the mixture of structures and to support transformations to homogeneous structures. Besides, dimension constraints support reasoning about aggregate navigation in heterogeneous OLAP data.

There are other forms of structural heterogeneity in OLAP models. It may be found in real data warehousing heterogeneity resulting from the nonvalidity of descriptive attributes attached to the categories of the dimensions. These attributes allow to describe elements of the category. As an example, we may have the attributes CEO, number of employees, total revenue, and so forth, to describe the elements of a category company (Jagadish et al., 1999). There is also another form of heterogeneity that involves the structure of fact tables, since different elements may require different measures. For example, while checking accounts have minimum balances, overdraft limits, and service charges, saving accounts have interest paid, and chargeable debits (Kimball, 1996). The development of techniques and tools to support transformations for different forms of heterogeneity and irregularities in the data is an open problem of practical significance for the improvement of current OLAP systems.

Acknowledgments

This work was supported by Millennium Nucleus, Center for Web Research (P04-067-F), Mideplan, Chile.

References

Abiteboul, S., & Vianu, V. (1999). Regular path queries with constraints. *Journal of Computer and System Science, 58*(3), 428-452.

Buneman, P., Fan, W., & Weinstein, S. (1998). Path constraints on semistructured and structured data. In *Proceedings of the Seventeenth ACM Symposium on Principles of Database Systems*, New York (pp. 129-138).

Copyright © 2007, Idea Group Inc. Copying or distributing in print or electronic forms without written permission of Idea Group Inc. is prohibited.

Cabibbo, L., & Torlone, R. (1998). Querying multidimensional databases. In *Proceedings of the Sixth International Workshop on Database Programming Languages*, London (pp. 319-335).

Chatziantoniou, D., & Ross, K. A. (1996). Querying multiple features of groups in relational databases. In *Proceedings of the Twenty-Second International Conference on Very Large Data Bases*, San Francisco (pp. 295-306).

Goldstein, B. S. (1981). Constraints on null values in relational databases. In *Proceedings of the Seventh International Conference on Very Large Data Bases*, Cannes, France (pp. 101-110).

Harinarayan, V., Rajaraman, A., & Ullman, J. (1996). Implementing data cubes efficiently. In *Proceedings of the 1996 ACM International Conference on Management of Data*, Montreal, Canada (pp. 205-216).

Hurtado, C., & Gutierrez, C. (2003). Computing cube view dependencies in OLAP datacubes. In *Proceedings of the Fifteenth IEEE International Conference on Scientific and Statistical Database Management*, Boston (pp. 33-43).

Hurtado, C., & Gutierrez, C. (2004). Equivalence of OLAP dimension schemas. In *Proceedings of the Third International Symposium on Foundations of Information and Knowledge Systems*, Wilhelminenburg Castle, Austria (pp. 176-195).

Hurtado, C., Gutierrez, C., & Mendelzon, A. (2005). Capturing summarizability with integrity constraints in OLAP. *ACM Transaction on Databases Systems, 30*(3), 854-886.

Hurtado, C., & Mendelzon, A. (2001). Reasoning about summarizability in heterogeneous multidimensional schemas. In *Proceedings of the Eighth International Conference on Database Theory* (pp. 375-389). London.

Hurtado, C., & Mendelzon, A. (2002). OLAP dimension constraints. In *Proceedings of the Twenty-First ACM Symposium on Principles of Database Systems*, New York (pp. 169-179).

Hurtado, C., Mendelzon, A., & Vaisman, A. (1999). Maintaining data cubes under dimension updates. In *Proceedings of the Fifteenth International Conference on Data Engineering*, Washington, DC (pp. 346-355).

Hurtado, C., Mendelzon, A., & Vaisman, A. (1999). Updating OLAP dimensions. In *Proceedings of the Second IEEE International Workshop on Data Warehousing and OLAP*, Kansas City, Missouri (pp. 60-66).

Huseman, B., Lechtenborger, J., & Vossen, G. (2000). Conceptual data warehouse design. In *Proceedings of the International Workshop on Design and Management of Data Warehouses*, Stockholm, Sweden (pp. 6-16).

Copyright © 2007, Idea Group Inc. Copying or distributing in print or electronic forms without written permission of Idea Group Inc. is prohibited.

Jagadish, H., Lakshmanan, L., & Srivastava, D. (1999). What can hierarchies do for data warehouses? In *Proceedings of the Twenty-Fifth International Conference on Very Large Data Bases*, San Francisco (pp. 530-541).

Jarke, M., Lenzerini, M., Vassiliou, Y., & Vassiliadis, P. (1997). *Fundamentals of data warehouses*. Berlin, Heidelberg; New York: Springer.

Kimball, R. (1995). The aggregate navigator. *DBMS and Internet Systems Magazine*. Retrieved May 26, 2006, from http://www.dbmsmag.com/9511d05.html

Kimball, R. (1996). *The data warehouse toolkit*. New York: John Wiley & Sons.

Kimball, R. (1997, August). A dimensional modeling manifesto. *DBMS and Internet Systems Magazine*. Retrieved May 26, 2006, from http://www.dbmsmag.com/9708d15.html

Lehner, W., Albrecht, J., & Wedekind, H. (1998). Normal forms for multidimensional databases. In *Proceedings of the Tenth International Conference on Scientific and Statistical Database Management*, Capri, Italy (pp. 63-72).

Lenz, H., & Shoshani, A. (1997). Summarizability in OLAP and statistical databases. In *Proceedings of the Ninth Scientific and Statistical Database Management Conference*, Olympia, Washington (pp. 132-143).

Malinowski, E., & Zimanyi, E. (2004). OLAP hierarchies: A conceptual perspective. In *Proceedings of the 16th International Conference Advanced Information Systems Engineering*, Riga, Latvia (pp. 447-491).

Mumick, I., Quass, D., & Mumick, B. (1997). Maintenance of data cubes and summary tables in a warehouse. In *Proceedings of the 1997 ACM SIGMOD International Conference on Management of Data*, Tucson, Arizona (pp. 100-111).

Pedersen, T., Jensen, C., & Dyreson, C. (1999). Extending practical pre-aggregation in on-line analytical processing. In *Proceedings of the Twenty-Fifth International Conference on Very Large Data Bases*, Edinburgh, Scotland (pp. 663-674).

Pedersen, T., Jensen, C., & Dyreson, C. (2001). A foundation for capturing and querying complex multidimensional data. *Information Systems, 26*(5), 383-423.

Rafanelli, M., & Shoshani, A. (1990). Storm: A statistical object representation model. In *Proceedings of the Fifth International Conference on Scientific and Statistical Database Management*, Charlotte, North Carolina (pp. 14-29).

West, D. B. (1996). *Introduction to graph theory*. Prentice Hall.

Copyright © 2007, Idea Group Inc. Copying or distributing in print or electronic forms without written permission of Idea Group Inc. is prohibited.

Chapter III

Data Quality-Based Requirements Elicitation for Decision Support Systems

Alejandro Vaisman
Universidad de Buenos Aires, Argentina

Abstract

Today, information and timely decisions are crucial for an organization's success. A decision support system (DSS) is a software tool that provides information allowing its users to make decisions timely and cost effectively. This is highly conditioned by the quality of the data involved, usually stored in a data warehouse, and by a sound and complete requirements analysis. In this chapter we show that conventional techniques for requirements elicitation cannot be used in DSS, and present a methodology denoted DSS-METRIQ, aimed at providing a single data quality-based procedure for complete and consistent elicitation of functional (queries) and nonfunctional (data quality) requirements. The outcomes of the process are a set

Copyright © 2007, Idea Group Inc. Copying or distributing in print or electronic forms without written permission of Idea Group Inc. is prohibited.

of requirement documents and a specification of the operational data sources that can satisfy such requirements. We review the state-of-the-art in the field, and show that in spite of the tools and methodologies already proposed for the modeling and design of decision support systems, DSS-METRIQ is the first one that supports the whole process by means of an integral technique.

Introduction

It is a well-known fact that, among the phases of the software development process, analysis and specification of functional and nonfunctional requirements is a crucial one. The lack of good requirements specification is a major cause of failure in software development (Thayer, 2002). The software engineering community has developed many useful tools for requirements analysis in transactional systems. These kinds of systems deal with the day-to-day operation of an organization. Decision support systems (DSS) are of a completely different kind: they are focused on integrating data and models in order to improve the decision-making process. The data that feed a DSS generally reside in a data warehouse. The software development cycle of DSS has particularities that require applying methodologies different than the ones used for operational systems. The reason for this is twofold: on the one hand, traditional methodologies have been thought and designed with transactional systems in mind; on the other hand, specific methodologies applicable to DSS arose as ad-hoc answers to practical needs, and most of them are just mere enumerations of activities that must take place in order to implement the system, focusing on populating the data repository while ignoring important issues like the impact of changes in the operational data sources, or worse, if these data sources satisfy the users' information requirements. New sources of failure are present in DSS: correctness and trustworthiness of the information are the basis of the decision-making process. We do not only need to understand the user's information needs, but also account for keeping the data repository up-to-date according to user specifications. Also, update processes and their frequency must be considered, as well as the analysis of the quality and completeness of the data sources.

It follows that there is a need for techniques that, besides accounting for the software process cycle and functional requirements, also consider the quality of the information the system will deliver. There are several reasons for this. For instance, most of the time, people developing information systems do not consider the impact of low quality data (Kimball, Reeves, Ross, & Thornthwaite, 1998). Low data quality is more a rule than an exception. Just to give an example, it has been detected in the U.S., that approximately 50 to 80% of the computerized criminal records are inaccurate, incomplete, or ambiguous (Strong, Yang, & Wang, 1997). So far, the contribution of software engineering for addressing the problems stated has been

Copyright © 2007, Idea Group Inc. Copying or distributing in print or electronic forms without written permission of Idea Group Inc. is prohibited.

limited, although many techniques have been proposed in order to analyze and measure a data quality requirement. Some examples of these techniques are GQM (goal question metric) (Basili, Caldiera, & Rombach, 1992) and QFD (quality function deployment) (Akao, 1997).

In summary, traditional software development methodologies do not apply to DSS, and focus on software correctness, paying little attention to the problem of data quality and completeness, given that, in general, this is not considered an issue in the requirement analysis phase of the software development cycle for operational systems. Based on these points, we propose a methodology called DSS-METRIQ that integrates concepts of requirements engineering and data quality, in order to provide a comprehensive solution to the requirements elicitation process specifically oriented to DSS.

Case Study

Throughout the chapter we will discuss the following case study. We must collect requirements for a DSS for a wholesale chain called "Los Andes" (specialized in food products). The chain has three branches in the Argentina countryside. The project involves the development of a data warehouse and a DSS for supporting the daily tasks of decision makers. The company has many different sources of operational data. We must carry out the requirements elicitation process, with the following goals in mind: discovery and documentation of user queries, addressing the information quality required by our customer (*that we must also help to define*). It will also be our task to analyze data quality in each one of the data sources, indicating for each piece of data, the data source from which we will obtain it and the data quality we can expect. Thus, we must specify the queries (functional requirements) that could be addressed by the system (given the available data sources) satisfying the data quality levels imposed by our customer (nonfunctional requirements). There will be a requirements engineering team, composed of a project leader, a training team, a team for carrying out the interviews, a data processing team, and a dictionary manager (more on dictionaries in the following sections). Our customer provided a list containing the contact information of the employees (belonging to different areas), who will cooperate in the process.

Contributions and Chapter Organization

We introduce a methodology (denoted DSS-METRIQ) for requirements elicitation in DSS, aimed at providing an integrated process specification for the complete and consistent analysis of functional (queries) and nonfunctional (data quality) requirements in DSS. We provide detailed mechanisms for collecting functional and

Copyright © 2007, Idea Group Inc. Copying or distributing in print or electronic forms without written permission of Idea Group Inc. is prohibited.

nonfunctional requirements as a whole, addressing data quality and completeness of the operational data sources. We give tools allowing answering the following questions: (a) *can we answer the set of queries required by the user with the data currently available in the data sources?* (b) *what is the quality of the answers we will obtain?* (c) *does this quality satisfy users' requirements?* This is a subject often ignored in other proposals. The outcomes of the process are a set of documents and a ranking of the operational data sources that can satisfy the users' quality and information requirements, based on two parameters denoted *local* and *global data source performance*. As far as we are aware of, no other proposal has addressed the problem in this way. Of course, the analysis may also trigger corrective actions over data that do not reach the required level of quality. Finally, each phase of this methodology needs a technical solution from the software engineering or data warehousing communities. For instance, for requirements elicitation we adapt the GQM (goal question metric) methodology. For data source selection we introduce a technique based on QFD (quality function deployment).

In this chapter we first review related work and study the differences between DSS and operational systems with respect to requirements elicitation. After presenting basic data quality concepts we introduce DSS-METRIQ and explain each phase of the methodology in detail. We conclude with a discussion on possible research directions.

Related Work

The software development cycle involves different stages or phases, each one of them composed of a set of activities. The final goal is obtaining a software product reflecting user requirements in the best possible way. *Waterfall* and *Baseline Management* are popular models for software development. There are five phases in these models: requirements analysis, design, coding, testing, and system integration, in sequential form. Modeling through *prototypes* consists in quickly developing a system for helping to determine software requirements. Another popular technique, the *Spiral model* emphasizes the idea that requirements cannot be determined in a precise way from the start, leading to the idea of a "spiral" which includes a complete cycle that must be revised iteratively until the final system satisfies the expected functionality. In all of these models, the requirements analysis phase is divided into four main activities: requirement elicitation, analysis and modeling, specification, and validation. During *requirements elicitation*, requirement engineers gain understanding of the user needs. A requirements engineer carries out interviews, classifies and integrates the information obtained. Techniques like IBIS (issue-based information system) (Christel & Kang, 1992), or JAD (joint application development), are widely used. The *analysis and modeling* outcome is the definition of user requirements. The most

Copyright © 2007, Idea Group Inc. Copying or distributing in print or electronic forms without written permission of Idea Group Inc. is prohibited.

popular methods for these tasks are enterprise modeling, data modeling (through entity-relationship modeling), object-oriented techniques, and structured methodologies like SADT (structured analysis and design techniques) (Ross & Schoman, 1979). *Specification* is the process of generating the requirements documentation. CORE (*c*ontrolled *r*equirements *e*xpression) (Mullery, 1979) can be used in this step. The purpose of *requirements validation* is to certify that requirements are an acceptable description of the system to be implemented. Inputs for the process are the requirements document, organizational standards, and organizational knowledge. The output is a list that contains the reported problems and the actions necessary to cope with them. Requirements reviews and requirements testing are common techniques used for this activity.

Decision support systems extract information from a database and use it to support the decision making process. A DSS usually requires processing great volumes of data for generating valuable information. Gill and Rao (1996) classify these kinds of systems as (a) data-driven, which emphasizes access and manipulation of large structured databases; (b) model driven, which emphasizes the access and manipulation of a model; (c) knowledge driven, which recommends actions to the managers, often customized for a certain domain; and (d) document driven, integrating a variety of storage and processing technologies. A DSS is made up of: (a) database (typically a data warehouse); (b) components for data extraction and filtering, used to extract and validate the data taken from the operational databases; (c) query tools; and (d) presentation tools. A *data warehouse* gathers data coming from different sources of an organization (Chaudhuri & Dayal, 1997). *Data warehousing* involves a series of processes that turn raw data into data suitable to be queried. A set of data transformation processes denoted ETL (Extraction, Transformation, Loading) exports data from the operational databases (generally in heterogeneous formats), and after some depuration and consolidation, load them into the data warehouse. OLAP (online analytical processing) tools are used for querying the warehouse.

System development involves three clearly defined phases: design, implementation, and maintenance. However, in the development cycle of traditional software system, activities are carried out sequentially, while in a DSS they follow a heuristic process (Cippico, 1997). Thus, methodologies for developing operational and DSS systems are different. For instance, in *operational systems* (a) the development cycle is *process driven*, based on a stable data model; (b) data must be normalized in order to support transaction processing; (c) hardware is defined in the planning phase, remaining quite stable; and (d) there is no periodic data loading. In DSS, we have (a) the development cycle is *data driven*; (b) data is generally denormalized; (c) hardware changes dynamically; and (d) periodical data loading is a typical process.

In spite of the popularity gained by DSS in the last decade, a methodology for software development has not been agreed upon. Thus, it is not surprising that most contributions on requirements analysis for DSS came from consulting companies and software vendors. The *NCR methodology* is aimed at developing and main-

Copyright © 2007, Idea Group Inc. Copying or distributing in print or electronic forms without written permission of Idea Group Inc. is prohibited.

taining the data warehouse infrastructure, assuring data quality, and improving performance encouraging the use of traditional database design techniques. The *SAS Institute Rapid Development methodology* is based on the argument that the two great sources of failure of data warehouse projects are the lack of experience and the development of very large projects. Thus, this methodology tries to handle such risk dividing the project into units called "builds." Each cycle of these builds consists of the following stages: valuation, requirements, design, implementation, final testing, and distribution. *Microsoft methodology* proposes eight activities: four devoted to creating the data warehouse and four to reviewing and maintaining it, with feedback from the processes. Kimball et al. (1998) propose a "federated" architecture, with data marts based on star schemas. All the methods are focused on the development of the infrastructure for decision support systems, but none of them handles data quality in a comprehensive fashion.

There are several proposals addressing the design of data warehouses and data marts. Many of them use some of the techniques we propose in this chapter. *However, these works do not compare with ours because the goals are different*: we are interested in the requirement elicitation process itself, and not in the design process, which belongs to a later stage. For example, the work by Moody and Kortink (2000) proposes the use of the entity-relationship model for data warehouse design. With a different approach, Bonifati, Cattaneo, Ceri, Fuggetta, and Paraboschi (2001) introduced an interesting requirements-driven design methodology for data marts. However, they focus on the design stage, and only address functional requirements in the requirements elicitation phase (they use GQM for this task). Vassiliadis, Bouzeghoub, and Quix (1999) also use GQM, but in this case for identifying metrics that allow evaluating the quality of a data warehouse once it has been developed. Closer to our proposal, Winter and Strauch (2003, 2004) introduced a demand-driven methodology (i.e., a methodology where end users define the business goals) for data warehousing requirement analysis. They define four steps where they identify users and application type, assign priorities, and match information requirements with actual information supply (i.e., data in the data sources). There are several differences with the methodology we present here. The main one resides in that our approach is based on data quality, which is not considered in the mentioned paper. Moreover, although the authors mention the problem of matching required and supplied information, they do not provide a way of *quantifying* the difference between them. On the contrary, we give a method for determining the data sources that best match the information needs for each query defined by the user. Paim and Castro (2003) introduced DWARF, a methodology that, like DSS-METRIQ, deals with functional and nonfunctional requirements. They adapt requirements engineering techniques and propose a methodology for requirements definition for data warehouses. For nonfunctional requirements, they use the extended-data warehousing NFR Framework (Paim & Castro, 2002). Although DWARF and this framework are close to the rationale of DSS-METRIQ, the main differences are (a) we give

Copyright © 2007, Idea Group Inc. Copying or distributing in print or electronic forms without written permission of Idea Group Inc. is prohibited.

a more detailed and concrete set of tools for nonfunctional requirements elicitation; (b) we provide a QFD-based method for data source ranking on a quantifiable basis; and (c) we give a comprehensive detail of all the processes and documents involved. Prakash and Gosain (2003) also emphasize the need for a requirements engineering phase in data warehousing development. This phase precedes the logical, conceptual, and physical design phases they propose as components of the data warehouse development process. They propose the GDI (goal decision information) model. However, the authors do not provide a level of detail that may allow a more in-depth analysis.

In summary, although our proposal intersects many other similar ones, it integrates the most popular techniques, resulting in a comprehensive and self-contained methodology where each phase has clearly defined steps, as we will see in the following sections. Most of all, DSS-METRIQ addresses the overlooked problem of data source qualification and selection.

Quality Concepts

When speaking about quality, people do not always refer to the same concept (Bobrowski, Marré & Yankelevich, 1999). Many techniques have been developed for measuring quality. In what follows, we survey the ones we are going to use in the remainder of this chapter.

Goal Question Metric (GQM)

GQM is a framework for metric definition (Basili et al., 1992). It defines a top-down procedure allowing for specifying what is going to be measured, and to trace how measuring must be performed, providing a framework for result interpretation. The outcome of the process is the specification of a system of measurements that consists of a set of results and a set of rules for the interpretation of the collected data. The model defines three levels of analysis: (a) conceptual (Goal), where a goal for a product, process, or resource is defined; (b) operational (Question): at this level, a set of questions is used for describing the way a specific goal will be reached; and (c) quantitative (Metric): the metric associated with each question. The model is a hierarchical structure that starts from a goal, follows with a set of questions refining the goal, and ends with the metrics that will help answer the questions. For example, if our goal consists in measuring the legibility of a certain text, the question would be "what is the level of readers' comprehension?" The metric will be the number of readers who understood the text.

Copyright © 2007, Idea Group Inc. Copying or distributing in print or electronic forms without written permission of Idea Group Inc. is prohibited.

Quality Function Deployment (QFD)

Quality function deployment (QFD) (Akao, 1997) is a method proposed in the 1960s by Yoji Akao in Japan. It was first conceived as a method for the development of new products under the framework of total quality control. QFD aims at assuring design quality while the product is still in its design stage. The central instrument of the methodology is a matrix called "House of Quality." This matrix is composed of information blocks, and it is filled out in a sequence of steps: first, interviews are used to model customer needs. Here, requirements are expressed in a vague or ambiguous way, and must be refined. Then, technical solutions for solving user needs are proposed. The process iterates until it finds all the solutions. With the results obtained in the previous steps, the matrix of interrelationships is completed. After identifying the relationships between technical factors, the roof of the *House of Quality* is completed and possible conflicts between technical solutions are detected. Two tables are completed: customer's valuations and the valuations of the technical solutions. The last two steps involve prioritizing user requirements and prioritizing technical requirements.

Data Quality

Organizations are conscious of data quality problems. Nevertheless, efforts generally focus on data accuracy, ignoring many other attributes and important quality dimensions (Wang & Strong, 1996). Thus, quality validation and verification techniques are still required. Usually, these techniques concentrate only on software and assume that external agents provide the data (Bobrowski et al., 1999). Poor information quality is due to several causes: (1) Problems in the processes: to understand the processes that generate, use, and store the data, it is essential to understand data quality. In an organization, the owners of the processes must be responsible for the quality of the data they produce or use. (2) Problems in the information systems: often related to poor system development (incomplete documentation or systems that have been extended beyond their original intention). (3) Problems of policies and procedures: a policy about data must cover security, privacy, inventory of the information that is controlled, or data availability. (4) Problems in data design: more often than not, data are used for tasks they were not defined for.

Data Quality Dimensions

There are basically two ways of defining data quality: the first one uses a *scientific approach* and defines data quality dimensions rigorously, classifying them as dimensions that are or are not *intrinsic* to an information system (Wang, Storey, & Firth,

Copyright © 2007, Idea Group Inc. Copying or distributing in print or electronic forms without written permission of Idea Group Inc. is prohibited.

Table 1. Quality dimensions

Proposal	Intrinsic	Contextual	Representation	Accessibility
Lee et al.	Accuracy Credibility Reputation Objectivity	Understandable data Concise representation Interpretability Consistency	Added value Relevance Completeness Timeliness	Accessibility Security Easy operation
Zmud	Accuracy	Reliability Timeliness	Order Legibility	
Jarke and Vassiliou	Accuracy Consistency Completeness Credibility	Relevance Timeliness Usefulness Up-to-date Volatility	Interpretability Syntax Semantics Alias Source	Accessibility Availability Privileges
Delone and McLean	Reliability Accuracy Precision	Relevance Timeliness Usefulness Content Completeness Opportunity	Understanding Legibility Clarity Format "Look and feel" Conciseness Uniqueness Comparability	Usefulness Accessibility Convenience
Wand and Wang	Correctness Ambiguity	Completeness	Meaning	

1995). The second one is a *pragmatic approach* aimed at defining data quality in an operational fashion (Wand & Wang, 1996). Wang & Strong (1996) identified four data quality categories after evaluating 118 variables (Wang & Strong, 1996): (1) *intrinsic* data quality; (2) *contextual* data quality (defines the quality of the information within the context of the task); (3) *data quality for data representation*: determines if the system presents the information in a concise, consistent, understandable way; and (4) data quality regarding *data access* (defines quality in terms of the role of the information system in the provision of the data). Table 1 summarizes the results of academic research on the multiple dimensions applicable to information quality, comparing results from Delone and McLean (1992), Hoxmeier (2000), Jarke and Vassiliou (1997), Lee, Strong, Kahn, and Wang (2002), Wand and Wang (1996), and Zmud (1978).

DSS-METRIQ Overview

In this section we introduce DSS-METRIQ. The methodology is composed of five phases: *scenario, information gathering, requirements integration, data source se-*

Copyright © 2007, Idea Group Inc. Copying or distributing in print or electronic forms without written permission of Idea Group Inc. is prohibited.

lection, and *document generation*, and from any phase it is possible to go back to any former one. The whole process can be summarized as follows: on the one hand, the data consumer's functional requirements are analyzed, unified, and documented. On the other hand, the quality of data in the data sources is collected from the data producer users. This information is then analyzed as a whole, and a collection of documents is produced. These documents will allow matching the requirements with the available data. In the remainder of this section we introduce the general framework of the methodology, and the conceptual basis over which it is built. Each phase of the methodology will be described in detail later in this chapter.

Framework

We first define the participants, concepts, techniques, and tools that will be used in the requirement analysis process.

- **Team:** The methodology defines the following roles and participants in the team that will carry out the project: (a) project leader: manages the working team and interacts with the customer; (b) training leader: carries out the training of the users on the concepts, methodologies, or technologies associated with the project; (c) requirements engineer: performs requirements elicitation, working jointly with the users (must be an experienced professional); (d) query and data manager: analyzes the queries; and (e) information administrator: deals with changes in the information that supports the methodology (dictionaries, forms, etc.).

- **Users:** Any person participating in the project is considered a *user*. Users to be interviewed are (a) *data producers*, who will participate in interviews aimed at understanding data; (b) *data consumers*, who will be interviewed for defining the queries that will be posed to the system; (c) *referent users* are users with a higher hierarchy in the organization than the ones defined in (a) and (b); referent users participate in interviews where the scope of the system and priorities are defined. She also solves conflicts between requirements of different users. Priorities are defined for users, ranging from 1 to 5. Users are associated to *domains* (sales, acquisitions). Each domain has a priority, also ranging between 1 and 5.

- **Data sources:** DSS-METRIQ defines two kinds of data sources: *physical* and *logical*. The former are sources where data are actually stored. The latter are sets of data sources producing a data element (i.e., set of physical data sources producing a view).

    Example 1: The attribute daily_sales is stored in the table Daily_Sales_ Summary, belonging to the operational database SalesCentral. This da-

Copyright © 2007, Idea Group Inc. Copying or distributing in print or electronic forms without written permission of Idea Group Inc. is prohibited.

tabase is a physical data source. The attribute buy_sell_daily_balance is computed as the difference of two attributes representing daily buys and sales, that are located in two different tables, in two different databases: the "BuysCentral" database and the "SalesCentral" database. Thus, buy_ sell_daily_balance is a logical data source. We will give this data source a name, say LDS_1 (standing for Logical Data Source 1).

- **Interviews:** DSS-METRIQ considers two kinds of interviews: (a) group interviews: in the requirements phase, JAD is used (Christel & Kang, 1992); and (b) individual interviews: the user requirements, mainly from the data consumers, can be obtained through traditional structured or unstructured interviews.

Supporting Elements

DSS-METRIQ provides elements for supporting the management of the information collected throughout the process. These elements are *forms, matrices, a data dictionary,* and *an aggregations dictionary*. Forms are elements that register the collected information. As usual, forms are divided in two main sections: the *heading* and the *body*. The heading contains name of form, phase of the methodology, step within the phase, version, and revision number. In the body of the form, the collected or generated information is written. Of course, forms can be updated during the process. Thus, requirements evolution is supported in this way (meaning that any change that occurs during the process can be reflected and documented in the forms). Matrices are equipped with a certain intelligence that allows weighting the information contained in the forms, in order to qualify and prioritize requirements. A data dictionary is a catalogue of data that contains names, aliases, and detailed descriptions of the atomic elements that compose the user queries, data sources, and the data warehouse. Its purpose is the definition of a common meaning for each one of these elements, allowing expression of user requirements on the basis of a common terminology. It can be updated throughout the process. The aggregations dictionary is a catalogue containing information on dimensions, dimension levels, and aggregations (Chaudhuri & Dayal, 1997).

Data Quality Requirements

DSS-METRIQ is a quality-based and quality-led methodology. Its main goal is to integrate functional requirements and data quality. As such, the data quality dimensions to be used must be defined. We adapted and integrated the main existing proposals commented previously, considering not only the relevance of each quality dimension, but also the possibility of quantifying it. Based on this, we will work

Copyright © 2007, Idea Group Inc. Copying or distributing in print or electronic forms without written permission of Idea Group Inc. is prohibited.

with the following quality dimensions: *accuracy, consistency, completeness, timeliness, query frequency, source availability,* and *accepted response time.* Associated with *timeliness,* we also add *currency* and *volatility.*

- **Accuracy:** Measures how close to the value in the real world the data under consideration are. Another vision, from the ontological point of view, defines *inaccuracy* as the probability that an information system represents an incorrect state of the real world (Wand & Wang, 1996). The accuracy of a data warehouse is influenced by two main factors: (a) accuracy of the data sources and (b) the error factor that the ETL process can introduce.

- **Consistency:** We adopt the ontological point of view, which describes consistency as the "logical consistency" of information. The underlying idea is that given two instances of representation for the same data, the value of the data must be the same. For example, if it is known that the sales of a company exceed a certain monthly value *v*, we expect the database to reflect this fact.

- **Completeness:** Is the information system able to represent every significant state of the real world. The methodology presented here emphasizes representation instead of structure. For instance, if there are 250 employees in the organization, we expect at least one record for each one of them to be in the database.

- **Timeliness:** It measures the delay between a change in the state of the real world and the corresponding data warehouse update. This dimension is tightly associated with other two: currency and volatility. Timeliness is affected by three main factors: (a) speed at which the state of the information system is updated after the changes occur in the real world; (b) frequency of change of the state of the real world; and (c) the instant when the data are actually used. The first aspect depends on the design of the system, while aspects (b) and (c) are design-independent.

- **Currency:** Measures the age of the data. It is computed as follows (Wang & Reddy, 1992)"

$$\text{Currency}(d) = t_c - t_0$$

Where d is the data element under consideration, t_c is the present time, and t_0 is the instant in the real world when the data element was created. An alternative definition is:

$$\text{Currency}(d) = t_r + (t_1 + t_e + t_q)$$

Copyright © 2007, Idea Group Inc. Copying or distributing in print or electronic forms without written permission of Idea Group Inc. is prohibited.

t_f = time in the data source: the time elapsed between the instant when the data were "born" in the real world and stored in the data source, and the moment when they are transferred to the data warehouse.

t_l = the duration of the loading process.

t_e = time elapsed between the moment when data are available for querying in the data warehouse, and the moment when the query is posed.

t_q = the query response time.

- **Volatility:** It represents the length of the interval during which data are valid in the real world (Wang & Reddy, 1992). Pipino, Lee, and Wang (2002) define *Timeliness* as a function of currency and volatility:

Timeliness (d)=MAX [1–currency (d)/ volatility (d), 0]^s, where s > 0

The coefficient *s* (not considered in our methodology) is denoted *sensitivity*; it reflects the criteria of the analyst, and depends on the task being performed. Timeliness ranges between 0 (worst case) and 1 (desirable value).

- **Data source availability:** It is the time during which the data source is available (Jarke, Lenzerini, Vassiliou, & Vassiliadis, 2003).

- **Expected query response time:** It is the maximum accepted time for getting the answer to a query.

- **Query frequency:** It is the minimum time between two successive queries.

Measuring Quality

There are many different ways of analyzing and measuring the required data quality parameters. Thus, it is necessary to define a common way of specifying user needs and measuring whether the DSS or the data warehouse will be able to fulfill the minimum levels of quality required. To this end, we propose to apply GQM to each one of the dimensions defined previously. This technique is used for specifying user requirements and measuring the actual values for data quality in the available data sources. Due to space constraints, next we only show how the technique is applied to the *accuracy, consistency,* and *completeness* dimensions. For *accuracy* we have the following:

a.   Specifying user requirements (*data consumer users*).

- **Goal:** Specify the level of accuracy required for each data element in a query.

Copyright © 2007, Idea Group Inc. Copying or distributing in print or electronic forms without written permission of Idea Group Inc. is prohibited.

- **Question:** What is the maximum acceptable difference between the answers obtained and the actual value of the data element in the real world?
- **Metric:** The user must specify the accepted difference (in %) between the value of a data element in the data warehouse and its value in the real world (Quix, Jarke, Jeusfeld, Vassiliadis, Lenzerini, Calvanese, & Bouzeghoub, 2002).

b.   Measuring accuracy in the data sources (*data producer users*).

- **Goal:** Determine the accuracy of the data in each source.
- **Question:** What is the divergence between the value of the data in the source and in the real world?
- **Metric:** Accuracy of the data source for a certain attribute.
- **Measuring methodology:** Given a representative sample of the data in the real world, we define the accuracy of the data source empirically as:

$$\text{Accuracy} = [\,\text{MAX} \quad \sqrt{((X - X\text{real})^2/X\text{real})}\,] * 100$$

where X and Xreal are the data in the sample and in the real world, respectively.

Regarding *consistency,* if the condition is mandatory for the data element under consideration, we require a 100% level of fulfillment. Consistency in the data sources is measured obtaining samples from each source and measuring the number of inconsistent records with respect to a user query. This means that the user knows in advance the answer to this query over the sample. Analogously, *completeness* is specified as in the previous case and measured from a data sample, posing a set of queries over this sample and applying the following formula:

(# of queries with incomplete answers / # of queries) * 100

where an incomplete answer is one such that a record (or a part of it) is missing (remember that we know in advance all the records from the sample that satisfy the query). We proceed analogously for the other quality dimensions. This allows determining which data sources can be considered apt for developing the DSS, meaning that if a data source does not fulfill the minimum bound for a quality dimension, either data cleaning methods are applied or the data source must be discarded.

Copyright © 2007, Idea Group Inc. Copying or distributing in print or electronic forms without written permission of Idea Group Inc. is prohibited.

Integrated Requirement Analysis

After finishing the interview phase, and when all functional and quality requirements have been obtained, information is consolidated, yielding a single requirements document that will be input for the later phases of design. In this process we need to establish priorities and solve conflicting requirements. Thus, we define a set of *priorities* for each functional and nonfunctional requirement. Conceptually, this priority indicates the level of importance of the requirement. Priorities are assigned a number between 1 and 5 as follows: optional requirement = 1; low importance requirement = 2; intermediate importance requirement = 3; high importance requirement = 4; mandatory requirement = 5. When two conflicting requirements have the same priority, a high-level user must decide which one will be considered. Once conflicts are solved, *requirements validation* is performed.

- **Data source selection and document generation:** With the information collected in the previous phases, interviews are carried out with data producer users in order to determine the quality of data in the data sources, with the goal of matching user requirements and available data. As this is the cornerstone of our methodology, we will explain it in detail in the next section.

DSS-METRIQ in Detail

In this section we describe the phases of the methodology, giving details of the processes within each phase. DSS-METRIQ can be adapted to the most used software development models, like waterfall, spiral, or prototyping. As we explained in the previous section, the methodology has five phases, each one grouping together tasks that are conceptually related: scenario, information gathering, requirements integration, data source selection, and document generation. Each phase consists of a set of atomic steps. In the following sections we describe each phase in terms of a set of *initial requirements*, a sequence of *steps,* a set of *forms,* and the *output* of the phase (the information obtained). During the process, several documents and forms will be manipulated, namely (a) master files, to be denoted with the prefix MAS; (b) hierarchy documents (e.g., dimension hierarchies, user hierarchies), with prefix HIE; (c) dictionaries (data and aggregation); (d) query forms, with prefix QRY, containing the most common queries that the user will pose to the system; (e) requirements forms, with prefix REQ; and (f) matrices for processing the information obtained (with prefix MAT). Due to space limitations we will not show all of these documents, but we will describe their content and give examples from our case study.

Copyright © 2007, Idea Group Inc. Copying or distributing in print or electronic forms without written permission of Idea Group Inc. is prohibited.

Phase I: Scenario

The goal of this phase is to introduce the project to the different levels of the company, building a consensus about the scope and boundaries of the project (e.g., users, domains), priorities, and the initial configuration of the information.

The *input* of this phase consists of (1) details of the project; (2) initial list of domains involved; and (3) scope and list of participants of the introductory meetings. The *output* of the phase is a set of documents containing (1) domains and domain hierarchy (MAS_DOM); (2) users and user hierarchy (MAS_USR); (3) quality dimensions (MAS_QTY); and (4) data dictionary (DIC_DATA); aggregation dictionary (DIC_AGGR). The steps of this phase are *skills acquisition* and *interviews with referent people.*

During *skills acquisition,* lectures are given to the project team in order to unify concepts to be addressed in the process. In the *project presentation* step, the project is presented to the company's decision levels, explaining goals, potential benefits, impact, and the working methodology. In the *global definitions* step, JAD meetings are carried out, aimed at obtaining consensus on:

a. **Domains:** sectors that will use the data warehouse (e.g., Sales Department). The form MAS_DOM is produced, with fields domain name, domain responsible, contact information, and relevance (a number between 1 and 5) of the domain within the organization. For example, in our case study, the MAS_DOM form contains the line *<D1, Sales, Jose Hernandez, ext. 2162, 5>,* stating that *Jose Hernandez* is responsible for the *Sales* domain (with domain id *D1*), can be contacted on phone *extension 2162,* and the domain has the highest importance (5).

b. **Quality dimensions:** The final set of quality dimensions to be considered, taking into account organizational policies, goals, scope, development time, and preferences. This may imply pruning the initial set of requirements. The form MAS_QTY is produced. In our running example, four quality dimensions were chosen: *Accuracy, Timeliness, Consistency,* and *Completeness.*

c. **Initial data dictionary:** An initial collection of terms that will become the common vocabulary to be used throughout the software development cycle. The form DIC_DATA is produced. A sample record in the data dictionary for the "Los Andes" project is *<D5, customer, customer name, account>,* stating that there is a data element with id = *D5,* denoted *customer,* representing a *customer's name,* and referred also with the alias *account.*

d. **Initial aggregations dictionary:** The goal of this dictionary is to record information regarding facts and dimensions to be used in later phases of the project, in order to produce the preliminary star schema. The form DIC_AGGR is produced. In our project, a record in the aggregations dictionary looks like

Copyright © 2007, Idea Group Inc. Copying or distributing in print or electronic forms without written permission of Idea Group Inc. is prohibited.

<D13, customerId, no, sale\purchase, Accounts, customer, 10, days>. This record states that there is a data element with id = D13, with name *customerId,* that does *not* represent a fact; the data element is a level in the *Accounts* dimension, denoted *customer*, having a volatility of *10 days.*

In the *referent people interviews* step, the users that will participate in the project are defined, and information about them is registered. The file MAS_USR is produced. In our project, a record in this file is <U1, Jose Hernandez, D1, referent, 5>, meaning that user *U1* named *Jose Hernandez* belongs to the domain *D1* and is a *referent user* with hierarchy level *5* (the highest one). For another user type we have <U2, Maria Lopez, D1, data consumer, 1>.

Phase II: Information Gathering

The phase's goal is capturing and documenting functional (queries) and nonfunctional (quality) requirements, taking into account the scope defined in Phase I. The *output* of the phase includes (1) a list of the queries expected to be posed to the system; (2) data quality requirements forms; and (3) a quality dimensions hierarchy. Next we describe the steps of this phase.

*   **Interviews with users and referent people:** Aimed at documenting queries and the associated quality parameters. Each user provides a list of queries (expressed as questions in English) the user needs for a daily task. Initially, the vocabulary is *unrestricted.* However, certain terms may have different meanings for different users, or team participants. For example, "the best customer" or "the largest source of buying orders." These expressions are disambiguated and converted to, for example, "best customer is the one averaging buying orders for more than $1000 monthly." The analyst must identify these kinds of ambiguous expressions and translate them as explained. The form QRY_USR is produced. This form contains, for each user and query, (1) *user ID*; (2) a *query ID* (a unique value of the form "Q" plus a sequential number); (3) the query expressed in English; (4) a *priority* for the query: the requirements engineer must guide the user in this task, avoiding overestimating the query hierarchy; (5) a *query frequency* (the minimum elapsed time between two instances of the same query); (6) the *accepted response time* (maximum time required for getting the query answer); and (7) a *global priority* for the query. The *global priority* is left blank and will be defined in a later phase. As an example, user U2 (Maria Lopez) has declared that a query she will be posing regularly is *"Number of monthly contracts per sales representative."*

Copyright © 2007, Idea Group Inc. Copying or distributing in print or electronic forms without written permission of Idea Group Inc. is prohibited.

The entry in QRY_USR, for user U2 will be <*Q1, Number of monthly...,5, 24hs,50sec*>.

- **Query analysis:** here we perform data recollection and validation against the data dictionary. The goal of the former is the discovery of atomic data required for satisfying each query defined in the previous step. However, initially the QRY_USR form may contain queries with redundant, ambiguous, or even incorrect terms. Thus, analysts and users review the queries and agree on a (possibly) new set of queries, using the information obtained from the data and aggregations dictionaries. For example, in query Q1 from user U2, the word *contracts* will be replaced by the word *sales*, according to the information in the data dictionary. These queries must be validated against the data diction-ary, and all terms not present in this dictionary must be added, using the form DIC_DATA. This is a cyclic process, which results in a final QRY_USR form where data referred in the queries are absolutely consistent with data in the dictionaries.

- **Preliminary identification of facts, dimensions, and aggregations:** The analyst tries to identify the underlying facts and dimensions from the queries. This is a manual or semiautomatic process (for example, this process can make use of one of the many algorithms that use an entity-relationship diagram for obtaining the star schema for the data warehouse), which includes the valida-tion against the aggregations dictionary DIC_AGGR (updating this dictionary, if necessary).

- **Quality survey interviews:** after the queries are validated, a list of data ele-ments will be extracted from the query definitions collected in the former step. These are the data elements that will be required for answering the queries. Recall that for each data element there is an entry in the data dictionary. The quality requirements for these data elements is then defined and registered in three forms: QRY_QTY I, QRY_QTY II, and QRY_QTY III. The first one contains, for each query, the following information: (1) Query ID and (2) Data ID: one for each data element in the query. This is the identifier of the element in the data dictionary. All data elements *directly or indirectly* related to the query must be included. For example, if a query asks for the "*Average monthly sales*," although it does not *directly* include the dollar value of each sale, this value is involved in the computation of the average, so we need to specify its quality requirement; (3) description of the element; (4) aggregation: indicates if the data expresses a dimension level; (5) range (valid range for the data element); (6) timeliness; and (7) accuracy. (Timeliness and accuracy apply to our case study, other cases may require different quality dimensions). The other two forms, QRY_QTY II and QRY_QTY III, specify consistency and completeness requirements respectively.

Copyright © 2007, Idea Group Inc. Copying or distributing in print or electronic forms without written permission of Idea Group Inc. is prohibited.

Example 2: In our case study, in the form QRY_USR, the entry for query Q2, informed by user U5 (George Martinez) reads: "Top 50 customers, among the customers with monthly average sales higher than $1500." This query includes the following data elements: D1 (sales), D4 (month), D5 (customer name), D7 (year), and D13 (customerId). For each of these elements, there is an entry in form QRY_QTY1. For instance, <Q2, D1, sales, NO, -, high, 10>, meaning that in query Q2, data element D1, representing sales, will not be used to aggregate, requires a "high" value for timeliness, and a minimum accuracy of 10% (i.e., maximum accepted divergence between data and real world value). Analogously, form QRY_QTYII contains the consistency conditions for data D5 in query Q2. The condition ID is Q2C, and the description is "the best customers must be the ones classified as 'international.'" For D5, consistency is mandatory. The form QRY_QTYIII records completeness conditions for data element D5 in query Q2. The condition states that "all customers registered since 2001 must be in the database," and it is also mandatory.

- **Prioritizing quality factors:** The user assigns a priority to quality dimensions. For instance, some departments may be more interested in the *accuracy* of the reported data than in *timeliness*. This criteria is determined for each user and applied to each query posed. The form HIE_QTY is filled out, containing, for each quality dimension, the dimension's name and a priority (a number between 1 and 5).

Example 3: In our running case study, we have four quality dimensions, denoted F1 to F4: accuracy, timeliness, consistency, and completeness. User U2, from the Sales Department (domain D1) has defined the following priorities: 5,5,4,3, respectively. User U3, from domain D2 (Purchasing Department) defined these other set of priorities: 4,3,5,1, respectively.

Phase III: Requirements Integration

In this phase, requirements from all users and domains are unified, using a criteria based on QFD (Akao, 1997). In the *input* of the phase we have (1) a query list; (b) a hierarchy of quality dimensions; (3) a data quality requirements form; (4) data and aggregation dictionaries; (5) a hierarchy of domains; and (6) a hierarchy of users. The *output* of the phase is a set of documents containing the unified data model, the query priorities, and the data requirements matrix. The steps of the phase are *analysis of query redundancy, unified query prioritizing,* and construction of the *data requirements matrix.*

Copyright © 2007, Idea Group Inc. Copying or distributing in print or electronic forms without written permission of Idea Group Inc. is prohibited.

- **Analysis of query redundancy:** Equivalent requirements are identified, that is, requirements such that queries and associated data quality are the same. Its goal is to reduce the number of requirements to the data sources. We do not have this situation in our case study.

- **Unified query prioritizing:** During the initial phases we worked with different domains. We now need to unify all requirements from these domains, and define priorities between them. DSS-METRIQ proposes the following order of priorities: *Priorities between domains -> Priorities between users -> Priorities between queries of the same user:* Intuitively, the idea is that the requirement with the least priority in a domain prevails over the requirement with the highest priority in the domain immediately following (in importance) the previous one. The following formula defines the global priority computation for a query "Q" denoted PriorityG(Q). This empirical expression is intends to capture the order of priorities defined previously:

PriorityG (Q) = PriorityD (D) * X^2 + PriorityU (U) * X + PriorityQ (Q)

where PriorityD (D), PriorityU (U), and PriorityQ (Q) are the domain, users, and query priorities. As a result of this step we obtain a set of queries ordered by priority. The form QRY_USR is updated in order to complete the *Global priority* field. These priorities are a tool for solving conflicting requirements. For example, in our case study, query *Q1* has priority 5 for user *U2* (with priority 1), who belongs to domain *D1* (with priority 5). Thus, the global priority for query *Q1* is *135*.

- **Data requirements matrix:** This is the integrated requirements form. This form is used for exchanging information with data producer users. The form MAT_REQ_DATA is filled out.

Example 4: Figure 1 shows a portion of the form MAT_REQ_DATA for our case study. Each triple domain-user-query has associated with it a set of data quality dimensions and values for these dimensions. Note that this form summarizes information obtained during the previous phases.

Phase IV: Data Source Selection

In this phase, data sources are studied in order to determine if they fulfill the information requirements collected in phases I to III. The *outputs* of the phase are (1) a query evaluation report and (2) a data source selection order for each data element. This process is central to our methodology. As far as we are aware of, this is the

Copyright © 2007, Idea Group Inc. Copying or distributing in print or electronic forms without written permission of Idea Group Inc. is prohibited.

Figure 1. Data requirements matrix

Origin (dom-usr)	ID Data (dictionary)	Description	Business Process	Aggregation	Range (description)	Ranking (description)	Timeliness	Accuracy	Consistency description	Consistency value	completeness description	completeness value
	Sale	contract	Sale		...	...	0,75	10	The sum of all Contracts must be equal to the sales total	100		
D1-U2-Q1-	Month	month	Sale	x	...	...	0,25					
	Year	year	Sale	x	...	...	0,25					
	Salesman	Sales rep.	...		...	...	0,50					
	Customer	Customer	...		Customers with sales average over $ 1500 monthly	...	0,50		The best customers must be the ones classified as "International"	100	All customers registered since 2001 must be in the database	100
D1-U5-Q2	Cust_cod	Customer code	...		...	...	0,75					
	Sale	Sale	Sale	x	...	top(50)	0,25	10				
	Month	Month	Sale		...	...	0,25					
	Year	Year	Sale	x	...	...						
D2-U3-Q3	Sale	Sale	Sale		...	...	0,50					
	Year	Year	Sale	x	...	...	0,25	12				

FORM
Name: MAT_REQ_DAT   Phase 3   Step 3
Page __ of __
Version __   Revision 0

SURVEY
Date 23 4 2005
Responsible Nancy Cepeda

Page 1/4

Notes:

first proposal addressing this topic in a quantitative fashion. Now we describe the steps of the phase.

- **Analysis of data sources:** Meetings with data producers are carried out (with the help of the documents produced so far), where the set of data sources and the quality of their data are documented. Also, information on source availability is collected. Two forms, MAS_DS_P and MAS_DS_L, are used for *physical*

Copyright © 2007, Idea Group Inc. Copying or distributing in print or electronic forms without written permission of Idea Group Inc. is prohibited.

and *logical* data sources, respectively. Each form contains a data source identifier, values for data source availability, and a source priority defined by the data producer user. In the case of logical data sources, for each data element the corresponding expression for obtaining the data must be specified. The following actions are taken: (a) the data producer user determines the priority criteria for data source usage, based on experience and technical issues. Priority ranges between 1 and 5. (b) The requirements engineer finds out if a physical source contains the required data; if so, it is registered in the form MAS_DS_P. (c) If a combination of fields yields some of the required data, this combination is considered a *logical data source*, and it is registered in the form MAS_DS_L. In our case study we have three physical data sources, which for simplicity we denote A, B, and C. Data source A is a proprietary system database, with transactional availability of 50% and priority 5 (contains the core data of the business processes). Data source B is a SAP repository with 50% availability and priority 4. Data source C is a stylesheet collection (containing monthly sales information) with availability 100% and priority 1.

- **Data source quality:** This step consists of three tasks that can be performed in parallel. The goal is obtaining the quality of the data source for each data-source combination. The data provider informs quality characteristics of the data source and a mapping for the required fields (i.e., where is the required data located, and under which name?).

- **Data source quality (data):** The form DS_QTY_I is completed. This form contains, for each query, for each data element in the query, and for each data source, the following information: (a) *mapping:* field in the data source containing the data element, or field to which a function must be applied. For instance, the month of a sale could be obtained as month(date). (b) *Aggregation:* tells if the aggregated data is or is not present in the source, or can be computed from the data in the source. (c) *Accuracy.* (d) *Timeliness.* The last two dimensions apply to our case study, but can be replaced by a different set of dimensions if the problem at hand requires it. In our case study, the record *<Q2, sales, B, amount, NO, 70, 5min>* tells that for query *Q2*, data element *sales* can be obtained from data source *B* (where it is in nonaggregated form), with 70% *accuracy* and with a *timeliness of* 5 minutes.

- **Data source quality (consistency):** The form DS_QTY_II is completed, with the consistency characteristics of the data source. There is one entry for each data source, containing an evaluation of the source's consistency. In our case study, consistency condition Q2C above is accomplished with a 100% precision by data source A, and 90% precision by data source B.

- **Data source quality (completeness):** The form DS_QTY_III is filled analogously to form DS_QTY_II, addressing completeness instead of consistency. In our case study, the completeness condition stating that all customers regis-

Copyright © 2007, Idea Group Inc. Copying or distributing in print or electronic forms without written permission of Idea Group Inc. is prohibited.

tered since 2001 must be in the database is accomplished with 100% precision by data source A, and 99% precision by data source B.

- **Data source quality assessment:** The goal of this step is the integration, in a single data source assessment matrix, of the three essential components of the methodology: (a) data requirements; (b) quality requirements; and (c) data sources. The output of the process is, for each data element, the best data source for obtaining it, and a range with the qualification for each data source. The *Global Data Source Performance* is computed, using a procedure that adapts the QFD methodology.

Example 5: The data source quality assessment matrix for our running case study is depicted in Figure 2. We only show the data element "sales" and two queries: Q1 (from user U2) and Q4 (from user U3). The information gathered so far is:

a.   Query Q1

Priorities of quality dimensions: accuracy: 5, consistency: 4, completeness: 3, timeliness: 5.

Global priority of the query: 135 (as explained in Phase III).

Aggregations required: month and salesman.

b.   Query Q4

Priorities of quality dimensions: accuracy: 4, consistency: 5, completeness: 1, timeliness: 3.

Global priority of the query: 31

Aggregations required: Country, province, city, neighborhood.

Finally, the data producer user provided the following information:

Available data sources: A, B, and C (c in Figure 2), with priorities 5,4,1 respectively, as explained previously (b in Figure 2).

Each matrix block is composed as follows: (1) Consumer users' requirements: data (h), query ID, quality dimensions (i), aggregations (j), global priority of the query (from Phase II), and quality dimension priorities given by the users in Phase III; (2) Data producer users' information, obtained in the previous step of this phase: a submatrix indicating requirements fulfillment for each available data source. According to the degree of fulfillment, a value is given (1, 3, or 9, d in Figure 2), using the following criteria: "1" is given if the condition is not fulfilled, "3" if the condition is not fulfilled, but can be computed from the data in the source; and "9" if the condition is fulfilled. For the sake of brevity we do not extend on how to de-

Copyright © 2007, Idea Group Inc. Copying or distributing in print or electronic forms without written permission of Idea Group Inc. is prohibited.

Figure 2. Quality assessment matrix

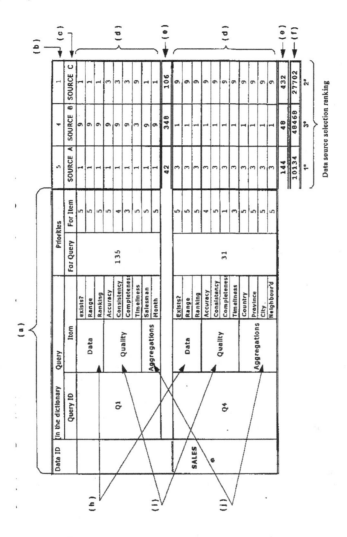

termine these values. (3) Data source performance for each query (e in Figure 2); (4) Global data source performance (f in Figure 2).

The data source performance for each query is computed as:

$$\textbf{PerfLocal(S,Q,D)} = \sum (pri_i * rel_i),$$

where

Copyright © 2007, Idea Group Inc. Copying or distributing in print or electronic forms without written permission of Idea Group Inc. is prohibited.

PerfLocal (S,Q,D): *Data source performance of source S for data D in query Q*

Pri$_i$: *Data, quality, and aggregations priorities, for data D in query Q*

Rel$_i$: *Degree of fulfillment of data source S for query Q and data element D*

The global data source performance is computed as:

PerfGlobal(F,Q) = $\sum$ HierGlobal(Qj) * PerfLocal(S,Q ,D)

For all queries Qj involving data element D, and given a set **F** of a data source and a set of queries **Q**. HierGlobal (Qj): Global priority of query Qj.

> **Example 6:** For the table in Example 5, the local performance for data source A and query Q1 is computed as 5 * 1 + 5 * 1 + 5 * 1 + 5 * 1 + 4 * 1 + 3 * 1 + 5 * 1 + 5 * 1 + 5 * 1 = 42. The global performance for source A is: 135 * 42 + 31 * 144 = 10134.

- **Data source selection:** Although the *final* source selection is beyond the scope of the methodology, a document is generated, with a ranking of data sources for each data. This document will be used in the final data source selection process. For our case study, the ranking is 1: data source B (global performance 48,468), 2: data source C (global performance 27,702), and 3: data source A (global performance 10,134).

Phase V: Document Generation

With the information collected on Phases I to IV, a set of requirements documents is produced. These documents are reviewed by the referent, data producer, and data consumer users, in order to reach a final agreement for closing the requirements elicitation phase. We describe these documents next.

- **Query requirements document:** Contains all the queries obtained in phases I to IV, ordered by global priority. Each query is qualified as follows: a value of "1" means that the query can be answered with the information contained in the data sources; "2" means that the query involves values not in the data sources, thus, it cannot be answered; "3" means that a query "close" to the original one can be answered with the data available in the sources (e.g., modi-

Copyright © 2007, Idea Group Inc. Copying or distributing in print or electronic forms without written permission of Idea Group Inc. is prohibited.

fying the required granularity or the required accuracy). In the "Los Andes" project, queries Q1 to Q3 were rated "1."

- **DSS requirements document:** Summarizes all the requirements collected during the process. Contains, for each query: the query identifier, the name of the user who specified the requirement, the query expressed in English, the same query after disambiguation, the query frequency, the query's global priority, and the expected response time. For each data attribute associated to each query, the form includes the identifier in the data dictionary, description, name to be displayed when showing the data, and all the quality conditions required. *Data warehouse requirements documents:* There are two documents: a metrics document and a quality document. The *metrics* document specifies, for each quality dimension, the range of values that are acceptable for each attribute involved in a requirement, and the metrics to be used in the data warehouse design. The *quality* document specifies the range of values acceptable for each requirement. For each required attribute, the document defines (1) maximum time for data loading; (2) minimum value for data currency (i.e., the age of the data); and (3) acceptable values for consistency and completeness. For each dimension, the report includes the formula for obtaining maximum or minimum values.

- **Preliminary data model:** With the collected information building a preliminary version of the star schema model for the data warehouse is straightforward.

- **Data source requirements document:** With the information obtained in Phase IV a document containing the data sources is produced. This document contains for each data source an identifier, a description, and the data source availability.

- **ETL process requirements document:** A complete listing of the required data and a mapping from the required data to the data source fields from which these data are obtained is provided, possibly including formulas involving more than one data field. This information will be used for the design and implementation of the ETL process.

Summary and Research Directions

In this chapter we showed that methodologies for software development in operational systems do not apply in the DSS setting. Based on this conclusion, we presented a methodology for requirements elicitation with focus on data quality dimensions and data source selection. The methodology aims at finding out if the data currently available in the operational data sources allow answering a set of queries (functional requirements) satisfying certain data quality conditions (nonfunctional requirements). In order to quantify the answer to such question, we adapted the quality

Copyright © 2007, Idea Group Inc. Copying or distributing in print or electronic forms without written permission of Idea Group Inc. is prohibited.

function deployment (QFD) technique. Finally, DSS-METRIQ specifies the set of forms needed to support the requirements elicitation process.

Future research directions include a Web-based implementation of the framework, currently in progress, and developing a data source selection engine that can deliver different combinations of data sources fulfilling the requirements with different levels of quality. Data quality evolution, and how it affects data source selection, allowing dynamically changing the data source being selected, must also be accounted for in future work.

References

Akao, Y. (1997). *QFD, past, present and future.* Presented at the Third International QFD Symposium (QFD'97), Linköpin, Sweden.

Basili, V., Caldiera, G., & Rombach, H. (1992). *The goal question metric approach* (Computer Science Technical Report Series CS-TR-2956). College Park: University of Maryland.

Bobrowski, M., Marré, M., &Yankelevich, D. (1999). An homogeneous framework to measure data quality. In Y. W. Lee & G. K. Tayi (Eds.), *Proceedings of IQ'99* (pp. 115-124). Cambridge, MA: MIT Press.

Bonifati, A., Cattaneo, F., Ceri, S., Fuggetta, A., & Paraboschi, S. (2001). Designing data marts for data warehouses. *ACM Transactions on Software Engineering and Methodology, 10*(4), 452-483.

Chaudhuri, S., & Dayal, U. (1997). An overview of data warehousing and OLAP technology. *SIGMOD Record, 26*(1), 65-74.

Christel, M. G., & Kang, K. C. (1992). *Issues in requirements elicitation* (Tech. Rep. No. CMU/SEI-92-TR-12). Carnegie Mellon University.

Cippico, V. (1997). Comparison of the decision support systems and transaction support system development methodologies. In *Advances in database and information systems* (pp. 416-426). St. Petersburg, FL: Nevsky Dialect.

Delone, W. H., & Mclean, E. R. (1992). Information systems success: The quest for the dependent variable. *Information Systems Research, 3*(1), 60-95.

Gill, H., & Rao, P. (1996). *Data warehousing.* Indianapolis, IN: Prentice Hall.

Hoxmeier, J. A. (2000). Database quality dimensions. *Journal of Business and Management, 7*(1).

Jarke, M., Lenzerini, M., Vassiliou, Y., & Vassiliadis, P. (2003). *Fundamentals of data warehouse.* Berlin, Germany: Springer-Verlag.

Copyright © 2007, Idea Group Inc. Copying or distributing in print or electronic forms without written permission of Idea Group Inc. is prohibited.

Jarke, M., & Vassiliou, Y. (1997). Data warehouse quality: A review of the DWQ project. In D. Strong & B. Kahn (Eds.), *Proceedings of the 1997 Conference on Information Quality* (pp. 299-313). Cambridge, MA: MIT Press.

Kimball, R., Reeves, L., Ross, M., & Thornthwaite, W. (1998). *The data warehouse lifecycle toolkit.* New York: John Wiley & Sons.

Lee, Y. W., Strong, D., Kahn, B., & Wang, R. (2002). AIMQ: A methodology for information quality assessment. *Information & Management, 40*(2), 133-146.

Moody, D., & Kortink, M. (2000, June 5-6). From enterprise models to dimensional models: A methodology for data warehouse and data mart design. In *Proceedings of the International Workshop on Design and Management of Data Warehouses (DMDW2000)* (pp. 5:1-5:12). Stockholm, Sweden.

Mullery, G. P. (1979, September). CORE: A method for controlled requirement specification. In *Proceedings of the 4ᵗʰ international conference on Software engineering*, Munich, Germany (pp. 126-135).

Paim, F., & Castro, J. (2002). Enhancing data warehouse design with the NFR framework. In *Proceedings of the 5ᵗʰ Workshop on Requirements Engineering (WER2002)* (pp. 40-57).

Paim, F., & Castro, J. (2003, September 8-12). DWARF: An approach for requirements definition and management of data warehouse systems. In *Proceedings of the 11ᵗʰ IEEE International Conference on Requirements Engineering* (pp. 75-84).

Pipino, L., Lee, Y. W., & Wang, R. (2002). Data quality assessment. *Communications of the ACM, 45*(4), 211-218.

Prakash, N., & Gosain, A. (2003, June 16-20). Requirements driven data warehouse development. In *Proceedings of the 15ᵗʰ Conference on Advanced Information Systems Engineering,* Klagenfurt / Velden, Austria.

Quix, C., Jarke, M., Jeusfeld, M., Vassiliadis, P., Lenzerini, M., Calvanese, D., & Bouzeghoub, M. (2002). *Data warehouse architecture and quality model* (Tech. Rep. No. DWQ-RWTH-002). LuFg Theoretical Computer Science, RWTH Aachen.

Ross, D., & Schoman, K. (1979). Structured analysis for requirements definition. *IEEE Transactions on Software Engineering, 3*(1), 6-15.

Strong, D., Yang, W., & Wang, R. (1997). Data quality in context. *Communications of the ACM, 40*(5), 103-110.

Thayer, R. (2002). Software requirements engineering: A tutorial. *IEEE Computer, 35*(4), 68-73.

Vassiliadis, P., Bouzeghoub, M., & Quix, C. (1999). Towards quality-oriented data warehouse usage and evolution. In *Proceedings of the International Conference on Advanced Information Systems Engineering* (pp. 164-179).

Copyright © 2007, Idea Group Inc. Copying or distributing in print or electronic forms without written permission of Idea Group Inc. is prohibited.

Wand, Y., & Wang, R. Y. (1996). Anchoring data quality dimensions in ontological foundations. *Communications of the ACM, 39*(11), 86-95.

Wang, R. Y., & Reddy, M. P. (1992). *Quality data objects.* (Total Data Quality Management Research Program, TDQM-92-06). MIT Sloan School of Management.

Wang, R., Storey, Y., & Firth, C. (1995). A framework for analysis of data quality research. *IEEE Transactions on Data and Knowledge Engineering, 7*(4), 623-640.

Wang, R. Y., & Strong, D. M. (1996). Beyond accuracy: What data quality means to data consumers. *Journal of Management Information Systems, 12*(4), 5-34.

Winter, R., & Strauch, B. (2003). A method for demand-driven information requirements analysis in data warehousing projects. In *HICSS-36*, Hawaii (pp. 231-231). IEEE Press.

Winter, R., & Strauch, B. (2004). Information requirements engineering for data warehouse systems. In H. Haddad, A. Omicini, R. L. Wainwright, & L. M. Liebrock (Eds.), *Proceedings of SAC'04*, Nicosia, Cyprus (pp. 1359-1365). ACM Press.

Zmud, R. (1978). Concepts, theories and techniques: An empirical investigation of the dimensionality of the concept of information. *Decision Sciences, 9*(2), 187-195.

Copyright © 2007, Idea Group Inc. Copying or distributing in print or electronic forms without written permission of Idea Group Inc. is prohibited.

Section II

Loading and Refreshing

Chapter IV

Extraction, Transformation, and Loading Processes

Jovanka Adzic
Telecom Italia, Italy

Valter Fiore
Telecom Italia, Italy

Luisella Sisto
Telecom Italia, Italy

Abstract

ETL stands for extraction, transformation, and loading, in other words, for the data warehouse (DW) backstage. The main focus of our exposition here is the practical application of the ETL process in real world cases with extra problems and strong requirements, particularly performance issues related to population of large data warehouses. In a context of ETL/DW with strong requirements, we can individuate the most common constraints and criticalities that one can meet in developing an ETL system. We will describe some techniques related to the physical database design, pipelining, and parallelism which are crucial for the whole ETL process. We will propose our practical approach, "infrastructure based ETL"; it is not a tool but a set of functionalities or services that experience has proved to be useful and widespread enough in the ETL scenario, and one can build the application on top of it.

Copyright © 2007, Idea Group Inc. Copying or distributing in print or electronic forms without written permission of Idea Group Inc. is prohibited.

Introduction

ETL stands for extraction, transformation, and loading, in other words, for the data warehouse backstage. A variety of commercial ETL tools exist in the market (IBM, 2005; Informatica, 2005; Microsoft, 2005; Oracle, 2005), with a recent market review of Gartner Research (Gartner, 2005). A lot of research efforts exist (Golfarelli & Rizzi, 1998; Husemann, Lechtenborger, & Vossen, 2000; Tryfona, Busborg, & Christiansen, 1999; Vassiliadis, Simitsis, & Skiadopoulos, 2002, May; Vassiliadis, Simitsis, & Skiadopoulos, 2002, November) mostly targeting modeling (conceptual, logical) and methodology issues (like logical modeling of ETL workflows). Some works are focused on the end-to-end methodology for the warehouse and ETL projects (Kimball & Caserta, 2004; Kimball, Reeves, Ross, & Thornthwaite, 1998; Vassiliadis, Simitsis, Georgantas, & Terrovitis, 2003) targeting the complete life cycle of the DW project, describing how to plan, design, build, and run the DW and its ETL backstage. The main focus of our exposition here is the practical application of the ETL process in real world cases with extra problems and strong requirements, particularly performance issues related to population of large data warehouses (one case study is described in Adzic & Fiore, 2003).

In this chapter, we will first discuss the ETL scenario, requirements, criticalities, and so forth that constitute the general framework for ETL processes. Then we will describe some techniques related to the physical database design, pipelining, and parallelism which are relevant for performance issues. Finally, we will describe our practical approach, "infrastructure based ETL"; it is not a tool but a set of functionalities or services that experience has proved to be useful and widespread enough in the ETL scenario, and one can build the application on top of it.

ETL Scenario

The primary scenario in which ETL takes place is a wide area between the sources of data and a target database management system (DBMS); in the middle, there are all the required functionalities to bring and maintain historical data in a form well suited for analysis (Figure 1).

All the work to collect, transform, and load data from different and multiple sources to a target DBMS structured for analysis is what we call ETL.

A DW project consists of three main technical tasks: ETL, database design, and analysis techniques and tools; each of them has particular issues and requirements. Above all, we must consider the problems in accessing data owned by other departments, groups, and so on; obtaining the necessary grants to access data is not always easy for both technical and nontechnical reasons. These political problems

Copyright © 2007, Idea Group Inc. Copying or distributing in print or electronic forms without written permission of Idea Group Inc. is prohibited.

Figure 1. ETL scenario

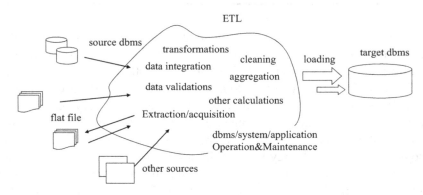

can impose constraints and work-around that make the ETL process more complex. Another topic is the absence of internal enterprise standardization. It can be very difficult to find the same rules (even in the same department) in naming files, in expressing a date, in choosing a structure for files, and so forth. These problems, involve very general questions like standardization, metadata, and so forth, and cover a relevant part in the ETL process design.

Requirements, Constraints, and Criticalities

In a DW project (as in every project), the most important step is the requirements collection. A well-defined set of requirements is essential in order to individuate the best approach to ETL. If the DW must be loaded once a week, with limited transformation complexity and volumes, then one can choose any preferred approach and hence skip this chapter entirely. In this case, ETL means loading data into DBMS with simple transformation; a normal knowledge of SQL and expertise in programming/scripting is enough to achieve the objective in many cases. On the contrary, if DW loading frequency, volumes, and complexity are high, then a more structured approach becomes necessary.

In these cases it is necessary to find out sophisticated ETL techniques, whereas in other cases the more usual approach is the best solution. It is true, however, that if a company has bought licenses for a commercial tool or has developed its own infrastructure (as we propose here), then it is strongly recommended to use them in all kinds of DW projects.

In a context of strong requirements, we can individuate the most common constraints and criticalities that one can meet in developing an ETL system:

Copyright © 2007, Idea Group Inc. Copying or distributing in print or electronic forms without written permission of Idea Group Inc. is prohibited.

- **Volumes:** High volumes imply specialized loading techniques (classic SQL is not suited) and require a good efficiency of transformation code.

- **Near real time (NRT):** In these contexts, loading and analysis processes must coexist together, and that implies strong constraints on loading techniques; massive loading mechanisms are not directly applicable, indexes must be active, and so on.

- **Strict time constraints:** Especially true in NRT where the population cycle can have a period of 10 or less minutes, but also in traditional batch systems in particular circumstances.

- **Reliability/availability:** Reliability is important, because in some contexts not even one data item is allowed to be lost, which means that any missing data must be recovered. The other face of reliability is availability, in our context, the ability to recover from external/internal error (data loss or corrupted, etc.) to maintain data integrity and consistency.

- **Loading atomicity:** The system must be able to manage partial load in atomic fashion (manage a sort of *global commit*) in order to allow partial recovery.

- **Source instability:** In some contexts the sources of data are not stable (e.g., due to network problems or systems unavailability) and acquisition process must be able to retry.

- **Nonstandard/complex transformation:** DW techniques are not only applied in "sales and revenue" contexts; in many cases one needs to implement complex transformations or specialized calculations that differ from standard analytical functions.

We have not yet mentioned issues like metadata and cleaning which are vastly debated. Metadata are data that describe other data: for example, a column named "price" obviously refers to the price of an article but many other pieces of information may also be useful for understanding its exact meaning. Does the price include VAT or not? Is that price for wholesale or retail dealers? Which department has established it? When was it modified last? These, and many other questions, may stay behind data, simple and clear only in appearance.

In our mind, data always exist together with their metadata: when we look at prices of goods at the grocery store, we know the answers to all the questions, because we are aware of the context (goods in a little retail store). But when we look at the column "price" in a table and nothing else, the context is unknown, and data may have several different meanings. In the case of "enterprise data warehouse" there could be a lot of information/metadata to manage, so the need for metadata management is clearly visible. One must know the exact meaning of any single data item contained in DW, otherwise one cannot do any reliable analysis (that is the goal of a DW). In other contexts, where the domain is limited and well known, the need

Copyright © 2007, Idea Group Inc. Copying or distributing in print or electronic forms without written permission of Idea Group Inc. is prohibited.

of metadata is less relevant because the operators are familiar with their own data (e.g., in a system that collects Telco measures, it is useless to specify what column "erlang" means). In these cases, the data are stored in the DBMS and metadata could continue to stay in the mind of the persons.

However, when the metadata management is necessary, there are still lots of questions: how to design, store, and display metadata. Some high-end ETL tools have a support for storing metadata more or less comprehensively, although rarely interchangeable with others (limits in metadata federations).

We have not got a great expectation in these techniques, we believe that a good, well-structured traditional documentation may constitute a valid metadata support; the human language has the flexibility, the undertones, and the richness to depict and contextualize any kind of information. The main problem is that paper documentation is not linked with the data scheme, and also stored metadata need a human intervention to reflect changes. This is a problem concerning the organization of the "productive process" more than an IT problem. Accordingly, it could be extremely useful to have something like a structured language for metadata representation.

Another aspect of interest in ETL is cleaning, that is, the ability to check, filter, and correct mistakes or corruption that can be found in the source data. A typical case in which a cleaning process is mandatory is in the address (location) processing: "street," "st," "st.," and so forth; all indicate the word "street" and an automatic process must be able to recognize it. For this particular purpose, there are specialized tools that apply ad-hoc algorithms and have their own topographic database where to store/retrieve the correct name of every street, and so forth. In this case, cleaning is a specific stage in the ETL process.

Nevertheless, the problem of assuring data correctness may be considered from different perspectives. Data sources do not have the same risks of errors: one is a well defined and certified file produced by another system, another is data inserted directly by users, or data sent via an unstable line or coming from unreliable systems, and so forth. The risk of data corruption in these examples is different in quantity and quality; in the case of a certified file, one can process them without any check; Web form data must be checked and interpreted according to the application logic, while in the last case, we must pay attention to *hardware* corruption, loss/inconsistency/duplication of some information and so on. It is impossible to find a general rule for "cleaning" due to the wide spectrum of possible types of errors. Apart from specific cases where a dedicated processing phase is mandatory, is it better to process the files twice (a first scan for cleaning and a second for transforming) or to incorporate the optimal level of checks in the transformation phase? In our experience, with large volumes and strict time constraints, the second solution is better because it saves computational and I/O time, however, loosing in the implementation conceptual separation between the cleaning and transform processes.

Copyright © 2007, Idea Group Inc. Copying or distributing in print or electronic forms without written permission of Idea Group Inc. is prohibited.

Physical Database Design

Many important works related to the database modeling and design for DW are available in Kimball et al. (1998); in this chapter, we focus on physical database design and correlated techniques because this aspect is crucial for the whole ETL process; a powerful transformation engine working on a not-well structured database may be a cause of problems for the entire ETL process. In this chapter, we will describe some important issues in physical database design, in particular, the relevance of partitioning (range, hash, composite) for managing history and for performance issues that must be taken into account in building a DW/ETL project.

Partitioning is a very important issue in a database design, in OLTP and DW for scalability reasons and, in the case of DW, for managing history. Partitioning is the ability to divide/organize data in separate subsets, for example, the ability to split a table into several ones still viewing it as a whole. When we have more than one database in different locations, we have done some kind of partitioning, when we use different tables to contain the same types of data. In all these cases, there is partitioning, and it does not matter if we use or do not use the partitioning constructions.

Modern DBMS support some kind of partitioning with unique techniques and constructions. The first way to achieve partitions in the Oracle DBMS was with the use of views; a partitioned table was defined as a view of many tables with the same layout connected together in "union all." Partitioning pruning, the ability of the query optimizer to involve only the few necessary partitions in a query instead of the all partitions, was achieved via an initialization parameter. Starting with Oracle8 and further releases, partitioning constructions were introduced in SQL as specific "partitioning clauses." Each partition can have its storage attributes like distinct tables, and there is information stored in the dictionary that permits a unified view of them. Nowadays, in the Oracle DBMS there are three types of partitions: range, hash, and list, with the possibility of subpartitioning by hash or list.

Partitioning is a fundamental issue in the DW and ETL design because this technique permits an easy management of history, loading, and query performance. Each row in a DW fact table has columns named "date-of-fact" or "loading-date"; when one wants to maintain data for a certain period of time (one month, one year, etc.), one must label the rows with a date (date-of-fact) and then, via management operation on tables at every loading cycle, delete old rows, making space for the new records. The "SQL delete" operation, when involving many thousands or millions of rows, is very expensive in terms of time and disk space (rows must be saved in before-image space and destroyed only after commit) but also involve heavy indexes reorganization. Suppose that a fact table has 1 billion rows and a 10-day history; deleting the rows related to 1 day (100 million) is just heavy, but this is nothing compared to the job of rearranging five to six indexes that own 1 billion rows. Without partitions (or without some surrogate techniques), it is practically impossible to manage

Copyright © 2007, Idea Group Inc. Copying or distributing in print or electronic forms without written permission of Idea Group Inc. is prohibited.

large and very large fact tables, especially due to the index reorganization costs. Enlarging history involves increasing the size of global indexes and so increasing, in a nonlinear way, the cost of its access/reorganization. The local indexes resolve this problem maintaining constant index reorganization costs at the level of a single partition cost (accessing the entire table via a local index has indeed a linear cost). In this way, it is possible to enlarge the history at the cost of increased disk storage requirement. In the following section, we will see the different types of partitioning and how they are suited for history management and for performance.

The main type of partitioning used in DW design is range partition; a table is usually partitioned on a date column (partition key) and each partition contains rows that fall in a range expressed by a start_date and end_date. As mentioned previously, one can partition by "date-of-fact" or by "loading-date": partitioning by date-of-fact is well suited for analysis, in that the optimizer can make an effective partition pruning when the queries (as usual) have a "where clause" on the date-of-fact; partition by "loading-date" is best suited for the ETL application, but can limit the benefit of partition pruning. In any case, a table partitioned by date is optimal for history management. At every loading cycle, (when necessary) a new partition is added and the oldest one is dropped with a SQL operation that is very fast and guarantees transaction consistency (the drop operation waits for in-course selection on partition).

The hash partitioning means that data are split over a specified number of partitions on the base of the value of a column and is useful for performance reasons (striped data across multiple files/disks/devices allow parallelization and then improve performance). Composite partition range-hash means that the single partitions will be further split on hash base (not controlled by application) or on list base (controlled by application) in range-list partitioning. When the volumes are high, splitting a single partition by hash or list is very useful also with respect to better disks utilization (Figure 2).

Here, we have a range (logical) partition that is striped over n table spaces, each of them containing one subpartition of every range partition; this organization (when table spaces are allocated on different volumes) gives good performance and easy manageability. Performance improves due to subpartitions (better I/O parallelization). Manageability is simpler because we have a *1:n* relation between table space and partitions, so space allocation constraints are relaxed.[1]

As Figure 2 shows, indexes are partitioned in the same way as the table. Partitioned or local indexes (an index that is in relation *1:1* with its partition) are the normality in DW because they can be dropped/added as table partition, thus avoiding index rebuilding. Different kinds of indexes (B*Tree and bitmap) can be defined as local, but not all types are well suited for DW; in particular, bitmap indexes are only useful with low cardinality and read-only access.

Copyright © 2007, Idea Group Inc. Copying or distributing in print or electronic forms without written permission of Idea Group Inc. is prohibited.

Figure 2. Subpartitioning schema

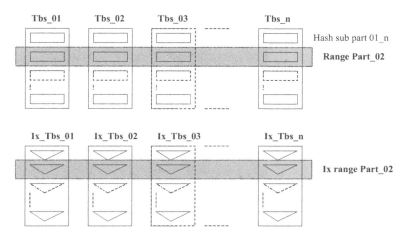

When we have to build indexes, should it be done after load or during load? In the case of high volumes, it is always preferable to build indexes after load (better performance); for small/medium volumes, loading with active indexes is the simplest way. Depending on the DBMS used, one can find some problems to build indexes leaving the table always accessible (this is a problem only in NRT), so one must use some work-around, but when the volumes are high, loading data with active indexes is impossible (direct path, or similar, and bitmap indexes cannot be used). A simple work-around to load a large volume of data is to use a temporary table. One must add a new partition on the fact table and create a temporary table, without indexes, with the same layout of the target table and laying on the same table space. Then one can load it in the direct path, create the indexes on this temporarily, and then exchange it, without validation, with the empty partition, and finally drop the empty table. At the end, one has a new partition full with its valid indexes. The exchange operation mentioned can be done with or without validation, in the sense that DBMS verifies or not if the data in the table to swap are correct according to the partition bound.

In DW, where the load of data is managed by an application, further validations are not necessary; this is true for particular operations like "exchange partition," but also for primary key, foreign key, check, and so forth. These checks and constraints that guarantee the "data integrity and consistency," must exist and must be verified, but inside the application, before the load operations occur, and not at the DBMS level. The choice between validating the integrity check in application or in DBMS does not exist in practice because, usually, the fast procedures for loading massive data do not support a check of any type. Then, fact tables must be free of primary key and other heavy constraints; in some cases, it is only useful to declare referential integrity check merely on behalf of optimizer (with no validate or similar clauses).

Copyright © 2007, Idea Group Inc. Copying or distributing in print or electronic forms without written permission of Idea Group Inc. is prohibited.

Figure 3. Thin-fat partitioning schema

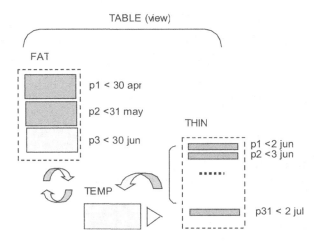

In the NRT context when the loading frequency is high and history is deep, creating a new partition every cycle implies a total number of partitions which DBMS, in general, does not support. If volumes are not so high, then it is possible to define partitions that span many loading cycles (e.g., a partition per day), but in these cases fast loading techniques cannot be used.

If volumes are high, and hence the use of fast loading is mandatory, then some ad-hoc techniques must be "invented" (Figure 3).

Our fact table consists of two partitioned tables named "thin" and "fat" merged by a view in "union all." The *thin* table is partitioned in a coherent way with loading cycle, while the *fat* one has a lower granularity partitioning. The *thin* table is massively loaded with the mentioned method of the temporary table exchange and, periodically, the *thin* partitions will be compacted together in a new partition of the *fat* table. With this method, complex only in appearance, we can contain the number of partitions to a reasonable value, loading data with the most efficient techniques, and defer the time-consuming compact operations to the optimal time window. All these operations can be done while querying the data; the view ensures the transactional consistency.

Pipelining and Parallelism for Performance

Performance is one of the most important issues in ETL processing. Due to a high volume of data, NRT time constraints, or hardware limits (not even the budget for

Copyright © 2007, Idea Group Inc. Copying or distributing in print or electronic forms without written permission of Idea Group Inc. is prohibited.

a DW project is large enough), it is always necessary to pay attention to the efficiency of code.

Loading records into a DBMS with some transformations is not a complex job; complexity results from a very great number of times that these simple operations must be repeated. Dividing a job into many sequential stages (each with its input and output on disk) is a good technique that simplifies the coding and debugging, but reading and writing the same data many times is very expensive. Processing many files (or extracting) sequentially is the simplest way but does not permit a good utilization of computational resources.

To achieve high performance, there are only two ways:

- execute the minimum number of machine instructions and avoid useless I/O
- do not waste the wait time that occurs in I/O operations

These elementary rules imply a not always simple balance between the readability and maintainability, on one hand, and an efficient but complex coding, on the other.

To avoid reading and writing the same data many times, split workload in conformity to the application logic to exploit parallel features of the machines. Use pipelining and parallelism as the main objective in ETL.

Parallelism is the ability to split workload in many tasks that work concurrently and synchronize each other. Split workload is obviously useful when we have more than one processor, but is even useful in a single processor machine; in the latter case, we can utilize the I/O idle time (orders of magnitude of CPU time) to do other useful jobs. In ETL, parallelism primarily means the full utilization of multiprocessor machines and minimization of waste of time correlated to I/O operations.

Pipelining, in the processors technology, is the ability to execute an instruction while fetching the next; in this context, we mean passing an output stream to the next stage without intermediate steps (involving useless write and read operations) and without waiting for the completion of any stage. This is another complementary way to save time and better utilize processing power.

Infrastructure-Based ETL

There are two main approaches to ETL: to resolve it implementing a set of scripts and ad-hoc programs or to buy a commercial ETL tool that simplifies the job of proposing a methodology, a graphical interface, and a language to solve specific problems. In the market, many of these tools exist, with different levels in terms of

Copyright © 2007, Idea Group Inc. Copying or distributing in print or electronic forms without written permission of Idea Group Inc. is prohibited.

performance (some of them are interpreted engines, some compiled and parallel), completeness, usability, and, of course, different costs.

In our experience, we have analyzed these products and some of them almost seemed to be quite adequate for our needs. Quite but not completely, some specific aspects were not covered, tool methodology imposed some workaround, or the tool was too complex/expensive for application, and so forth. The problem is that ETL scenarios are so heterogeneous, so case-by-case specific, without any general rule, that it is not possible to comprise them into one well-defined scheme. It is *impossible* to recognize a *language* for ETL and build software as a consequence (e.g., for SQL); it is always (or almost) necessary to write from scratch the code that performs *that* extraction and *that* transformation. Only in the loading phase (for a specific target DBMS), it is possible to establish some rules. On the other hand, ad-hoc scripts/programs have poor flexibility, reusability, and maintainability. An infrastructure suited for the specific business/application context seems to us the best solution.

The infrastructure is not a tool; it is a set of functionalities or services that experience has proved to be useful and widespread enough in the ETL scenario, and one can build the application on top of them thus saving coding and debugging time. The infrastructure layer implements, for example, an API to access DBMS and manage partitions, functions for lookup operations, file acquisition, parallel read/write, and so on as shown in Figure 4. Then, on top of this infrastructural layer, one can write simpler and more readable code that implements the application specific logic, resolving each possible *trick* not covered by the lower layer. The infrastructure is, in fact, a library, so one can pick only what is needed; some constraints on how to organize the application may exist or not, but in general these are not so strict as a well-structured tool imposes. This *weak model* gives one major chances to achieve a good solution suited for the specific case.

With these concepts in mind, we developed an infrastructure written in C for the best performance, using OCI[2] to access Oracle for flexibility and OS API Posix[3] for

Figure 4. ETL infrastructure modules

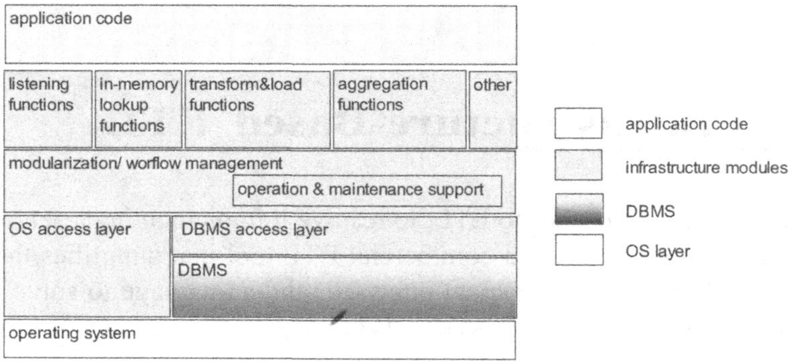

Copyright © 2007, Idea Group Inc. Copying or distributing in print or electronic forms without written permission of Idea Group Inc. is prohibited.

portability. We also decided to give a modular structure and utilize, where possible, a declarative approach. From the design point of view, whatever infrastructure or tool used is generally better than a fully programmatic approach, in that it constrains to provided guidelines or formalisms.

Modularization and Workflow Management

A typical ETL application may be decomposed in many correlated jobs; some of them need to be executed sequentially and others may be parallelized. In certain cases, a job can start only on a certain condition, and so forth. The ability to package jobs and synchronize them is fundamental for an ETL infrastructure for both performance and recovery reasons.

We have chosen to define the "processUnit" as an elementary piece of code that can be implemented both as thread or process in the specified number of instances, without formal parameters, but with an exit code. The processUnit is the basic element of synchronization graph; each processUnit has a dependence list based on its exit code. These processUnits and dependences are all declared (via a simple API) in a main module called "master" and these definitions are then stored (at startup) in a memory segment shared across all jobs (processes/threads) that constitute the application. The master supervises all application activities and forks the processes/threads when necessary according to the graph maintained in the shared memory segment. Each processUnit registers its status in the appropriate structure; the master, at polling interval, checks them, and verifying the dependences, starts or cancels the appropriate processUnits and so on up to the completion of the execution of defined graph. For recovery reasons, as detailed in the Operation and Maintenance Issues section, the processUnit status is also registered on DBMS.

Whenever it is possible, useful, and quite simple, we have adopted a "declarative approach" for implementing the defined functionality. We have a set of *declarative functions* that can be seen as a sort of language that describes the *data of the problem* and a *control function*, the engine, that applies certain rules on these data.

This modularization concisely fits the demand of parallelism (a logical operation in more threads, and correlated operation managed in parallel) and a fine-grained application design. But, generally speaking, for medium-large applications, organizing the code in small units may involve a great number of them (processUnit) and a dependency graph too complex to maintain and evolve.

To overcome these problems, we implemented the concept of "component." The components are logical structures embedding one or more processUnits with their dependences, but at a higher level of granularity. The concept of component addresses a top-down approach to the problem; first, one can individuate the logical

Copyright © 2007, Idea Group Inc. Copying or distributing in print or electronic forms without written permission of Idea Group Inc. is prohibited.

blocks (components) and the relation between them (dependences), then "drill down" designing and organizing the specific problem in detail using the thin, more flexible, and *near implementation* processUnits.

As an example, the whole structure of the application (processUnit, component, dependence) consists of a set of functions as shown in the following fragment of code:

```
...
SYNCComponentDefine("comp1", <compAttr>);
SYNCComponentDefine("comp2", <compAttr>);
... ...
SYNCCompDependenceDefine("comp2","comp1");
...
SYNCProcessUnitDefine("comp1","pU0",<pUAattr>);
SYNCProcessUnitDefine("comp1","pU1",<pUAattr>);
SYNCProcessUnitDefine("comp1","pU2",<pUAattr>);
SYNCDependenceDefine("pU0",NULL,NULL,NULL);
SYNCDependenceDefine("pU1","pU0",SUCCESS,NULL);
SYNCDependenceDefine("pU2","pU0",FAILURE,NULL);

SYNCProcessUnitDefine(«comp2»,»pUc2»,<pUAattr>);
SYNCDependenceDefine(«pUc2»,NULL,NULL,NULL);
... ...
SYNCControl();
```

The functions "*Define" describe the problem (storing the data in memory). The function "*Control" loops on these data applying predefined semantic rules; in this case it starts a processUnit when the event declared (termination of another processUnit with a certain state) occurs. This approach, here seen for synchronization module, is the same for acquire, transform and load hub, aggregation function, and so forth. This declarative approach has been preferred to others, in that it allows synthetic and clear application code and some standardization in developing several infrastructural modules.

Structuring the code in components and processUnits is a way to implement a sufficiently clear workflow. The "master" module provides the overall structure of the whole application giving evidence to the logical tasks involved and how these correlate to each other. The application is therefore logically structured in components, and single components are then organized/implemented in processUnits. This two-level modularization is also useful for operations and maintenance issues as described later.

Copyright © 2007, Idea Group Inc. Copying or distributing in print or electronic forms without written permission of Idea Group Inc. is prohibited.

Main-Memory Support

In any ETL application, a main-memory support is essential because of lookup operations. In a fact table, there are always some foreign keys, and these must be set in the loading phase with the corresponding value in the dimensional table. This operation is very simple and looks like "select key from tab where value = ..." but must be repeated many, many times: 10 foreign key and 10 millions rows to load implies 100 millions of "select." It is clear that these operations cannot be performed on DBMS. The solution is to bring the dimensional tables into memory, indexing them (with simple hash structure or binary search) and so perform the lookup operation without involving DBMS.

These main-memory functions are adequate for simple cases, but often a more sophisticated support should be useful. Sometimes a dimensional table must be updated in consequence of information contained in fact records; the same dimensional tables are big and it would be useful to manage them in memory; the application logic imposes some processing of temporary data in memory, and so on. To cover these cases in great measure the main-memory support must be read/write (with a minimal but effective concurrency control) and support not only "select" but also "insert," "delete," and "update." This does not mean that main-memory support for ETL purposes must be a commercial main-memory database. An SQL interface, ACID properties, full data type set, and so forth are rarely useful in our context and are expensive; an ad-hoc main-memory support often performs better than a well-structured main-memory DBMS.

In a data warehouse, the fact tables are big (often millions or billions of records) because they contain detail records; consider the single carton, canned foods, and so forth bought at the supermarket, which are useful for certain types of analysis (basket analysis in this case) but useless for others. It could be too expensive to access the fact table every time, so we need some form of *summary* or aggregation. These aggregations are the dataset resulting from a SQL "group by" performed on the fact table. The simplest way to do this is to run a SQL at the end of the loading phase, but this approach implies a serialization and a double scan of the data (the first read for loading, the second for aggregation). How can one avoid it? In the loading phase, when one processes a record and the corresponding aggregate row in memory does not exist, one can create a new one and copy the record data into it; otherwise, one has to update the existent aggregate row with its calculation (sum, count, etc.). This is exactly a "group by" operation, but performed on the fly.

The aggregation operation is conceptually simple, but very complex in practice; memory allocation and indexing, for example, are not at all prosaic when the volume grows and with compound aggregation keys. Building a complete set of functions to perform these operations with the necessary flexibility is hard and expensive compared with the facility of the SQL "group by" clause. This is generally true in

Copyright © 2007, Idea Group Inc. Copying or distributing in print or electronic forms without written permission of Idea Group Inc. is prohibited.

batch systems where the loading phase occurs in the night hours, and spending one or two hours to perform all the required aggregation is acceptable. However, in near real time contexts, we have small volume but strict timing constraints; further, it is also necessary to manage alarm tables that often require some aggregation. In this area, a set of functions to perform simple aggregation on the fly can be useful and not too hard to implement. Saving up some queries (after the loading) and avoidng useless read/write can give significant advantage in NRT where ETL processing has a time-slot of 5-10 minutes.

Acquire, Transform, and Load Hub

The core of every ETL system is the engine that brings together various data flows, makes the transformations, and loads them into DBMS. In our solution, all of this is done in a "hub" with the intent to minimize and parallelize I/O, saving elapsed time and resource usage as much as possible. However, before dealing with the issue in the whole (the hub), let us look at the several specific aspects: acquisition scenario and loading techniques.

Acquisition Scenario

We can acquire data from files, directly from DBMS, or listening to incoming messages, but this last eventuality is more typical in mediation systems than in ETL. In the scholastic ETL examples, there is always a source db, a target db, and in the middle, the ETL processes. In our experience, we never had the opportunity to acquire the data we needed directly from the source DBMS. It is politically hard obtaining access to a system owned by another division, group or department, and this is the typical organizational scenario in a DW project. It should not be very reasonable for a system manager to open a system to others and allow the installation of foreign agents for many understandable reasons. A better and more usual way is to define (the owner of data defines) an interface in order to decouple the source from the target system. The simplest method to do that is the use of flat files. Direct extraction from source DBMS often is not possible; it does not permit decoupling systems, DBMS may be different (e.g., DB2 and Oracle), the data almost always need transformations and must be stored in a staging table, but storing data in a table is more expensive than storing them in files. Another important issue is that data sometimes come from a DBMS, but sometimes do not, or come from a *closed* system where interface types, emission criterion, naming rules, and so on are predefined and typically not negotiated.

An ETL acquisition process, even if limited to file acquisition, must be able to manage a great variety of situations, for example, a big file one time a day (zipped,

Copyright © 2007, Idea Group Inc. Copying or distributing in print or electronic forms without written permission of Idea Group Inc. is prohibited.

Figure 5. Entity schema for data acquisition

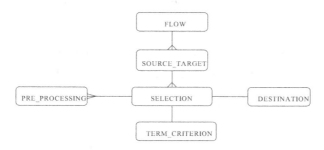

compressed, or none) or many little files every few minutes. Some types of files are positional, other CSV, or coded in XML; sometimes they are plan files or in master-detail fashion, in ASCII or binary format. Naming and location rules have a limit only in the human imagination.

It is very difficult to achieve a context formalization/generalization useful to closely define a model for data acquisition in ETL, but one can define a loose schematization as a base for application software. As one can see in Figure 5, the highest entity is the flow, a set of logically correlated data; an application may need more than one flow. Many source-to-target mappings may refer to a flow; in other words, a logical flow may comprise files coming from several distinct systems. In each source-to-target mapping there can reside several types of files, each of them identifiable with a selection criterion (usually Unix-like selection but also others specific for the application). These files may need or not need some preprocessing actions like uncompress, split in smaller chunks, merge, and other application specific action. Then, these files must be delivered to their destination (another stage of the process). For each selection at least one termination criterion must be defined; examples of these criteria may be "try selection once," "repeat selection until condition," or "other criterion."

As one can see, this model comprises, in every entity, an escape "other" in order to leave the possibility to insert ad-hoc code when necessary. In our infrastructure, we used this schematization to build a set of functions to manage file acquisition. In analogy with synchronization functions, even in this case, we have adopted the previously described declarative approach.

Loading Techniques

Every DBMS has its own proprietary techniques for massive loading; here we briefly treat Oracle, since it is one of the most widespread industrial DBMS. Oracle offers

Copyright © 2007, Idea Group Inc. Copying or distributing in print or electronic forms without written permission of Idea Group Inc. is prohibited.

two methods to programmatically interact with a server: Pro*C/Fortran/Cobol and so forth, which are a set of precompilers in order to embed SQL into the specific language and OCI which are an API callable from C/C++. Pro*C is quite easy to use but has several limitations (e.g., massive loading) while the OCI is more difficult (or better speaking, prolix) to use, but constitutes a flexible and complete interface.

Loading data in Oracle, also in massive parallel mode, can be simply done with the utility *SQLldr* which takes a file as input (or many files in parallel mode) and loads them into specified tables. Another more elegant way to do the same thing is to use the *external tables*; this method is substantially analogous to *SQLldr* with the difference managed in SQL. Using these simple techniques in ETL has the drawback to add the cost to write a file and to read and parse it by *SQLldr*. When data sum to dozens of gigabytes, it becomes convenient to use Direct path OCI[4] to load data directly into the database avoiding useless write and read to file.

As the whole OCI, these sets of functions for direct path are too complex/prolix to be utilized directly in the code. A common way to solve this problem is to use an OCI wrapper, in other words, to build a set of functions suited for its own purposes over the OCI layer (some wrappers are also available via the Internet).

Massive loading into a database may impose heavy constraints; indexes must be inactive, referential constraints cannot be used, particular criterion in extents allocation occurs, and so forth. Not all these limits can be escaped because the use of traditional SQL insert is not suited for massive loading (millions of rows and more). In ETL, one can use SQL only for managing dimension or loading fact in NRT with small volumes. Massive loading does not generally support commit/rollback statements, so one needs to build one's own error checks and perform rollback *by hand*. How to manage and recover errors, in loading, but even in other cases, will be discussed in the "Operation and Maintenance Issue" section.

Transform and Load Hub

Acquisition, especially transform and load, are operations that involve I/O and CPU-bound operations tightly correlated with each other and so they are well suited to be parallelized for performance. Only in very special cases, the data must be processed in sequential order; normally, records need to be transformed and loaded in relational tables in an independent way. This assumption makes a single row parallelization possible; each row can be acquired, transformed, and loaded independently, having many pipelines in parallel. This "row pipelined" model, very clean in theory, has a drawback in implementation; passing rows through many stages involves a lot of synchronization that can become relevant compared with the cost of single stage itself. A better solution is to extend the "row pipeline" model to a "block pipeline" one, where single blocks contain a certain number of rows. In this manner, we maintain parallelism/pipeline mechanism reducing the weight of synchronization,

Copyright © 2007, Idea Group Inc. Copying or distributing in print or electronic forms without written permission of Idea Group Inc. is prohibited.

memory passing, and routines invocation times. Working with blocks of data more-over paves the way for treating master-detail and other strange formats in which records are correlated. In summary, the block pipeline model contains the cost of synchronization, preserves a general parallel/pipeline mechanism, and leaves the possibility to manage some form of sequential order.

Transforming a record essentially means working with strings and performing lookup operations in memory (foreign keys valorization). One can use the well-known string functions available in Unix, but a more efficient way is to write ad-hoc simple macros that copy tokens from input to output buffer, save it in local variables, pad the output string with blanks, and so on, thus increasing the set every time one needs some new basic functionality. Working with blocks of data implies that the transformation code must be structured in nested loops (an outer "while <incoming_blocks>" and an inner "while <records_in_block>"), inside which the transformation macros can take place. The main implementation problem is, how-ever, how to pass a block of data from one stage to the next and how to exploit the waiting time correlated to I/O operations.

In Figure 6 we depict the basic scheme we adopted in our infrastructure.

We have two pools of buffers: one for input data and one for output data. A pool of thread readers fill the input buffers; a pool of processUnits pick the filled buffers, transform, and write them into the output buffers; and finally another pool of thread writers downloads the filled buffers into database or flat files.

Aside from implementation details concerning the multibuffer pool, there is the capability to link one input channel to many output channels, the possibility to

Figure 6. Schema of the transformation hub

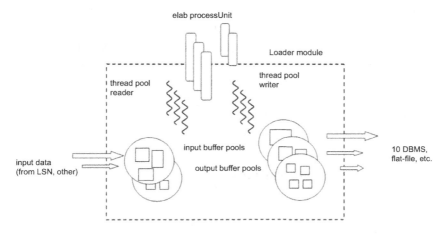

Copyright © 2007, Idea Group Inc. Copying or distributing in print or electronic forms without written permission of Idea Group Inc. is prohibited.

Figure 7. An example of pseudocode for the transformation hub

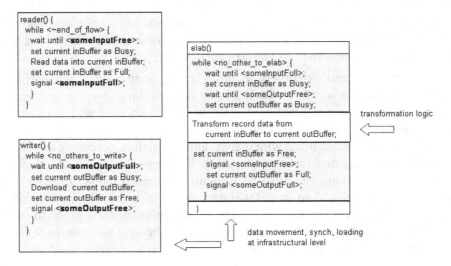

integrate in this scheme the listening functionalities, and so forth. The core of this solution is the use of condition variables to manage synchronization. As one can see in Figure 7, pseudocode, the synchronization scheme, is quite simple.

This mechanism gives one complete parallelism in reading/elab/writing (read-ahead and write-behind) using simple read() and write() functions.

This approach gives a clear definition of the data flow, where these come from, where their transformation code resides, and what their target is. All the transformation code is contained in a processUnit ("elab()" in the schema above) where the incoming data, at application level, are viewed record by record, but internally processed block by block for performance reasons.

We have spoken about a "hub" because this architecture with several buffer pools, several groups of specialized threads (for reading from file or another database, for writing in direct path or SQL or to file, etc.), several groups of transformation threads (in which application code resides) is well suited to be viewed as a hub, in which many flows converge and other data flows are delivered to different DBMS tables or other destinations.

Operation and Maintenance Issues

One of the most critical aspects in a DW project is "operation and maintenance" (O&M). Even the best ETL application can fail for many reasons, sometimes due

Copyright © 2007, Idea Group Inc. Copying or distributing in print or electronic forms without written permission of Idea Group Inc. is prohibited.

to a DBMS problem, an always possible application bug, or a hardware failure; but above all, a loading process can fail due to an external problem: absence or corruption of data, unavailability of some source systems, and so forth. In any case, a failure anywhere in the process causes a corruption, data inconsistency, or data loss. But we have to be straight; sometimes a loss of data is allowed, sometimes not. Sometimes one can skip a loading phase and retry it later, and sometimes data must be loaded without "holes." DW requirements, even in this perspective, are wide-ranging, so one system can meet its requirements almost ignoring the O&M issues, and for another stability and "fault-tolerance" are mandatory.

Even in a quiet scenario like a population in nightly window, when in the morning one sees that a failure has occurred, it is really hard to detect the bug, localize the corrupted or incomplete data, clean them, and restart the application at the old point-in-time. It is hard because one is under stress, the time in hand is constrained, and the users claim to access the DW. In an ETL application that does not consider the aspects of efficient managing, the interrupted DW loads cannot be defined as "robust." Some works in the literature discuss the problems related to resumption of interrupted DW loads (Labio, Wiener, Garcia-Molina, & Gorelik, 2000).

The simplest way to guarantee the data consistency in case of failure is to manage a *global rollback* involving all loaded and modified data, quite easy for loaded data (all the loaded partitions need to be truncated), a bit more difficult for the modified data (tables must be restored with the previously saved data). This approach is functional in case of serious and complex failures, but when a problem involves only the data portion of the ETL process (e.g., an updating of a dimensional table), it could be unacceptable to throw out all jobs just done, especially when the entire process requires hours.

A better way to manage partial failures is to organize the ETL process in functional components (even useful for documentation/modularization purposes) that can be individually recovered. Previously, we described processUnits (small blocks of code) and the synchronization engine that starts them according to predefined rules. This modularization is too fine-grained for recovery purposes (how can one recover from a failure of a single processUnit instance), so we built over them a logical container of processUnit called *component*. These components look like a processUnit, but on a higher level they have a termination status; their dependency rules are structured in simple trees and not in graphs. Each component can then have an associated *recoveryProcessUnit*, so called because it keeps the undo code (e.g., truncate partition).

The synchronization engine keeps track (on the DBMS) of the termination status of a single processUnit, so the engine can evaluate the status of each component and of the entire ETL process itself. At the end, we have a status table that says if some failure has occurred (the process needs recovery) and which component has failed. With this information, we can recover only the failed components and, which is

Copyright © 2007, Idea Group Inc. Copying or distributing in print or electronic forms without written permission of Idea Group Inc. is prohibited.

important, in an automatic way. Simplifying, the synchronization engine, running in recovery mode, has to do a *reversal* of the component status and then start only the failed components (or to be more precise, the processUnits of the failed components). In practice, there are some further complications; a component in recovery mode can depend on a previous one that has not failed but must be rerun because it does an initialization job (and so we have introduced the onRecovery dependence); then the process running in recovery mode must always use a point-in-time date and so on with other little complications.

The technique briefly depicted above fits in the batch scenario; a population occurs at night, in the morning O&M operators see the errors, remove the cause, and rerun the application in recovery mode. All the undo operations are coded in the recoveryProcessUnit, and, if the causes of failure were transient or have been removed, the system can recover the failed portion of the ETL job without human intervention on DBMS.

In the NRT context, where a population cycle occurs every hour or less, the recovery process needs to be managed in an automatic way as much as possible. An H24 operator can hardly check the result of every cycle; the solution is to use a standby recovery application. Therefore, there are two running applications: a *primary* application instance that does its job at scheduled intervals and a *recovery* application instance that checks the status of the primary and, if required, performs the recovery, otherwise sleeps until next check. The recovery mechanism and the status table are the same as we have seen before. Obviously, due to the absence of human intervention, this mechanism can recover only transient errors (e.g., a lack in the network).

Future Trends and Conclusion

As the computational power of today's equipments grows, the performance constraints become less strong. That is clear evidence in the whole computer science also valid for ETL. In the near future, it may be possible to see ETL tools/system written in Java with sophisticated metadata support that works well in an application context where today we have *cryptic* C programs. But, if it is true that machines run faster and faster, even the volumes of data grow, so that there will always be the "border line" applications where the performance constraints are again strong.

With regard to the possible spread of some kind of intersystems communication standards/guidelines, we are a little more skeptical; these forms of standardization do not have a strong economic boost, involve delicate internal organization balance, and are really a too complex job. In our opinion, the ETL complexity is also directly correlated to high volumes, timing constraints, reliability requirements,

Copyright © 2007, Idea Group Inc. Copying or distributing in print or electronic forms without written permission of Idea Group Inc. is prohibited.

and so forth that need very sophisticated techniques. One of the main criticalities in facing an ETL project consists in evaluating the impact of different choices in order to weigh their costs in different perspectives (performance, etc.), and making decisions respecting the balance of the system in its wholeness.

In this chapter, we have proposed an infrastructural approach to ETL as an optimal solution for a specific class of problems in large DW; we have given some practical suggestions in order to address typical implementation issues, leaving other aspects and points of view in the background.

References

Adzic, J., & Fiore, V. (2003, September). Data warehouse population platform. In *Proceedings of the International Workshop on Design and Management of Data Warehouses (DMDW03).* Berlin, German. Retrieved May 27, 2006, from http://ftp.informatik.rwth-aachen.de/Publications/CEUR-WS/Vol-77/08_Adzic.pdf

Gartner. (2005, May). *ETL Magic Quadrant update.* Retrieved May 25, 2006, from http://www.gartner.com/displaydocument?doc_cd=127170

Golfarelli, M., & Rizzi, S. (1998, November). *Methodological framework for data warehouse design.* Paper presented at the ACM First International Workshop on Data Warehousing and OLAP (DOLAP '98), Bethesda, Maryland.

Husemann, B., Lechtenborger, J., & Vossen, G. (2000). Conceptual data warehouse modeling. In *Proceedings of the 2nd International Workshop on Design and Management of Data Warehouses (DMDW00),* Stockholm, Sweden.

IBM. (2005). *IBM Data Warehouse Manager overview.* Retrieved May 27, 2006, from http://www-306.ibm.com/software/data/db2/datawarehouse/

Informatica. (2005). *PowerCenter 6.* Retrieved May 27, 2006, from http://www.informatica.com/products/powercenter/default.htm

Kimball, R., & Caserta, J. (2004). *The data warehouse ETL toolkit: Practical techniques for extracting, cleaning, conforming, and delivering data warehouse.* New York: John Wiley & Sons.

Kimball, R., Reeves, L., Ross, M., & Thornthwaite, W. (1998). *The data warehouse lifecycle toolkit: Expert methods for designing, developing, and deploying data warehouses.* New York: John Wiley & Sons.

Labio, W., Wiener, J. L., Garcia-Molina, H., & Gorelik, V. (2000). Efficient resumption of interrupted warehouse loads. In *Proceedings of the SIGMOD '00,* Texas (pp. 46-57).

Copyright © 2007, Idea Group Inc. Copying or distributing in print or electronic forms without written permission of Idea Group Inc. is prohibited.

Microsoft Corp. (2005). *SQL Server 2005: Data management and analysis solution.* Retrieved May 27, 2006, from http://www.microsoft.com/sql/default.mspx

Oracle Corp. (2005). *Oracle Warehouse Builder 10G.* Retrieved May 27, 2006, from http://www.oracle.com/technology/products/warehouse/index.html

Tryfona, N., Busborg, F., & Christiansen, J. G. B. (1999, November 6). starER: A conceptual model for data warehouse design. In *Proceedings of the ACM Second International Workshop on Data Warehousing and OLAP (DOLAP'99),* Missouri (pp. 3-8).

Vassiliadis, P., Simitsis, A., Georgantas, P., & Terrovitis, M. (2003, June). *A framework for the design of ETL scenarios.* Paper presented at the 15th Conference on Advanced Information Systems Engineering (CAiSE '03), Klagenfurt, Austria.

Vassiliadis, P., Simitsis, A., & Skiadopoulos, S. (2002). Modeling ETL activities as graphs. In *Proceedings of the Design and Management of Data Warehouses (DMDW'2002) 4th International Workshop in conjunction with CAiSE'02,* Toronto, Canada (pp. 52-61).

Vassiliadis, P., Simitsis, A., & Skiadopoulos, S. (2002, November). Conceptual modeling for ETL processes. In *Proceedings of the Data Warehousing and OLAP (DOLAP2002) ACM 5th International Workshop in conjunction with CIKM'02,* McLean, VA.

Endnotes

[1]   If the relationship between partitions and table space is 1:1, then one must dimension all the table spaces to be large enough to contain the biggest partition; in the proposed configuration many partitions share the same table space and so it must be dimensioned to contain "n" average weight partitions.

[2]   Oracle Call Interface: a set of low level functions (API) to access DBMS functionality.

[3]   OS API Posix: Posix is a family of open standards based on Unix; following Posix model guarantees portability especially in the case of thread API (SUN, for example, besides Posix, has a proprietary threading model).

[4]   Direct path OCI are an API allowing massive loading in Oracle in the same way as SQLldr.

Copyright © 2007, Idea Group Inc. Copying or distributing in print or electronic forms without written permission of Idea Group Inc. is prohibited.

Chapter V

Data Warehouse Refreshment

Alkis Simitisis
National Technical University of Athens, Greece

Panos Vassiliadis
University of Ioannina, Greece

Spiros Skiadopoulos
University of Peloponnese, Greece

Timos Sellis
National Technical University of Athens, Greece

Abstract

In the early stages of a data warehouse project, the designers/administrators have to come up with a decision concerning the design and deployment of the backstage architecture. The possible options are (a) the usage of a commercial ETL tool or (b) the development of an in-house ETL prototype. Both cases have advantages and disadvantages. However, in both cases the design and modeling of the ETL workflows have the same characteristics. The scope of this chapter is to indicate the main challenges, issues, and problems concerning the manufacturing of ETL workflows, in order to assist the designers/administrators to decide which solution suits their data warehouse project better and to help them construct an efficient, robust, and evolvable ETL workflow that implements the refreshment of their warehouse.

Copyright © 2007, Idea Group Inc. Copying or distributing in print or electronic forms without written permission of Idea Group Inc. is prohibited.

Introduction

In the past, research has treated data warehouses as collections of materialized views. Although this abstraction is elegant and possibly sufficient for the purpose of examining alternative strategies for view maintenance, it is sufficient enough to describe the structure and contents of a data warehouse in real-world settings. Vassiliadis, Quix, Vassiliou, and Jarke (2001) bring up the issue of *data warehouse operational processes* and deduce the definition of a table in the data warehouse as the outcome of the combination of the processes that populate it. This new kind of definition complements existing approaches, since it provides the operational semantics for the content of a data warehouse table, whereas the existing definitions give an abstraction of its intentional semantics. Indeed, in a typical mediation scheme one would pose a query to a "virtual" data warehouse, dispatch it to the sources, answer parts of it there, and then collect the answers. On the contrary, in the case of data warehouse operational processes, the objective is to carry data from a set of source relations and eventually load them in a target (data warehouse) relation. To achieve this goal, we have to (a) specify data transformations as a workflow and (b) optimize and execute the workflow.

Data warehouse operational processes normally compose a labor intensive workflow and constitute an integral part of the backstage of data warehouse architectures. To deal with this workflow and in order to facilitate and manage the data warehouse operational processes, specialized workflows are used under the general title extraction transformation loading (ETL) workflows. ETL workflows are responsible for the extraction of data from several sources, their cleansing, their customization and transformation, and finally, their loading into a data warehouse.

ETL workflows represent an important part of data warehousing, as they represent the means by which data actually get loaded into the warehouse. To give a general idea of the functionality of these workflows we mention their most prominent tasks, which include:

- The *identification* of relevant information at the source side
- The *extraction* of this information
- The *transportation* of this information to the DSA
- The *transformation* (i.e., customization and integration) of the information coming from multiple sources into a common format
- The *cleaning* of the resulting dataset, on the basis of database and business rules
- The *propagation* and loading of the data to the data warehouse and the refreshment of data marts

Copyright © 2007, Idea Group Inc. Copying or distributing in print or electronic forms without written permission of Idea Group Inc. is prohibited.

Figure 1. The environment of extraction-transformation-loading processes (Simitsis, 2004)

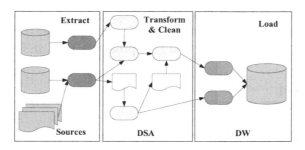

In the sequel, we will adopt the general acronym ETL for all kinds of in-house or commercial tools, and all the aforementioned categories of tasks/processes.

In Figure 1, we abstractly describe the general framework for ETL processes. On the left side, we can observe the original data stores (sources) that are involved in the overall process. Typically, data sources are relational databases and files. The data from these sources are extracted by specialized routines or tools, which provide either complete snapshots or differentials of the data sources. Then, these data are propagated to the data staging area (DSA) where they are transformed and cleaned before being loaded into the data warehouse. Intermediate results, again in the form of (mostly) files or relational tables are part of the data staging area. The data warehouse (DW) is depicted in the right part of Figure 1 and comprises the target data stores, that is, fact tables for the storage of information and dimension tables with the description and the multidimensional rollup hierarchies of the stored facts. The loading of the central warehouse is performed from the loading activities depicted in the right side before the data warehouse data store.

Despite the plethora of commercial solutions that offer ad-hoc capabilities for the creation of an ETL scenario, a designer/administrator needs a concrete method to develop an efficient, robust, and evolvable ETL workflow. Therefore, this chapter intends to point out the main challenges and issues concerning the generic construction of ETL workflows. As an outline, in the rest of the chapter, we proceed with a brief presentation about the state of the art in ETL technology. Afterwards, we discuss why the modeling of ETL workflows is important and we indicate the main problems that arise during all the phases of an ETL process. Moreover, we present a modeling approach for the construction of ETL workflows, which is based on the life cycle of the data warehouse, along with an exemplary research framework named Arktos II. Finally, we list several open research challenges that proclaim ETL as a commodity of future research.

Copyright © 2007, Idea Group Inc. Copying or distributing in print or electronic forms without written permission of Idea Group Inc. is prohibited.

Background

In this section, we present ETL methodologies that are proposed by (a) commercial studies and tools and (b) the research community. Then, we present the reasons and the motives that signify the research on ETL processes is a valid research goal.

State of the Art

*   **Commercial studies and tools:** In terms of technological aspects, the main characteristic of the area is the involvement of traditional database vendors with ETL solutions built in the DBMS. The three major database vendors that practically ship ETL solutions "at no extra charge" are pinpointed: Oracle with Oracle Warehouse Builder (Oracle, 2001), Microsoft with Data Transformation Services (Microsoft, 2003), and IBM with the Data Warehouse Center (IBM, 2003). Still, the major vendors in the area are Informatica's Powercenter (Informatica, 2003) and Ascential's DataStage suites (Ascential, 2003) (the latter part of the IBM recommendations for ETL solutions). As a general comment, we emphasize the fact that the former three have the benefit of the minimum cost, because they are shipped with the database, while the latter two have the benefit to aim at complex and deep solutions not envisioned by the generic products. The aforementioned discussion is supported from a second recent study (Gartner, 2003), where the authors note the decline in license revenue for pure ETL tools, mainly due to the crisis of IT spending and the appearance of ETL solutions from traditional database and business intelligence vendors. The Gartner study discusses the role of the three major database vendors (IBM, Microsoft, Oracle) and points out that they slowly start to take a portion of the ETL market through their DBMS-built-in solutions.

*   **Research focused specifically on ETL:** The *AJAX* system (Galhardas, Florescu, Shasha & Simon, 2000) is a data cleaning tool developed at INRIA France. It deals with typical data quality problems, such as *the object identity problem* (Cohen, 1999)*, errors due to mistyping,* and *data inconsistencies* between matching records. AJAX provides a framework wherein the logic of a data cleaning program is modeled as a directed graph of data transformations that start from some input source data. AJAX also provides a declarative language for specifying data cleaning programs, which consists of SQL statements enriched with a set of specific primitives to express mapping, matching, clustering, and merging transformations. Finally, a interactive environment is supplied to the user in order to resolve errors and inconsistencies that cannot be automatically handled and support a stepwise refinement design of data cleaning programs. The theoretic foundations of this tool can be found in Galhardas, Florescu, Shasha, and Simon (1999), where apart from the presentation

Copyright © 2007, Idea Group Inc. Copying or distributing in print or electronic forms without written permission of Idea Group Inc. is prohibited.

of a general framework for the data cleaning process, specific optimization techniques tailored for data cleaning applications are discussed.

The *Potter's Wheel* system (Raman & Hellerstein, 2001), is targeted to provide interactive data cleaning to its users. The system offers the possibility of performing several algebraic operations over an underlying dataset. Optimization algorithms are also provided for the CPU usage for certain classes of operators. The general idea behind Potter's Wheel is that users build data transformations in iterative and interactive ways. In the background, Potter's Wheel automatically infers structures for data values in terms of user-defined domains, and accordingly checks for constraint violations. Users gradually build transformations to clean the data by adding or undoing transforms on a spreadsheet-like interface; the effect of a transform is shown at once on records visible on screen. These transforms are specified either through simple graphical operations, or by showing the desired effects on example data values.

- **Data quality and cleaning:** Jarke, List, and Koller (2000) present an extensive review of data quality problems and related literature, along with quality management methodologies. Rundensteiner (1999) offers a discussion on various aspects on data transformations. Sarawagi (2000) presents a similar collection of papers in the field of data cleaning including a survey (Rahm & Hai Do, 2000) that provides an extensive overview of the field, along with research issues and a review of some commercial tools and solutions on specific problems (Borkar, Deshmuk, & Sarawagi, 2000; Monge, 2000). In a related but different context, we would like to mention the IBIS tool (Calì, Calvanese, De Giacomo, Lenzerini, Naggar, & Vernacotola, 2003). IBIS is an integration tool following the global-as-view approach to answer queries in a mediated system. Departing from the traditional data integration literature though, IBIS brings the issue of data quality into the integration process. The system takes advantage of the definition of constraints at the intentional level (e.g., foreign key constraints) and tries to provide answers that resolve semantic conflicts (e.g., the violation of a foreign key constraint).

- **Workflow and process models:** In general, research on workflows is focused around the following reoccurring themes: (a) modeling (Eder & Gruber, 2002; Kiepuszewski, ter Hofstede, & Bussler, 2000; Sadiq & Orlowska, 2000; Van der Aalst, ter Hofstede, Kiepuszewski, & Barros, 2000; Workflow Management Coalition, 1998), where the authors are primarily concerned in providing a metamodel for workflows; (b) correctness issues (Eder & Gruber, 2002; Kiepuszewski et al., 2000; Sadiq & Orlowska, 2000), where criteria are established to determine whether a workflow is well formed, and (c) workflow transformations (Eder & Gruber, 2002; Kiepuszewski et al., 2000; Sadiq & Orlowska, 2000) where the authors are concerned with correctness issues in the evolution of the workflow from a certain plan to another.

Copyright © 2007, Idea Group Inc. Copying or distributing in print or electronic forms without written permission of Idea Group Inc. is prohibited.

- **Applications of ETL workflows in data warehouses:** Finally, the literature reports several efforts (both research and industrial) for the management of processes and workflows that operate on data warehouse systems. Jarke, Quix, Blees, Lehmann, Michalk, and Stierl (1999) describe an industrial effort where the cleaning mechanisms of the data warehouse are employed in order to avoid the population of the sources with problematic data in the first place. The described solution is based on a workflow which employs techniques from the field of view maintenance. Schafer, Becker, and Jarke (2000) describe an industrial effort at Deutche Bank, involving the import/export, transformation and cleaning, and storage of data in a terabyte-size data warehouse. The authors explain also the usage of metadata management techniques, which involves a broad spectrum of applications, from the import of data to the management of dimensional data and more importantly for the querying of the data warehouse. Jarke et al. (2000) present a research effort (and its application in an industrial application) for the integration and central management of the processes that lie around an information system. A metadata management repository is employed to store the different activities of a large workflow, along with important data these processes employ.

Motivation

All engineering disciplines employ blueprints during the design of their engineering artifacts. Modeling in this fashion is not a task with a value, per se; as Booch, Rumbaugh, and Jacobson (1998) mention "we build models to communicate the desired structure and behavior of our system ... to visualize and control the system's architecture ... to better understand the system we are building ... to manage risk."

Discussing the modeling of ETL workflows is important for several reasons. First, the data extraction, transformation, integration, and loading process is a key part of a data warehouse. The commercial ETL tools that are available on the market the last few years increased their sales from US$101 million dollars in 1998 to US$210 million dollars in 2002, having a steady increase rate of approximately 20.1% each year (Jarke, Lenzerini, Vassiliou, & Vassiliadis, 2003). The same survey indicates that ETL tools are in the third place of the annual sales of the overall components of a data warehouse with the RDBMS sales for data warehouses in the first place (40% each year since 1998) and data marts (25%) in the second place.

Also, ETL processes constitute the major part of a data warehouse environment, resulting in the corresponding development effort and cost. Data warehouse operational processes are *costly* and *critical* for the success of a data warehouse project, and their design and implementation has been characterized as a labor-intensive and lengthy procedure (Demarest, 1999; Shilakes & Tylman, 1998; Vassiliadis, 2000). Several reports mention that most of these processes are constructed through

Copyright © 2007, Idea Group Inc. Copying or distributing in print or electronic forms without written permission of Idea Group Inc. is prohibited.

an in-house development procedure that can consume up to 70% of the resources for a data warehouse project (Giga, 2002; Strange, 2002). Complementary reports (Friedman, 2002; Strange, 2002a) address the factors that influence the cost of its implementation and support: (a) *staff* (development, application support teams, on-going support and maintenance, and operations); (b) *computing resources* (dedicated ETL server, disk storage for "temporary" or staging files, CPU use of servers hosting source data, and annual maintenance and support); (c) *tools acquisition* (annual maintenance support and training); (d) *latency* (timeliness of the delivery of data to the target environment impacts the overall effectiveness of BI); and (e) *quality* (flaws in data distilled from ETL processes can severely limit BI adoption). Each of these components directly influences the total cost of ownership of a data warehouse implementation and operation.

For example, Strange (2002) mentions the development of a data warehouse realized in the Fortune 500 financial institution. This development included the support of the data warehouse for applications to perform customer retention analysis, bank loan risk management, customer contact history, and many other applications. There were 100 people on the data warehouse team (approximately 8.5% of the overall IT staff)—55 from ETL, four database administrators, four architects, four systems administrators, nine BI competency center workers (assisting end users), five report writers, nine managers, and nine hardware, operating system, and operations support staff members. These 55 individuals were responsible for building and maintaining the ETL process, which includes 46 different source systems. Responsibilities include updates of data marts on a weekly and monthly basis. This does not include staff from operations to support the execution of the ETL processes. They used a large parallel server platform that is consisted of multiple silver nodes (four processors per node) and four terabytes or more of disk storage, at an acquisition cost over three years of US$5 million. The cost of the ETL tool used was US$1 million, excluding the yearly maintenance and support costs.

Moreover, these processes are *important* for the correctness, completeness, and freshness of data warehouse contents, since not only do they facilitate the population of the warehouse with up-to-date data, but they are also responsible for homogenizing their structure and blocking the propagation of erroneous or inconsistent entries.

In addition, these data intensive workflows are quite *complex* in nature, involving dozens of sources, cleaning and transformation activities, and loading facilities. Bouzeghoub, Fabret, and Matulovic (1999) mention that the data warehouse refreshment process can consist of many different subprocesses, like data cleaning, archiving, transformations, and aggregations, interconnected through a complex schedule. For instance, Adzic and Fiore (2003) report a case study for mobile network traffic data, involving around 30 data flows and 10 sources, while the volume of data rises to about 2 TB, with the main fact table containing about 3 billion records. The throughput of the (traditional) population system is 80 million records per hour for the entire process (compression, FTP of files, decompression, transformation, and

Copyright © 2007, Idea Group Inc. Copying or distributing in print or electronic forms without written permission of Idea Group Inc. is prohibited.

loading), on a daily basis, with a loading window of only 4 hours. The request for performance is so pressing that there are processes hard-coded in low level DBMS calls to avoid the extra step of storing data to a target file to be loaded to the data warehouse through the DBMS loader. In general, Strange (2002a) notes that the complexity of the ETL process, as well as the staffing required to implement it, depends mainly on the following variables: (a) the number and variety of data sources; (b) the complexity of transformation; (c) the complexity of integration; and (d) the availability of skill sets. Also, the same report suggests considering "one person per source" as a guide to accomplishing the ETL implementation effectively.

Based on the previous discussion, we can identify key factors underlying the main problems of ETL workflows:

- Vastness of the data volumes
- Quality problems, since data are not always clean and have to be cleansed
- Performance, since the whole process has to take place within a specific time window and it is necessary to optimize its execution time
- Evolution of the sources and the data warehouse can eventually lead to daily maintenance operations

Visualizing and understanding this kind of system is another issue. In fact, traditional modeling approaches need to be reconsidered: we need interactive, multiview modeling frameworks that abstract the complexity of the system and provide complementary views of the system's structure to the designer (apart from simply providing the big picture, like the traditional ER/DFD approaches did). Moreover, we need to be able to manage risk through our modeling artifacts. For example, we would like to answer questions like:

- Which attributes/tables are involved in the population of a certain attribute?
- What part of the scenario is affected if we delete an attribute?
- How good is the design of my ETL workflow?
- Is variant A better than variant B?

Main Thrust of the Chapter

In this section, we identify the main problems that arise during all the phases of an ETL process. Then, we propose a modeling approach for the construction of ETL workflows, which is based on the life cycle of the ETL processes.

Copyright © 2007, Idea Group Inc. Copying or distributing in print or electronic forms without written permission of Idea Group Inc. is prohibited.

Problems and Issues of DW Refreshment

In all the phases of an ETL process (extraction and transportation, transformation and cleaning, and loading), individual issues arise, making data warehouse refreshment a very troublesome task. In the sequel, in order to clarify the complexity and the special characteristics of the ETL processes, we briefly review several issues, problems, and constraints that turn up in each phase separately.

*   **Global problems and constraints:** Scalzo (2003) mentions that 90% of the problems in data warehouses arise during the loading of the data at the nightly batch cycles. At this period, the administrators have to deal with problems such as (a) efficient data loading and (b) concurrent job mixture and dependencies. Moreover, ETL processes have global time constraints including the initiation time and their completion deadlines. In fact, in most cases, there is a tight "time window" in the night that can be exploited for the refreshment of the data warehouse, since the source system is off-line or not heavily used during this period.

    Consequently, a major problem arises with the scheduling of the overall process. The administrator has to find the right execution order for dependent jobs and job sets on the existing hardware for the permitted time schedule. On the other hand, if the OLTP applications cannot produce the necessary source data in time for processing before the data warehouse comes online, the information in the data warehouse will be out of date. Still, since data warehouses are used for strategic purposes, this problem can sometimes be afforded, due to the fact that long-term reporting/planning is not severely affected by this type of failures.

*   **Extraction and transportation:** During the ETL process, one of the very first tasks that must be performed is the extraction of the relevant information that has to be further propagated to the warehouse (Theodoratos, Ligoudistianos, & Sellis, 2001). In order to minimize the overall processing time, this involves only a fraction of the source data that has changed since the previous execution of the ETL process, mainly concerning the newly inserted and possibly updated records. Usually, change detection is physically performed by the comparison of two snapshots (one corresponding to the previous extraction and the other to the current one). Efficient algorithms exist for this task, like the snapshot differential algorithms presented by Labio and Garcia-Molina (1996). Another technique is log "sniffing," that is, the scanning of the log file in order to "reconstruct" the changes performed since the last scan. In rare cases, change detection can be facilitated by the use of triggers. However, this solution is technically impossible for many of the sources that are legacy systems (such a technique adds an enormous load to the source systems) or plain flat files.

Copyright © 2007, Idea Group Inc. Copying or distributing in print or electronic forms without written permission of Idea Group Inc. is prohibited.

In numerous other cases, where relational systems are used at the source side, the usage of triggers is also prohibitive both due to the performance degradation that their usage incurs and the need to intervene in the structure of the database. Moreover, another crucial issue concerns the transportation of data after the extraction, where tasks like FTP, encryption-decryption, compression-decompression, and so forth, can possibly take place.

- **Transformation and cleaning:** It is possible to determine typical tasks that take place during the transformation and cleaning phase of an ETL process. Rahm and Hai Do (2000) further detail this phase in the following tasks: (a) data analysis; (b) definition of transformation workflow and mapping rules; (c) verification; (d) transformation; and (e) backflow of cleaned data. In terms of the transformation tasks, we distinguish two main classes of problems (Lenzerini, 2002): (a) conflicts and problems at the *schema level* (e.g., naming and structural conflicts) and (b) *data level* transformations (i.e., at the instance level). The main problems with respect to the schema level are (a) *naming conflicts*, where the same name is used for different objects (homonyms) or different names are used for the same object (synonyms) and (b) *structural conflicts*, where one must deal with different representations of the same object in different sources. In addition, there are a lot of variations of data-level conflicts across sources: duplicated or contradicting records, different value representations (e.g., for marital status), different interpretation of the values (e.g., measurement units dollar vs. euro), different aggregation levels (e.g., sales per product vs. sales per product group), or reference to different points in time (e.g., current sales as of yesterday for a certain source vs. as of last week for another source). The list is enriched by low-level technical problems like data type conversions, applying format masks, assigning fields to a sequence number, substituting constants, setting values to NULL or DEFAULT based on a condition, or using simple SQL operators, for instance, UPPER, TRUNC, SUBSTR. The integration and transformation programs perform a wide variety of functions, such as reformatting, recalculating, modifying key structures, adding an element of time, identifying default values, supplying logic to choose between multiple sources, summarizing, merging data from multiple sources, and so forth.

- **Loading:** The final loading of the data warehouse has its own technical challenges. A major problem is the ability to discriminate between new and existing data at loading time. This problem arises when a set of records has to be classified to (a) the new rows that need to be appended to the warehouse and (b) rows that already exist in the data warehouse, but their value has changed and must be updated (e.g., with an UPDATE command). Modern ETL tools already provide mechanisms towards this problem, mostly through language predicates, for example, Oracle's MERGE command (Oracle, 2002). Also,

Copyright © 2007, Idea Group Inc. Copying or distributing in print or electronic forms without written permission of Idea Group Inc. is prohibited.

simple SQL commands are not sufficient since the open-loop-fetch technique, where records are inserted one by one, is extremely slow for the vast volume of data to be loaded in the warehouse. An extra problem is the simultaneous usage of the rollback segments and log files during the loading process. The option to turn them off contains some risk in the case of a loading failure. So far, the best technique seems to be the usage of the batch loading tools offered by most RDBMS that avoids these problems. Other techniques that facilitate the loading task involve the creation of tables at the same time with the creation of the respective indexes, the minimization of interprocess wait states, and the maximization of concurrent CPU usage.

Research Problems and Challenges

The previous discussion demonstrates the problem of designing an efficient, robust, and evolvable ETL workflow is relevant and pressing. To be more specific and understand the requirements of the design and evolution of a data warehouse, we have to clarify how ETL workflows fit in the data warehouse life cycle.

As we can see in Figure 2, the life cycle of a data warehouse begins with an initial reverse engineering and requirements collection phase where the data sources are analyzed in order to comprehend their structure and contents. At the same time, any requirements on the part of the users (normally a few power users) are also collected. The deliverable of this stage is a conceptual model for the data stores and the processes involved. In a second stage, namely the logical design of the warehouse, the logical schema for the warehouse and the processes are constructed. Third, the logical design of the schema and processes are optimized and refined to the choice

Figure 2. The life cycle of a data warehouse and its ETL processes (Vassiliadis, Simitsis, & Skiadopoulos, 2002a)

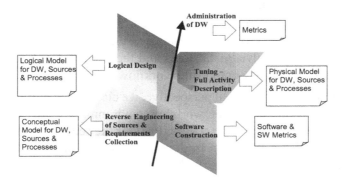

Copyright © 2007, Idea Group Inc. Copying or distributing in print or electronic forms without written permission of Idea Group Inc. is prohibited.

of specific physical structures in the warehouse (e.g., indexes) and environment-specific execution parameters for the operational processes. We call this stage *tuning* and its deliverable is the physical model of the environment. In a fourth stage, software construction, the software is constructed, tested, evaluated, and a first version of the warehouse is deployed. This process is guided through specific software metrics. Then, the cycle starts again, since data sources, user requirements, and the data warehouse state are under continuous evolution. An extra feature that comes into the scene after the deployment of the warehouse is the administration task, which also needs specific metrics for the maintenance and monitoring of the data warehouse. Consequently, in order to achieve our goal we have to deal with the phases of the life cycle of a data warehouse.

- **Conceptual model:** A conceptual model for ETL processes deals with the earliest stages of the data warehouse design. During this period, the data warehouse designer is concerned with two tasks which are practically executed in parallel: (a) the collection of requirements from the part of the users, and (b) the analysis of the structure and content of the existing data sources and their intentional mapping to the common data warehouse model. The design of an ETL process aims at the production of a crucial deliverable: the mapping of the attributes of the data sources to the attributes of the data warehouse tables through the appropriate intermediate transformations. The production of this deliverable involves several interviews that result in the revision and redefinition of original assumptions and mappings; thus it is imperative that a simple conceptual model should be employed in order to facilitate the smooth redefinition and revision efforts and to serve as the means of communication with the rest of the involved parties.

  From our point of view, a conceptual model for ETL processes shall not be another process/workflow model for the population of the data warehouse. There are two basic reasons for this approach. First, in the conceptual model for ETL processes, the focus is on documenting/formalizing the particularities of the data sources with respect to the data warehouse and not in providing a technical solution for the implementation of the process. Second, the ETL conceptual model is constructed in the early stages of the data warehouse project during which the time constraints of the project require a quick documentation of the involved data stores and their relationships, rather than an in-depth description of a composite workflow.

- **Logical model:** In the logical perspective, we classify the design artifacts that describe an abstraction of the workflow environment. First, the designer is responsible for defining an Execution Plan for the scenario. The definition of an execution plan can be seen from various views. The Execution Sequence involves the specification of (a) which process runs first, second, and so on;

Copyright © 2007, Idea Group Inc. Copying or distributing in print or electronic forms without written permission of Idea Group Inc. is prohibited.

(b) which processes run in parallel; or (c) when a semaphore is defined so that several processes are synchronized at a rendezvous point. ETL processes normally run in batches, so the designer needs to specify an Execution Schedule, that is, the time points or events that trigger the execution of the workflow as a whole. Finally, due to system crashes, it is imperative that a recovery plan exists, specifying the sequence of steps to be taken in the case of failure for a certain process (e.g., retry to execute the process, or undo any intermediate results produced so far). In the ETL case, due to the data centric nature of the process, the designer must deal with the relationship of the involved processes with the underlying data. This involves the definition of a primary data flow that describes the route of data from the sources towards their final destination in the data warehouse, as they pass through the processes of the workflow. Also, due to possible quality problems of the processed data, the designer is obliged to define a data flow for logical exceptions, which is responsible for the flow of the problematic data, that is, the rows that violate integrity or business rules. Moreover, a very crucial topic is the semantics of the ETL workflow. These semantics are generated by the combination of the data flow and the execution sequence: the data flow defines what each process does and the execution plan defines in which order and combination.

- **Mapping conceptual to logical models:** Another issue that has to be solved is the transition between the aforementioned phases (i.e., conceptual and logical) of the data warehouse life cycle. On one hand, there exists a simple model, sufficient for the early stages of the data warehouse design. On the other hand, there exists a logical model that offers formal and semantically founded concepts to capture the particularities of an ETL process.

The goal of this transition should be to facilitate the integration of the results accumulated in the early phases of a data warehouse project into the logical model, such as the collection of requirements from the part of the users, the analysis of the structure and content of the existing data sources, along with their intentional mapping to the common data warehouse model. The deliverable of this transition is not expected to be always a complete and accurate logical design. The designer/administrator in the logical level should examine, complement, or change the outcome of this methodology, in order to achieve the goals.

In the context of finding an automatic transition from one model to the other, there are several problems that should be addressed. Since the conceptual model is constructed in a more generic and high-level manner, each conceptual entity has a mapping to a logical entity. Thus, there is a need for the determination of these mappings. Moreover, we have stressed that the conceptual model is not a workflow as it simply identifies the transformations needed in an ETL process. Therefore, it does not directly specify the execution order of these

Copyright © 2007, Idea Group Inc. Copying or distributing in print or electronic forms without written permission of Idea Group Inc. is prohibited.

transformations. On the other hand, the execution order is a very important property of the logical model. So, there is a necessity for finding a way to specify the execution order of the transformations in an ETL process during the transition between the two models.

- **Optimization of ETL workflows:** In order to design an efficient, robust, and evolvable ETL workflow, we have to optimize its execution plan. In other words, we have to optimize the sequence of the ETL operations involved in the overall process.

Up to now, the research community has confronted the problem of the optimization of data warehouse refreshment as a problem of finding the optimal strategy for view maintenance. But this is not sufficient with respect to mechanisms that are employed in real-world settings. In fact, in real-world data warehouse environments, this procedure differs to the point that the execution of operational processes (which is employed in order to export data from operational data sources, transform them into the format of the target tables, and finally, load them to the data warehouse) does not like as a "big" query; rather it is more realistic to be considered a complex transaction. Thus, there is a necessity to deal with this problem for a different perspective by taking into consideration the characteristics of an ETL process presented in the previous subsection. One could argue that we can possibly express all ETL operations in terms of relational algebra and then optimize the resulting expression as usual. But, the traditional logic-based algebraic query optimization can be blocked, basically due to the existence of data manipulation functions.

However, if we study the problem of the optimization of ETL workflows from its logical point of view, we can identify several interesting research problems and optimization opportunities. At first, there is a necessity for a framework that will allow the application of several well-known query optimization techniques to the optimization of ETL workflows. For example, it is desirable to push selections all the way to the sources, in order to avoid processing unnecessary rows. Moreover, it is desirable to determine appropriate techniques and requirements, so that an ETL transformation (e.g., a filter) can be pushed before or after another transformation involving a function. Additionally, there is a need to tackle the problem of homonyms. For example, assume the case of two attributes with the same name, COST, where the first one has values in European currency, while the other contains values in American currency. Clearly, in this case it is not obvious if a transformation that involves the first attribute (e.g., a transformation that converts the values from American to European currency) can be pushed before or after another transformation that involves the second attribute (e.g., a transformation that filters the values over a certain threshold).

Copyright © 2007, Idea Group Inc. Copying or distributing in print or electronic forms without written permission of Idea Group Inc. is prohibited.

- **Software construction:** To conclude the discussion about the life cycle of the data warehouse presented in Figure 2, one anticipates that the outcome of the aforementioned analysis should be used for the construction of a software prototype. This construction phase includes the development, testing, and deployment of a first version of the data warehouse. This process has to be guided through specific metrics for the maintenance and monitoring of the data warehouse.

A Roadmap for a Data Warehouse Designer/Administrator

We summarize the previously mentioned issues in Table 1, where we present a set of steps for the data warehouse designers towards constructing the backstage of the data warehouse. We organize the tasks of the designers in four phases (requirements, design, tuning, and implementation) of the software project. For each

Table 1. Typical tasks for a data warehouse designer/developer organized by phase and stage

	Extract	Transform	Load	Deliverable
Phase 1a: Reverse Engineering of Sources & Requirements Collection	▪ collection of requirements from the part of the users ▪ analysis of the structure and content of the existing data sources and their intentional mapping to the common data warehouse model	▪ mapping of the attributes of the data sources to the attributes of the data warehouse tables through the appropriate intermediate transformations	▪ identification of data targets	▪ conceptual schema
Phase 1b: Define Sources and Processes	▪ concepts map to logical recordsets	▪ transformations map to logical activities ▪ definition of a proper execution order	▪ concepts map to logical recordsets ▪ ETL constraints map to logical activities	▪ a set of steps for the transition of conceptual to logical schemas
Phase 2: Logical Design	▪ definition of a plan for the population of the Data Staging Area w.r.t. schemata mappings ▪ choice of extraction policy: incremental or full extraction	▪ description of ETL activities w.r.t. schemata mappings and internal semantics ▪ identification of an optimal execution plan	▪ appropriate schemata mappings	▪ logical schema

Copyright © 2007, Idea Group Inc. Copying or distributing in print or electronic forms without written permission of Idea Group Inc. is prohibited.

phase, we present the issues and the steps to follow concerning the main tasks of the warehouse architecture (extraction, transformation, cleaning). The fundamental deliverable that guides this process is also listed.

Arktos II: A Framework towards the Modeling and the Optimization of ETL Workflows

In this subsection, we present a framework for traditional data warehouse flows, named Arktos II, as an exemplary ETL modeling methodology that follows the life cycle of a data warehouse as we previously presented it. Below, we briefly present the main contributions of Arktos II, grouped by the phases of the life cycle of a data warehouse.

Arktos II (Simitsis, Vassiliadis, & Sellis, 2005a; Vassiliadis, Simitsis, Georgantas, Terrovitis, & Skiadopoulos, 2005) is a framework that studies the design, development, and optimization of ETL workflows. The uttermost goal of this framework is to facilitate, manage, and optimize the design and implementation of the ETL workflows during the initial design and deployment stage and during the continuous evolution of the data warehouse. Despite the fact that its prototype is only a design environment, at least for the moment, it benefits compared to the commercial ETL tools due to the logical abstraction that it offers; on the contrary, commercial tools are concerned directly with the physical perspective of an ETL scenario (at least to the best of our knowledge).

Arktos II proposes a novel conceptual model for the early stages of a data warehouse project (Vassiliadis, Simitsis, & Skiadopoulos, 2002). This model focuses on (a) the interrelationships of attributes and concepts and (b) the necessary transformations that need to take place during the loading of the warehouse. Also, it is able to capture constraints and transformation composition. Due to the nature of the design process, the features of the conceptual model are presented in a set of design steps that constitute a methodology for the design of the conceptual part of the overall ETL process. The construction of the model is realized in a customizable and extensible manner, so that the designer can enrich it with the designer's own reoccurring patterns for ETL transformations. Furthermore, it is enriched with a "palette" of frequently used ETL transformations, like the assignment of surrogate keys, the check for null values, and so on.

Additionally, Arktos II presents a formal logical model for the ETL environment that concentrates on the flow of data from the sources towards the data warehouse through the composition of activities and data stores (Vassiliadis et al., 2002). The flow of data from producers towards their consumers is achieved through the usage of provider relationships that map the attributes of the former to the respective attributes of the latter. A serializable combination of ETL activities, provider relation-

Copyright © 2007, Idea Group Inc. Copying or distributing in print or electronic forms without written permission of Idea Group Inc. is prohibited.

ships, and data stores constitutes an ETL workflow. Also, a reusability framework that complements the genericity and customization of the metamodel is provided. Finally, Arktos II introduces techniques for the measurement of ETL workflows.

Furthermore, Arktos II proposes a semiautomatic transition from conceptual to logical model for ETL processes (Simitsis, 2005). The constituents of the conceptual model are mapped to their respective constituents of the logical model. Also, it presents a method for the determination of a correct execution order of the activities in the logical model, wherever feasible, by grouping the transformations of the conceptual design into stages.

Moreover, Arktos II delves into the logical optimization of ETL workflows, having as its uttermost goal the finding of the optimal ETL workflow (Simitsis, Vassiliadis, & Sellis, 2005). The method proposed reduces the execution cost of an ETL workflow, by changing either the total number or the execution order of the processes. The problem is modeled as a state space search problem, with each state representing a particular design of the workflow as a graph. The tuning of an ETL workflow is realized through several algorithms for the optimization of the execution order of the activities.

Finally, to replenish the aforementioned issues, an ETL tool has prototypically been implemented with the goal of facilitating the design, the (re)use, and the optimization of ETL workflows. The general architecture of Arktos II comprises a GUI, an ETL library, a metadata repository, and an optimizer engine. The GUI facilitates the design of ETL workflows in both the conceptual and logical level, through a workflow editor and a template palette. The ETL library contains template code of built-in functions and maintains a template code of user-defined functions. After its creation, the ETL workflow is propagated to the optimizer in order to achieve a better version with respect to the execution time. All the aforementioned components are communicating with each other through the metadata repository.

Future Trends

In our opinion, there are several issues that are technologically open and present interesting topics of research for the future in the field of data integration in data warehouse environments. This opinion is supported by the results of a recent workshop located in Dagstuhl, Germany in the Summer of 2004 (Dagstuhl Perspective Workshop, 2004), where several researchers tried to articulate the most pressing issues for the next directions of data warehousing research. A research agenda describing opportunities and challenges for promising new areas in data warehousing research was proposed that focuses on architecture, processes, modeling and design, and novel applications. Out of these, the participants discuss the future role of ETL

Copyright © 2007, Idea Group Inc. Copying or distributing in print or electronic forms without written permission of Idea Group Inc. is prohibited.

in a threefold categorization: traditional ETL, stream ETL, and on-demand ETL. We adopt this classification, and for each one of these categories, we present a list of several future directions.

- **Traditional ETL:** Traditional ETL processes are responsible for the extraction of data from several sources, their cleansing, customization, and insertion into a data warehouse. These tasks are repeated on a regular basis, and in most cases, they are asynchronous. As research challenges in this area, we mention the following issues:
  - o A formal description of ETL processes with particular emphasis on an algebra (for optimization purposes) and a formal declarative language.
  - o The optimization of ETL processes on logical and physical levels. A challenge will be either the optimization of the whole ETL process or of any individual transformation. Parallel processing of ETL processes is of particular importance.
  - o The propagation of changes back to the sources. Potential quality problems observed at the end-user level can lead to clean data being propagated back to the sources, in order to avoid the repetition of several tasks in future application of the ETL process. Clearly, this idea has already been mentioned in the literature as "backflow of cleaned data" (Rahm & Hai Do, 2000), but the problem is not solved yet.
  - o The provision of standard-based metadata for ETL processes. There does not exist common model for the metadata of ETL processes. CWM is not sufficient for this purpose and it is too complicated for real-world applications.
  - o The integration of ETL with XML adapters, EAI (Enterprise Application Integration) tools (e.g., MQ-Series), and data quality tools.
  - o The extension of the ETL mechanisms for nontraditional data, like XML/ HTML, spatial, and biomedical data.
  - o The treatment of security issues in ETL; source data and data in transit are security risks (Friedman, 2002a).
- **Stream ETL:** Streams are sequences of data, continuously flowing from a data source with the particular characteristic that, due to their volume, each tuple is available only for a limited time window for querying. Stream examples would involve stock rates extracted from the Web, packets going through a router, clickstreams from a Web site, and so forth. Stream ETL is an ETL process involving the possible filtering, value conversion, and transformations of this incoming information in a relational format. Although, streams cannot be stored, some patterns or snapshot aggregates of them can be stored

Copyright © 2007, Idea Group Inc. Copying or distributing in print or electronic forms without written permission of Idea Group Inc. is prohibited.

for subsequent querying. As research challenges in this area, we can mention the following issues:

- o   The necessity of maintaining data in the DW as much "online" as we can, but without adding an extra load to sources or DW.

- o   The provision of correctness guarantees.

- o   The necessity of cost models for the tuning of the incoming stream within specified time window.

- o   The audit of the incoming stream data for several constraints or business rules, also with respect to stored data (e.g., primary key violations).

- **On-Demand ETL:** An ETL process of this kind is executed sporadically, and it is manually initiated by some user demand. The process is responsible for retrieving external data and loading them in the DW after the appropriate transformations. For instance, consider the case that some users request data to be brought in from the Web. The administrator/programmer is assigned the task of constructing an ETL process that extracts the dates from the specified sites, transforms them, and ultimately stores them in some (possibly novel) part of the warehouse. Any time the user needs this data, this on-demand ETL process brings in the relevant information. As research challenges in this area, we mention the following issues:

- o   The need for appropriate operators, since this process is mostly focused towards Web data.

- o   The computation of minimum effort/time/resources for the construction of the process.

- o   The provision of a framework easily adaptable to the changes of the external data.

- o   The finding of efficient algorithms, due to the fact that this process is initiated by the user.

Conclusion

In this chapter, we have delved into a crucial part of the data warehouse architecture: the backstage area. We have presented the state of the art concerning the existing ETL technology. In practice, a designer/administrator uses a commercial ETL tool or an in-house developed software artifact to create ad-hoc ETL workflows. We have stressed the fact that there is not a unified approach that concretely deals with the modeling and the optimization of ETL workflows.

Copyright © 2007, Idea Group Inc. Copying or distributing in print or electronic forms without written permission of Idea Group Inc. is prohibited.

Additionally, we have indicated the main challenges and problems concerning the manufacturing of ETL workflows. In all the phases of an ETL process (extraction and transportation, transformation and cleaning, and loading) individual issues arise, making data warehouse refreshment a very troublesome task. In general, ETL workflows are characterized as quite complex, costly, critical, and important for the success of a data warehouse project. The key factors underlying the main problems of ETL workflows are vastness of the data volumes, quality problems, performance, evolution of the sources, and the data warehouse.

Moreover, we have presented a modeling approach for the construction of ETL workflows, which is based on the life cycle of the ETL processes. This life cycle consist of four phases: reverse engineering and requirements collection, logical design, tuning and physical design, and software construction. As a result, in order to construct an efficient, robust, and evolvable ETL workflow, we have to deal with all the phases of the life cycle of a data warehouse.

Finally, we have pointed out a list of open research issues arranged in three basic categories: traditional ETL, stream ETL, and on-demand ETL; and we have provided several future directions.

References

Adzic, J., & Fiore, V. (2003, September). Data warehouse population platform. In *Proceedings of 5th International Workshop on the Design and Management of Data Warehouses (DMDW'03),* Berlin, Germany.

Ascential. (2003). *Data warehousing technology.* Retrieved May 27, 2006, from http://www.ascentialsoftware.com/products/datastage.html

Booch, G., Rumbaugh, J., & Jacobson, I. (1998). *The unified modeling language user guide.* Addison-Wesley.

Borkar, V., Deshmuk, K., & Sarawagi, S. (2000). Automatically extracting structure from free text addresses. *Bulletin of the Technical Committee on Data Engineering, 23*(4).

Bouzeghoub, M., Fabret, F., & Matulovic, M. (1999). Modeling data warehouse refreshment process as a workflow application. In *Proceedings of 1st International Workshop on the Design and Management of Data Warehouses (DMDW'99),* Heidelberg, Germany.

Calì, A., Calvanese, D., De Giacomo, G., Lenzerini, M., Naggar, P., & Vernacotola, F. (2003). IBIS: Semantic data integration at work. In *Proceedings of the 15th International Conference on Advanced Information Systems Engineering (CAiSE 2003)*, Klangefurt, Austria (pp. 79-94).

Copyright © 2007, Idea Group Inc. Copying or distributing in print or electronic forms without written permission of Idea Group Inc. is prohibited.

Cohen, W. (1999). Some practical observations on integration of Web information. In *Proceedings of SIGMOD Workshop on the Web and Databases (WebDB '99)*, Philadelphia, Pennsylvania.

Dagstuhl Perspective Workshop. (2004). *Data warehousing at the crossroads.* Dagstuhl, Germany.

Demarest, M. (1999). *The politics of data warehousing.* Retrieved May 27, 2006, from http://www.hevanet.com/demarest/marc/dwpol.html

Eder, J., & Gruber, W. (2002). A meta model for structured workflows supporting workflow transformations. In *Proceedings of the 6ᵗʰ East European Conference on Advances in Databases and Information Systems (ADBIS '02)*, Bratislava, Slovakia (pp. 326-339).

Friedman, T. (2002). *Reducing the cost of ETL for the data warehouse* (Tech. Rep. No. COM-16-8237). Gartner Group.

Friedman, T. (2002a). *Security issues in ETL for the data warehouse* (Tech. Rep. No. COM-17-8459). Gartner Group.

Galhardas, H., Florescu, D., Shasha, D., & Simon, E. (1999). *An extensible framework for data cleaning* (Tech. Rep. No. INRIA RR-3742).

Galhardas, H., Florescu, D., Shasha, D., & Simon, E. (2000). Ajax: An extensible data cleaning tool. In *Proceedings of ACM International Conference on the Management of Data (SIGMOD '00)*, Dallas, Texas (p. 590).

Gartner. (2003). *ETL Magic Quadrant update: Market pressure increases* (Gartner's Strategic Data Management Research Note M-19-1108). Author.

Giga. (2002). *Market overview update: ETL* (Tech. Rep. No. RPA-032002-00021). Author.

IBM. (2003). *IBM Data Warehouse Manager.* Retrieved May 27, 2006, from http://www-3.ibm.com/software/data/db2/datawarehouse

Informatica. (2003). *PowerCenter.* Retrieved May 27, 2006, from http://www.informatica.com/products/data+integration/powercenter/default.htm

Jarke, M., Lenzerini, M., Vassiliou, Y., & Vassiliadis, P. (Eds.). (2003). *Fundamentals of data warehouses* (2ⁿᵈ ed.). Germany: Springer-Verlag.

Jarke, M., List, T., & Koller, J. (2000). The challenge of process warehousing. In *Proceedings of the 26ᵗʰ International Conference on Very Large Databases (VLDB '00)*, Cairo, Egypt.

Jarke, M., Quix, C., Blees, G., Lehmann, D., Michalk, G., & Stierl, S. (1999). Improving OLTP data quality using data warehouse mechanisms. In *Proceedings of ACM International Conference on Management of Data (SIGMOD '99)*, Philadelphia (pp. 537-538).

Copyright © 2007, Idea Group Inc. Copying or distributing in print or electronic forms without written permission of Idea Group Inc. is prohibited.

Labio, W., & Garcia-Molina, H. (1996). Efficient snapshot differential algorithms for data warehousing. In *Proceedings of the 22ⁿᵈ International Conference on Very Large Data Bases (VLDB'96)*, Bombay, India (pp. 63-74).

Kiepuszewski, B., Ter Hofstede, A. H. M., & Bussler, C. (2000). On structured workflow modeling. In *Proceedings of the 12ᵗʰ International Conference on Advanced Information Systems Engineering (CAiSE'00)*, Stockholm, Sweden (pp. 431-445).

Lenzerini. (2002). Data integration: A theoretical perspective. In *Proceedings of the 21ˢᵗ Symposium on Principles of Database Systems (PODS'02)*, Wisconsin (pp. 233-246).

Microsoft. (2003). *Data transformation services.* Retrieved May 27, 2006, from http://www.microsoft.com

Monge, A. (2000). Matching algorithms within a duplicate detection system. *Bulletin of the Technical Committee on Data Engineering, 23*(4).

Oracle. (2001). Oracle9i™ Warehouse Builder user's guide (Release 9.0.2). Retrieved May 27, 2006, from http://otn.oracle.com/products/warehouse/content.html

Oracle. (2002). *Oracle9i™ SQL reference* (Release 9.2, pp. 17.77-17.80). Author.

Rahm, E., & Hai Do, H. (2000). Data cleaning: Problems and current approaches. *Bulletin of the Technical Committee on Data Engineering, 23*(4).

Raman, V., & Hellerstein, J. (2001). Potter's Wheel: An interactive data cleaning system. In *Proceedings of 27ᵗʰ International Conference on Very Large Data Bases (VLDB'01)*, Roma, Italy (pp. 381-390).

Rundensteiner, E. (Ed.). (1999). Special issue on data transformations. *Bulletin of the Technical Committee on Data Engineering, 22*(1).

Sadiq, W., & Orlowska, M. E. (2000). On business process model transformations. In *Proceedings of the 19ᵗʰ International Conference on Conceptual Modeling (ER'00)* (pp. 267-280), Salt Lake City, Utah.

Sarawagi, S. (2000, December). Special issue on data cleaning. *Bulletin of the Technical Committee on Data Engineering, 23*(4).

Scalzo, B. (2003). *Oracle DBA guide to data warehousing and star schemas.* Prentice Hall.

Schafer, E., Becker, J.-D., & Jarke, M. (2000). DB-Prism: Integrated data warehouses and knowledge networks for bank controlling. In *Proceedings of the 26ᵗʰ International Conference on Very Large Databases (VLDB'00),* Cairo, Egypt.

Shilakes, C., & Tylman, J. (1998). Enterprise information portals. Retrieved May 27, 2006, from http://www.sagemaker.com/company/downloads/eip/indepth.pdf

Simitsis, A. (2004). *Modeling and optimization of extraction-transformation-loading (ETL) processes in data warehouse environments.* Doctoral Thesis, NTU Athens, Greece.

Copyright © 2007, Idea Group Inc. Copying or distributing in print or electronic forms without written permission of Idea Group Inc. is prohibited.

Simitsis, A. (2005). Mapping conceptual to logical models for ETL processes. In *Proceedings of the 8th ACM International Workshop on Data Warehousing and OLAP (DOLAP '05)*, Bremen, Germany.

Simitsis, A., Vassiliadis, P., & Sellis, T. (2005). Optimizing ETL processes in data warehouse environments. In *Proceedings of the 21st IEEE International Conference on Data Engineering (ICDE '05)*, Tokyo, Japan.

Simitsis, A., Vassiliadis, P., & Sellis, T. (2005a). State-space optimization of ETL workflows. *IEEE Transactions on Knowledge and Data Engineering, 17*(10), 1404-1419.

Strange, K. (2002). *ETL was the key to this data warehouse's success* (Tech. Rep. No. CS-15-3143). Gartner Group.

Strange, K. (2002a). *Data warehouse TCO: Don't underestimate the cost of ETL* (Tech. Rep. No. DF-15-2007). Gartner Group.

Theodoratos, D., Ligoudistianos, S., & Sellis, T. (2001). View selection for designing the global data warehouse. *Data & Knowledge Engineering, 39*(3), 219-240.

Trujillo, J., & Luján-Mora, S. (2003). A UML based approach for modeling ETL processes in data warehouses. In *Proceedings of 22nd International Conference on Conceptual Modeling (ER 2003)*, Chicago (pp. 307-320). LNCS, 2813.

Van der Aalst, W. M. P., ter Hofstede, A. H. M., Kiepuszewski, B., & Barros, A. P. (2000). *Workflow patterns* (BETA Working Paper Series WP 47). Eindhoven University of Technology, Eindhoven.

Vassiliadis, P. (2000). Gulliver in the land of data warehousing: Practical experiences and observations of a researcher. In *Proceedings of 2nd International Workshop on Design and Management of Data Warehouses (DMDW'00)*, Stockholm, Sweden.

Vassiliadis, P., Quix, C., Vassiliou, Y., & Jarke, M. (2001). Data warehouse process management. *Information Systems, 26*(3), 205-236.

Vassiliadis, P., Simitsis, A., Georgantas, P., Terrovitis, M., & Skiadopoulos, S. (2005). A generic and customizable framework for the design of ETL scenarios. *Information Systems, 30*(7), 492-525.

Vassiliadis, P., Simitsis, A., & Skiadopoulos, S. (2002). Conceptual modeling for ETL processes. In *Proceedings of the 5th ACM International Workshop on Data Warehousing and OLAP (DOLAP '02)*, McLean, Virginia.

Vassiliadis, P., Simitsis, A., & Skiadopoulos, S. (2002a). Modeling ETL activities as graphs. In *Proceedings of the 4th International Workshop on the Design and Management of Data Warehouses (DMDW '02)*, Toronto, Canada (pp. 52-61).

Copyright © 2007, Idea Group Inc. Copying or distributing in print or electronic forms without written permission of Idea Group Inc. is prohibited.

Workflow Management Coalition. (1998). *Interface 1: Process definition interchange process model* (Doc. No. WfMC TC-1016-P).

Copyright © 2007, Idea Group Inc. Copying or distributing in print or electronic forms without written permission of Idea Group Inc. is prohibited.

Section III

Efficiency of
Analytical Processing

Chapter VI

Advanced Ad Hoc Star Query Processing

Nikos Karayannidis
National Technical University of Athens, Greece

Aris Tsois
National Technical University of Athens, Greece

Timos Sellis
National Technical University of Athens, Greece

Abstract

Star queries are the most prevalent kind of queries in data warehousing, online analytical processing (OLAP), and business intelligence applications. Thus, there is an imperative need for efficiently processing star queries. To this end, a new class of fact table organizations has emerged that exploits path-based surrogate keys in order to hierarchically cluster the fact table data of a star schema. In the context of these new organizations, star query processing changes radically. In this chapter, we present a complete abstract processing plan that captures all the necessary steps in evaluating such queries over hierarchically clustered fact tables. Furthermore, we realize the abstract operations in terms of physical operations over the CUBE File data structure. Finally we discuss star query optimization issues over the presented abstract plan.

Copyright © 2007, Idea Group Inc. Copying or distributing in print or electronic forms without written permission of Idea Group Inc. is prohibited.

Introduction

Star queries are the most prevalent kind of queries in data warehousing, online analytical processing (OLAP), and business intelligence applications. Star queries impose restrictions on the dimension tables that are used for selecting specific facts from the fact table; these facts are further grouped and aggregated according to the user demands. Furthermore, advanced decision support calls for *ad hoc analysis*, in contrast to using predefined reports that are constructed periodically, or have already been precomputed. The foundation for this kind of analysis is the support of *ad hoc star queries*, which comprise the real essence of OLAP. Efficient processing of ad hoc star queries is a very difficult task considering, on one hand, the native complexity of typical OLAP queries, which potentially combine huge amounts of data, and on the other, the fact that no a priori knowledge for the query exists and thus no precomputation of results or other query-specific tuning can be exploited. The only way to evaluate these queries is to access directly the base data in an efficient way.

Traditionally, the major bottleneck in evaluating star queries has been the join of the central (and usually very large) fact table with the surrounding dimension tables (also known as a *star join*). To cope with this problem various indexing schemes have been developed (Chan & Ioannidis, 1998; O'Neil & Grafe, 1995; O'Neil & Quass, 1997; Sarawagi, 1997; Wu & Buchmann, 1998). Also precomputation of aggregation results has been studied extensively—mainly as a view maintenance problem—and is used as a means of accelerating query performance in data warehouses (Roussopoulos, 1998; Srivastava, Dar, Jagadish & Levy, 1996).

However, for ad hoc star queries the usage of precomputed aggregation results is extremely limited or even impossible in some cases. Even when elaborate indexes are used, due to the arbitrary ordering of the fact table tuples, there might be as many disk page accesses as are the tuples resulting from the fact table. The only alternative one can have for such queries is a good physical clustering of the data, and it is exactly for this reason that a new class of primary organizations for the fact table has emerged (Karayannidis, Sellis, & Kouvaras, 2004; Markl, Ramsak, & Bayern, 1999). These organizations exploit a special kind of key that is based on the hierarchy paths of the dimensions, in order to achieve hierarchical clustering of the facts. This physical clustering results in a reduced I/O cost for the majority of star queries, which are based on the dimension hierarchies. Moreover, in a dimensional data warehouse it is natural to exploit a multidimensional index for storing the tuples. A typical star join is transformed then into a multidimensional range query, which is very efficiently computed using the underlying multidimensional data structures. The combination of the two: hierarchical clustering of data and a multidimensional structure for accessing the fact table tuples results in a very efficient method for ad hoc star query processing.

Copyright © 2007, Idea Group Inc. Copying or distributing in print or electronic forms without written permission of Idea Group Inc. is prohibited.

In this chapter, we discuss the processing of ad hoc star queries over hierarchically clustered fact tables. In particular, we present a complete abstract processing plan that covers all the necessary steps for answering such queries. This plan directly exploits the benefits of hierarchically clustered fact tables and opens the road for new optimization challenges. Then we proceed in realizing this abstract plan for the case of a multidimensional storage structure that achieves hierarchical clustering, namely the *CUBE File*. We continue with a discussion on star query optimization for the presented abstract plan and present the *hierarchical pregrouping transformation*. This is a very elegant transformation that exploits dimension hierarchy semantics to speed up query processing significantly. Finally, we conclude with a discussion on main conclusions of the presented methods, and future trends in star query processing.

Background

Preliminary Concepts

In a relational OLAP (ROLAP) implementation, a dimension is stored into one or more *dimension tables*, each having a set of attributes. Dimension attributes usually form one or more classification hierarchies. For example, the h_1 attribute is classified by the h_2 attribute, which is further classified by the h_3 attribute, and so forth. We call the attributes $h_1, h_2, h_3, \ldots$ *hierarchical attributes* because they participate in the definition of the hierarchy. For example, *day*, *month*, and *year* can be a hierarchical classification in the *DATE* dimension. For the purposes of this chapter we will assume a single hierarchy for each dimension.[1] A dimension table may also contain one or more *feature attributes f*. Feature attributes contain additional information about a number of hierarchical attributes and are always functionally dependent on one (or more) hierarchical attribute. For example, *population* could be a feature attribute dependent on the *region* attribute of dimension *LOCATION*.

Measures (or *facts*) are stored in *fact tables*. A fact table may contain one or more *measure attributes* and is always linked (by foreign key attributes) to some dimension tables. This logical organization consisting of a central table (the fact table) and surrounding tables (the dimension tables) that link to it through 1:N relationships is known as the *star schema* (Chaudhuri & Dayal, 1997). In a typical scenario, the hierarchical attribute representing the most detailed level will be the primary key of the respective dimension. Each such attribute will have a corresponding foreign key in the fact table.

In Figure 1(a) we depict an example schema of a simplified data warehouse. The data warehouse stores sales transactions recorded per item, store, customer, and

Copyright © 2007, Idea Group Inc. Copying or distributing in print or electronic forms without written permission of Idea Group Inc. is prohibited.

Figure 1. (a) The schema of the data warehouse; (b) the dimension hierarchies of the example

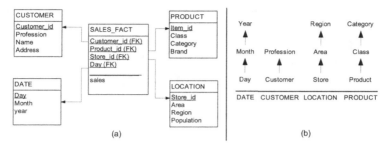

(a)   (b)

date. It contains one fact table *SALES_FACT*, which is defined over the dimensions: *PRODUCT*, *CUSTOMER*, *DATE*, and *LOCATION* with the obvious meanings. The single measure of *SALES_FACT* is *sales* representing the sales value for an item bought by a customer at a store on a specific day. The dimension hierarchies are depicted in Figure 1(b).

The dimension *DATE* is organized in three levels: Day-Month-Year. Hence, it has three hierarchical attributes (*Day, Month, Year*). The PRODUCT dimension is organized into three levels (Item-Class-Category) with three hierarchical attributes and one feature attribute (*Brand*). The dimension *CUSTOMER* is organized in only two levels (Customer-Profession) with two hierarchical attributes and two feature attributes (*Name, Address*). The *LOCATION* dimension is organized into three levels: store-area-region, meaning that stores are grouped into geographical areas and the areas are grouped into regions. For each area, the population is stored as feature attribute. Therefore, the dimension has three hierarchical attributes (*Store_id, Area, Region*) and one feature attribute (*Population*) that is assigned to the Area level.

Note that the key attributes of the dimension tables are *Customer_id*, *Item_id*, *Store_id*, and *Day* and the corresponding foreign keys (*Customer_id, Product_id, Store_id, Day*) define the fact table's primary key.

In order to create a fact table that is clustered according to the dimension hierarchies we first need to apply a *hierarchical encoding* (*HE*) on each dimension table. To achieve this we use the *hierarchical surrogate key* (or *h-surrogate*) attribute, a special attribute which is defined for each dimension table. The value of this attribute is computed based on the value of the hierarchical attributes of the dimension. The h-surrogate encodes not only the values of the hierarchical attributes but also the hierarchical relationships defined among the levels of the dimension. Although there are several equivalent ways to define such an encoding, it is sufficient to present only one such technique for the reader to understand how h-surrogates are used. All the query processing and optimization techniques presented in this chapter work regardless of the particular encoding technique used.

Copyright © 2007, Idea Group Inc. Copying or distributing in print or electronic forms without written permission of Idea Group Inc. is prohibited.

Definition 1 (Hierarchical Surrogate Key).

Assume a dimension table D containing the hierarchical attributes $h_m, h_{m-1}, ..., h_1$ (h_m the most aggregated level and h_1 the most detailed one). Each tuple t of D assigns the values $t.v_m, t.v_{m-1}, ..., t.v_1$ to the corresponding hierarchical attributes. Let $\{oc_i\}$ be a set of m bijective functions so that $oc_i: V_i \rightarrow \{0, ..., |Vi|-1\}$, where $1 \leq i \leq m$ and V_i is the set of values of the hierarchical attribute h_i and $|V_i|$ is the total number of values in this set. The *hierarchical surrogate key* (or h-surrogate) of D is a computed attribute of D so that for each tuple t of D the value of the h-surrogate is $hsk=oc_m(t.v_m).\ oc_{m-1}(t.v_{m-1}).\ ....\ oc_1(t.v_1).$ □

The value assigned by a oc_i function to a hierarchical attribute value is called an *order-code* and since these functions are 1-1 the order-codes uniquely identify a hierarchical attribute value. In Figure 2(b) we depict the hierarchy-tree formed from the values of the hierarchy attributes (equivalently *levels*) of dimension LOCATION. Below each value appears in parentheses its assigned order-code. In the same figure we depict the h-surrogate value for the leaf-value "storeC." Note that an h-surrogate conveys all the hierarchical semantics (i.e., the genealogy) of a specific value. Moreover it is indeed an alternate key, since it determines all hierarchical attributes, which in turn functionally determine all feature attributes. Note also that leaf-values under the same parent have a common h-surrogate prefix. For example the prefix "0.1" in Figure 2(b) is the same for the two stores in "AreaB" and the prefix "0." is common to all stores in "RegionA." We use the notation $hsk:L$ to refer to the prefix of the h-surrogate that corresponds to the level L of the hierarchy.

Figure 2. (a) The schema of the data warehouse enhanced with h-surrogates; (b) each value of a hierarchical attribute is assigned an order-code, which preserves hierarchical proximity.

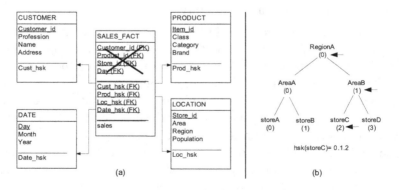

(a)   (b)

Note: An h-surrogate is essentially a path of order-codes in the hierarchy tree.

Copyright © 2007, Idea Group Inc. Copying or distributing in print or electronic forms without written permission of Idea Group Inc. is prohibited.

Each h-surrogate can trigger the creation of a foreign key in the fact table. The concatenation of all these foreign keys produces the fact table's primary key. This is depicted in Figure 2(a). Note that for the fact table we have two alternative composite keys: (a) (*Customer_id, Product_id, Store_id, Day*) that links to the corresponding lowest hierarchical attribute of each dimension and (b) (*Cust_hsk, Prod_hsk, Loc_hsk, Date_hsk*) that links to the corresponding h-surrogate attribute. Note that the former is not necessary to achieve hierarchical clustering of the data, and thus could be omitted, in order to reduce storage overhead.

The h-surrogates play a central role in processing ad hoc star queries, first because they enable the clustering of the fact table according to the dimension hierarchies, and second because they can be exploited to optimize the query evaluation plans. Experiments in Karayannidis et al. (2002) have shown speed-ups up to a factor of 20, over the state of the art bitmap-based star join processing (see section on other methods for star query processing). Even more interestingly, this factor doubled when query optimization techniques that are discussed later in this chapter were exploited.

The h-surrogates should be system assigned and maintained attributes, and typically they should be made transparent to the user. The actual implementation of the h-surrogates depends heavily on the underlying physical organization of the fact table. Proposals for physical organizations (Karayannidis et al., 2004; Markl et al., 1999) exploit such path-based surrogate keys, in order to achieve hierarchical clustering of the fact table data.

In this chapter, we adopt a denormalized approach for the design of a dimension; that is, we represent each dimension with only one table. The hierarchical attributes $(h_1, h_2, ..., h_m)$, the feature attributes $(f_1, f_2, ..., f_k)$, as well as the hierarchical surrogate key *hsk* of the dimension are stored in a unique dimension table. However, the presented methods are fully applicable to normalized schemata (i.e., *snowflaked schemata*) as well, with the only difference that extra joins between the several dimension tables (corresponding to separate hierarchy levels) must be included in the plan. In addition, we assume a special physical organization for the fact table. The fact table is stored hierarchically clustered in a multidimensional data structure such as the CUBE File (Karayannidis et al., 2004) or the UB-tree (Markl et al., 1999). The index attributes of these structures are the h-surrogates.

Star Queries

OLAP queries typically include restrictions on multiple dimension tables that trigger restrictions (via the foreign key relationships) on the (usually very large) fact table. This is known as a *star join* (O'Neil & Grafe, 1995). We use the term *star query* to refer to flat SQL queries, defined over a single star schema, that include a star join. Star queries represent the majority of OLAP queries. In particular, we are

Copyright © 2007, Idea Group Inc. Copying or distributing in print or electronic forms without written permission of Idea Group Inc. is prohibited.

Figure 3. The ad hoc star query template

SELECT	<grouping attributes and/or aggregation functions>
FROM	<fact table>, D_1, D_2, ..., D_k
WHERE	<star join conditions: equalities on key-f.key> AND LP_1 AND LP_2 AND ... AND LP_k AND <restrictions on attributes of the fact table>
GROUP BY	<grouping attributes>
HAVING	<group selection predicate>
ORDER BY	<sorting attributes>

interested in *ad hoc* OLAP star queries. With the term "ad hoc" we refer to queries that are not known in advance and therefore the administrator cannot optimize the DBMS specifically for these.

In Figure 3 we depict the SQL query template for the ad hoc star queries considered. The template defines the most complex query structure supported and uses abstract terms that act as placeholders. Note that queries conforming to this template have a structure that is a subset of the template in Figure 3 and instantiate all abstract terms.

The terms D_1, D_2, ..., D_k are the dimension tables of the star join and LP_1, LP_2, .., LP_k are the corresponding *local predicates*. Thus, the term LP_i is a *local predicate* on the dimension table D_i. The characterization "local" is because this predicate includes restrictions only on D_i and not on other dimension tables or the fact table. This predicate is very important for the h-surrogate processing phase explained later, and is used to produce the necessary *h-surrogate specification* accessing the fact table discussed later.

The vast majority of OLAP queries contains an equality restriction on a number of hierarchical attributes and more commonly on hierarchical attributes that form a complete path in the hierarchy (i.e., starting from the most aggregated level to some lower level without "gaps" in between). For example, the query "show me sales for area A in region B for each month of 1999" contains two whole-path restrictions, one for a dimension *LOCATION* and one for a *DATE*: (a) *LOCATION.Region* = 'A' AND *LOCATION.Area* = 'B' and (b) *DATE.Year* = 1999. This is reasonable since the core of analysis is conducted along the hierarchies. We call this kind of restriction *hierarchical prefix path* (HPP) restrictions. Note also that even if we impose a restriction solely on an intermediate level hierarchical attribute, we can still have an HPP restriction, as long as hierarchical attributes functionally determine higher level ones. For example, the restriction *Month* = *'AUG-99'* implies also that *Year = 1999*.

Let us now define an example query on the schema of Figure 1: We want to see the sum of sales by area and month for areas with population more than 1 million, for

Copyright © 2007, Idea Group Inc. Copying or distributing in print or electronic forms without written permission of Idea Group Inc. is prohibited.

Figure 4. Example query

```
SELECT L.area, D.month, SUM(F.sales)
FROM SALES_FACT F, LOCATION L, DATE D, PRODUCT P
WHERE F.day = D.day AND F.store_id = L.store_id AND
        F.product_id = P.item_id AND D.year = 1999 AND
L.population>1000000 AND P.category = "air condition"
GROUP BY L.area, D.month
```

the months of the year 1999 and for products that belong to the category "air condition." Figure 4 shows the corresponding SQL expression of this query. One can easily see that the query is an instance of the query template of Figure 3.

Star Query Processing

Methods of Ad-Hoc Star Query Processing

The most well known technique for star-query processing is based on a star-join via bitmap index intersections. Star join processing has been studied extensively and specific solutions have been implemented in commercial products. See also Chaudhuri and Dayal (1997) for an overview.

The standard query processing algorithm for a star join over n dimensions first evaluates the predicates on the dimension tables, either on a normalized (snowflake) or a denormalized (star) schema, resulting in a set R_i of n_i tuples of dimension D_i ($1 \leq i \leq n$). It then builds a *Cartesian product* of the dimension result tuples ($R_1 \times R_2 \times \ldots \times R_n$). The cardinality of the Cartesian product is $n_1 \cdot n_2 \cdot \ldots \cdot n_n$ for the n restricted dimensions. With these Cartesian product tuples, we perform a direct index access on the composite index built on the fact table. For nonsparse fact tables and queries that restrict most dimensions of the composite index in the order of the index attributes, the access to the fact tuples is quite fast. However, for large sparse fact tables and high dimensionality, such a query processing plan does not work efficiently enough. The cardinality of the Cartesian product resulting from the dimension predicates grows very fast, whereas the number of affected tuples in the fact table may be relatively small. This is the point where a call is made for specialized indexing or clustering methods.

Bitmapped join indices (O'Neil & Graefe, 1995; O'Neil & Quass, 1997) are often used to speed up the access to the fact table. This type of star-join evaluation has also been incorporated into a popular commercial system (Oracle, 2005). The so-

Copyright © 2007, Idea Group Inc. Copying or distributing in print or electronic forms without written permission of Idea Group Inc. is prohibited.

called *star transformation* rewrites a star-join so as the dimension restrictions are expressed as direct restrictions on the fact table column. For example, following query containing a star-join:

SELECT dim2.dim2_attr, dim3.dim3_attr, dim5.dim5_attr, fact.fact1

FROM fact, dim2, dim3, dim5

WHERE fact.dim2_key = dim2.dim2_key /* joins */

AND fact.dim3_key = dim3.dim3_key

AND fact.dim5_key = dim5.dim5_key

AND dim2.dim2_attr IN ('c','d') /* dimension restrictions */

AND dim3.dim3_attr IN ('e','f')

AND dim5.dim5_attr IN ('l','m')

is rewritten in the following form:

SELECT ... FROM fact

WHERE fact.dim2_key IN (SELECT dim2.dim2_key FROM dim2 WHERE dim2.dim2_attr IN ('c','d'))

AND fact.dim3_key IN (SELECT dim3.dim3_key FROM dim3 WHERE dim3.dim3_attr IN ('e','f'))

AND fact.dim5_key IN (SELECT dim5.dim5_key FROM dim5 WHERE AND dim5.dim5_attr ('l','m'))

In this way, the evaluation of the individual dimension restrictions takes place in the beginning, as if these were separate queries. From this evaluation *only the dimension keys* of the qualifying tuples are extracted; and for large dimensions, the results are saved into temporary tables. In the mean time, a separate bitmap index has been created on each fact table attribute that is a foreign key referencing a dimension table key. Then, the extracted list of qualifying dimension keys, for each dimension, is used to access the bitmap index on the corresponding fact table column. The created bitmaps are merged (i.e., ANDed) and a final bitmap, indicating the qualifying fact table tuples, is produced. Next, bits set on the final bitmap are converted to the corresponding row ids and the fact table tuples are retrieved. Finally, these tuples have to be joined to the dimension tables in order to retrieve the dimension attribute values required in the final result.

The main advantage of this method is that the bitmap operations can be executed very efficiently. However, the lack of appropriate data clustering might lead to a significant number of I/Os. When the query selectivity is high (small output), then only a few bits in the final bitmap are set. If there is no particular order among the fact table tuples, we can expect each bit to correspond to a tuple on a different page. Thus, there will be as many I/Os as there are bits set. Moreover, bitmap indexes become inefficient if the number of distinct values for a column is large (O'Neil & Quass, 1997). In this case the "bitmap density" (i.e., the number of bits

Copyright © 2007, Idea Group Inc. Copying or distributing in print or electronic forms without written permission of Idea Group Inc. is prohibited.

set per bitmap) becomes low and the storage overhead is significantly increased. Therefore, compression techniques have to be used that will reduce the efficiency of the bitmap operations.

An Abstract Plan for Star Query Processing

In this section, we will describe the major processing steps entailed when we want to answer star queries over a hierarchically clustered fact table.

- **Step 1. Identifying relevant fact table data:** The processing begins with the evaluation of the restrictions on the individual dimension tables, that is, the evaluation of the local predicates (operations *Create_Range* in Figure 5(a)). This step performed on a hierarchically encoded dimension table will result in a set of h-surrogate values that will be used in order to access the corresponding fact table data. Due to the hierarchical nature of the h-surrogate, this set can be represented by a number of h-surrogate intervals called the *h-surrogate specification*. Using the notation of Karayannidis et al. (2004), an interval will have the form *1999.*.** for the restriction on the DATE dimension in our running example. This denotes that we need to access all values under *1999* at the *Month* level and all values of each such month at the *Day* level.

  Once the h-surrogate specifications are determined for *all* dimensions, the evaluation of the star join follows. In hierarchically clustered fact tables, this translates to one or more simple multidimensional range queries on the underlying multidimensional structure that is used to store the fact table data (operator *MD_Range_Access* in Figure 5(a)). Moreover, since data are physically clustered according to the hierarchies and the ranges originate from hierarchical restrictions, this will result in a low-I/O evaluation of the range selection.

- **Step 2. Computing necessary joins:** The tuples resulting from the fact table contain the h-surrogate values and the measure values. At this stage, there might be a need for joining these tuples with a number of dimension tables in order to retrieve certain hierarchical or feature attributes that the user wants to have in the final result and might also be needed for the grouping operation. We call these joins *residual joins*. Note that all these join operations (the *Residual_Join* nodes in Figure 5(a)) are equi-joins on key-foreign key attributes and therefore each fact table tuple is joined with *exactly one* dimension table tuple.

- **Step 3. Performing grouping, filtering, and ordering:** Finally, the resulting tuples may be grouped and aggregated and the groups further filtered and ordered for delivering the result to the user. The *Group_Select* operator in Figure 5(a) performs these actions.

Copyright © 2007, Idea Group Inc. Copying or distributing in print or electronic forms without written permission of Idea Group Inc. is prohibited.

Figure 5. (a) The abstract processing plan; (b) the abstract processing plan for the example query

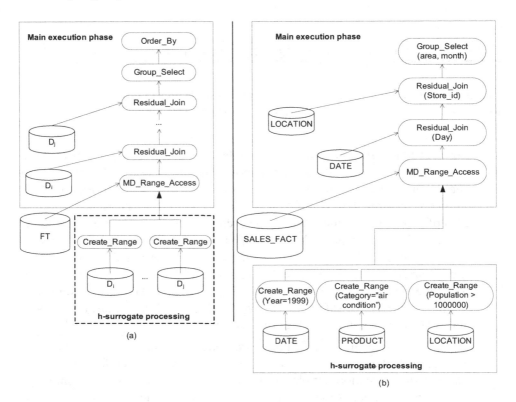

(a)

(b)

The abstract processing plan comprising of the phases is illustrated in Figure 5(a) and can be used to answer the star queries that belong to the query template of Figure 3. This plan is abstract in the sense that it does not determine specific algorithms for each processing step; it just defines the processing that needs to be done. That is why it is expressed in terms of *abstract operators* (or *logical operators*), which in turn can be mapped to a number of alternative *physical operators* that correspond to specific implementations.

An example abstract processing plan is shown in Figure 5(b) and it corresponds to the query of Figure 4.

Having described the framework for query processing of OLAP queries, we move next to discuss how this can be materialized on a hierarchical clustering-preserving data structure, namely the CUBE File.

Copyright © 2007, Idea Group Inc. Copying or distributing in print or electronic forms without written permission of Idea Group Inc. is prohibited.

Figure 6. (a) A cube hierarchically chunked; (b) the whole subtree up to the data chunks under chunk 0|0 (corresponding to the grayed cells on the left figure)

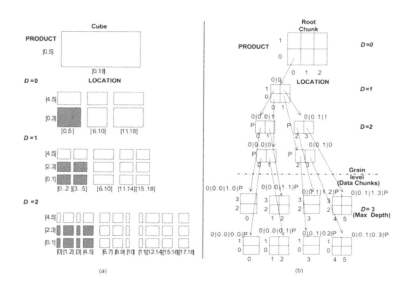

(a)   (b)

Processing Star Queries over CUBE File Organized Fact Tables

The CUBE File (Karayannidis et al., 2004) is a multidimensional data structure for storing the most detailed data of a fact table. Thus it could be exploited as an alternative primary organization to heap files for fact tables. It provides fast indexing on data, when these are accessed via restrictions on the hierarchies. Moreover, it physically clusters data w.r.t. dimension hierarchies (i.e., hierarchical clustering), which reduces significantly the I/O cost for star query evaluation.

The CUBE File partitions the multilevel-multidimensional data space of an OLAP cube in disjoint subspaces, called *chunks*, which are formed by all hierarchy value combinations per hierarchy-level. This process is called *hierarchical chunking* (Figure 6(a)) and results in a *chunk-tree representation* of the cube (Figure 6(b)). Note that prior to applying hierarchical chunking all hierarchies have to be normalized to the same length with the insertion of *pseudo-levels* to the shorter ones. The main advantage of hierarchical chunking is that it results in a structure that is highly adaptive to the cube's inherent extreme sparseness. The intuition is that the underlying data clusters are located naturally during the chunking process, exactly because hierarchy value combinations form the dense and sparse data areas. For example, a

Copyright © 2007, Idea Group Inc. Copying or distributing in print or electronic forms without written permission of Idea Group Inc. is prohibited.

Figure 7. The chunk-to-bucket allocation for a chunk-tree where the size of a bucket is $S_B = 30$ units of storage

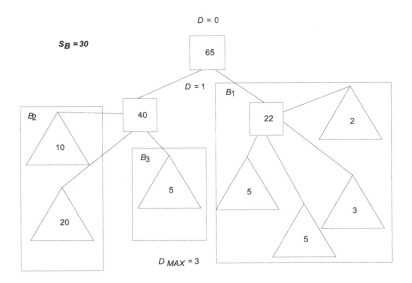

sparse area would be formed in a 3-dimenisonal cube, along the subspace (Sept00-Dec00, Books, Italy) if we did not sell any books during Sept00-Dec00 in Italy.

A subtree at *chunking-depth D* corresponds to a "family" (i.e., a subspace) of hierarchy-related data points. In fact the taller this subtree is (i.e., the smaller *D* is), the larger is the subspace of hierarchy-related data points that it "covers." Based on this observation, the CUBE File construction algorithm tries to "pack" into buckets (i.e., disk pages) *whole* subtrees of the smaller possible depth. This is the basic heuristic exploited by the CUBE File for achieving hierarchical clustering of the data. Note that the packing of chunks into buckets, so as to preserve hierarchical clustering, is an NP-Hard problem (Karayannidis, 2003).

In Figure 7 we depict such an allocation of chunks into buckets. In this figure we depict an arbitrary chunk-tree, where subtrees appear as triangles and specific nodes (i.e., chunks) as squares. The number within a triangle denotes the size of the corresponding subtree. The number within a square denotes the size of all subtrees under this node, plus the size of the node itself. In the figure, we have assumed a bucket size of 30 storage units. The lowest depth subtree that has been stored in a bucket corresponds to depth $D = 1$ (see bucket B_1). This bucket has the maximum *hierarchical clustering degree* among all buckets of the specific chunk-to-bucket allocation. Essentially this means that HPP queries that need to access B_1 will have reduced I/O cost, since this bucket has stored a larger subspace.

Copyright © 2007, Idea Group Inc. Copying or distributing in print or electronic forms without written permission of Idea Group Inc. is prohibited.

Note that the upper nodes (including the root node) that "fail" to be allocated to some bucket comprise the *root-directory* of the CUBE File. The root-directory is usually cached in main memory or it is further allocated into buckets as if it is a chunk-tree on its own.

The CUBE File requires the assignment of h-surrogates to the dimension values. Moreover, for each cell of a chunk, the interleaving of the corresponding h-surrogates yields a path-based key called the *chunk-id*, which is a unique identifier of a data point in the multilevel multidimensional data space of a cube. For example, $0|0.0|0$ is the chunk-id of the low-left cell of the chunk at depth $D = 1$ in Figure 6(b) (in the figure, it is depicted as a label on the corresponding chunk). "P" in a chunk-id denotes a pseudo-level.

In Figure 8(a), we depict the abstract processing plan of Figure 5(b) as a physical execution plan over a CUBE File organized fact table. We can see the evaluation of the local predicate on the *DATE* dimension consisting of an HPP restriction solely

Figure 8. (a) The abstract processing plan of our running example expressed as a physical execution plan over a CUBE File organized fact table; (b) the optimized abstract plan

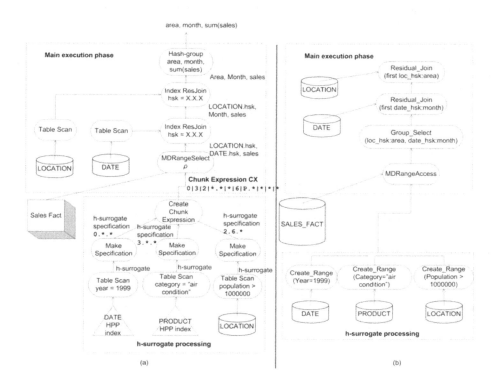

Copyright © 2007, Idea Group Inc. Copying or distributing in print or electronic forms without written permission of Idea Group Inc. is prohibited.

on the HPP-Index (a B-tree index defined on the hierarchy attributes of a dimension) without the need to access the base table (i.e., the *DATE* dimension table). The restriction *Year = 1999* has been translated to the h-surrogate specification *0.*.** (assuming that the order-code of *1999* is *0*). Note that only the first matching index-tuple (corresponding to the *Day* level) suffices for generating the corresponding h-surrogate specification, since all days of *1999* have the same h-surrogate prefix: *0..* This single index-tuple retrieval is an extremely fast implementation of the *Create_Range* abstract operation of Figure 5(a).

The same holds for the *PRODUCT* dimension also, since another HPP restriction is imposed there. The corresponding h-surrogate specification for the restriction *Category = 'Air Condition'* is *3.*.** (assuming that the order-code of the 'Air Condition' value is *3*). For dimension *LOCATION* things are a bit different since we have to perform a full table scan directly on the base table and then select the tuples that match the restriction on the feature attribute *Population*, which is functionally dependent on the hierarchical attribute *Area*. The corresponding h-surrogate specification is *2.6.** assuming that only one area (with order-code *6*) in a single region (with order-code *2*) satisfies the restriction on the *Population* feature attribute.

As soon as the h-surrogate specifications are extracted from each dimension, they are combined into a single *chunk expression (CX)* that is passed as input to an *MDRangeSelect* operator. A chunk expression is essentially an access pattern describing the cells that must be accessed in each depth of the chunk-tree and exploits the chunk-id notation. The chunk expression is created from the interleaving of the h-surrogate specifications. The depicted chunk expression $0|3|2|*.*|*|6|P.*|*|*|*$ is built from the interleaving of the aforementioned h-surrogate specifications, plus the h-surrogate specification for the *CUSTOMER* dimension, which is **.P.**, since this dimension is left unrestricted in the query of Figure 4 ("*P*" denotes a pseudo-level). The interleaving order is *DATE, PRODUCT, LOCATION,* and *CUSTOMER* and was chosen arbitrarily.

The *MDRangeSelect* will access the CUBE File in order to efficiently retrieve the relevant detailed data (described in the CX). Each *sales* value retrieved will be augmented with two h-surrogates, one corresponding to the *DATE* dimension and the other to *LOCATION*, which are dynamically computed from the corresponding data cell chunk-id (which is *not* stored along with the measure values, since the chunks are essentially multidimensional arrays, but retrieved from the current position/data point in the cube's data space). This provides the "impression" of tuples coming out of the *MDRangeSelect* operator.

Furthermore, these tuples will need to be joined with the *DATE* dimension in order to retrieve the *Month* values required in the final result. This join is implemented by a physical operator named *IndexResJoin* in the figure. Essentially, this is an index-based join that utilizes the primary organization of the dimension tables to efficiently retrieve the *single* join tuple from the dimension side. A dimension table

Copyright © 2007, Idea Group Inc. Copying or distributing in print or electronic forms without written permission of Idea Group Inc. is prohibited.

is organized as a B+ tree with the h-surrogate attribute as the search key. Each tuple coming from the CUBE File side contains an *hsk* attribute (i.e., an h-surrogate) corresponding to the *DATE* dimension. We use this value as a key for accessing directly the *DATE* dimension and retrieving the single tuple that matches. Indeed, since *hsk* is a primary key of the dimension table, there will be only a single tuple match. Therefore, the number of tuples in the output of the *IndexResJoin* operator is the same as the one in the input.

Similarly, for each *hsk* value corresponding to dimension *LOCATION* we access the corresponding tuple and retrieve the appropriate *Area* value. Finally, the grouping and aggregation has to take place. We depict a *hash-group* operator that groups the incoming tuples by *Area* and *Month*.

Star Query Optimization

An interesting feature of the database schema is the hierarchical structure of the h-surrogate attributes and the fact that they encode all the hierarchical attributes of the dimensions. Therefore, a number of functional dependencies exist in the schema, along with inclusion dependencies defined through the key-foreign key relationships. These functional and inclusion dependencies can be combined and used for the optimization of the grouping and join operations. The complex optimization technique that exploits these existing integrity constraints is the *hierarchical pregrouping* and it is presented next. Experimental results have shown that this technique can drastically reduce the execution time of the examined OLAP queries (Pieringer et al., 2003).

Other optimization opportunities exist and pertain to the *Create_Range* operation of the abstract processing plan (Figure 5(a)), or the exploitation of the sort-order of the tuples coming from the fact table (*MD_Range_Access* operation). Due to lack of space, these techniques will not be described here. The interested reader can find details in Karayannidis et al. (2002), Tsois and Sellis (2003), Pieringer et al. (2003), and Tsois (2005) for the former and in Theodoratos and Tsois (2003) and Tsois (2005) for the latter.

The Hierarchical Pregrouping technique is based on the properties of the join and grouping operations. The grouping operation uses the values of the grouping attributes only to group tuples that have the same value. However, the actual value of a grouping attribute is not important. Therefore, an attribute X that is used only in a grouping operation, like *Group_Select*, can be replaced with any other attribute Y when there is a bijective (1-1 and onto) mapping among the values of X and Y. Therefore, one can use the functional (and inclusion) dependencies in order to replace grouping attributes. In a similar manner functional and inclusion dependencies

Copyright © 2007, Idea Group Inc. Copying or distributing in print or electronic forms without written permission of Idea Group Inc. is prohibited.

allow the modification of join conditions, as explained in detail by Tsois (2005) and Tsois and Sellis (2003). By replacing grouping attributes and join conditions, the hierarchical pregrouping technique can group the fact table tuples very efficiently before the residual join operations, it can push join operations above the grouping operations and it can even remove completely some of the join operations.

The key idea used in the hierarchical pregrouping transformation is the following: if a hierarchical attribute h_k of a dimension D_i is used in the query evaluation plan just for grouping or just for an equi-join operation, then this attribute can be replaced by its encoded form which *exists within* (as a prefix) the corresponding h-surrogate. If hsk_i is the corresponding h-surrogate, the encoded value of h_k is denoted as $hsk_i{:}h_k$.

For example, for the *LOCATION* dimension in our running example of Figure 4, we can use the prefix part of the h-surrogate to group on the *Area* attribute, instead of using the actual *Area* attribute. This is because all tuples of *LOCATION* with the same values in the *Region* and *Area* attributes will have the same prefix in the h-surrogate value. Furthermore, since the foreign key *loc_hsk* exists in the fact table we can group the fact table tuples according to the *Area* attribute without having to join them with the *LOCATION* dimension table.

Lets see how this transformation affects the abstract plan shown in Figure 5(b) for our example query of Figure 4. The hierarchical pregrouping transformation modifies this initial plan by changing the grouping attributes and pushing both residual join operations after the *Group_Select* operation. This is possible because grouping is done on hierarchical attributes only (attributes *Area* and *Month*) that have a corresponding encoded form in the h-surrogates found in the fact table (*loc_hsk: area*, *date_hsk:month*). The residual join operations are modified so that each tuple in the output of the *Group_Select* operation is joined with only one tuple from the *DATE* dimension and one tuple from the *LOCATION* dimension. The resulting plan is shown in Figure 8(b).

By exploiting the above properties of the h-surrogates the hierarchical pregrouping transformation can achieve three different types of modifications to the proposed abstract processing plan for star queries (Figure 5(a)):

1. It can eliminate a residual join operation completely. This case happens when the removed dimension table was joined only to obtain access to hierarchical attributes that where then used only for the grouping operation.

2. It can split the grouping operation of the initial plan into two stages: in the first stage, a pregrouping of the fact table tuples is performed before invoking them in residual join operations. The grouping is performed using the h-surrogates contained in the fact table (the foreign keys). In the second stage, which is executed after performing the required residual joins, the tuples are once again grouped to obtain the required result. This second grouping operation

Copyright © 2007, Idea Group Inc. Copying or distributing in print or electronic forms without written permission of Idea Group Inc. is prohibited.

uses some of the attributes that where acquired with the residual join operations performed. This transformation reduces drastically the number of tuples involved in the residual join operations and therefore it reduces significantly the cost of the query evaluation plan.

3.   It can push join operations above the grouping operation by carefully modifying the grouping attributes and the join condition. The result of this transformation is similar to the previous one: it reduces the number of tuples involved in the affected residual join operations and therefore it improves the overall cost of the evaluation plan.

Note that in order to push a residual join operation above a grouping operation the join must be carefully modified. This can be done either by grouping the dimension table and modifying the join condition or by using special join algorithms that join each fact table tuple with only one tuple (the first matching tuple) from the dimension table. This is because all initial residual joins are equi-joins on the key attribute.

The details of the hierarchical pregrouping transformation and its definition as an algorithm appear in Karayannidis et al. (2002) and Tsois (2005). A theoretical analysis of the transformation, its generalization as well as a proof of correctness can be found in Tsois (2005) and Tsois and Sellis (2003).

Future Trends

Speculating about the future trends in data warehouse query processing in general, we believe that there are two main factors that will drive the processing requirements in the near future:

1.   Continuously increasing data volumes that one needs to analyze.

2.   Continuously increasing rates by which data for analysis are generated on the one hand and increasing need for up to date information on the other.

The first factor calls for extremely scalable storage organizations that exploit a plethora of successful techniques such as semantic based physical data clustering, precomputation of aggregates, and fast indexing. It also requires even more elaborate semantic-based optimization transformations that will reduce the amount of data processed at each step. The second calls for storage structures that are extremely adaptive to updates, and for processing techniques "borrowed" from the field of data stream processing.

Copyright © 2007, Idea Group Inc. Copying or distributing in print or electronic forms without written permission of Idea Group Inc. is prohibited.

Conclusion

In this chapter, we discussed the processing of ad hoc star queries over hierarchically clustered fact tables. We presented a complete abstract processing plan that covers all the necessary steps for answering such queries. This plan directly exploits the benefits of hierarchically clustered fact tables and opens the road for new optimization challenges. We showed how this abstract plan can be "materialized" for the case of a multidimensional storage structure that achieves hierarchical clustering, namely the *CUBE File*. Finally, we presented the hierarchical pregrouping transformation as a powerful optimization technique for this type of query processing.

Clearly, star query processing over hierarchically clustered fact tables is significantly different from other approaches. The most remarkable difference is that the fact table access is transformed to a multidimensional range query through the use of h-surrogates (i.e., surrogate keys with hierarchy semantics). Moreover, fact table physical organizations such as the CUBE File exploit h-surrogates to provide physical data clustering w.r.t the dimension hierarchies, resulting in a reduced I/O fact table access. Finally, the exploitation of the hierarchy semantics that h-surrogates convey can lead to efficient query optimization techniques such as the hierarchical pregrouping transformation.

The abstract processing plan can be easily incorporated in a DBMS provided that a hierarchical clustering-preserving fact table organization is supported. For example the methods introduced in this chapter have been fully implemented in the commercial relational DBMS TransBase HyperCube® (TransBase HyperCube®, 2005), which utilizes the UB-tree (Bayer, 1997) as a fact table primary organization.

References

Bayer, R. (1997). The universal B-tree for multi-dimensional indexing: General concepts. *Proceedings of the Worldwide Computing and Its Applications, International Conference,* Tsukuba, Japan (pp. 198-209).

Chan, C. Y., & Ioannidis, Y. (1998). Bitmap index design and evaluation. *Proceedings of the ACM SIGMOD International Conference on Management of Data,* Seattle, WA (pp. 355-366).

Chaudhuri, S., & Dayal, U. (1997). An overview of data warehousing and OLAP technology. *SIGMOD Record, 26*(1), 65-74.

Karayannidis, N. (2003). *Storage structures, query processing, and implementation of on-line analytical processing systems.* PhD doctoral thesis, *National Techni-*

Copyright © 2007, Idea Group Inc. Copying or distributing in print or electronic forms without written permission of Idea Group Inc. is prohibited.

cal University of Athens. (2003). Retrieved May 29, 2006, from http://www.dblab.ece.ntua.gr/~nikos/thesis/PhD_thesis_en.pdf

Karayannidis, N., Sellis, T., & Kouvaras, Y. (2004, March 14-18). CUBE file: A file structure for hierarchically clustered OLAP cubes. In *Proceedings of the 9ᵗʰ International Conference on Extending Database Technology* (pp. 621-638), Heraklion, Crete, Greece. EDBT.

Karayannidis, N., Tsois, A., Sellis, T. Pieringer, R., Markl, V. Ramsak, F., et al. (2002). Processing star-queries on hierarchically-clustered fact-tables. *Proceedings of the 28th International Conference on Very Large Data Bases (VLDB),* Hong Kong (pp. 730-741).

Markl, V., Ramsak, F., & Bayern, R. (1999). Improving OLAP performance by multidimensional hierarchical clustering. *Proceedings of the International Database Engineering and Applications Symposium,* Montreal, Canada (pp. 165-177).

O'Neil, P. E., & Graefe, G. (1995). Multi-table joins through bitmapped join indices. *SIGMOD Record, 24*(3), 8-11.

O'Neil, P. E., & Quass, D. (1997). Improved query performance with variant indexes. *Proceedings of the ACM SIGMOD International Conference on Management of Data,* Tucson, AZ (pp. 38-49).

Oracle® 10g. (2005). Documentation.

Pieringer, R., Elhardt, K. Ramsak, F., Markl, V., Fenk, R., Bayer, R., et al. (2003). Combining hierarchy encoding and pre-grouping: Intelligent grouping in star join processing. *Proceedings of the 19th International Conference on Data Engineering (ICDE),* Bangalore, India (pp. 329-340).

Roussopoulos, N. (1998). Materialized views and data warehouses. *SIGMOD Record, 27*(1), 21-26.

Sarawagi, S. (1997). Indexing OLAP data. *Data Engineering Bulletin, 20*(1), 36-43.

Sarawagi, S., & Stonebraker, M. (1994, February 14-18). Efficient organization of large multidimensional arrays. In *Proceedings of the 11ᵗʰ International Conference on Data Engineering,* Houston, Texas (pp. 326-336).

Srivastava, D., Dar, S., Jagadish, H. V., & Levy, A. Y. (1996). *Answering queries with aggregation using views.* Paper presented at the VLDB Conference 1996 (pp. 318-329).

Theodoratos, D., & Tsois, A. (2003, May). Processing OLAP queries in hierarchically clustered databases. *Data & Knowledge Engineering, 45*(2), 205-224.

TransBase HyperCube® Relational Database System. (2005). Retrieved May 29, 2006, from http://www.transaction.de

Copyright © 2007, Idea Group Inc. Copying or distributing in print or electronic forms without written permission of Idea Group Inc. is prohibited.

Tsois, A. (2005). *Optimization of on-line analytical processing systems: Conceptual data modeling and query processing techniques.* Unpublished doctoral dissertation, National Technical University Of Athens.

Tsois, A., & Sellis, T. (2003). *The generalized pre-grouping transformation: Aggregate-query optimization in the presence of dependencies* (Tech. Rep. No. TR-2003-4). Retrieved May 29, 2006, from http://www.dbnet.ece.ntua.gr/pubs/uploads/TR-2003-4.pdf

Weber, R., Schek, H.-J., & Blott, S. (1998). A quantitative analysis and performance study for similarity-search methods in high-dimensional spaces. VLDB, 194-205.

Wu, M. C., & Buchmann, A. P. (1998). Encoded bitmap indexing for data warehouses. *ICDE,* 220-230.

Yan, W. P., & Larson, P.-A. (1995). Eager aggregation and lazy aggregation. *VLDB,* 345-357.

Endnote

[1]   Naturally, the only way to favor more than one hierarchy (per dimension) in clustering is to maintain redundant copies of the cube (Sarawagi & Stonebraker, 1994), or to treat different hierarchy paths as separate dimensions (Markl, 1999). The latter results in an increase of the cube dimensionality, rendering clustering even more difficult (Weber, 1998).

Copyright © 2007, Idea Group Inc. Copying or distributing in print or electronic forms without written permission of Idea Group Inc. is prohibited.

Chapter VII

Bitmap Indices for Data Warehouses

Kurt Stockinger
Lawrence Berkeley National Laboratory, University of California, USA

Kesheng Wu
Lawrence Berkeley National Laboratory, University of California, USA

Abstract

In this chapter we discuss various bitmap index technologies for efficient query processing in data warehousing applications. We review the existing literature and organize the technology into three categories, namely bitmap encoding, compression, and binning. We introduce an efficient bitmap compression algorithm and examine the space and time complexity of the compressed bitmap index on large datasets from real applications. According to the conventional wisdom, bitmap indices are only efficient for low-cardinality attributes. However, we show that the compressed bitmap indices are also efficient for high-cardinality attributes. Timing results demonstrate that the bitmap indices significantly outperform the projection index, which is often considered to be the most efficient access method for multidimensional queries. Finally, we review the bitmap index technology currently supported by commonly used commercial database systems and discuss open issues for future research and development.

Copyright © 2007, Idea Group Inc. Copying or distributing in print or electronic forms without written permission of Idea Group Inc. is prohibited.

Introduction

Querying large datasets to locate some selected records is a common task in data warehousing applications. However, answering these queries efficiently is often difficult due to the complex nature of both the data and the queries. The most straightforward way of evaluating a query is to sequentially scan all data records to determine whether each record satisfies the specified conditions. A typical query condition is as follows: "Count the number of cars sold by producer P in the time interval T". This search procedure could usually be accelerated by indices, such as variations of B-Trees or kd-Trees (Comer, 1979; Gaede & Guenther, 1998). Generally, as the number of attributes in a dataset increases, the number of possible indexing combinations increases as well. To answer multidimensional queries efficiently, one faces a difficult choice. One possibility is to construct a separate index for each combination of attributes, which requires an impractical amount of space. Another possibility is to choose one of the multidimensional indices, which is only efficient for some of the queries. In the literature, this dilemma is often referred to as the curse of dimensionality (Berchtold, Boehm, & Kriegl, 1998; Keim & Hinneburg, 1999).

In this chapter we discuss an indexing technology that holds a great promise in breaking the curse of dimensionality for data warehousing applications, namely the bitmap index. A very noticeable character of a bitmap index is that its primary solution to a query is a bitmap. One way to break the curse of dimensionality is to build a bitmap index for each attribute of the dataset. To resolve a query involving conditions on multiple attributes, we first resolve the conditions on each attribute using the corresponding bitmap index, and obtain a solution for each condition as a bitmap. We then obtain the answer to the overall query by combining these bitmaps. Because the operations on bitmaps are well supported by computer hardware, the bitmaps can be combined easily and efficiently. Overall, we expect the total query response time to scale linearly in the number of attributes involved in the query, rather than exponentially in the number of dimensions (attributes) of the dataset, thus breaking the curse of dimensionality.

These statements omitted many technical details that we will elaborate in this chapter. In the next section we give a broad overview of the bitmap index and its relative strengths and weaknesses to other common indexing methods. We then describe the basic bitmap index and define the terms used in the discussions. We devote a large portion of this chapter to review the three orthogonal sets of strategies to improve the basic bitmap index. After reviewing these strategies, we give a more in-depth discussion on how the word-aligned-hybrid (WAH) bitmap compression technique reduces the bitmap index sizes. We will also present some timing results to demonstrate the effectiveness of the WAH compressed bitmap indices for two different application datasets. Our performance evaluation is deliberately based on datasets

Copyright © 2007, Idea Group Inc. Copying or distributing in print or electronic forms without written permission of Idea Group Inc. is prohibited.

with high-cardinality attributes, since for low-cardinality attributes the performance advantage of bitmap indices is well known. We conclude with a short review of bitmap indices available in commercial DBMS products and discuss how to make bitmap indices better supported in these commercial products.

Background

By far the most commonly used indexing method is the B-Tree (Comer, 1979). Almost every database product has a version thereof since it is very effective for online transaction processing (OLTP). This type of tree-based indexing method has nearly the same operational complexities for searching and updating the indices. This parity is important for OLTP because searching and updating are performed with nearly the same frequencies. However, for most data warehousing applications such as online analytical processing (OLAP), the searching operations are typically performed with a much higher frequency than that of updating operations (Chaudhuri & Dayal, 1997; Chaudhuri, Dayal, & Ganti, 2001). This suggests that the indexing methods for OLAP must put more emphasis on searching than on updating. Among the indexing methods known in the literature, the bitmap index has the best balance between searching and updating for OLAP operations.

Frequently, in OLAP operations each query involves a number of attributes. Furthermore, each new query often involves a different set of attributes than the previous one. Using a typical multidimensional indexing method, a separate index is required for nearly every combination of attributes (Gaede & Guenther, 1998). It is easy to see that the number of indices grows exponentially with the number of attributes in a dataset. In the literature this is sometimes called the curse of dimensionality (Berchtold et al., 1998; Keim & Hinneburg, 1999). For datasets with a moderate number of dimensions, a common way to cure this problem is to use one of the multidimensional indexing methods, such as R-Trees or kd-trees. These approaches have two notable shortcomings. Firstly, they are effective only for datasets with a modest number of dimensions, say, < 15. Secondly, they are only efficient for queries involving all indexed attributes. However, in many applications only some of the attributes are used in the queries. In these cases, the conventional indexing methods are often not efficient. For ad hoc range queries, most of the known indexing methods do not perform better than the projection index (O'Neil & Quass, 1997), which can be viewed as one way to organize the base. The bitmap index, on the other hand, has excellent performance characteristics on these queries. As shown with both theoretical analyses and timing measurements, a compressed bitmap index can be very efficient in answering one-dimensional range queries (Stockinger, Wu, & Shoshani, 2002; Wu, Otoo, & Shoshani, 2004, 2006). Since answers to one-dimensional range queries can be efficiently combined to answer arbitrary

Copyright © 2007, Idea Group Inc. Copying or distributing in print or electronic forms without written permission of Idea Group Inc. is prohibited.

multidimensional range queries, compressed bitmap indices are efficient for any range query. In terms of computational complexity, one type of compressed bitmap index was shown to be theoretically optimal for one-dimensional range queries. The reason for the theoretically proven optimality is that the query response time is a linear function of the number of hits, that is, the size of the result set. There are a number of indexing methods, including B*-tree and B+-tree (Comer, 1979), that are theoretically optimal for one-dimensional range queries, but most of them cannot be used to efficiently answer arbitrary multidimensional range queries.

The bitmap index in its various forms was used a long time before relational database systems or data warehousing systems were developed. Earlier on, the bitmap index was regarded as a special form of inverted files (Knuth, 1998). The bit-transposed file (Wong, Liu, Olken, Rotem, & Wong, 1985) is very close to the bitmap index currently in use. The name bitmap index was popularized by O'Neil and colleagues (O'Neil, 1987; O'Neil & Quass, 1997). Following the example set in the description of Model 204, the first commercial implementation of bitmap indices (O'Neil, 1987), many researchers describe bitmap indices as a variation of the B-tree index. To respect its earlier incarnation as inverted files, we regard a bitmap index as a data structure consisting of keys and bitmaps. Moreover, we regard the B-tree as a way to layout the keys and bitmaps in files. Since most commercial implementations of bitmap indices come after the product already contains an implementation of a B-tree, it is only natural for those products to take advantage of the existing B-tree software. For new developments and experimental or research codes, there is no need to couple a bitmap index with a B-tree. For example, in a research program that implements many of the bitmap indexing methods discussed later in this chapter (FastBit, 2005), the keys and the bitmaps are organized as simple arrays in a binary file. This arrangement was found to be more efficient than implementing bitmap indices in B-trees or as layers on top of a DBMS (Stockinger et al., 2002; Wu et al., 2002).

The basic bitmap index uses each distinct value of the indexed attribute as a key, and generates one bitmap containing as many bits as the number of records in the dataset for each key (O'Neil, 1987). Let the attribute cardinality be the number of distinct values present in a dataset. The size of a basic bitmap index is relatively small for low-cardinality attributes, such as "gender," "types of cars sold per month," or "airplane models produced by Airbus and Boeing." However, for high-cardinality attributes such as "temperature values in a supernova explosion," the index sizes may be too large to be of any practical use. In the literature, there are three basic strategies to reduce the sizes of bitmap indices: (1) using more complex bitmap encoding methods to reduce the number of bitmaps or improve query efficiency, (2) compressing each individual bitmap, and (3) using binning or other mapping strategies to reduce the number of keys. In the remaining discussions, we refer to these three strategies as encoding, compression, and binning, for short.

Copyright © 2007, Idea Group Inc. Copying or distributing in print or electronic forms without written permission of Idea Group Inc. is prohibited.

Figure 1. Simple bitmap index with six bitmaps to represent six distinct attribute values

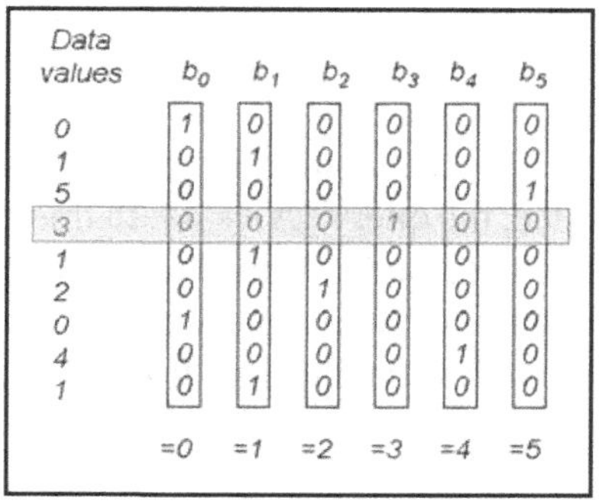

Bitmap Index Design

Basic Bitmap Index

Bitmap indices are one of the most efficient indexing methods available for speeding up multidimensional range queries for read-only or read-mostly data (O'Neil, 1987; Rotem, Stockinger & Wu, 2005b; Wu et al., 2006). The queries are evaluated with bitwise logical operations that are well supported by computer hardware. For an attribute with c distinct values, the basic bitmap index generates c bitmaps with N bits each, where N is the number of records (rows) in the dataset. Each bit in a bitmap is set to "1" if the attribute in the record is of a specific value; otherwise the bit is set to "0". Figure 1 shows a simple bitmap index with six bitmaps. Each bitmap represents a distinct attribute value. For instance, the attribute value 3 is highlighted to demonstrate the encoding. In this case, bitmap 3 is set to "1", all other bits on the same horizontal position are set to "0".

Encoding

The basic bitmap index introduced is also called equality-encoded bitmap index since each bitmap indicates whether or not an attribute value equals to the key. This strategy is the most efficient for equality queries such as "temperature = 100." Chan and Ioannidis (1998, 1999) developed two other encoding strategies that are called range encoding and interval encoding. These bitmap indices are optimized for one-sided and two-sided range queries, respectively. An example of a one-sided range query is "pressure < 56.7". A two-sided range query, for instance, is "35.8 < pressure < 56.7".

Copyright © 2007, Idea Group Inc. Copying or distributing in print or electronic forms without written permission of Idea Group Inc. is prohibited.

A comparison of an equality-encoded and range-encoded bitmap index is given in Figure 2 (based on Chan & Ioannidis, 1999). Let us look at the encoding of value 2, which is highlighted in the figure. For equality encoding, the third bitmap is set to "1" (E2), whereas all other bits on the same horizontal line are set to "0". For the range-encoded bitmap index, all bits between bitmap R2 and R8 are set to "1", the remaining bits are set to "0". This encoding is very efficient for evaluating range queries. Consider, for instance, the query "A <= 4". In this case, at most one bitmap, namely bitmap R4, has to be accessed (scanned) for processing the query. All bits that are set to "1" in this bitmap fulfill the query constraint. On the other hand, for the equality-encoded bitmap index, the bitmaps E0 to E4 have to be ORed together (via the Boolean operator OR). This means that 5 bitmaps have to be accessed, as opposed to only 1 bitmap for the case of range encoding. In short, range encoding requires at most one bitmap scan for evaluating range queries, whereas equality encoding requires in the worst case $c/2$ bitmap scans, where c corresponds to the number of bitmaps. Since one bitmap in range encoding contains only "1"s, this bitmap is usually not stored. Therefore, there are only $c-1$ bitmaps in a range-encoded index.

Assuming each attribute value fits in a 32-bit machine word, the basic bitmap index for an attribute with cardinality 32 takes as much space as the base data (known as user data or original data). Since a B-tree index for a 32-bit attribute is often observed to use three or four times the space as the base data, many users consider only attributes with cardinalities less than 100 to be suitable for using bitmap indices. Clearly, controlling the size of the bitmap indices is crucial to make bitmap indices practically useful for higher cardinality attributes. The interval-encoding scheme (Chan & Ioannidis, 1999) reduces the number of bitmaps only by a factor 2. Thus, other techniques are needed to make bitmap indices practical for high cardinality attributes.

Figure 2. Equality-encoded bitmap index (b) compared with range-encoded bitmap index (c). The leftmost column shows the row ids (RID) for the data values represented by the projection index shown in (a).

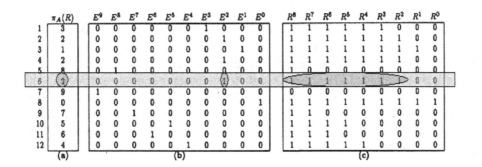

Copyright © 2007, Idea Group Inc. Copying or distributing in print or electronic forms without written permission of Idea Group Inc. is prohibited.

The encoding method that produces the least number of bitmaps is binary encoding introduced by Wong et al. (1985). Binary encoding was later used by various authors (O'Neil & Quass, 1997; Wu & Buchmann, 1998) in the context of bitmap indices. This encoding method uses only   rather than c/2 bitmaps, where c is the attribute cardinality. For an integer attribute in the range of 0 and c-1, each bitmap in the bitmap index is a concatenation of one of the   binary digits for every record. For an attribute with c=1000, it only needs 10 bitmaps. The advantage of this encoding is that it requires much fewer bitmaps than interval encoding. However, to answer a range query, using interval encoding one has to access only two bitmaps whereas using binary encoding one usually has to access all bitmaps.

A number of authors have proposed strategies to find the balance between the space and time requirements (Chan & Ioannidis, 1999; Wong et al., 1985). A method proposed by Chan and Ioannidis (1999) called multicomponent encoding can be thought of as a generalization of binary encoding. In the binary encoding, each bitmap represents a binary digit of the attribute values; the multicomponent encoding breaks the values in a more general way, where each component could have a different size. Consider an integer attribute with values ranging from 0 to c-1. Let b1 and b2 be the sizes of two components c1 and c2, where b1*b2>=c. Any value v can be expressed as v = c1*b2+c2, where c1 = v / b2 and c2 = v % b2, where '/' denotes the integer division and '%' denotes the modulus operation. One can use a simple bitmap encoding method to encode the values of c1 and c2 separately. Next, we give a more specific example to illustrate the multicomponent encoding.

Figure 3 illustrates a 2-component encoded bitmap index for an attribute with cardinality c = 1000. In our example, the two components have base sizes of b1 = 25 and b2 = 40. Assume the attribute values are in the domain of [0; 999]. An attribute value v is decomposed into two components with c1 = v / 40 and c2 = v % 40. The component c1 can be treated as an integer attribute in the range of 0 and 24; the component c2 can be viewed as an integer attribute in the range of 0 and 39. Two bitmap indices can be built, one for each component, for example, c1 with the equality encoding and c2 with range encoding. If range encoding is used for both components, it uses 24 bitmaps for Component 1, and 39 bitmaps for Component 2. In this case, the 2-component encoding uses 63 bitmaps, which is more than the 10 bitmaps used by binary encoding. To answer the same query "v < 105" using the 2-component index, the query is effectively translated to "c1<2 OR (c1=2 AND

Figure 3. An illustration of a 2-component bitmap index

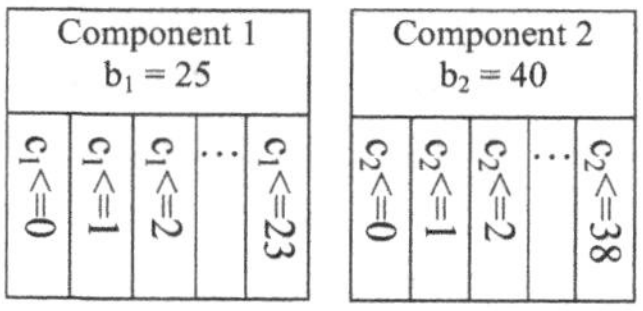

Component 1 $b_1 = 25$				Component 2 $b_2 = 40$			
$c_1 <= 0$	$c_1 <= 1$	$c_1 <= 2$	$\cdots$ $c_1 <= 23$	$c_2 <= 0$	$c_2 <= 1$	$c_2 <= 2$	$\cdots$ $c_2 <= 38$

Copyright © 2007, Idea Group Inc. Copying or distributing in print or electronic forms without written permission of Idea Group Inc. is prohibited.

c2<25)." Evaluating this expression requires three bitmaps representing "c1<=1," "c1<=2," and "c2<=24." In contrast, using the binary encoded bitmap index to evaluate the same query, all 10 bitmaps are needed.

Using more components can reduce the number of bitmaps and therefore reduces the total index size. However, using more components will also increase the number of bitmaps accessed in order to answer a query, hence increasing the query response time. Clearly, there is a trade-off between the index size and the query response time. Without considering compression, Chan and Ioannidis (1999) have analyzed this space-time trade-off. They suggested that the inflection point of the trade-off curve is at two components. They further suggested that the two components should have nearly the same base sizes to reduce the index size.

Binning

The simplest form of bitmap indices works well for low-cardinality attributes, such as "gender," "types of cars sold per month," or "airplane models produced by Airbus and Boeing." However, for high-cardinality attributes such as "distinct temperature values in a supernova explosion," simple bitmap indices are impractical due to large storage and computational complexities. We have just discussed how different encoding methods could reduce the index size and improve query response time. Next, we describe a strategy called binning to reduce the number of bitmaps. Since the encoding methods described before only take certain integer values as input, we may also view binning as a way to produce these integer values (bin numbers) for the encoding strategies.

The basic idea of binning is to build a bitmap for a bin rather than each distinct attribute value. This strategy disassociates the number of bitmaps from the attribute cardinality and allows one to build a bitmap index of a prescribed size, no matter how large the attribute cardinality is. A clear advantage of this approach is that it allows one to control the index size. However, it also introduces some uncertainty in the answers if one only uses the index. To generate precise answers, one may need to examine the original data records (candidates) to verify that the user-specified conditions are satisfied. The process of reading the base data to verify the query conditions is called candidate check (Rotem et al., 2005b; Stockinger, Wu, & Shoshani, 2004).

A small example of an equality-encoded bitmap index with binning is given in Figure 4. In this example we assume that an attribute A has values between 0 and 100. The values of the attribute A are given in the second leftmost column. The range of possible values of A is partitioned into five bins [0, 20), [20, 40).... A "1-bit" indicates that the attribute value falls into a specific bin. On the contrary, a "0-bit" indicates that the attribute value does not fall into the specific bin. Take the example of evaluating the query "Count the number of rows where 37 <= A < 63."

Copyright © 2007, Idea Group Inc. Copying or distributing in print or electronic forms without written permission of Idea Group Inc. is prohibited.

Figure 4. Range query "37 <= A < 63" on a bitmap index with binning

The correct result should be 2 (rows 5 and 7). We see that the range in the query overlaps with bins 1, 2, and 3. We know for sure that all rows that fall into bin 2 definitely qualify (i.e., they are hits). On the other hand, rows that fall into bins 1 and 3 possibly qualify and need further verification. In this case, we call bins 1 and 3 edge bins. The rows (records) that fall into edge bins are candidates and need to be checked against the query constraint.

In our example, there are four candidates, namely rows 1 and 3 from bin 1, and rows 5 and 6 from bin 3. The candidate check process needs to read these four rows from disk and examine their values to see whether or not they satisfy the user-specified conditions. On a large dataset, a candidate check may need to read many pages and may dominate the overall query response time (Rotem et al., 2005b).

There are a number of strategies to minimize the time required for the candidate check (Koudas, 2000; Rotem et al., 2005a, 2005b; Stockinger et al., 2004). Koudas (2000) considered the problem of finding the optimal binning for a given set of equality queries. Rotem et al. (2005a, 2005b) considered the problem of finding the optimal binning for range queries. Their approaches are based on dynamic programming. Since the time required by the dynamic programming grows quadratic with the problem size, these approaches are only efficient for attributes with relatively small attribute cardinalities (Koudas, 2000) or with relatively small sets of known queries (Stockinger et al., 2004). Stockinger et al. (2004) considered the problem of optimizing the order of evaluating multidimensional range queries. The key idea is to use more operations on bitmaps to reduce the number of candidates checked. This approach usually reduces the total query response time. Further improvements to this approach are to consider the attribute distribution and other factors that influence the actual time required for the candidate check.

Copyright © 2007, Idea Group Inc. Copying or distributing in print or electronic forms without written permission of Idea Group Inc. is prohibited.

To minimize number of disk page accesses during the candidate check, it is necessary to cluster the attribute values. A commonly used clustering (data layout) technique is called the vertical partition or otherwise known as projection index. In general, the vertical data layout is more efficient for searching, while the horizontal organization (commonly used in DBMS) is more efficient for updating. To make the candidate check more efficient, we recommend the vertical data organization.

Compression

Compression is the third strategy to reduce the size of bitmap indices. Since each bitmap of the bitmap index may be used separately from others, compression is typically applied on each individual bitmap. Compression is a well-researched topic and efficient compression software packages are widely available. Even though these general-purpose compression methods are effective in reducing the size of bitmaps, query-processing operations on compressed bitmaps are often slower than on uncompressed bitmaps (Johnson, 1999). This motivated a number of researchers to improve the efficiency of compressed bitmap indices. Two of the most notable compression methods are byte-aligned bitmap code (BBC) (Antoshenkov, 1994; Antoshenkov & Ziauddin, 1996) and word-aligned hybrid (WAH) code (Wu et al., 2004, 2006). Bitmaps compressed with BBC are slightly larger in size than those compressed with the best available general-purpose compression methods. However, operations on BBC compressed bitmaps are usually faster (Johnson, 1999). Clearly, there is a worthwhile space-time trade-off. The WAH compression takes this space-time trade-off one step further. More specifically, WAH compressed bitmaps are larger than BBC compressed ones, but operations on WAH compressed bitmaps are much faster than on BBC compressed ones. Therefore, WAH compressed bitmap indices can answer queries much faster as demonstrated in a number of different experiments (Stockinger et al., 2002; Wu et al., 2006). In the next section we provide a detailed description of the WAH compression. For more information on BBC, we refer the reader to Antoshenkov (1994) and Antoshenkov & Ziauddin (1996).

WAH Bitmap Compression

The WAH bitmap compression is based on run-length encoding, where consecutive identical bits are represented with their bit value (0 or 1) and a count (length of the run). In WAH each such run consists of a fill and a tail. A fill is a set of consecutive identical bits that is represented as a count plus their bit value. A tail is a set of mixed 0s and 1s that is represented literally without compression. One key idea of

Copyright © 2007, Idea Group Inc. Copying or distributing in print or electronic forms without written permission of Idea Group Inc. is prohibited.

Figure 5. An example of WAH encoding of a sequence of 5456 bits on a 32-bit machine

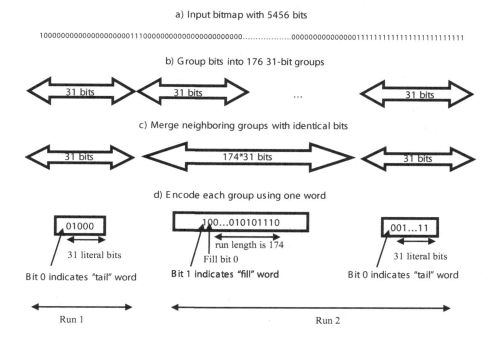

a) Input bitmap with 5456 bits

1000000000000000000001110000000000000000000000000.................0000000000000001111111111111111111111111

b) Group bits into 176 31-bit groups

c) Merge neighboring groups with identical bits

d) Encode each group using one word

WAH is to define the fills and tails so that they can be stored in words – the smallest operational unit of modern computer hardware.

The WAH compression is illustrated in Figure 5. Assuming that a machine word is 32 bits long, the example shows how a sequence of 5456 bits (see Figure 5(a)) is broken into two runs and encoded as three words. Conceptually, the bit sequence is first broken into groups of 31 bits each (see Figure 5(b)). Next, the neighboring groups with identical bits are merged (Figure 5(c)). Finally, these three groups are encoded as 32-bit machine words (Figure 5(d)). The first run contains a fill of length 0 and a tail. There is no fill word but only a literal word representing the 31 tail bits for this run. Since a literal word has 32 bits, we use the first bit to indicate it is a literal word, and the rest to store the 31 tail bits. The second run contains a fill of length 174 (and thus represents 174 groups of 31 bits each) plus a tail. This run requires a fill word and a tail word. As illustrated, the first bit of a fill word indicates that it is a fill word, the second bit stores the bit value of the fill, which is 0 in this example. The remaining 30 bits store the binary version of the fill length, which is 10101110 (174) in this example.

Copyright © 2007, Idea Group Inc. Copying or distributing in print or electronic forms without written permission of Idea Group Inc. is prohibited.

In theoretical analysis, the query response time on one-dimensional range queries using WAH compressed indices was shown to grow linearly in the number of hits. This time complexity is optimal for any searching algorithm since one has to return at least the hits, which takes $\Omega(h)$ time (where h is the number of hits). A variety of well-known indexing methods such as B+-trees and B*-trees have the same optimal scaling property. However, compressed bitmap indices have the unique advantage that they can be easily combined to answer multidimensional ad hoc range queries, while B+-trees or B*-trees cannot be combined nearly as efficiently.

In general, the query response time can be broken into I/O time and CPU time. Since WAH compressed bitmaps are larger in size than BBC compressed bitmaps, we would expect that WAH require more I/O time to read compressed bitmaps. For many database operations, the CPU time is negligible compared with the I/O time. It turns out that this is not the case when answering queries with compressed bitmap indices. In a performance experiment Stockinger et al. (2002) compared WAH compressed indices with two independent implementations of BBC compressed indices, one based on Johnson's (1999) code and the other by Wu et al. (2002). The results showed that the total query response time was smaller with WAH compressed bitmap indices than with BBC compressed bitmaps, even on a relatively slow disk system that can only sustain 5 MB/s for reading files from disk. On faster disk systems, the performance advantage of WAH compressed bitmap indices is even more pronounced. Using WAH could be 10 times faster than using BBC.

Bitmap Index Tuning

Unless one uses binary encoding, it is important to compress the bitmap indices. To build an efficient compressed bitmap index, the three main parameters to consider are: (1) encoding, (2) number of bins, and (3) binning strategy. In the following we present a rule-of-thumb for choosing these three parameters.

The optimal bitmap encoding technique depends on the kind of queries that are evaluated. Chan and Ioannidis (1999) showed that range encoding is the best bitmap encoding technique for range-queries. However, range encoding might not always be practical for high-cardinality attributes or for a large number of bins. As we will show in the next section, range-encoded bitmap indices do not compress as well as equality-encoded bitmap indices.

The general rule for choosing the number of bins is as follows: The more bins, the less work during the candidate check. The reason is fairly straightforward. In general, as the number of bins increases, the number of candidates per bin decreases. Let us consider the following example. Assume the base data follows a uniform random distribution. With a typical page size of 8KB, using the projection index,

Copyright © 2007, Idea Group Inc. Copying or distributing in print or electronic forms without written permission of Idea Group Inc. is prohibited.

a page could hold 2048 4-byte words. If one in 1000 words is accessed during the candidate check, it is likely that every page containing the attribute values would be touched (Stockinger et al., 2004). We, thus, suggest using 1000 bins or more.

For equality encoding there is an additional trade-off, namely using more bins may also increase the cost of the index scan. For range encoding the cost of the index scan is not significantly affected by the number of bins because one needs to access no more than two bitmaps to evaluate a range query (Chan & Ioannidis, 1999). Without compression, one would clearly favor range encoding. However, with compression, the relative strength is not as obvious. With a WAH compressed equality-encoded index, it was shown that the cost of the index scan is proportional to the number of hits, independent of the number of bitmaps involved (Wu et al., 2006). Because the equality-encoded indices are much easier to compress, this could make the WAH compressed equality-encoded index a preferred choice.

Finally, the binning strategy has an impact on the candidate check. The simplest kind of binning, called equi-width binning, partitions the domain of the indexed attribute into bins of equal size. As a result, each bin might have a different number of entries. Equi-depth binning, on the other hand, distributes the number of entries equally among the bins. This technique has a better worst-case behavior than equi-width binning but is more costly to build because one typically has to scan the data first to generate the exact histogram before starting with the binning.

One approach to reduce the cost of building a set of equi-depth bins is to use a sampled histogram instead of the exact histogram. Another approach is to first build an equi-width binned index with more bins than desired, and then combine the neighboring bins to form approximate equi-depth bins. However, the second approach might not produce well-balanced bins. For example, the attribute mass fraction from a supernova simulation is expected to be in the range of 0 and 1. If, for some reason, the mass fraction is not known, scientists typically enter the value -999 to represent a bad or missing value. In this example, equi-width binning would produce bins starting from -999. This results in too many empty bins and thus cannot be combined to produce well-balanced equi-depth bins. In contrast, the approach of sampled histograms is generally more reliable in detecting this type of unusual outliers and typically produces well-balanced bins.

Space Complexity: Sizes of Compressed Bitmap Indices

The space complexity of uncompressed bitmap indices was studied in Chan and Ioannidis (1998, 1999). In this section, we analyze the size of compressed bitmap indices. Our discussion mainly focuses on the WAH compression method since BBC

Copyright © 2007, Idea Group Inc. Copying or distributing in print or electronic forms without written permission of Idea Group Inc. is prohibited.

Figure 6. Size of base data compared with bitmap indices

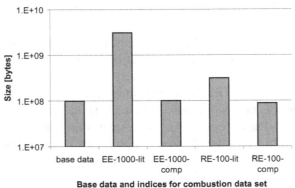

Base data and indices for combustion data set

Note: EE = equality encoding; RE = range encoding; lit = literal (no compression); comp = with compression

compression was extensively studied in Johnson (1999). We give an upper bound of the worst-case size and provide an experimental study of compressed bitmap indices for various application datasets.

Index Size: Worst-Case Behavior

In the previous section we defined a WAH run to be a fill followed by a tail. To make the discussion more concrete, let us assume that a machine word is 32 bits. In this case, a WAH tail contains exactly 31 bits from the input bitmap and a WAH fill contains a multiple of 31 bits that are all the same (either 0 or 1). Because the bitmap index is known to be efficient for low cardinality attributes, we further restrict our discussion to high cardinality attributes only, say, $c > 100$. In an equality-encoded bitmap index, there are c keys (distinct values of the attribute) and thus c bitmaps. We do not know exactly how many bits are set to 1 in each individual bitmap. However, we know that the total number of bits that are 1 is exactly N (the number of rows in the dataset). In the worst case, there are $(N+c)$ WAH runs in the bitmaps, where N refers to maximum number of tail words (each containing a single bit set to 1) and c refers to the maximum number of runs at the end of each bitmap that are not terminated with a tail word. Each WAH run is encoded by two machine words. Therefore, we need a total of $2(N+c)$ words to represent the bitmaps. Assuming each key is encoded by one word along with one additional word to associate the key with the bitmap, the total index size is $2N+4c$ words. In most cases, the attribute cardinality c is much smaller than N. In these cases, the WAH compressed equality-encoded bitmap index size is at worst 2N words. With binning, one may

Copyright © 2007, Idea Group Inc. Copying or distributing in print or electronic forms without written permission of Idea Group Inc. is prohibited.

use many thousands of bins and the maximum index size would still be no more than 2N. Since a number of commercial implementations of B-trees are observed to use 3N to 4N words, the maximum size of compressed bitmap indices is relatively modest. As we will show for real application data, the WAH compressed index is often much smaller than the predicted worst-case sizes.

For WAH compression, in the worst case, about 90% of the bitmaps in a range-encoded bitmap index will not be compressible (Wu et al., 2006). Unless one can tolerate very large indices or one knows beforehand that compression would be effective, we generally recommend using no more than 100 bins for range-encode bitmap indices. This guarantees that the size of the bitmap index is at worst the size of a B-tree.

Index Size for Real Application Datasets

We will now analyze experimentally the size of compressed bitmap indices for various application datasets.

Combustion Dataset

The combustion dataset is from a simulation of the auto-ignition of turbulent Hydrogen-air mixture from the TeraScale High-Fidelity Simulation of Turbulent Combustion with Detailed Chemistry (Tera Scale Combustion, 2005). The dataset consists of 24 million records with 16 attributes each. For this dataset we built equality-encoded and range-encoded bitmap indices with various numbers of equi-depth bins. Figure 6 shows the average size of the compressed bitmap indices per attribute. We can see that equality-encoded bitmap indices with 1000 bins and the range-encoded bitmap indices with 100 bins have about the same size as the base data. Note that the size of an uncompressed bitmap index with 100 bins is about 3 times as large as the base data. With 1000 bins, the size of the uncompressed bitmap index is about 30 times larger. This shows that the WAH compression algorithm works well on this dataset.

High-Energy Physics Dataset

Our second dataset is from a high-energy physics experiment at the Stanford Linear Accelerator Center. It consists of 7.6 million records with 10 attributes. Figure 7 shows the size of the compressed bitmap indices. We notice that the size of the range-encoded bitmap index with 100 bins is about twice as large as the base data. The equality-encoded bitmap index with 1000 bins is about 30% smaller than the

Copyright © 2007, Idea Group Inc. Copying or distributing in print or electronic forms without written permission of Idea Group Inc. is prohibited.

Figure 7. Size of base data compared with bitmap indices

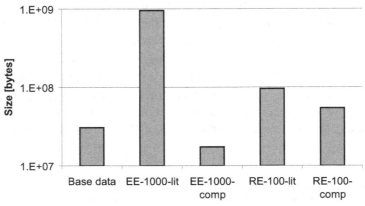

Base data and indices for high-energy physics data set

Note: For an explanation of the legend, see Figure 6.

base data. Typically, the records from these high-energy physics experiments are not correlated with each other. Thus, it is generally hard for the run-length encoding to be effective. This is why the index sizes for range encoding are relatively large compared with the previous datasets. However, equality encoding compresses very well for this physics dataset.

Overall, we see that the actual bitmap index sizes are considerably smaller than the base data sizes and less than the sizes of typical commercial implementations of B-trees (that are often three to four times the size of the base data).

Time Complexity: Query Response Time

In this section we are focusing on the two basic encoding methods, namely equality encoding and range encoding. We have chosen these two encoding methods for the following reason. Equality encoding showed to be the most space efficient method. Range encoding, on the other hand, is the most time efficient method for one-sided range queries (Chan & Ioannidis, 1998) that we use in our experiments.

Analyses have shown that the worst case query response time to answer a one-dimensional range query using a WAH compressed basic bitmap index (equality-encoded without binning) is a linear function of the number hits (Wu et al., 2006). The analyses also indicate that the worst-case behavior is for attributes following

Copyright © 2007, Idea Group Inc. Copying or distributing in print or electronic forms without written permission of Idea Group Inc. is prohibited.

Figure 8. Time (in seconds) to answer a one-dimensional range query using a WAH compressed bitmap index is a linear function of the number of hits

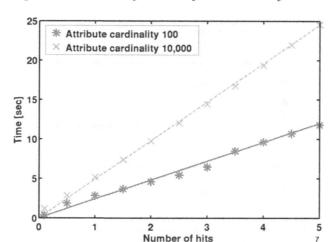

a uniform random distribution. Figure 8 plots the query response time against the number of hits for a set of queries on two attributes with different attribute cardinalities. The data values for the two attributes are randomly distributed in the range of [0;100] and [0; 10,000] respectively. We see that in both cases the timing measurements follow straight lines, which is theoretically optimal.

In the remainder of this section we present more timing measurements to compare the query response time of equality-encoded and range-encoded bitmap indices. All indices are compressed with WAH compression. Since the results for the two datasets are similar, we only report on the measurements based on the larger and thus more challenging combustion dataset. We use the projection index as the base line for all the comparisons. We note that this is a good base line since the projection index is known for outperforming many multidimensional indices.

In the next set of experiments we measure the query size with the query box size. A query box is a hypercube formed by the boundaries of the range conditions in the attribute domains. We measure the query box size as the fraction of the query box volume to the total volume of the attribute domains. If all attributes have uniform distribution, then a query box size of 0.01 indicates that the query would select 1% of the dataset. We say a query is more selective if the query box size is smaller.

Figure 9 shows the response time (in seconds) for 2- and 10-dimensional queries with various query box sizes. For all experiments the query box size was chosen randomly and covers the whole domain range. In general, we see that the query processing time for the bitmap indices decreases as the queries become more selective. On the

Copyright © 2007, Idea Group Inc. Copying or distributing in print or electronic forms without written permission of Idea Group Inc. is prohibited.

Figure 9. Multidimensional queries with various bitmap indices. EE-1000: equality encoding with 1000 bins, RE-100: range encoding with 100 bins

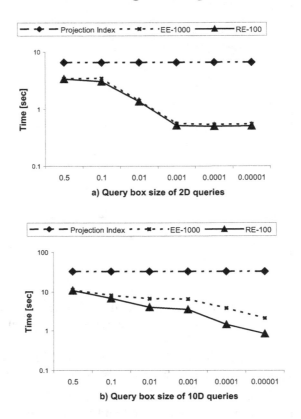

other hand, the query processing time for the projection index stays constant as the selectivity changes. For all query dimensions the range-encoded bitmap index with 100 bins shows the best performance characteristics, however, sometimes at the cost of a larger index. In case the storage space is a limiting factor, it is better to choose equality-encoded bitmap indices with 1000 bins (see Figure 7). As we can see in Figure 9, the performance of equality-encoded bitmap indices is not significantly different from the performance of range-encoded bitmap indices.

Key Features in Commercial Products

Due to the considerable amount of work involved in producing and maintaining a robust commercial software system, only the most efficient and proven indexing

Copyright © 2007, Idea Group Inc. Copying or distributing in print or electronic forms without written permission of Idea Group Inc. is prohibited.

technologies make their way into a commercial DBMS. In this section, we give a short review of the key bitmap indexing technologies currently used by various well-known commercial products. This is not meant to be an exhaustive survey. Our main interest is to see what kind of bitmap indexing technology is missing and which technology may likely make an impact on commercial products.

The first commercial product to use the name bitmap index is Model 204. O'Neil (1987) has published a description of the indexing method. Model 204 implements the basic bitmap index. It has no binning or compression. Currently, Model 204 is marketed by Computer Corporation of America. Oracle has a version of compressed bitmap indices in its flagship product since version 7.3. They implemented a proprietary compression method. Based on the observed performance characteristics, it appears to use equality encoding without binning.

Sybase IQ implements the bit-sliced index (O'Neil & Quass, 1997). Using the terminology defined in the second and third sections, Sybase IQ supports unbinned, binary encoded, uncompressed bitmap indices. In addition, it also has the basic bitmap index for low-cardinality attributes. IBM DB2 implements a variation of the binary encoded bitmap index called Encode Vector Index. IBM Informix products also contain some versions of bitmap indices for queries involving one or more tables. These indices are specifically designed to speed up join-operations and are commonly referred to as join indices (O'Neil & Quass, 1997). InterSystems Corp's Cache also has bitmap index support since version 5.0.

Even though we do not have technical details on most of these commercial products, it is generally clear that they tend to use either the basic bitmap index or the bit-sliced index. Strategies like binning and multicomponent encoding are not used partly because there is no robust strategy to select parameters like the number of bins or the number of components that suits different applications.

Summary and Open Problems

In this chapter, we reviewed a number of recent developments in the area of bitmap indexing technology. We organized much of the research work under the three orthogonal categories of encoding, compression, and binning. We also provided a brief overview of commercial bitmap index implementations by major vendors.

Most of the indexing methods reviewed were designed to efficiently answer multidimensional range queries. However, they are also efficient for other types of queries, such as joins on foreign keys and computations of aggregates (O'Neil & Quass, 1997).

Despite the success of bitmap indices, there are a number of important questions that remain to be addressed. For example, is there an efficient bitmap index for similar-

Copyright © 2007, Idea Group Inc. Copying or distributing in print or electronic forms without written permission of Idea Group Inc. is prohibited.

ity queries? How can we automatically select the best combination of encoding, compression and binning techniques? How can we use bitmap indices to answer more general join queries?

Research work on bitmap indices so far has concentrated on answering queries efficiently, but has often neglected the issue of updating the indices. Clearly, there is a need to update the indices as new records are added. Efficient solutions to this issue could be the key to gain a wider adaptation of bitmap indices in commercial applications.

References

Antoshenkov, G. (1994). *Byte-aligned bitmap compression* (Tech. Rep., U.S. Patent number 5,363,098). Oracle Corp.

Antoshenkov, G., & Ziauddin, M. (1996). Query processing and optimization in ORACLE RDB. *VLDB Journal, 5*, 229-237.

Berchtold, S., Boehm, C., & Kriegl, H.-P. (1998). The pyramid-technique: Towards breaking the curse of dimensionality. *SIGMOD Record, 27*(2), 142-153.

Chan, C.-Y., & Ioannidis, Y. E. (1998, June). Bitmap index design and evaluation. *International Conference on Management of Data, SIGMOD*, Seattle, Washington (pp. 355-366). ACM Press.

Chan, C.-Y., & Ioannidis, Y. E. (1999, June). An efficient bitmap encoding scheme for selection queries. *International Conference on Management of Data, SIGMOD*, Philadelphia (pp. 215-226). ACM Press.

Chaudhuri, S., & Dayal, U. (1997). An overview of data warehousing and OLAP technology. *ACM SIGMOD Record, 26*(1), 65-74.

Chaudhuri, S., Dayal, U., & Ganti, V. (2001). Database technology for decision support systems. *Computer, 34*(12), 48-55.

Comer, D. (1979). The ubiquitous B-tree. *Computing Surveys, 11*(2), 121-137.

FastBit. (2005). Retrieved May 31, 2006, from http://sdm.lbl.gov/fastbit

Gaede, V., & Guenther, O. (1998). Multidimensional access methods. *ACM Computing Surveys, 30*(2), 170-231.

Johnson, T. (1999, September). Performance measurements of compressed bitmap indices. In *International Conference on Very Large Data Bases (VLDB)*, Edinburgh, Scotland (pp. 278-289). Morgan Kaufmann.

Keim, D., & Hinneburg, A. (1999, September). Optimal grid-clustering: Towards breaking the curse of dimensionality in high-dimensional clustering. In *Pro-*

Copyright © 2007, Idea Group Inc. Copying or distributing in print or electronic forms without written permission of Idea Group Inc. is prohibited.

ceedings of the International Conference on Very Large Data Bases (VLDB), San Francisco (pp. 506-517). Morgan Kaufmann.

Kiyoki, Y., Tanaka, K., Aiso, H., & Kamibayashi, N. (1981, May). Design and evaluation of a relational data base machine employing advanced data structures and algorithms. Paper presented at the *Symposium on Computer Architecture,* Los Alamitos, California (pp. 407-423). IEEE Computer Society Press.

Knuth, D. E. (1998). *The art of computer programming* (vol. 3). Addison-Wesley.

Koudas, N. (2000, November). Space efficient bitmap indexing. In *Proceedings of the Conference on Information and Knowledge Management (CIKM),* McLean, Virginia (pp. 194-201). ACM Press.

O'Neil, P. (1987, September). Model 204 architecture and performance. *Workshop in High Performance Transaction Systems,* Asilomar, California (pp. 40-59). Springer-Verlag.

O'Neil, P. (1997). Informix indexing support for data warehouses. *Database Programming and Design, 10*(2), 38-43.

O'Neil, P., & Quass, D. (1997, May). Improved query performance with variant indexes. In *Proceedings of the International Conference on Management of Data (SIGMOD 1997),* Tucson, Arizona (pp. 38-49). ACM Press.

Rotem, D., Stockinger, K., & Wu, K. (2005a, September). Optimizing I/O costs of multidimensional queries using bitmap indices. In *Proceedings of the International Conference on Database and Expert Systems Applications (DEXA),* Copenhagen, Denmark (pp. 220-229). Springer Verlag.

Rotem, D., Stockinger, K., & Wu, K. (2005b, November). Optimizing candidate check costs for bitmap indices. In *Proceedings of the Conference on Information and Knowledge Management (CIKM),* Bremen, Germany (pp. 648-655). ACM Press.

Stockinger, K., Shalf, J., Bethel, W., & Wu, K. (2005, June). DEX: Increasing the capability of scientific data analysis pipelines by using efficient bitmap indices to accelerate scientific visualization. In *Proceedings of the International Conference on Scientific and Statistical Database Management (SSDBM),* Santa Barbara, California (pp. 35-44). IEEE Computer Society Press.

Stockinger, K., Wu, K., & Shoshani, A. (2002). Strategies for processing ad hoc queries on large data sets. In *Proceedings of the International Workshop on Data Warehousing and OLAP (DOLAP),* McLean, Virginia (pp. 72-79).

Stockinger, K., Wu, K., & Shoshani, A. (2004). Evaluation strategies for bitmap indices with binning. In *Proceedings of the International Conference on Database and Expert Systems Applications (DEXA),* Zaragoza, Spain (pp. 120-129). Springer-Verlag.

Copyright © 2007, Idea Group Inc. Copying or distributing in print or electronic forms without written permission of Idea Group Inc. is prohibited.

TeraScaleCombustion. (2005). *TeraScale High-fidelity simulation of turbulent combustion with detailed chemistry.* Retrieved May 31, 2006, from http://www.scidac.psc.edu

Wong, H. K. T., Liu, H. -F., Olken, F., Rotem, D., & Wong, L. (1985, August). Bit transposed files. In *Proceedings of the International Conference on Very Large Databases (VLDB)*, Stockholm, Sweden (pp. 448-457). Morgan Kaufmann.

Wu, K., Otoo, E. J., & Shoshani, A. (2002, July). Compressing bitmap indexes for faster search operations. In *Proceedings of the International Conference on Scientific and Statistical Database Management (SSDBM)*, Edinburgh, Scotland (pp. 99-108). Computer Society Press.

Wu, K., Otoo, E. J., & Shoshani, A. (2004, September). On the performance of bitmap indices for high cardinality attributes. In *Proceedings of the International Conference on Very Large Data Bases (VLDB),* Toronto, Canada (pp. 24-35). Morgan Kaufmann.

Wu, K., Otoo, E., & Shoshani, A. (2006). *An efficient compression scheme for bitmap indices* (Tech. Rep. LBNL-49626). ACM Transactions on Database Systems (TODS).

Wu, M.-C., & Buchmann, A. P. (1998, February). Encoded bitmap indexing for data warehouses. In *Proceedings of the International Conference on Data Engineering (ICDE),* Orlando, Florida (pp. 220-230). IEEE Computer Society Press.

Copyright © 2007, Idea Group Inc. Copying or distributing in print or electronic forms without written permission of Idea Group Inc. is prohibited.

Chapter VIII

Indexing in
Data Warehouses:
Bitmaps and Beyond

Karen C. Davis
University of Cincinnati, USA

Ashima Gupta
University of Cincinnati, USA

Abstract

Bitmap indexes (BIs) allow fast access to individual attribute values that are needed to answer a query by storing a bit for each distinct value and tuple. A BI is defined for a single attribute and the encodings are based solely on data values; the property map (PMap) is a multidimensional indexing technique that precomputes attribute expressions for each tuple and stores the results as bit strings. In order to determine whether the PMap is competitive with BIs, we conduct a performance study of the PMap with the range encoded bit sliced index (REBSI) using cost models to simulate storage and query processing costs for different kinds of query types. We identify parameters that have significant effect on index performance and determine situations in which either index is more suitable. These results could be useful for improving the performance of an analytical decision making system.

Copyright © 2007, Idea Group Inc. Copying or distributing in print or electronic forms without written permission of Idea Group Inc. is prohibited.

Introduction

A data warehouse is a repository of information collected from different sources. Querying of data warehouses for decision-making in areas such as sales and marketing planning is referred to as online analytical processing (OLAP). In the write-once-read-many environment of OLAP applications, multidimensional data analysis is now increasingly used for decision support systems (DSS). Complex DSS queries are often submitted interactively and reducing their response time is a critical issue in the data warehousing environment (Vanichayobon & Gruenwald, 1999; Jurgens & Lenz, 2001). Bitmap indexes are widely used for indexing warehouse data.

A bitmap index (BI) allows fast access to tuples based on values of attributes. Bitmap indexes consume only a fraction of the size of the indexed data and provide dramatic performance gains. Boolean operations such as AND, OR and NOT are extremely fast for bitmap vectors, also called bitmaps or bit-vectors (O'Neil & Quass, 1997). Bitmaps indicate whether an attribute in a tuple is equal to, greater than or less than (depending upon the type of BI) a specific value or not. The length of a bit-vector is equal to the cardinality of the indexed table. The position of a bit in a bit-vector denotes the position of a tuple in the table. For example, a simple bitmap index (SBI) on an attribute status, with domain {backorder, shipped}, results in two bitmap vectors, say B_b and B_s. For B_b, the bit is set to 1 if the corresponding tuple has the value "backorder" for the attribute status, otherwise the bit is set to 0. Similarly for B_s, the bit is set to 1 if the associated tuple has the value "shipped" for the attribute status, otherwise the bit is set to 0. For another attribute, say product-category having values from 1-5, there is a bitmap vector corresponding to each of the five values, say B_1-B_5. Tuples that have product-category value as 1 have the bit corresponding to bit-vector B_1 set; the rest of the bits for that tuple are 0. Table 1 shows an SBI on status and product-category for 5 tuples with two bitmap vectors for status and five for product-category. These indexes can be interpreted as follows: tuple number 2

Table 1. Example of two simple bitmap indexes

Tuple	status		product-category				
	B_s	B_b	B_1	B_2	B_3	B_4	B_5
1	1	0	0	1	0	0	0
2	1	0	0	0	0	0	1
3	1	0	0	0	0	1	0
4	0	1	1	0	0	0	0
5	1	0	0	0	1	0	0

Copyright © 2007, Idea Group Inc. Copying or distributing in print or electronic forms without written permission of Idea Group Inc. is prohibited.

corresponds to a shipped order (B_s is set) with product-category 5 (B_5 is set). To illustrate query processing with an SBI, consider a simple SQL query that retrieves all tuples corresponding to shipped orders for product category 5:

SELECT * FROM Inventory WHERE status = "shipped" AND product-category = "5"

In order to evaluate this query using the example SBIs, a query optimizer takes the bitmaps for "status = shipped" and "product-category = 5" and performs a logical AND operation. Tuple 2 in Table 1 is the only tuple in the query answer.

We survey bitmap indexing techniques in the next section. Then we propose a novel multidimensional indexing technique that precomputes attribute expressions for data items and stores the results as bit strings. We study performance issues for this technique and a comparable bitmap index and recommend scenarios where one may be preferable to the other. We conclude with guidelines for improving query processing performance for complex range queries.

Background

Bitmap indexes are designed for different query types including range, aggregation and join queries. Figure 1 shows tree diagrams of bitmap indexes, which we classify into three categories based on their main features. Figure 1(a) shows bitmap indexing methods that use the simple bitmap index (SBI) representation described in the previous section. The techniques that use clustering of attribute values are

Figure 1. Classification of bitmap indexing techniques

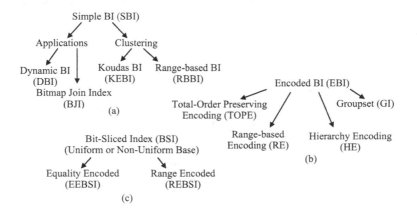

Copyright © 2007, Idea Group Inc. Copying or distributing in print or electronic forms without written permission of Idea Group Inc. is prohibited.

grouped in one category. The other category consists of techniques that are basically applications of SBI. Figure 1(b) shows encoded bitmap index (EBI) techniques that use binary encoding along with a mapping table and retrieval functions. Each attribute is encoded in such a way that the number of bitmap vectors retrieved to answer a query is reduced compared to the SBI. Bit-sliced index techniques are shown in Figure 1(c). They are based on the idea of attribute value decomposition, that is, decomposition of an attribute value in digits according to some base, either uniform or non-uniform. They can be either range or equality encoded.

BIs comparable to the novel technique introduced in the third section are discussed in further detail below. We select one technique for comparison in the fourth section based on three criteria: suitability for processing range queries, published design algorithms for the index, and research results indicating that the technique is competitive with other known techniques. Note that bitmap compression techniques are not considered here; they are discussed in the future work section.

Simple Bitmap Index

The basic idea of a simple bitmap index (also called Pure BI) (O'Neil & Quass, 1997) is to use a bit (0 or 1) to indicate whether an attribute in a tuple is equal to a specific value or not. The sparsity of the bit-vectors increases with increasing cardinality of the indexed attribute and number of tuples in the database, resulting in poor space utilization and high processing cost. Hence, as the cardinality of the indexed attribute and the database size increases, both time and space complexity of building and maintaining an SBI rapidly becomes higher (Wu & Buchmann, 1998). Thus, an SBI is best for database tables with a small number of records and small cardinality attributes. For these reasons, SBIs are not considered in our performance comparison.

Applications of Bitmap Indexes

We describe two techniques, dynamic bitmap indexes and bitmap join indexes, that are referred to as bitmap indexes in the literature but are really applications of BIs. They can use the SBI or any other kind of BI that we present in this chapter; we discuss them here for the sake of completeness.

The dynamic bitmap index (DBI) (Sarawagi, 1997) is a temporary structure that is built from a permanent index as needed by a query optimizer to include or eliminate records for selection. It is constructed dynamically from a vertically partitioned table in which each column stores a compressed representation of the values in the

Copyright © 2007, Idea Group Inc. Copying or distributing in print or electronic forms without written permission of Idea Group Inc. is prohibited.

corresponding attribute column. For example, if there are n different values of an attribute, they are mapped to continuous integers and each value is represented by $\log_n$ bits, which represents its integer map. When a predicate requires a subset of values in that column, the required values are converted to their integer maps and represented in an in-memory array or hash table. The column partition is scanned and for each value, the in-memory array is probed. Depending on whether a match is found or not, a 1 or a 0 is stored at the corresponding row position of a bitmap. This process is repeated for predicates on other columns. At the end of scanning all queried columns, individual bitmaps are obtained, which can be ANDed or ORed resulting in a bitmap with 1 at row positions that satisfy all predicates. Tuples corresponding to these row positions can be retrieved.

A bitmap join index (BJI) (Vanichayobon & Gruenwald, 1999) is built by creating a bitmap index on a table T based on a single column A of table S, where A is a join attribute; hence, the actual join need not be performed. It is usually used with low cardinality data.

Koudas' Encoded Bitmap Index

Koudas (2000) proposes a technique to index large cardinality attributes using less storage space compared to SBIs, taking into account both the query and data distribution of the attribute instances. We call this technique Koudas' encoded bitmap index (KEBI). The idea is to encode sequences of attribute values together in the bitmap index, as opposed to creating one bitmap per attribute value. The information returned from the bitmap may be a superset of a query answer. Table 2 shows an example of this approach. The attribute *WorkYears* has five distinct values. If they are encoded separately as in an SBI, it results in five bitmaps. By encoding more than one value in a bitmap, the number of vectors is reduced to two. Attribute values {1, 2} and {3, 4, 5} are jointly encoded. A query referencing attribute value 2 retrieves tuples having the attribute value 1 along with the ones having the value 2. Therefore, it is vital to minimize the number of false hits that each bitmap returns, since these tuples have to be retrieved and filtered out in a post-processing phase. The essential idea is the same as the SBI in that a bit (1 or 0) is used to indicate

Table 2. Koudas' encoded bitmap index

A	{1,2}	{3,4,5}
2	0	1
4	0	1
1	1	0
5	0	1
3	1	0

Copyright © 2007, Idea Group Inc. Copying or distributing in print or electronic forms without written permission of Idea Group Inc. is prohibited.

Table 3. Range-based bitmap indexing

Bucket Number	Ranges on *Age*	Number of Persons
1	[1, 16)	21
2	[16, 28)	22
3	[28, 40)	21
4	[40, 60)	22
5	[60, 65)	23

Tuple	[1, 16)	[16, 28)	[28, 40)	[40, 60)	[60, 65)
1	1	0	0	0	0
2	0	0	0	1	0
3	0	0	1	0	0
4	0	1	0	0	0
5	0	0	0	0	1

(a) Population of Each Bucket   (b) Bitmap Representation of Example Tuples

whether an attribute in a tuple is equal to a specific value (here, a set of values) or not. The choice of attribute values to jointly encode depends on the frequency of access of each attribute value as well as the frequency of occurrence of the value in the attribute instances. The mutually exclusive range of consecutive attribute values encoded together in the same bitmap is called the range of that bitmap.

The author compares KEBI with a strategy in which the attribute values are divided into approximately equal length ranges. The number of false hits is large for KEBI under uniform data distribution, but reduces sharply as the skew in data distribution increases. As compared to the SBI, KEBI saves index storage space, reducing the number of index pages retrieved, although filtering excess tuples requires additional processing time and could increase the number of data pages retrieved. We do not consider KEBI for comparison here as it has only been studied for equality or point queries and DSS queries typically include complex range queries.

Range-Based Bitmap Indexing

SBIs can cause significant storage overhead if the attributes to be indexed have high cardinality. This is the motivation for range-based bitmap indexing (RBBI) (Wu & Yu, 1998). In RBBI, the attribute values are partitioned into a small number of ranges and a bitmap vector is constructed to represent each range and not each distinct value. A bit (1 or 0) is used to indicate whether an attribute in a tuple is within a specific range or not.

Unless the distribution of the attribute values is known, ranges can be unevenly populated resulting in highly unbalanced query access times. RBBI utilizes the distribution of attribute values in the data to construct a range-based bitmap index for high cardinality attributes with skew. It uses a dynamic bucket expansion and contraction approach in which data are first scanned into the buffer to construct the

Copyright © 2007, Idea Group Inc. Copying or distributing in print or electronic forms without written permission of Idea Group Inc. is prohibited.

bucket ranges by counting the data points falling into each bucket. If the bucket grows beyond a threshold, it is expanded into smaller-range buckets. Adjacent buckets are then combined into the final required number of buckets that are approximately balanced. The bitmap vectors are built with another scan of the data.

Table 3(a) shows five nearly-equally populated bucket ranges on the attribute Age, constructed by the RBBI technique. The range-based bitmap index for the first 5 tuples of a database with 109 tuples is shown in Table 3(b). Note that the records are nearly evenly distributed in the 5 buckets.

The ranges are continuous-valued intervals and mutually exclusive. Thus, RBBI can effectively answer range and point queries, though it results in retrieval of excess tuples since all the tuples within the queried range are retrieved and the excess has to be filtered out. While RBBI is designed for range queries, it is not chosen for the performance study discussed in this chapter; we choose a BSI technique because its developers give compelling results regarding its competitive performance.

Encoded Bitmap Index

The encoded bitmap index (EBI) (Wu & Buchmann, 1998) has been proposed to index large cardinality domains since they are not efficiently indexed by SBI. The basic idea is to encode each value of the attribute domain as a binary number, rather than have a bit-vector for each value as in an SBI. Each distinct value of an attribute is encoded using a number of bits, each of which is stored in a bitmap vector. For example, if attribute A has 12,000 different values, then an SBI has 12,000 bitmap vectors. Encoded bitmap indexing uses only $\lceil \log_2 12000 \rceil$, i.e., 14 bitmap vectors and a mapping table. A lookup table stores the mapping between A and its encoded representation. Cases for NULL values or non-existing tuples are encoded together with other domain values so separate existence vectors are not required, as in the case of SBIs. An EBI on a column A of table T consists of a set of bitmap vectors,

Table 4. Encoded bitmap indexing

A	B_2	B_1	B_0
b	0	1	1
a	0	1	0
d	1	0	1
c	1	0	0
$NULL$	0	0	0

NULL	000
NotExist	001
a	010
b	011
c	100
d	101

f_a	$B_2'B_1B_0'$
f_b	$B_2'B_1B_0$
f_c	$B_2B_1'B_0'$
f_d	$B_2B_1'B_0$

(a) Bitmap vector   (b) Mapping table for A   (c) Retrieval functions

Copyright © 2007, Idea Group Inc. Copying or distributing in print or electronic forms without written permission of Idea Group Inc. is prohibited.

a one-to-one mapping and a set of retrieval Boolean functions. Table 4 shows an EBI for an attribute A with domain {a, b, c, d}. NULL and non-existing values are encoded with the domain, so that the total number of domain values is 6 (NotExist, NULL, a, b, c, and d.) The number of bit-vectors required is $\lceil \log_2 6 \rceil = 3$.

To retrieve data, a Boolean function is defined for each value. If a value v with a domain of size k is encoded as $b_i b_0$ ($b_i \in \{0, 1\}$, $i = 0$ to $\lceil \log_2 k \rceil -1$), then the retrieval function for v is defined as $x_1 x_0$, where $x_i = B_i$ if $b_i = 1$, otherwise x_i is equal to the negation of B_i, i.e., $x_i = B_i'$. The number of bitmap vectors accessed is minimized as a result of a well-defined encoding.

Compared to SBI, the EBI improves space utilization and solves sparsity problems. It performs efficiently with wide-range queries. In an environment where selection patterns can be pre-defined, the main idea of EBI is to establish a well-defined encoding so that time efficiency can be improved without sacrificing space efficiency. Encoding schemes are crucial since Boolean operations can be performed on the retrieval functions before retrieving the data, reducing the total number of operations performed and bitmap vectors accessed. Defining a good encoding scheme is a difficult and open problem. In addition, EBI performance degrades for equality queries since all the bitmap vectors have to be searched. Due to these drawbacks, we do not consider EBI for further comparison here. Variations of the EBI for specific scenarios are given by Wu and Buchmann (1998) and listed in our classification in Figure 1 under EBI techniques.

Bit-Sliced Index

A bit-sliced index (BSI) (O'Neil & Quass, 1997; Chan & Ioannidis, 1998) is a set of bitwise projections of an attribute. BSIs are total-order preserving, hence they are suitable for representing numeric (fixed-point) or ordinal types of attributes, and are especially good for wide-range searches. The design space of a BSI is defined by two factors, attribute value decomposition and encoding scheme (Chan & Ioannidis, 1998).

The first factor, attribute value decomposition (AVD), defines the arithmetic to represent the values of an attribute. It is the decomposition of an attribute's values in digits according to a chosen base. For example, 124 can be decomposed into <1, 2, 4> according to base <10, 10, 10>. The second factor that defines a BSI is the encoding scheme. Consider the ith component of an index with a base value b_i. There are two schemes to directly encode the corresponding values v_i ($0 <= v_i <= b_i -1$) in bits, equality encoding and range encoding. In equality encoding, the bit in a component is set if equality condition is satisfied and there are b_i bits, one for each possible value. The representation of value v_i has all bits set to 0, except for

Copyright © 2007, Idea Group Inc. Copying or distributing in print or electronic forms without written permission of Idea Group Inc. is prohibited.

the bit corresponding to v_i, which is set to 1. Thus, an equality encoded bit-sliced index (EEBSI) component with base b_i consists of b_i bitmaps.

In range-encoding, there are b_i bits (one for each possible value) set so as to satisfy an inequality condition between the value represented by them and the decomposed attribute value of the corresponding record for that component. The representation of value v_i has the v_i rightmost (or leftmost) bits set to 0 and the remaining bits (starting from the one corresponding to v_i, and to the left (or right)) are set to 1. In the example shown in Table 5, the bitmaps are less than or equal to encoded. For the attribute value 124, 1 is represented by component 3, 2 by component 2 and 4 by component 1. The representation of 1 has one rightmost bit set to 0 and the rest set to 1, the representation of 2 has two rightmost bits set to 0 and the rest set to 1, and so on. Intuitively, each bitmap $B_i v_i$ has 1 in all the records whose i^{th} component value is less than or equal to v_i. Since the bitmap $B_i b_i - 1$ has all bits set to 1, it does not need to be stored, so a range-encoded bit-sliced index (REBSI) component consists of $(b_i - 1)$ bitmaps. For the decimal base all digits are less than or equal to 9, thus bit 9 of all components is set and can be ignored, as shown in Table 5.

Non-binary, uniform base BSIs are often less efficient in both space and time than non-uniform base BSIs with the same number of components (Chan & Ioannidis, 1998). For BSIs with a uniform base, as the magnitude of the base increases, the index requires more space but performs better. The effort of performing range retrieval can be reduced if a larger number of bitmaps are stored, for example, base 10 instead of base 2.

We consider range-encoded non-uniform base bit-sliced index (REBSI) for our performance comparison, as it is one of the most efficient indexes to answer range as well as equality queries and has clearly defined design algorithms (Chan & Ioannidis, 1998). Its performance has been compared with that of tree-based indexes and is shown to be better suited for a data warehousing environment (Jurgens & Lenz, 2001). It is more efficient than the equality-encoded BSI in the case of range as well as equality queries (Chan & Ioannidis, 1998). Since range selections are a common class of queries in OLAP, we choose this technique for our performance study.

Table 5. A range-encoded decimal (base-10) bit-sliced index

	Component 3						Component 2							Component 1							
A	B^8	B^7		B^2	B^1	B^0	B^8	B^7		B^3	B^2	B^1	B^0	B^8	...	B^5	B^4	B^3	B^2	B^1	B^0
124	1	1	...	1	1	0	1	1	...	1	1	0	0	1	...	1	1	0	0	0	0
...																					

Copyright © 2007, Idea Group Inc. Copying or distributing in print or electronic forms without written permission of Idea Group Inc. is prohibited.

Beyond Bitmaps: The Property Map

There are two characteristics of bitmap indexes that we modify in order to consider a new kind of bitmap. One is that bitmap indexes generally create encodings based on values only; we propose encodings based on values and driven by application knowledge, e.g., queries. In this respect, our technique is similar to EBI (Wu & Buchmann, 1998), however, how to design the encoding of an EBI is an open question. The second is that bitmap indexes are generally single attribute-only; we propose a solution that supports multi-attribute queries directly. RBBI (Wu & Yu, 1998) has a similar notion of range-encoding, but our technique supports additional encoding schemes. The novel technique introduced here is called a Property Map. The basic concept is defined and illustrated below and then its performance is compared to the REBSI technique in the following section.

A property map (PMap) defines properties on each attribute depending on knowledge of the application, such as a known set of queries. The value of each property is computed as a bit string for each data instance, and these are concatenated to form a pstring. To illustrate a PMap, consider an example relation Inventory with attributes quantity, status, and product-category with a PMap having the following properties:

- **Property 1:** Range on quantity; contains range intervals on the quantity attribute from 20-29, 30-39, 40-49, and 49-59. Each interval is represented by a bit string. For example, the interval 20-29 is represented by 00, 30-39 by 01, 40-49 by 10, and 50-59 by 11. Thus, Property 1 requires 2 bits.

- **Property 2:** Enumerated on product-category; has the enumerated values of the product-category attribute (1, 2, 3, 4 and 5). A bit string represents each value. Therefore, 1 is represented 000, 2 by 001, 3 by 010, 4 by 011, and 5 by 100. Therefore, this property requires 3 bits.

- **Property 3:** Boolean on status = "shipped," property value is true (or 1) when a record's attribute status is "shipped" and false (or 0) otherwise. This property requires 1 bit.

The pstrings for this example are 6 bits long; two bits for Property 1, three bits for Property 2, and one bit for Property 3. Table 6 shows 5 records of an Inventory table with the corresponding values for each property and the resulting pstring. The properties are constructed based on some knowledge about the application (e.g., frequently executed queries), and can be used to answer multi-attribute queries directly.

The example PMap given here is handcrafted in order to illustrate terminology and concepts. In practice, designing an efficient PMap is not a trivial task. We have

Copyright © 2007, Idea Group Inc. Copying or distributing in print or electronic forms without written permission of Idea Group Inc. is prohibited.

proposed algorithms that rely on heuristics to reduce the design space and create efficient PMaps and are currently implementing them in an automated design tool (Darira et al., 2006). One example of a design heuristic is how we determine the details of range properties. We group all of the predicates over a single attribute in a frequent query set together and create range intervals based on numeric constants that appear in inequality comparisons. We create Boolean properties on equality predicates and for attribute expressions that do not evaluate to numeric values. Enumerated properties are created for attributes where the number of bits to represent ranges over the attribute exceeds $\log_2$ of the number of values in the domain (since this is the size of an enumerated property pstring.) Combinations of properties and their ordering are evaluated based on reducing the number of excess tuples that would be retrieved when evaluating the query set.

In order to illustrate how PMaps are used for query evaluation, consider the query used earlier:

SELECT * FROM Inventory WHERE status = "shipped" AND product-category = "5"

The query processor determines the pmask, which is obtained by setting the bits corresponding to the properties covering the query predicates to 1 (status and product-category) and setting all other bits to 0 (quantity), yielding the pmask 001111 in this case. The pfilter is obtained by setting all bits corresponding to properties covering the query predicate to the desired value, and setting all other bits to 0. The pfilter here is 001001, since the queried product-category value is equal to 5 (property value 100) and status value is equal to "shipped" (property value 1.) The tuples for which the filter formula "pstring AND pmask = pfilter" is TRUE are in the result set. For tuple 2 in Table 6, the filter formula evaluates to TRUE since the pstring (001001) ANDed with 001111 (pmask) is equal to 001001 (pfilter). Since no other tuple in this example satisfies the filter formula, only tuple 2 is in the result set. To answer a range query such as "product-category > 5," the equals sign in the filter formula is changed to greater than.

Table 6. Example of property strings (pstrings)

Tuple ID	(qty, prod-cat, status)	Property 1	Property 2	Property 3	pstring
1	(49, 2, s)	01	001	1	010011
2	(24, 5, s)	00	100	1	001001
3	(52, 4, s)	11	011	1	110111
4	(37, 1, b)	01	000	0	010000
5	(28, 3, s)	00	010	1	000101

Copyright © 2007, Idea Group Inc. Copying or distributing in print or electronic forms without written permission of Idea Group Inc. is prohibited.

Detailed definitions, algorithms, and cost models for storage and query processing are introduced for PMaps (Gupta et al., 2002) and REBSI (Chan & Ioannidis, 1998; Jurgens & Lenz, 2001). The next section discusses simulations to compare performance and their results. Observations and analysis of the performance results follow.

Performance Study

In this section, the methodology for conducting simulations and performing analysis is described, followed by a discussion of some representative results. General observations over all of the simulation results are offered in conclusion.

Methodology

The simulation methodology includes a synthetic query benchmark that forms the basis of our investigation along with parameters that are varied to study the impact of different database environments. The analysis is based on observations of index page retrievals and relative performance for each set of queries derived from the benchmark. Components of the methodology are described in the three sections below.

1. **Queries:** The set query benchmark (Gray, 1993) is designed to measure the performance of systems that strategically analyze data repositories in commercial enterprises. Computer resource usage by such queries can be extremely high, and hence we use this benchmark to compare the performance of PMap indexing and REBSI. The set query benchmark has the following key characteristics.

    *   The queries for the benchmark are specified in SQL, and the data used is representative of real applications.

    *   These queries are chosen to span the tasks performed by different strategic data applications (e.g., document search, direct marketing, and decision support).

    *   The benchmark specifies measurements for a wide range of selectivity values within each query type.

    The database has a single table called BENCH that contains 1 million rows of 200 bytes each (224 with overhead). Besides using the given size to measure performance for large databases, we also use a size of 50,000 rows to mea-

Copyright © 2007, Idea Group Inc. Copying or distributing in print or electronic forms without written permission of Idea Group Inc. is prohibited.

sure the performance for a smaller database size. Each of the 13 attributes has integer values ranging from 1 to its cardinality, which is represented in the attribute name. Thus K2 has 2 values: 1 and 2, K4 has 4 values: 1, 2, 3 and 4, K100k has 100,000 values: 1, 2, ..., 100,000. One indexed attribute, KSEQ, is a clustered primary key, with values: 1, 2, ..., 1,000,000. The remaining twelve attributes are unordered and out of these, we do not consider K40, K250k and K500k in our selected queries to limit the number of queries. The attributes included for each query set are sufficient to provide a variety of cardinality and selectivity values for that set, limiting the number of experiments at the same time. In our simulations, we assume uniform data distribution and this is consistent with the BENCH table. We identify a subset of the set query benchmark that consists of document search and direct marketing queries. We omit the management reporting queries as we do not take into consideration aggregation and join queries in our study. The performance study here focuses on selection costs and we simulate the selection conditions (SQL WHERE clause) in each chosen query.

The total number of queries that we consider is 43, and from these we create subsets based on different criteria, such as cardinality of attributes and query selectivities. The six query sets are based on queries embodying high cardinality attributes, very high cardinality attributes, low cardinality attributes, low selectivity, high selectivity, and mixed queries. For each of these query sets, we vary input parameters to study their impact, while we fix other factors to limit the number of simulations. The values of parameters are given in Table 7.

Apart from data and system specific parameters, we define a parameter called scaling factor (sf), to facilitate the comparison between PMap and REBSI. We consider REBSIs that are time-optimal under a given space constraint (Chan & Ioannidis, 1998). REBSIs occupy a large amount of disk space because a separate REBSI has to be created for each attribute to be indexed, so more space is allotted to it than space occupied by the corresponding PMap. The space constraint for REBSI is equal to the space occupied by the corresponding PMap multiplied by a scaling factor. For example, a scaling factor of 2 means that the bitmap index occupies twice the space used by the PMap. The minimum scaling factor is the smallest value for which a REBSI corresponding to the PMap can be constructed. We vary scaling factors to compare PMap performance with faster REBSIs; greater storage allocation reduces the number of bitmaps that need to be scanned to answer a query. Apart from the minimum scaling factor (sf_min) needed to create a REBSI, we consider one or two other suitable sf values to create REBSI with increased space consumption but faster performance. In other words, to create a REBSI with the same attributes as the PMap requires four times the space (sf = 4) of the PMap. Since that is the baseline performance for REBSI, we also create a REBSI that is 10 times the

Copyright © 2007, Idea Group Inc. Copying or distributing in print or electronic forms without written permission of Idea Group Inc. is prohibited.

Table 7. Parameter values

	VAR	DESCRIPTION	TYPE	VALUES
Data Specific	d	dimensionality of index	integer	Number of unique attributes referenced in the query set
	t	number of tuples	integer	50,000 and 1,000,000
	c	attribute cardinality	integer	n, where Kn is the attribute
	S_{REC}	size of a data record	bytes	224
System Specific	S_B	block size	bytes	2048, 4096 and 8192
	ws	word size	bits	16 and 32
User Defined	sf	scaling factor	integer	minimum sf (*sf_min*) depending upon the corresponding PMap, up to 10

size of our PMap to investigate how the PMap competes with a more efficient REBSI.

2. **Measuring PMap performance:** The pstrings of a PMap are stored in a B+ tree for efficient searching. A query with multiple predicates can be rewritten in disjunctive normal form and processed as separate queries whose results are OR'd together to obtain the query answer (we call this strategy A) or processed as a single query (strategy B). In either case, multiple pfilters are generated; we call the one with the lowest value pfilter low ($pfilter_l$) and the one with the highest value pfilter high ($pfilter_h$). Only the pstrings with values between $pfilter_l$ and $pfilter_h$ need to be searched in the B+ tree. For our performance study, the more efficient strategy is chosen in each individual case. A minimum number of record pointers to answer a query is computed based on the utilization of a pstring; for example, a range property may only utilize 20 different values even though 32 have to be allocated to store it (5 bits). A maximum number of record pointers is computed based on the number of leaf level blocks that appear between the lower and upper pfilters. The minimum represents best case performance and the maximum is worst case performance. Since the real performance lies in between, we also compute an average of the two.

3. **Simulation framework:** Our experiments study the impact of parameters such as block size, database size, scaling factor, query selectivity, and attribute cardinality that affect index performance. For each of the query sets, we create PMaps and REBSIs and measure their performance in terms of the number

Copyright © 2007, Idea Group Inc. Copying or distributing in print or electronic forms without written permission of Idea Group Inc. is prohibited.

of index pages retrieved. A PMap is created using heuristic design algorithms (Darira et al., 2006). As a result of the design heuristics, PMap ranges are designed to exactly cover the query predicates and hence no excess tuples are retrieved. We calculate the PMap storage requirements and index pages retrieved for each of the queries, for this query set. In other words, for each of the two pstring sizes (ws) for a query set, we vary the number of tuples (t) and block size (Sb) and calculate the space occupied by the corresponding PMap and the minimum and maximum number of index pages retrieved to answer the queries in this set. For each database size and block size combination corresponding to a PMap, we find 3 different REBSIs by varying the scaling factor and using algorithms FindSmallestN and RefineIndex (Chan & Ioannidis, 1998). In the REBSI for a query set, a separate REBSI is created for every attribute that is present in the query set to be able to answer each query completely. Then we determine the index pages retrieved using each of these bitmaps for the particular query set using the Time formula (Chan & Ioannidis, 1998). Thus, the inputs to the REBSI storage and performance measurement simulator are tuple size, block size and the scaling factor with respect to the corresponding PMap. The results of these experiments for the PMap and REBSI techniques with one query set (very high cardinality attributes) are presented and analyzed here to illustrate the methodology and develop intuition for the general observations we offer. Cost models and results for different query sets are detailed elsewhere (Gupta et al., 2002).

Very High Cardinality Attribute Query Set

The very high cardinality attribute query set (VHCAQS) consists of high cardinality attribute queries (Gupta et al., 2002) along with the queries containing the attribute KSEQ, in which case we substitute only the high cardinality attributes for KN so that these queries contain only high cardinality attributes. Even though the HCAQS is a subset of VHCAQS, a different PMap is obtained here as the additional attribute KSEQ is included. The number of bits allotted to each property in the pstring is different from the PMap generated for the HCAQS, as is the space consumption. Table 8 shows the 12 queries in VHCAQS.

Property Map

The PMap for this set of queries constitutes five properties on the five attributes accessed in the queries. In this example, the dimensionality of the PMap index is 5 and pstring size is 11. For each query, the pmask, $pfilter_l$, and $pfilter_h$ are shown in Table 9. The properties in the VHCAQS PMap are as follows:

Copyright © 2007, Idea Group Inc. Copying or distributing in print or electronic forms without written permission of Idea Group Inc. is prohibited.

Table 8. Very high cardinality attribute query set

ID	Query
HC1	K1k = 2
HC2	K10k = 2
HC3	K100k = 2
HC7	KSEQ = 2
HC4	K2 = 2 AND K1k = 3
HC5	K2 = 2 AND K10k = 3
HC6	K2 = 2 AND K100k = 3
HC8	K2 = 2 AND KSEQ = 3
HC9	KSEQ >= 400000 AND KSEQ <= 500000 AND K10k = 3
HC10	KSEQ >= 400000 AND KSEQ <= 500000 AND K100k = 3
HC11	KSEQ >= 400000 AND KSEQ <= 410000 OR KSEQ >= 420000 AND KSEQ <= 430000 OR KSEQ >= 440000 AND KSEQ <= 450000 OR KSEQ >= 460000 AND KSEQ <= 470000 OR KSEQ >= 480000 AND KSEQ <= 500000 AND K10k = 3
HC12	KSEQ >= 400000 AND KSEQ <= 410000 OR KSEQ >= 420000 AND KSEQ <= 430000 OR KSEQ >= 440000 AND KSEQ <= 450000 OR KSEQ >= 460000 AND KSEQ <= 470000 OR KSEQ >= 480000 AND KSEQ <= 500000 AND K100k = 3

- **Property 1:** Range property on K100k utilizing 2 bits: $[0, 2)$, $[2, 3)$, $[3, 4)$ and $[4, 100000]$,

- **Property 2:** Range property on K10k utilizing 2 bits: $[0, 2)$, $[2, 3)$, $[3, 4)$ and $[4, 10000]$,

- **Property 3:** Range property on K1k utilizing 2 bits: $[0, 2)$, $[2, 3)$, $[3, 4)$ and $[4, 1000]$,

- **Property 4:** Boolean property on "K2 = 2" utilizing 1 bit, and

- **Property 5:** Range property on KSEQ utilizing 4 bits: $[0, 2)$, $[2, 3)$, $[3, 4)$, $[4, 400000)$, $[400000, 410001)$, $[410001, 420000)$, $[420000, 430001)$, $[430001, 440000)$, $[440000, 450001)$, $[450001, 460000)$, $[460000, 470001)$, $[470001, 480000)$, $[480000, 490001)$, $[490001, 500001)$ and $[500001, 1000001)$.

Copyright © 2007, Idea Group Inc. Copying or distributing in print or electronic forms without written permission of Idea Group Inc. is prohibited.

Range-Encoded Bit-Sliced Index

A separate REBSI is created for each attribute referenced in the query set, i.e., for K2, K1k, K10k, K100k and KSEQ; the dimensionality of the bit-sliced index is 5. In order to create a REBSI with the same attributes as the PMap, four times the space is required (min_sf = 4). Table 10 shows the average number of bitmap scans for each attribute for both database sizes, with the min_sf and 8K blocksize. The size of each bitmap in blocks (z) is also given for both cases.

Observations

Figure 2 shows a performance comparison graph for the two techniques and the VHCAQS for the database size of 1,000,000 tuples and 8K blocksize. The x-axis shows the queries and the y-axis shows the index pages retrieved for each query. The queries are ordered in decreasing order of the difference between the average number of index pages retrieved by the PMap (PAvg) and the number of pages retrieved by the REBSI with the smallest scaling factor (min_sf), i.e., occupying the minimal required space. To simplify the figure, performance results for HC11 and HC12 are not shown. In both cases, the number of index blocks exceeds 3,000 for the smaller REBSI (sf = 4) and 1,000 for the larger REBSI (sf = 10); the PMap average number of blocks is 36 and 113, respectively.

Table 9a. pmasks for queries in the VHCAQS

ID	K100k		K10k		K1k		K2	KSEQ			
HC1	0	0	0	0	1	1	0	0	0	0	0
HC2	0	0	1	1	0	0	0	0	0	0	0
HC3	1	1	0	0	0	0	0	0	0	0	0
HC7	0	0	0	0	0	0	0	1	1	1	1
HC4	0	0	0	0	1	1	1	0	0	0	0
HC5	0	0	1	1	0	0	1	0	0	0	0
HC6	1	1	0	0	0	0	1	0	0	0	0
HC8	0	0	0	0	0	0	1	1	1	1	1
HC9	0	0	1	1	0	0	0	0	0	0	0
HC10	1	1	0	0	0	0	0	1	1	1	1
HC11	0	0	1	1	0	0	0	1	1	1	1
HC12	1	1	0	0	0	0	0	1	1	1	1

Copyright © 2007, Idea Group Inc. Copying or distributing in print or electronic forms without written permission of Idea Group Inc. is prohibited.

Table 9b. pfilters for queries in the VHCAQS

ID	K100k		K10k		K1k		K2	KSEQ				K100k		K10k		K1k		K2	KSEQ			
HC1	0	0	0	0	0	1	0	0	0	0	0	1	1	1	1	0	1	1	1	1	1	1	1
HC2	0	0	0	1	0	0	0	0	0	0	0	1	1	0	1	1	1	1	1	1	1	1	1
HC3	0	1	0	0	0	0	0	0	0	0	0	0	1	1	1	1	1	1	1	1	1	1	1
HC7	0	0	0	0	0	0	0	0	0	0	1	1	1	1	1	1	1	1	1	0	0	0	1
HC4	0	0	0	0	1	0	1	0	0	0	0	1	1	1	1	1	0	1	1	1	1	1	1
HC5	0	0	1	0	0	0	1	0	0	0	0	1	1	1	0	1	1	1	1	1	1	1	1
HC6	1	0	0	0	0	0	1	0	0	0	0	1	0	1	1	1	1	1	1	1	1	1	1
HC8	0	0	0	0	0	0	1	0	0	1	0	1	1	1	1	1	1	1	1	0	0	1	0
HC9	0	0	1	0	0	0	0	0	1	0	0	1	1	1	0	1	1	1	1	1	1	0	1
HC10	1	0	0	0	0	0	0	0	1	0	0	1	0	1	1	1	1	1	1	1	1	0	1
HC11	0	0	1	0	0	0	0	0	1	0	0	1	1	1	0	1	1	1	1	1	1	0	1
HC12	1	0	0	0	0	0	0	0	1	0	0	1	0	1	1	1	1	1	1	1	1	0	1

We offer three specific observations pertaining to the VHCAQS:

1. **Relative performance per query:** The performance of PMap and REBSI in the case of K1k queries (HC2 and HC5) is similar for both database sizes. Queries with higher cardinality attributes (KSEQ, K100k) have better average PMap performance in all cases for the VHCAQS. In the case of database size of 1,000,000 tuples with a blocksize of 8K (Figure 2), the least space that the REBSI requires to be able to create bitmaps for all the attributes is 4 times the space required by the PMap (min_sf = 4). For the min_sf, the average

Table 10. Number of bitmap scans for attributes in VHCAQS

Attribute	1,000,000 tuples ($min\_sf=4$, $z=16$)	50,000 tuples ($min\_sf=5$, $z=1$)
K2	1	1
K1k	9	8
K10k	12	11
K100k	15	14
KSEQ	18	17

Copyright © 2007, Idea Group Inc. Copying or distributing in print or electronic forms without written permission of Idea Group Inc. is prohibited.

PMap performance is better than REBSI for most of the queries in this set, and comparable for the remaining two. For the REBSI occupying 10 times the space of the PMap, the average performance of the PMap is better in eight of the queries, comparable in two (HC5 and HC2) and worse in the case of two queries, HC4 and HC1. The minimum number of pages (PMin) retrieved by

Figure 2. PMap and REBSI performance comparison: VHCAQS

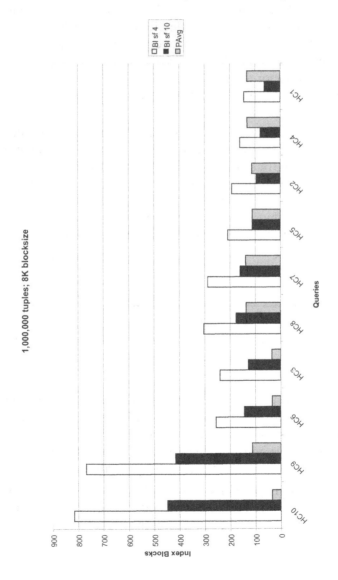

Copyright © 2007, Idea Group Inc. Copying or distributing in print or electronic forms without written permission of Idea Group Inc. is prohibited.

the PMap (not shown here) is less than the number of pages retrieved by any of the REBSIs.

2.   **Impact of cardinality:** For the queries with attribute KSEQ and K100k, the PMap performance is better for both database sizes and all scaling factors. Queries with K1k (HC1 and HC4) show similar performance for both database sizes. As the attribute cardinality decreases, REBSI performance improves. For the PMap, performance for similar queries varies according to the position of attribute properties in the pstring rather than attribute cardinalities, as in the case of HCAQS (Gupta et al., 2002). Though KSEQ has cardinality 10 times that of K100k, the savings in the case of queries accessing K100k (HC3 and HC6) compared to similar queries accessing KSEQ (HC7 and HC8) are greater. This is because of the relative positions of the properties covering these attributes in the pstring. The difference between $pfilter_h$ and $pfilter_l$ is the main contributing factor to the cost of index page retrieval in the worst case, i.e., PMax. The relative position of properties in the pstring has significant impact on performance of a PMap.

3.   **Multi-attribute queries:** For each high cardinality attribute KN, the PMap retrieves fewer than or the same number of pages for queries of the form K2 AND KN as the ones with only KN. Multiple conditions increase the number of bits that are set in the $pfilter_l$, which reduces the difference between pfilterh and $pfilter_l$, resulting in fewer pages retrieved. For the REBSIs, a higher number of attributes results in more pages retrieved as the number of scans increases. Thus, PMaps perform better than REBSI for multi-attribute queries for the VHCAQS.

Analysis

In general, we conclude the following based on our simulations and analysis over all 6 query sets.

1.   The storage cost of REBSI is higher than that of PMap because separate REBSIs have to be created for each of the attributes accessed in the frequently used queries. Due to the trade-off between space and time, the scaling factor (sf) has a predictable impact on the performance of a REBSI. REBSI performance increases proportionally to increased space allocation.

2.   The position of a property covering a predicate in the pstring significantly affects the number of pages retrieved for a query accessing that predicate. The closer the property to the beginning of the pstring, the higher the $pfilter_l$ value, which reduces the PMax value, i.e., the number of pages retrieved

Copyright © 2007, Idea Group Inc. Copying or distributing in print or electronic forms without written permission of Idea Group Inc. is prohibited.

by the PMap in the worst case. This is illustrated in all query set observations.

3. PMap performance is not significantly affected by attribute cardinality or query selectivity.

4. REBSI retrieval cost increases as the number of attributes accessed in the query increases, even for a very small cardinality attribute like K2. On the other hand, PMap retrieval cost remains the same or decreases with multi-attribute queries, as the additional attributes limit the pstring search by changing $pfilter_l$ and $pfilter_h$ values.

5. As the database size decreases, REBSI performance becomes better and the relative savings of the PMap are reduced. This is intuitive since the number of tuples directly impacts bit-vector length and the number of blocks to read one bitmap decreases significantly. Savings for PMaps over REBSI are higher for the larger database sizes and high cardinality attributes, essentially since the REBSI performance deteriorates in these cases.

6. We identify two strategies to evaluate a disjunctive query, i.e., a query with one or more OR operators. Strategy A splits a high level query into two or more separate queries by rewriting it in disjunctive normal form and processing each disjunct as a separate query, taking the union of the result set as the final answer. These disjuncts are processed individually and the results for both constitute the answer to the query. Strategy B processes a high level query as a single query using multiple pfilters, without separating the disjuncts. We experiment with both strategies for all the query sets having disjunctive queries (VHCAQS, LCAQS, HSQS and MQS) and choose the best strategy in each case in our performance studies. Strategy A performs better in general, except for the queries HC11 and HC12 in the VHCAQS. These queries have multiple conditions on the attribute KSEQ and Strategy B performs much better for them.

Conclusion

In this section we present techniques and enhancements that emerge from analyzing query processing performance of PMaps. Further study of these techniques could result in improved PMaps and guidelines for using different PMap creation techniques and query processing strategies in different scenarios. Based on all observations and analyses, we give the following general guidelines for the use of PMaps and applications where they may be useful and provide extra savings in query processing.

Copyright © 2007, Idea Group Inc. Copying or distributing in print or electronic forms without written permission of Idea Group Inc. is prohibited.

- From our analysis, we learn that PMap performance is not affected by attribute cardinality; however the property position in the pstring is a significant factor. Since performance for most other indexing techniques deteriorates for high cardinality attributes, we can achieve significant savings for these by creating PMaps on high and very high cardinality attributes. The property ordering should be in decreasing order of savings desired for the attributes. Thus, the attributes for which we desire maximum savings have properties at the beginning of the pstring.

- PMaps are beneficial when there is limited space for index creation, as they occupy much less space compared to bitmaps indexing the same set of attributes.

- PMaps perform well for multi-attribute queries, even better than single attribute queries, unlike REBSIs and many other known techniques. Hence, it is useful to create PMaps for frequently used multi-attribute queries.

- PMap savings increase in the case of large databases. Therefore, PMaps could be created for very large databases where SBIs are inefficient. PMap savings also increase for larger block sizes when the database size is large.

- PMaps perform very well in the case of inequality queries or high selectivity queries. This result could be used to create PMaps for specific applications.

Extensions to the research reported here are summarized as follows:

- Currently, PMaps are not designed to represent aggregation and grouping queries. Grouping attributes are usually low cardinality attributes, and can be covered by enumerated properties in a PMap. After processing the WHERE clause, the pstrings of the tuples in the intermediate result need to be scanned for the ones satisfying the grouping property. Future research could extend the PMap to solve aggregation and grouping queries.

- Index maintenance, including deletions and updates, is an area for future investigation.

- A solution to the problem of finding a well-defined encoding discussed by Wu and Buchmann (1998) can be used to make PMaps more efficient. Bit string representations of properties and their ordering can be decided using a well-defined encoding so that fewer pstrings have to be searched. Vertical partitioning of pstrings may be another way to improve PMap performance.

- Although useful for our study of the impact of parameters on performance, the database sizes used here are small compared to real data warehouse applications. Further investigation into the scalability of PMaps is a topic for future study.

Copyright © 2007, Idea Group Inc. Copying or distributing in print or electronic forms without written permission of Idea Group Inc. is prohibited.

- Techniques for compressing bitmap indexes (Wu et al., 2006) increase efficiency of in-memory logical operations. The impact of these techniques on query processing with PMaps is an open question.

References

Chan, C. Y., & Ioannidis, Y. (1998). Bitmap index design and evaluation. *Proceedings of the ACM SIGMOD International Conference,* Seattle, WA (pp. 355-366).

Darira, R., Davis, K. C., & Grommon-Litton, J. (2006). Heuristic design of property maps. *Proceedings of the 9th ACM Workshop on Data Warehousing and On-Line Analytical Processing,* McLean, VA.

Gray, J. (1993). *The benchmark handbook for database and transaction processing systems.* Morgan Kaufmann Publishers.

Gupta, A., Davis, K. C., & Grommon-Litton, J. (2002). A performance comparison of property map and bitmap indexing. *Proceedings of the Fifth ACM Workshop on Data Warehousing and On-Line Analytical Processing,* McLean, VA (pp. 65-71).

Jurgens, M., & Lenz, H. J. (2001). Tree based indexes vs. bitmap indexes: A performance study. *International Journal of Cooperative Information Systems.* *10*(3), 355-376.

Koudas, N. (2000). Space efficient bitmap indexing. *Proceedings of the 9th International Conference on Information and Knowledge Management,* McLean, Virginia (pp. 194-201).

O'Neil, P., & Quass, D. (1997). Improved query performance with variant indexes. *Proceedings of the ACM SIGMOD Conference,* Tucson, AZ (pp. 38-49).

Sarawagi, S. (1997). Indexing OLAP Data. *Data Engineering Bulletin, 20*(1), 36-43.

Vanichayobon, S., & Gruenwald, L. (1999). *Indexing techniques for data warehouses'queries.* The University of Oklahoma, School of Computer Science, Technical Report.

Wu, K., Otoo, E., & Shoshani, A. (2005). An efficient compression scheme for bitmap indices. *ACM Transactions on Database Systems, 31*(1), 1-38.

Wu, K. L., & Yu, P. S. (1998). Range-based bitmap indexing for high cardinality attributes with skew. *Proceedings of the 22nd International Computer Software and Application Conference,* Vienna, Austria (pp. 61-67.

Copyright © 2007, Idea Group Inc. Copying or distributing in print or electronic forms without written permission of Idea Group Inc. is prohibited.

Wu, M. C., & Buchmann, A. (1998). Encoded bitmap indexing for data warehouses. *Proceedings of the 14ᵗʰ International Conference on Data Engineering,* Orlando, FL (pp. 220-230).

Copyright © 2007, Idea Group Inc. Copying or distributing in print or electronic forms without written permission of Idea Group Inc. is prohibited.

Chapter IX

Efficient and Robust Node-Partitioned Data Warehouses

Pedro Furtado
Universidade de Coimbra, Portugal

Abstract

Running large data warehouses (DWs) efficiently over low cost platforms places special requirements on the design of system architecture. The idea is to have the DW on a set of low-cost nodes in a nondedicated local area network (LAN). Nodes can run any relational database engine, and the system relies on a partitioning strategy and query processing middle layer. These characteristics are in contrast with typical parallel database systems, which rely on fast dedicated interconnects and hardware, as well as a specialized parallel query optimizer for a specific database engine. This chapter describes the architecture of the node-partitioned data warehouse (NPDW), designed to run on the low cost environment, focusing on the design for partitioning, efficient parallel join and query transformations. Given the low reliability of the target environment, we also show how replicas are incorporated in the design of a robust NPDW strategy with availability guarantees and how the replicas are used for always-on, always efficient behavior in the presence of periodic load and maintenance tasks.

Copyright © 2007, Idea Group Inc. Copying or distributing in print or electronic forms without written permission of Idea Group Inc. is prohibited.

Introduction

Data warehouses (DWs) are specialized databases storing historical data pertaining to an organization. The objective is to allow business analysis on varied perspectives. They have been applied in many contexts, for instance, insurance companies keeping track of individual events on insurance policies, telecom companies with terabytes of data tracking individual phone calls or individual machine events in production factories, generating gigabytes of detailed data per day. The degree of detail over which the data is stored in the data warehouse can vary, but from the examples given, it is easy to see that data warehouses can become extremely large. As such, multiple performance optimization strategies can be sought after, ranging from specialized indexing, materialized views for faster computation over predicted query patterns, to parallel architectures and parallel processing. Parallel database systems are implemented on one of the alternative parallel architectures: shared-memory, shared-disk, shared nothing, hierarchical, or NUMA (Valduriez & Ozsu, 1999), which have implications on parallel query processing algorithms, data partitioning, and placement. In practice, parallel environments involve several extra overheads related to data and control exchanges between processing units and also concerning storage, so that all components of the system need to be designed to avoid bottlenecks that would compromise the whole processing efficiency. Some parts of the system have to account for the aggregate flow into/from all units. For instance, in shared-disk systems the storage devices and interconnections should be sufficiently fast to handle the aggregate of all accesses without becoming a significant bottleneck. To handle these requirements, a significant initial and continuous investment is necessary in specialized, fast, and fully-dedicated hardware. An attractive alternative is to use a number of low-cost computer nodes in a shared-nothing environment, possibly in a nondedicated local network. The only requirement is that each node has some database engine and connectivity, while a middle layer provides parallel processing. This system must take into consideration partitioning and processing, as the computer nodes and interconnects are not specially designed to that end. The node-partitioned data warehouse (NPDW) is a generic architecture for partitioning and processing over the data warehouse in such an environment. The objective of this chapter is to discuss and analyze partitioning, processing, and availability issues in the design of the NPDW.

Background

Typical data warehouse schemas have some distinctive properties: they are mostly read-only, with periodic loads. This characteristic minimizes consistency issues

Copyright © 2007, Idea Group Inc. Copying or distributing in print or electronic forms without written permission of Idea Group Inc. is prohibited.

which are a major concern regarding the parallelization of transactional schemas and workloads; data warehouse schemas usually have multidimensional characteristics (Kimball, Reeves, Ross, & Thornthwaite, 1998), with large central fact relations containing several measurements (e.g., the amount of sales) and a size of up to hundreds or thousands of gigabytes, and dimensions (e.g., shop, client, product, supplier). Each measurement is recorded for each individual combination of dimension values (e.g., sales of a product from a supplier, in one shop and for an individual client). While there are specific analysis-oriented data marts stored and analyzed using some nonrelational multidimensional engine (Kimball, Reeves, Ross, & Thornthwaite, 1998), our focus is on the large central repository warehouses stored in a relational engine; warehouses are used for online analytical processing (OLAP), including reporting and ad-hoc analysis patterns. OLAP involves complex query patterns, with joins involving multiple relations and aggregations. These query patterns can pose difficulties to the performance of shared-nothing partitioned environments, especially when nodes need to exchange massive quantities of data. While very small dimensions can be replicated into every node and kept in memory to speed up joins involving them, much more severe performance problems appear when many large relations need to be joined and processed to produce an answer. We use the schema and query set of the decision support performance benchmark TPC-H (TPC) as an example of such a complex schema and query workload and also as our experimental testbed. Performance and availability are relevant issues in data warehouses in general and pose specific challenges in the NPDW context (standard computer nodes and nonspecialized interconnects).

Some research in recent years has focused on ad-hoc star join processing in data warehouses. Specialized structures such as materialized views (Rousopoulos, 1998) and specialized indexes (Chan & Ioannidis, 1998; O'Neil & Graefe, 1995) have been proposed to improve response time. Although materialized views are useful in a context in which queries are known in advance, this is not the case when ad-hoc queries are posed. Parallel approaches are therefore important as they can be used alone or in conjunction with specialized structures to provide efficient processing for any query pattern at any time. In the past, there has also been a lot of work on implementing database systems over conventional shared-nothing architectures, as reviewed in DeWitt and Gray (1992). A shared-nothing architecture consists of a set of independent computer nodes that are connected through some network. Each node has its own storage devices and there is no expensive local area storage network with shared storage devices. Additionally, the NPDW does not assume any specialized fast interconnects between nodes, as it should work over a nondedicated local area network. In this context, performance is very dependent on strategies to partition data into nodes' storage devices and processing into nodes' processing units, respectively. It is also very dependent on achieving a balance between data exchange requirements and autonomous processing among nodes. The lack of fast specialized hardware and interconnects in the target environment means that there

Copyright © 2007, Idea Group Inc. Copying or distributing in print or electronic forms without written permission of Idea Group Inc. is prohibited.

would be too large a penalty if relations were not carefully placed among nodes to explore parallelism power and reduce bottlenecks. This is the reason why one of the major concerns is to decide how to partition or cluster relations into nodes both on initial placement and subsequent reorganizations.

Partitioning, Parallel Join, and Cost Models

Several strategies have been proposed for efficient distributed placement and query processing. The semi-join operator (Bernstein & Chiu, 1981) applies selection and projection operations before sending data through the network. Other proposed strategies for efficient distributed query processing include placement dependency (Liu, Chen, & Krueger, 1996), which uses dependency relationships between relations to co-locate fragments for faster processing. This and other alternative strategies are compared experimentally in Liu and Yu (1993). The most promising solutions to extra join overheads that characterize many successful parallel and distributed database systems in shared-nothing environments involve hash-partitioning large relations into nodes in order to minimize data exchange requirements (DeWitt & Gerber, 1985; Kitsuregawa, Tanaka, & Motooka, 1983). Parallel hash-join algorithms, also reviewed in Yu and Meng (1998), consider partitioning and allocating intervening relation fragments into processors or computer nodes for fast join processing. These strategies typically allocate a hash range to each processor, which builds a hash table and hashes relation fragments accordingly. In a shared-nothing environment, it often becomes necessary to exchange data between nodes in order to send tuples into the node that has been allocated the corresponding hash-value range for the join attribute. This process is called partitioning, if the relation is not partitioned yet, or repartitioning, if the relation is already partitioned but must be reorganized. Both operations can be costly because they may require heavy data exchange over the network connecting the nodes. In this work we will refer to partitioning (and placement) not as the operation of partitioning while processing a join but rather as an initial placement and sporadic reorganization task that decides which relations are to be divided or replicated into nodes and which partitioning attributes are to be used. Williams and Zhou (1998) review five major data placement strategies (size-based, access frequency-based, and network traffic based) and conclude experimentally that the way data is placed in a shared-nothing environment can have considerable effect on performance. Hua and Lee (1990) use variable partitioning (size and access frequency-based) and conclude that partitioning increases throughput for short transactions but complex transactions involving several large joins result in reduced throughput with increased partitioning.

Some of the most promising partitioning and placement approaches focus on query workload-based partitioning choice (Rao, Zhang, & Megiddo, 2002; Zilio, Jhingram, & Padmanabhan, 1994). These strategies use the query workload to determine the

Copyright © 2007, Idea Group Inc. Copying or distributing in print or electronic forms without written permission of Idea Group Inc. is prohibited.

Figure 1. Join and query graphs for the example: (a) join graph and (b) join graph for query workload (JGQW)

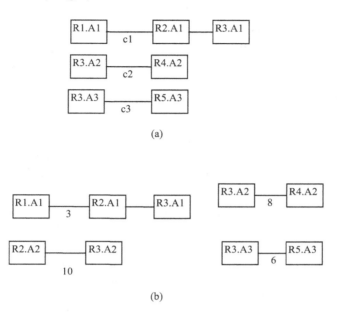

(a)

(b)

most appropriate partitioning attributes, which should be related to typical query access patterns. But while they are targeted at generic parallel databases and may require tight integration with a specific cost predictor and optimizer (Rao et al., 2002), we discuss generic data partitioning that is independent of the underlying database server and targeted at node partitioned data warehouses (Furtado, 2004a, b, c). Consider the query $Q = \{ R_1.A_2, R_2.A_4 \mid R_1.A_1=R2.A_1 \land R_2.A_1=R_3.A_1 \land R_3.A_2=R_4.A_2 \land R_3.A_3=R_5.A_3 \}$, where R_i are relations and A_i are attributes. The join graph of Figure 1a is a graph where vertices correspond to attributes R.A participating in equi-joins and the edges depict the set of equi-joins between those attributes. A component is a set of interconnected vertices and its edges. The join graph of the query workload (JGQW) shown in Figure 1b adds every join pattern occurring in the workload—the set of historical or expected queries—with a weight on each edge representing the frequency of occurrence of the corresponding join on the query workload (either a percentage or number of occurrences) (Furtado, 2004a).

Nodes of a component of a join graph form a set of relations that can be joined without requiring repartitioning and redistribution. The focus of the workload-based algorithms in Furtado (2004a, 2004b, 2004c) is to partition the whole relations in the join graph in a way that results in reduced repartitioning cost and redistribution requirements. Given this JGQW graph, a simple partitioning algorithm can assign partitioning attributes starting by the most frequent join (R3.A2, R2.A2 in the fig-

Copyright © 2007, Idea Group Inc. Copying or distributing in print or electronic forms without written permission of Idea Group Inc. is prohibited.

ure), to reduce the amount of repartitioning. More complex algorithms may search in the space of possible alternative execution plans, evaluating a cost for each possible plan (Kossman & Stocker, 2000).

In a data warehouse, there are an additional set of patterns that are important to guide the partitioning algorithm. Data warehouses have facts and dimensions, facts reference dimensions, and queries almost always join dimensions by their primary key. As a result, the algorithm we proposed in Furtado (2004c) partitions dimensions by primary keys (except small ones, which are replicated) and applies workload-based partitioning to facts.

Several works refer to the cost of processing queries over a distributed database or query optimization (query plan selection) in such context (Kossman & Stocker, 2000; Sasha, Wang, & Tsong-Li, 1991; Steinbrunn, Moerkotte, & Kemper, 1997; Yu, Guh, Brill, & Chen, 1989).

Yu et al. (1989) consider partitioning, local processing, and data communication costs in their cost model, to determine which relations should be partitioned and replicated, considering that no relation is prepartitioned. Algorithms and optimizations for parallel processing of multiway joins over hash-partitioned relations are considered by Sasha et al. (1991). The authors also introduce a cost model and propose algorithms to determine the most efficient join order for multiway joins over fully partitioned relations in a shared-nothing cluster. Some works (Kossman & Stocker, 2000; Steinbrunn et al., 1997) consider heuristic search for the best overall execution plan, considering that the search for the optimal plan is an NP-hard problem.

Low Bandwidth and Early Selection

Another factor that affects the efficiency of partitioning schemes is the "available bandwidth." Given that the network interconnecting the computer nodes may be slow, nondedicated, or the system may be running several queries simultaneously, it is important to take into account the possibility of low available bandwidth. This is a motivation for also considering partitioning schemes that favor replication such as strategies based on the partition and replicate strategy (PRS) of Yu et al. (1989), which partitions a single relation and replicates all others to process joins without repartitioning requirements.

Another relevant approach to reduce both the amount of repartitioning and also of local processing at each node is to apply early-selection strategies. These apply selection conditions as early as possible to datasets so that much less tuples need to be processed and exchanged. A bitmap index (Chan & Ioannidis, 1998) contains one bitmap per possible value of a given attribute (or a coded bitmap with b bits for 2^b possible values); the bitmap consists of one bit (or code) per row to indicate whether or not that row matches the respective attribute value. Chan and Ioannidis

Copyright © 2007, Idea Group Inc. Copying or distributing in print or electronic forms without written permission of Idea Group Inc. is prohibited.

(1998) describe and analyze the use of bitmap indexes. When accessing a relation to answer a query, bitmaps are read and bitwise-operated (e.g., logical AND of bitmaps) to determine which relation tuples qualify for the query before even reading the relation itself. All processing and data exchanging is then applied to this reduced subset of tuples.

Bitmap join indexes (O'Neil & Graefe, 1995) are very efficient materialized structures for avoiding costly joins. When bitmap join indexes are applied to a data warehouse schema, each bitmap indicates which fact rows correspond to each attribute value of a dimension table, representing the precomputed result of a join between the fact and a dimension table. Consider the simple example of a "Sales" fact, a "Product" dimension, and a "Brand" attribute within "Product." A bitmap for Brand "X" associates a bit with each row of the Sales fact with a "1" bit if that row is a sale of Brand "X" and a "0" bit otherwise. A query for sales of brand "X" may scan the bitmap and then read only rows of Sales corresponding to that Brand. More importantly, it also avoids the need to join Sales with Product and therefore the need to repartition Part if it is partitioned and not co-located with Sales. In summary, the use of early-selection and in particular bitmap join indexes reduces the amount of data that must be exchanged very significantly, as long as there are selective conditions on the query patterns.

Next we review replication for availability issues, as it is also a major concern in the low-reliability environment of the NPDW.

Replication for Availability

A discussion of availability for node-partitioned data warehouses brings up several issues like network failures, data loading failures, or availability monitoring. Each of these issues requires specific solutions. For instance, network failures can be accommodated using backup connections. We concentrate on handling the possible unavailability of computing nodes, guaranteeing efficient availability, and promoting manageability. The objective is that the system be always-on and always efficient even when nodes are unavailable or entire parts of it are taken off-line for maintenance and management functions, such as loading with new data or other DBA functionality. Efficient node availability can be achieved via the use of replicas. A replica is a "standby" copy of some data that can be activated at any moment in case of unavailability or failure of the node holding the "original," so that processing resumes as usual. If processing with unavailable nodes is implemented efficiently, unavailability becomes less onerous to the whole system and it becomes feasible to have nodes unavailable or to stop a set of nodes for data loading, maintenance, upgrading, or other management activities without any major repercussions to processing. Replica placement has been studied in different contexts, from RAID disks (Patterson, Gibson, & Katz, 1998) to the context of generic parallel

Copyright © 2007, Idea Group Inc. Copying or distributing in print or electronic forms without written permission of Idea Group Inc. is prohibited.

and distributed databases. Replication strategies for shared-nothing systems range from mirrored disk drives (Tandem, 1987) to chained declustering (Hsiao & De-Witt, 1990a, b, 1991) or interleaved declustering (Teradata, 1985). Copeland and Keller (1989) compare some of these high-availability media recovery techniques. There are also recent works on replication (Coloun, Pacitti, & Valduriez, 2004; Lin, Kemme, & Jimenez-Peris, 2005; Pacitti, Özsu, & Coulon, 2003), but the emphasis is on transaction-related consistency issues. In general, most works focus generic replication strategies for availability considering nonpartitioned relations and OLTP workloads, while in this chapter we briefly discuss and evaluate replication on the specific node-partitioned data warehouse context. An extended discussion on the subject is available in Furtado (2005c).

Partitioning and Processing over the NPDW

In a partitioning scheme, each relation can either be partitioned (divided into partitions or fragments), copied in its entirety, or placed into a single node of a group of nodes. We simplify the discussion by considering only one group (all nodes) and homogeneity between nodes, in order to concentrate on the core partitioning and processing issues. Generically, if a relation is large or very large, partitioning is the choice that drives faster processing. On the other hand, very small relations can be replicated to avoid the need to repartition other very large datasets that may need to be joined with them. In practice the decision on replication vs. partitioning for each relation can be taken by a cost-based optimizer that evaluates alternative execution plans and partitioning scenarios to determine the best one. Horizontally-partitioned relations can typically be divided using a round-robin, random, range, or hash-based scheme. We assume horizontal hash-partitioning, as this approach facilitates key-based tuple location for parallel operation. Partitioning is intimately related to processing issues. Therefore, first we describe generic query processing over the NPDW. Then we focus on parallel join and partitioning alternatives.

Generic Processing over the NPDW

Query processing over a parallel shared-nothing database, and in particular over the NPDW, follows roughly the steps in Figure 2(b). Figure 2(a) illustrates a simple sum query example over the NPDW. In this example the task is divided into all nodes, so that each node needs to apply exactly the same initial query on its partial data, and the results are merged by applying a merge query again at the merging node with the partial results coming from the processing nodes. If the datasets could be

Copyright © 2007, Idea Group Inc. Copying or distributing in print or electronic forms without written permission of Idea Group Inc. is prohibited.

Figure 2. Query processing steps in NPDW: (a) example query (b) query processing steps

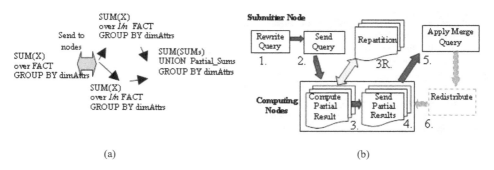

(a)   (b)

divided into N nodes and processed independently, each node would process its part (1/N) independently with a speedup of approximately N, and only the merge part of the query would represent extra overhead.

More generically, the typical query processing cycle implemented by the query processing middle layer is shown in Figure 2(b) and an example is given in Figure 3. A query is executed in steps. Step 1 "Rewrite Query" prepares the node and merge query components from the original submitted query. Step 2 "Send Query" forwards the node query into all nodes, which process the query locally in step 3. Each node then sends its partial result into the submitter node (step 4), which applies the merge query in step 5. Step 6 redistributes results into processing nodes if required (for some queries containing subqueries, in which case more than one processing cycle may be required). The query processing middle layer transforms queries into node queries and controls repartitioning requirements for processing operations such as parallel join.

In steps 1 and 2 of Figure 3 we can see that query aggregation expressions are replaced by aggregation primitives to be computed at each node and merged afterwards to obtain the results. The most common primitives are: Linear sum (LS=SUM(X)); Sum of squares (SS=SUM(X^2)); Number of elements (N); and Extremes (MAX and MIN).

Although in Figure 3 every node computes partial aggregations for all aggregation groups, aggregation can also be computed by assigning the computation of specific aggregation groups to specific nodes (Shatdal & Naughton, 1995). A detailed study and evaluation of query processing issues in the NPDW is available in Furtado (2005a).

The repartitioning operation of step 3R in Figure 2(b) is necessary whenever a partitioned dataset needs to participate in a join but is not partitioned by the join attribute. Each node is assigned a hash range for the join key, and every node needs to send to

Copyright © 2007, Idea Group Inc. Copying or distributing in print or electronic forms without written permission of Idea Group Inc. is prohibited.

Figure 3. Basic aggregation query steps

0. Query submission:
Select sum(a), count(a), average(a), max(a), min(a), stddev(a), group_attributes
From fact, dimensions (join)
Group by group_attributes;

3. Nodes compute partial results:
Select sum(a), count(a), sum(a x a), max(a), min(a), group_attributes
From fact, dimensions (join)
Group by group_attributes;

4. Results collecting:
Create cached table
PRqueryX(node, suma, counta, ssuma, maxa, mina,
group_attributes)
as <insert received results>;

5. Results merging:
Select sum(suma), sum(counta),
sum(suma) / sum(counta), max(maxa), min(mina)
(sum(ssuma)-sum(suma)^2)/sum(counta), group_attributes
From UNION_ALL(PRqueryX), dimensions (join)
Group by group_attributes;

every other node the tuples it has that belong to the hash-range corresponding to that node. It should be implemented as efficiently as possible to minimize the cost. We assume a switched network (the cost of repartitioning would be larger on a shared-media hub-based network). A simple parallel repartitioning algorithm would be:

Number the N nodes sequentially;

For (i=1;i<N;i++)

Parallel: every node j sends data to node (j+i) mod N;

The objective of this algorithm is for nodes to exchange data in parallel, to reduce the repartitioning overhead. In practice, the fact that nodes and processing at nodes are not homogeneous and that both switch and nodes' network interfaces often limit full duplex capability and performance means that the data communication overhead is usually larger than the optimal case. Given the generic query processing architecture, we focus next on partitioning alternatives.

Partitioning vs. Replication in NPDW

Consider relations or more generically datasets R_1 and R_2 that must be joined by an equi-join key as part of the execution plan: $R_1 \bowtie_A R_2$. Consider also that R_1 is fully horizontally partitioned into all nodes or into a node group. Each node out of N should process only 1/N of the total work in order to take full advantage of parallel execution. If both relations are partitioned by the same equi-join key, the join can be processed as a "**Local or Co-located Join**" (LocalJ) and this is the fastest alterna-

Copyright © 2007, Idea Group Inc. Copying or distributing in print or electronic forms without written permission of Idea Group Inc. is prohibited.

tive. The expression $R_1 \bowtie_A R_2$ is processed as ($R_{11} \bowtie_A R_{21}$) U ... U ($R_{1n} \bowtie_A R_{2n}$
), each part of this expression in a different node, because as the two relations are partitioned by the equi-join key, the join between two fragments in different nodes is an empty set (e.g., $R_{11} \bowtie_A R_{22} = \phi$). Otherwise, at least one of the relations must be moved. If only one of the relations or neither is partitioned on the join key, we can dynamically repartition on the same join key and proceed with the parallel equi-join—this is the "**Repartitioned Join**" (RpartJ). The repartitioning is accounted as an extra overhead, which increases total work and response time and is dependent on data buffering and communication-related overheads. On the other hand, if one of the relations is replicated by placement, the join can proceed independently at all nodes regardless of the partitioning key for the other relation. This is the "**Replicated Join**" (ReplicaJ). In a replicated join, the expression $R_1 \bowtie_A R_2$ is processed as ($R_{11} \bowtie_A R_2$) U ... U ($R_{1n} \bowtie_A R_2$). LocalJ requires the datasets involved in the join to be co-located. When trying to co-locate partitions from multiple relations, the partitioning issue that arises is that it is often necessary to choose which join will be co-located. For example, consider the join $R_1 \bowtie_A R_2 \bowtie_B R_3$. In this case R_2 will either be partitioned on A, in which case it will be co-located with R_1, or on B, in which case it will be co-located with R_3 (we can also partition R_2 by both attributes, but this does not result in co-location).

In multidimensional schemas of data warehouses, the partitioning issue is raised as some relations (e.g., facts) typically hold several foreign keys to other relations (e.g., dimensions). Furtado (2004c) searches partitioning keys for facts that increase the amount of LocalJ as opposed to RpartJ by looking at the query workload.

If the interconnections are slow or the available bandwidth is small, a replication strategy using ReplicaJ may be preferable, as it requires no or little data exchange between nodes. Processing with replicas follows the logic of the "partition and replicate strategy" (PRS) (Yu et al., 1989), where a single relation is partitioned and the remaining ones replicated. The actual decision on whether to partition or replicate relations requires a cost model that we review later.

Partitioning Strategies

In this section we define a set of strategies that take into consideration partitioning and replication. In the following section a generic cost model will also be presented. Consider the TPC-H data warehouse schema of Figure 4 from TPC (1999). It contains several large relations, which are frequently involved in joins. The schema represents ordering and selling activity (LI-lineitem, O-orders, PS-partsupp, P-part, S-supplier, C-customer), where relations such as LI, O, PS, and even P are quite large. There are also two very small relations, NATION and REGION, not depicted in the figure as they are very small and can be readily replicated into all nodes.

Copyright © 2007, Idea Group Inc. Copying or distributing in print or electronic forms without written permission of Idea Group Inc. is prohibited.

Figure 4. Summary of TPC-H schema: (a) TPC-H schema and (b) relation sizes (100GB)

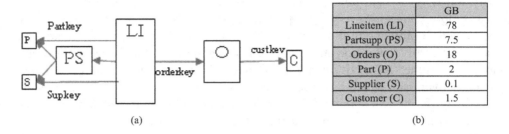

	GB
Lineitem (LI)	78
Partsupp (PS)	7.5
Orders (O)	18
Part (P)	2
Supplier (S)	0.1
Customer (C)	1.5

(a)   (b)

Figure 5. Example query and possible execution plan (TPC-H): (a) generic query Qa and (b) part of execution plan for Qa

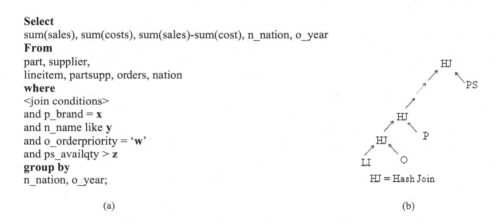

Select
sum(sales), sum(costs), sum(sales)-sum(cost), n_nation, o_year
From
part, supplier,
lineitem, partsupp, orders, nation
where
<join conditions>
and p_brand = **x**
and n_name like **y**
and o_orderpriority = '**w**'
and ps_availqty > **z**
group by
n_nation, o_year;

HJ = Hash Join

(a)   (b)

Figure 5(a) shows a generic query Qa, and a possible "star-join" execution plan for that query is shown in Figure 5(b).

Given this example schema, the challenge is how to partition, process, and provide availability to obtain an efficient low cost, platform-independent shared-nothing data warehouse. We wish to determine what would be a good partitioning strategy to process queries, considering that each relation could either be fully partitioned or replicated.

In the next figures we represent the contents of each node: filled relation boxes represent replicated relations and partially-filled ones represent partitioned relations. The following alternatives will be considered:

- **Partition and replicate strategy (PRS):** Partition the largest relation (LI in TPC-H) and replicate all the other ones, as shown in Figure 6. Each node stores

Copyright © 2007, Idea Group Inc. Copying or distributing in print or electronic forms without written permission of Idea Group Inc. is prohibited.

Figure 6. Node contents for PRS and PFRD-H partitioning strategies: (a) PRS partitioning, and (b) PFRD-H partitioning

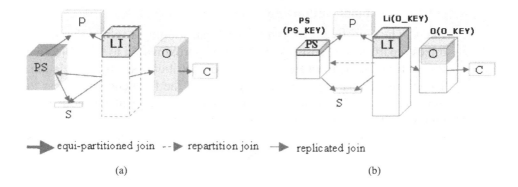

(a)   (b)

only a fraction of the largest relation (LI) and replicas of all other relations. All the joins are ReplicaJ in this case. This strategy allows joins to be processed without any data exchange between nodes, but the overhead of processing large replicated relations can be prohibitive.

With PRS, the join execution plan of Figure 5(b) would be executed without any data exchange between nodes, but each node would need to process full O and PS relations, which are 18 and 7.5 GB in size considering TPC-H with 100 GB (scale factor 100).

In order to avoid replicating very large relations, a modified strategy is to replicate dimensions and partition every fact, while also co-locating LI and O:

- **Hash-partition fact and replicate dimensions strategy (PFRD-H):** Partition relations identified as facts by the user (LI, O, and PS in TPC-H), co-locating LI and O. With PFRD-H, the execution plan of Figure 4b requires repartitioning of only two datasets: the intermediate result LI-O-P-S and relation PS. The join between LI and O is a LocalJ.

- **Workload-based partitioning (WBP):** A workload-based strategy where hash-partitioning attributes are determined based on schema and workload characteristics. We use the strategy proposed in Furtado (2004c). The partitioning algorithm is:

  1. **Dimensions:** Small dimensions are replicated into every node (and optionally cached into memory). Nonsmall dimensions can simply be hash-partitioned by their primary key. This is because that attribute is expected to be used in every equi-join with facts, as the references from facts to dimensions correspond to foreign keys.

     The determination of whether a dimension is small can be cost-based or, for simplicity, based on a user-defined threshold (e.g., every relation with

Copyright © 2007, Idea Group Inc. Copying or distributing in print or electronic forms without written permission of Idea Group Inc. is prohibited.

less than 250 MB is to be replicated and those with less than 100 MB are to be cached into memory for faster access). For our experiments we have used this simple approach, but we describe a cost model and discuss the search for optimal partitioning in the next section.

2.   **Facts:** The objective is to find the hash-partitioning attribute that minimizes repartitioning costs. A reasonable approximation to this objective is to determine the most frequent equi-join attribute used by the relation. To do this, the partitioning strategy looks at the frequency of access to other partitioned relations and chooses the most frequent equi-join attribute with those relations as the partitioning attribute. We have described this process in the second section. A more complex approach involves the search for optimal partitioning, as described in the next section.

By co-locating relation fragments that are frequent equi-join targets, this simple strategy reduces significantly repartitioning requirements (we have determined experimentally that WBP achieves an improvent of about 50% over straightforward primary-key based partitioning (PK) when executing the query of Figure 5 under the same conditions described later in the experiments).

Figure 7 shows the partitioning that resulted from applying the WBP strategy to TPC-H query set. Concerning the execution plan of Figure 4b, this strategy allows joins LI to O and LI-O-P-S to PS to be processed as LocalJ. Repartitioning is necessary only for intermediate dataset LI-O.

- **WBP with bitmap join indexes (WBP+JB):** We have materialized join bitmaps in every node for attributes (p_brand, n_name, o_orderpriority, ps_availqty) to speed up the query of Figure 5. For instance, before scanning the LI relation, the associated bitmap join indexes such as the one for Brand x is scanned. This way, only the LI rows associated with Brand x are processed any further, including repartitioning data.

Figure 7. WBP partitioning

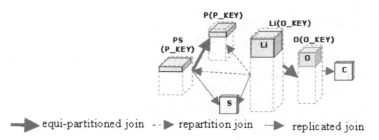

Copyright © 2007, Idea Group Inc. Copying or distributing in print or electronic forms without written permission of Idea Group Inc. is prohibited.

In the next section we review a generic cost model for the strategies, taking into account factors such as the number of nodes and network bandwidth.

Cost Model

The main processing costs (listed next) are repartitioning, data communication, local processing, and merging:

a. **Repartitioning cost (RC):** Partitioning a relation consists of retrieving the relation from secondary memory, dividing it into fragments by applying a hash function to a join attribute, and assigning buffers for the data to send to other nodes. Repartitioning is similar but involves a fragment in each node. Multiple nodes can rehash and exchange relation fragments simultaneously.

b. **Data communication cost (DC):** The data communication cost is monotonically increasing with the size of the data transferred. We assume a switched network, as this allows different pairs of nodes to send data simultaneously (with no collisions). This, in turn, allows the repartitioning algorithm to be implemented more efficiently.

c. **Local processing cost (LC):** The local processing cost for the join operation typically depends on whether the join is supported by fast access paths such as indexes and the size of the relations participating in the join. For simplicity, we assume these costs also increase monotonically on the relation sizes, although, in practice, this depends on several parameters, including memory buffer size.

d. **Merging cost (MC):** The merging cost is related to applying a final query to the collected partial results at the merging node. We do not consider this cost as it is similar in every case and independent of the other ones.

Given these items, the next objective is to represent the cost as an expression involving the local processing and repartitioning costs (here we consider the data communication cost within the repartitioning cost). We define weighting parameters as in Sasha et al. (1991): a partitioning cost weight, β, and a local processing cost weight, α, so that β/α denotes the ratio of partitioning costs to local processing costs, for example, ~2 (Sasha et al., 1991). A cost-based optimizer is used to determine the most appropriate execution plan (Kossman & Stocker, 2000; Steinbrunn et al., 1997). A join order determines the order by which relations are joined. Assuming the datasets are joined using an algorithm such as parallel hybrid hash-join, at each step an additional relation is joined to the current intermediate result set IR_i (selec-

Copyright © 2007, Idea Group Inc. Copying or distributing in print or electronic forms without written permission of Idea Group Inc. is prohibited.

tion and projection operators are applied as soon as possible to reduce the size of the datasets that need to be processed). Given the result set IR_i and a relation R_j, equations (1) and (2) represent the processing costs for a single server and a node-partitioned system where R_j is replicated into all nodes and IR_i is partitioned:

$$one\ server\ system:\ \alpha \times \left(IR_i + R_j \right) \tag{1}$$

$$replicated\ join:\ \alpha \times \left(\frac{IR_i}{N} + R_j \right) \tag{2}$$

Equations (3) and (4) represent the local processing cost (LC) and repartitioning cost (RC) when both datasets are partitioned. The RC cost in (4) is only incurred when the datasets are not co-located.

$$LC\ for\ local\ join:\ \alpha \times \left(\frac{IR_i}{N} + \frac{R_j}{N} \right) \tag{3}$$

$$RC\ non-colocated\ data\ sets:\ \beta \times \left(\frac{IR_i}{N} - \frac{IR_i}{N^2} \right) \tag{4}$$

The value IR_i/N in equation (4) is the fraction of the IR_i that is at each node and IR_i/N^2 is the fraction of that quantity that already has the correct hash-value for that node, therefore requiring no repartitioning.

By subtracting (3) from (2) we get the advantage of partitioning over replicating when both datasets are co-located. However, if the datasets are not co-located, we must subtract equation (4) from this value. If β is large (small available bandwidth), this RC cost can become dominant and replication becomes the best choice.

The WBP strategy improves the performance of the system by making each node process $1/N$ of relations and intermediate results as much as possible (3) and simultaneously reducing repartitioning requirements (4) by placing datasets based on the workload. On the other hand, PRS focuses on eliminating repartitioning requirements (4) to handle contexts with low bandwidth, but on the other hand, it needs to process whole relations (2). Finally, WBP-JB uses bitmaps over the nodes to avoid the repartitioning cost (4) (and simultaneously also reducing local processing costs). Given a cost model, a cost-based optimizer evaluates the cost of alternative execution plans (including join orders) for alternative partitioning options (partition or replicate relations). In practice, this cost model is replaced by evaluating the cost of operations as our simulator described next does.

Copyright © 2007, Idea Group Inc. Copying or distributing in print or electronic forms without written permission of Idea Group Inc. is prohibited.

Comparative Analysis of Partitioning Alternatives

The partitioning strategies described before can be characterized as more replication-oriented (PRS, PFRD-H) and more partitioning-oriented (WBP, WBP+JB) ones. Partitioning-oriented strategies are very efficient in an environment with fast interconnections and available bandwidth, because repartitioning is cheap in those environments. On the other hand, the advantage of PRS (and PFRD-H) is that it places lower requirements on the interconnections, with fewer data exchange requirements. However, the drawback is the size of replicated relations that must be processed in every node. Our comparative analysis is based both on a simulator environment, to test several possible configurations (e.g., number of nodes, available bandwidth) and actual executions to help validate the results and analyze the strategies for TPC-H query set.

We have built a discrete-event simulation environment, which uses a basic set of parameters listed in Figure 8. The simulator estimates the cost of individual operations that need to be performed to execute the query. Operation tasks are submitted as required and resource utilization for disk access, memory and bus, processor, and network send/receive are used to determine completion time for those tasks. For instance, the cost of a hybrid hash-join is related to the cost of scanning the relations from secondary storage, bucketizing them, building a hash table, and probing into the hash table. For instance, the cost to join relations R1 and R2 considering the individual scan costs is scanR1 + scanR2 + 2(scanR1 + scanR2) (1-q), where q denotes the fraction of R1 whose hash-table fits in memory (Steinbrunn et al., 1997). Disk access rates (measured in MB/sec) are then used to complete the evaluation of the cost. Similar strategies are applied to evaluate the repartitioning cost, which involves scanning the datasets, operating on them, assigning buffers, and sending to destination nodes (with given network bandwidth in MB/sec). A typical number of instructions used to process different low-level operations and to send and receive messages (Network) were included as a parameter to the simulator (Stöhr, Märtens & Rahm, 2000). For these experiments we used a TPC-H with 100 GB and generic query Qa of Figure 5a, with default selectivity for attribute values (x, y, w, z) of (0.7, 0.7, 0.2, 0.2) respectively.

Figure 9 shows the response time (a) and speedup (b) vs. the n° of nodes for query Qa.

The performance of replica-based strategies (especially PRS) is much worse than partitioning-based ones (WBP, WBP+JB), because nodes have to process large replicated datasets. Additionally, (WBP+JB) improves response time further, as early-selection functionality reduces the amount of data that must be processed and repartitioned. Of course bitmap join indexes must be available and their usefulness depends on the selectivity of query select conditions. On the other hand, if the

Copyright © 2007, Idea Group Inc. Copying or distributing in print or electronic forms without written permission of Idea Group Inc. is prohibited.

Figure 8. Basic parameters for simulation

Disk		Processing	N° Instrs.	Network	
seek time	10 ms	read page	3,000	connection speed (default)	100 MB/s
settle time + ctrller delay	per access 3 ms + 1 ms per page	process bitmap page	1,500	send message	1,000 + #B instructions
Seq. transfer rate / node	100MB/s	extract & hash/probe table row	250	receive message	1,000 + #B instructions
CPU speed	50 MIPS			message size (small)	128 B
Memory Buffer	500MB/node			message size (large)	1 page (4 KB)

Figure 9. Response time and speedup VS N° of nodes (100 MB/s) (log-plots): (a) RT vs N° of nodes and (b) speedup vs n° of nodes

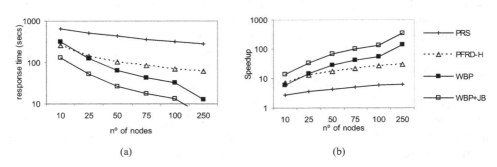

(a)   (b)

available network bandwidth is low, strategies using replicas (e.g., PRS, PFRD-H) can exhibit better performance relative to those relying on partitioning (WBP), as shown in Figure 10a. Still, early-selection (WBP+JB) was the best strategy because it is not very dependent on repartitioning.

We also subjected our simulator to conformance tests, to evaluate whether its simulation is sufficiently accurate for our purposes. Figure 11 shows a result from those tests. We ran WBP and PRS on a system with the characteristics: TPC-H 25GB; commercial DBMS; each node with 3 GHz Intel Pentium 4 processor; 1 GB memory; 200 GB SATA II disk; 1 GB/s network; query Qa). Cost-based optimization was used, the schema objects were analyzed and the best query plan suggestion was chosen (the default execution plan had very bad performance for PRS). The results show

Copyright © 2007, Idea Group Inc. Copying or distributing in print or electronic forms without written permission of Idea Group Inc. is prohibited.

Figure 10. RT vs. Mbps (100 nodes)

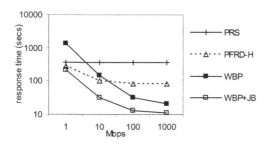

Figure 11. Simulation vs. real execution (25 GB, 1Gbps)

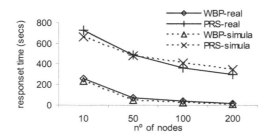

that the simulated response time was reasonably accurate. Although its prediction for PRS was slightly higher than the actual response time for a number of nodes above 100, the advantage of WBP is still very evident from these results.

Finally, we also ran the whole TPC-H query set against WBP and PRS to compare replication vs. partitioning on the following system: 25 nodes; TPCH 50 GB; each node with Pentium III 866 MHz CPU; 80 GB IDE hard disks; 512 MB of RAM; 100 MB/s switched network). For these results we consider TPC-H query set divided into groups (Figure 12) according to sizes of replicated relations accessed and processed by the joins. Group G1 accesses only a partitioned relation (LI or PS). The other groups include references to replicated relations with sizes in the following intervals:* Small: (0, 500MB); Medium: (500 MB, 5 GB); Large (5 GB, ∞).

The speedup intervals (T lines) of Figure 13 are the range of speedup values considering all queries in a group. From the results we can see that the larger the replicated relations, the smallest the PRS speedup (G2, G3, and G4), with a large penalty for processing heavy ReplicaJ joins. WBP achieved a near-to-linear speedup for all queries, while PRS revealed very low speedup for most queries.

Copyright © 2007, Idea Group Inc. Copying or distributing in print or electronic forms without written permission of Idea Group Inc. is prohibited.

Figure 12. Size and layout of relations involved in parallel join over PRS

G1	G2	G3	G4
Partitioned	Partitioned + Medium Replicated	Partitioned + Large Replicated	Partitioned + Large Replicated + Medium Replicated
Q1, Q6, Q15	Q11,Q14,Q19	Q3, Q5, Q7, Q9, Q10, Q12, Q16	Q4, Q8, Q13, Q22

Figure 13. Grouped speedup results for PRS and WBP over 25 nodes

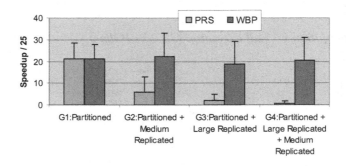

Replication for Nonstop Availability on NPDW

In this section we discuss briefly alternative replication choices within the NPDW for always-on, always efficient processing and allowing multiple nodes off-line simultaneously for data loading, maintenance, and other DBA functionality. Figure 14 shows the schema of a node X with availability-related replica from another node Y. Notice that some relations are already replicated by placement (S and C). Node X can now replace node Y in case of unavailability of Y by simply including Y partitions in the processing.

The simplest replica placement strategy involves replicating each node's data into at least one other node—full replicas (FRs). In case of failure of one node, a node containing the replica resumes the operation of the failed node. A simple placement algorithm considering R replicas is:

Number nodes linearly;

For each node i

      For (replica =1 to R) data for node i is also placed in node (i+R) MOD N;

Copyright © 2007, Idea Group Inc. Copying or distributing in print or electronic forms without written permission of Idea Group Inc. is prohibited.

Figure 14. Schema in node X with replicated schema from node Y

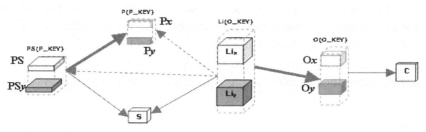

This simple strategy allows the system to work with unavailable nodes and it is possible to take more than one node off-line simultaneously. The major drawback is processing efficiency when unavailability of a few nodes occur: consider a NPDW system with N homogeneous nodes. Although normally each node contains and processes about 1/N of the data, if one node fails, the node replacing it with a replica will have to process twice as much data (2/N), even though all the other nodes will process only 1/N. The replica effort is placed on a single node, even though other nodes are less loaded.

An alternative to full replicas is to use fully partitioned replicas (FPR)—replicas are partitioned into as many slices as there are nodes minus one. If there are N nodes, a replica is partitioned into N-1 slices and each slice is placed in one node. The replica of node *i* is now dispersed into all nodes except node i. In order to allow up to R nodes to become unavailable, there must be R nonoverlapping replica slice sets. Two replicas are nonoverlapped *if* the equivalent slices of the two replicas are not placed in the same node. The following placement algorithm is used:

Number nodes linearly;

The copy of the data of node i is partitioned into N-1 numbered slices, starting at 1.

For j=0 to R:

      For (slice x from 1 to N-1) Place slice x in node (i+j+ x) MOD N

This strategy is the most efficient because, considering N nodes, each replica slice has 1/(N-1) of the data and each node has to process only that fraction in excess in case of a single node becoming unavailable. However, all nodes that remain active are needed to process a slice from the replica. In order to allow up to R nodes to become unavailable, there must be R nonoverlapping replica slice sets.

If we desire *y* nodes to be able to be off-line simultaneously when a single replica

Copyright © 2007, Idea Group Inc. Copying or distributing in print or electronic forms without written permission of Idea Group Inc. is prohibited.

is used, then the y nodes must not contain replica slices of each other. Partitioned replicas (PRs) guarantee this by creating groups and placing replica slices from one group in a different group. This way we can take a whole group off-line simultaneously for maintenance or other functionality, because the complete set of replica slices are elsewhere. This strategy is a hybrid between FPR and FR.

If replicas are partitioned into x slices, we denote it by PR(x). If x = N, we have a fully partitioned replica. A very simple algorithm to generate less than N slices is:

Number nodes linearly;

The data for node i is partitioned into X slices starting at 1;

For slice set j = 0 to R

    For (slice x from 1 to X) Place slice x in node (i+j+ x) MOD N

Figure 15 compares the response time <min:sec> (line) for query TPC-H Q9 and the minimum number of replicas needed (bars) when 5 out of 20 nodes are off-line using full replicas (FRs), fully partitioned replicas (FPRs), and partitioned replicas (PRs). These results were obtained in a system with the characteristics: 50 GB TPC-H; 20 nodes, each with 866 MHz processor; 512 MB RAM). The alternatives compared are: online—every node is online; FPR—fully partitioned replicas; PR(10)—partitioned replicas with two groups of 10 nodes; PR(5)—partitioned replicas with 4 groups of 5 nodes. These results show the much larger penalty incurred by FR and the excessive number of replicas required for FPR to allow 5 nodes off-line simultaneously. PR(10) (partitioned replicas with two 10 element groups) is a good choice, as it requires a single replica and obtains a good response time simultaneously.

Given these results, we conclude that replicas partitioned by groups are the most advantageous alternative for NPDW if we consider both performance and flexibility in allowing multiple nodes to be taken off-line simultaneously for maintenance and loading reasons.

Figure 15. Response time and replicas when 5 out of 20 nodes are off-line (average over TPC-H)

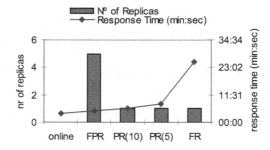

Copyright © 2007, Idea Group Inc. Copying or distributing in print or electronic forms without written permission of Idea Group Inc. is prohibited.

Future Trends

The NPDW is the basic design for the Data Warehouse Parallel Architecture Project (DWPA, 2005), which focuses on architectural characteristics, automatic reorganization, load balancing, response time prediction, and automatic adaptability for the low-cost node-partitioned data warehouse. These are in line with current and future trends on database research in related issues, which include database self-tuning and autoconfiguration (Chaudhuri & Weikum, 2002; Schiefer & Valentin, 1999; Weikum, Moenkeberg, Hasse, & Zabback, 2002). Runtime prediction is also an important objective for current and future research on database engines. There are very interesting recent works on runtime estimation and improvement (Chaudhuri, Narasayya, & Ramamurthy, 2004; Luo, Naughton, Ellmann, & Watzke, 2004) that can be usefully adapted to parallel settings and in particular to the NPDW environment. There is nowadays a market trend towards more and more open-source software, including open-source database engines being deployed in organizations and cost-consciousness in both hardware and software platforms is increasingly important. In this context, the DWPA concept of an architecture that can run anywhere efficiently and adaptively also seems to be in line with current trends. Besides, many of the issues discussed in this chapter can also be applied to other parallel architectures that are increasingly deployed, in particular symmetric multiprocessors (SMP) and clusters of SMPs.

Conclusion

We have discussed design issues for low-cost alternatives to specialized, fast, and fully-dedicated parallel hardware to handle large data warehouses. The idea is to design the system with special care concerning partitioning for placement and re-organization and also concerning availability. Alternative partitioning strategies were proposed and their performance compared. We have tested replica-based and partitioned-based strategies and analyzed their performance vs. the number of nodes and available network bandwidth. We also tested the use of early selection with join bitmaps as an approach to overcome extra overheads related to repartitioning and overall processing. We concluded that workload-based partitioning is a suitable strategy, and join bitmaps not only improve speedup but also prevent significant slowdown when the available network bandwidth is low. We have also described replication-based availability that allows always-on behavior and efficiency when multiple nodes are taken off-line.

Copyright © 2007, Idea Group Inc. Copying or distributing in print or electronic forms without written permission of Idea Group Inc. is prohibited.

Acknowledgments

This work was supported in part by the Portuguese "Fundação para a Ciência e Tecnologia," under project POSC/EIA/57974/2004.

References

Bernstein, P. A., & Chiu, D. M. (1981). Using semi-joins to solve relational queries. *Journal of the ACM, 28*(1), 25-40.

Chan C.-Y., & Ioannidis, Y. E. (1998). Bitmap index design and evaluation. In *Proceedings of the International Conference on the Management of Data* (pp. 355-366).

Chaudhuri, S., Narasayya, V., & Ramamurthy, R. (2004). Estimating progress of execution for SQL queries. In *Proceedings of the ACM International Conference on Data Management*, Paris.

Chaudhuri, S., & Weikum, G. (2002). Rethinking database system architecture: Towards a self-tuning, RISC-style database system. In *Proceedings of Very Large Databases Conference*.

Copeland, G., & Keller, T. (1989). A comparison of high-availability media recovery techniques. In *Proceedings of the ACM International Conference on Management of Data*.

Coulon, C., Pacitti, E., & Valduriez, P. (2004, June 28-30). Scaling up the preventive replication of autonomous databases in cluster systems. In *Proceedings of the 6th International Vecpar Conference*, Valencia, Spain.

DeWitt, D., & Gray, J. (1992). The future of high performance database processing. *Communications of the ACM, 35*(6).

DWPA. (2005-2008). *Fundação para a Ciência e a Tecnologia* (Research and Development Project POSI/EIA/57974/2004 of FCT), Portugal.

Furtado, P. (2004a, July). Hash-based placement and processing for efficient node partitioned query-intensive databases. In *Proceedings of the Tenth International Conference on Parallel and Distributed Systems* (pp. 127-134). Newport Beach, California.

Furtado, P. (2004b, September). Workload-based placement and join processing in node-partitioned data warehouses. In *Proceedings of the International Conference on Data Warehousing and Knowledge Discovery* (pp. 38-47). Zaragoza, Spain.

Copyright © 2007, Idea Group Inc. Copying or distributing in print or electronic forms without written permission of Idea Group Inc. is prohibited.

Furtado, P. (2004c, November). Experimental evidence on partitioning in parallel data warehouses. In *Proceedings of the ACM DOLAP 04 Workshop of the International Conference on Information and Knowledge Management*, Washington.

Furtado, P. (2005a, May). Efficiently processing query-intensive databases over a non-dedicated local network. In *Proceedings of the 19th International Parallel and Distributed Processing Symposium*, Denver, Colorado.

Furtado, P. (2005b, April). The issue of large relations in node-partitioned data warehouses. In *Proceedings of the International Conference on Database Systems for Advanced Applications*, Beijing, China.

Furtado, P. (2005c, August). Replication in node partitioned data warehouses. In *Proceedings of the VLDB Ws. on Design, Implementation, and Deployment of Database Replication*, Trondheim, Norway.

Hsiao, H., & DeWitt, D. (1990a). *Chained declustering: A new availability strategy for multi-processor database machines.* Paper presented at the International Conference on Data Engineering.

Hsiao, H., & DeWitt, D. (1990b). *Replicated data management in the Gamma Database Machine.* Paper presented at the Workshop on the Management of Replicated Data.

Hsiao, H., & DeWitt, D. J. (1991). A performance study of three high availability data replication strategies. In *Proceedings of the Parallel and Distributed Systems.*

Hua, K. A., & Lee, C. (1990, August). An adaptive data placement scheme for parallel database computer systems. In *Proceedings of the Sixteenth Very Large Data Bases Conference* (pp. 493-506). Brisbane, Queensland, Australia.

Kimball, R., Reeves, L., Ross, M., & Thornthwaite, W. (1998). *The data warehouse life cycle toolkit.* John Wiley & Sons.

Kitsuregawa, M., Tanaka, H., & Motooka, T. (1983). Application of hash to database machine and its architecture. *New Generation Computing, 1*(1), 63-74.

Lin, Y., Kemme, B., & Jimenez-Peris, R. (2005, August 30-September 2). Consistent data replication: Is it feasible in WANs? In *Proceedings of the 11th International Europar Conference*, Lisboa, Portugal.

Luo, G., Naughton, J. F., Ellmann, C. J., & Watzke, M. W. (2004). Toward a progress indicator for database queries. In *Proceedings of the ACM International Conference on Data Management*, Paris.

O'Neil, P., & Graefe, G. (1995). Multi-table joins through bitmapped join indices. *SIGMOD Record, 24*(3), 8-11.

Copyright © 2007, Idea Group Inc. Copying or distributing in print or electronic forms without written permission of Idea Group Inc. is prohibited.

Pacitti, E., Özsu, M., & Coulon, C. (2003, August 26-29). Preventive multi-master replication in a cluster of autonomous databases. In *Proceedings of the 9th International Europar Conference*, Klagenfurt, Austria.

Patterson, D. A., Gibson, G., & Katz, R. H. (1998, June). A case for redundant arrays of inexpensive disks (raid). In *Proceedings of the International Conference on Management of Data* (pp. 109-116). Chicago.

Rao, J., Zhang, C., Megiddo, N., & Lohman, G. (2002, June). Automating physical database design in a parallel database. In *Proceedings of the ACM International Conference on Management of Data* (pp. 558-569). Madison.

Rousopoulos, R. (1998). Materialized views and data warehouses. *SIGMOD Record, 27*(1), 21-26.

Saborit, J. A., Mulero, V. M., & Pey, J. L. (2003). Pushing down bit filters in the pipelined execution of large queries. In *Proceedings of the International Conference Europar* (pp. 328-337).

Schiefer, B., & Valentin, G. (1999). DB2 universal database performance tuning. *IEEE Data Engineering Bulletin, 22*(2), 12-19.

Shatdal, A., & Naughton, J. (1995, May 22-25). Adaptive parallel aggregation algorithms. In *Proceedings of the 1995 International Conference on Management of Data*, San Jose, California (pp. 104-114).

Stöhr, T., Märtens, H., & Rahm, E. (2000). Multi-dimensional database allocation for parallel data warehouses. In *Proceedings of the 26th International Conference on Very Large Databases (VLDB)*, Cairo, Egypt.

Tandem. (1987, September). NonStop SQL, a distributed, high-performance, high-reliability implementation of SQL. Paper presented at the *Workshop on High Performance Transactional Systems*, California.

Teradata. (1985, November). *Teradata DBC/1012 Database Computer System Manual 2.0, C10-0001-02*. Author.

TPC. (1999, June). *TPC Benchmark H, Transaction Processing Council*. Retrieved June 13, 2006, from http://www.tpc.org/

Valduriez, P., & Ozsu, M. (1999). *Principles of parallel and distributed database systems* (3rd ed.). Prentice Hall.

Weikum, G., Moenkeberg, A., Hasse, C., & Zabback, P. (2002). Self-tuning database technology and information services: From wishful thinking to viable engineering. In *Proceedings of the Very Large Databases Conference*.

Williams, M., & Zhou, S. (1998). Data placement in parallel database systems: Parallel database techniques. *IEEE Computer Society Press* (pp. 203-219).

Yu, C. T., Guh, K. C., Brill, D., & Chen, A. L. P. (1989, June). Partition strategy for distributed query processing in fast local networks. *IEEE Transactions on Software Engineering, 15*(6), 780-793.

Copyright © 2007, Idea Group Inc. Copying or distributing in print or electronic forms without written permission of Idea Group Inc. is prohibited.

Yu, C. T., & Meng, W. (1998). *Principles of database query processing for advanced applications*. Morgan Kaufmann.

Zilio, D. C., Jhingran, A., & Padmanabhan, S. (1994). *Partitioning key selection for a shared-nothing parallel database system* (IBM Research Rep. No. RC 19820 (87739)). IBM.

Copyright © 2007, Idea Group Inc. Copying or distributing in print or electronic forms without written permission of Idea Group Inc. is prohibited.

Chapter X

OLAP with a Database Cluster

Uwe Röhm

University of Sydney, Australia

Abstract

This chapter presents a new approach to online decision support systems that is scalable, fast, and capable of analysing up-to-date data. It is based on a database cluster: a cluster of commercial off-the-shelf computers as hardware infrastructure and off-the-shelf database management systems as transactional storage managers. We focus on central architectural issues and on the performance implications of such a cluster-based decision support system. In the first half, we present a scalable infrastructure and discuss physical data design alternatives for cluster-based online decision support systems. In the second half of the chapter, we discuss query routing algorithms and freshness-aware scheduling. This protocol enables users to seamlessly decide how fresh the data analysed should be by allowing for different degrees of freshness of the online analytical processing (OLAP) nodes. In particular it becomes then possible to trade freshness of data for query performance.

Copyright © 2007, Idea Group Inc. Copying or distributing in print or electronic forms without written permission of Idea Group Inc. is prohibited.

Introduction

Online analytical processing (OLAP) systems must cope with huge volumes of data and at the same time must allow for short response times to facilitate interactive usage. They must also be capable to scale, meaning to be easily extensible with the increasing data volumes accumulated. Furthermore, the requirement that the data analysed should be up-to-date is becoming more and more important. However, not only are these contrary requirements, but they also run counter to the performance needs of the day-to-day business.

Most OLAP systems nowadays are kept separated from mission critical systems. This means that they offer a compromise between "up-to-dateness," that is, freshness (or currency) of data, and query response times. The data needed are propagated into the OLAP system on a regular basis, preferably when not slowing down day-to-day business, for example, during nights or weekends. OLAP users have no alternative but to analyse stale data.

But a decision support system that could provide decision makers insight into up-to-date data "hot off the press" would open exciting new possibilities. A stockbroker, for example, could analyse current trends in the market online. For e-commerce, the personalisation of Web shops could be much improved by more complex analysis of current browsing behaviour. Even for the so-called "old economy," new perspectives open up, because the update window has already become drastically small in a 24/7 setting of a worldwide operating company. However, up to now there is no solution that meets these performance and freshness requirements at the same time.

In this chapter, we present a new approach to online decision support systems that is capable of analysing up-to-date data. It is based on a database cluster: this is a cluster of commercial off-the-shelf computers as hardware infrastructure and off-the-shelf database management systems as transactional storage managers. A coordination middleware on top hides the details and provides a uniform, general-purpose query interface. The result is a "database of databases" following the vision of a hyperdatabase (Schek, Böhm, Grabs, Röhm, Schuldt, & Weber, 2000). An important design principle of a database cluster is its component-oriented nature. In particular, we want to be able to easily plug together and to expand the cluster using standard hardware and software components only. This results in a highly scalable system architecture.

We concentrate on central architectural issues and performance aspects of database clusters for usage in a decision support scenario. The objective is to develop a basic infrastructure for interactive decision support systems that are capable of analysing up-to-date data and that can give guarantees on how outdated data accessed might be. To be able to do so, we need different versions of data in the cluster, which we achieve by replicating data throughout the cluster. Replication also helps to avoid expensive distributed joins over huge amounts of data; as always several nodes can

Copyright © 2007, Idea Group Inc. Copying or distributing in print or electronic forms without written permission of Idea Group Inc. is prohibited.

evaluate an OLAP query. We will discuss query routing strategies for an optimal workload distribution of long running and I/O intensive OLAP queries over encapsulated standard components of a database cluster.

Furthermore, we explicitly allow that not all cluster nodes are up-to-date all the time. This is reflected by the notion of freshness of data, which is a measure for the deviation of a certain component as compared to an up-to-date component. We present an innovative approach to replication management, called freshness-aware scheduling (FAS). The intention of freshness-aware scheduling is to trade query performance for freshness of data. Consequently, FAS introduces a new quality-of-service parameter that allows queries to specify an explicit freshness limit for the data accessed. If some queries agree to be evaluated on older data, update propagation can be interleaved with query processing more efficiently. This results in an overall better system performance and only a minimal slowdown of both queries and updates. In particular, it enables clients to request and access up-to-date data.

The remainder of this chapter is organised as follows: In the next two sections, we will first present a scalable infrastructure for an unified OLTP/OLAP database cluster and discuss physical data design alternatives for cluster-based online decision support systems. The subsequent two sections introduce query routing and freshness-aware scheduling, and also discuss related work. Both techniques have been prototypically implemented as part of the PowerDB project at ETH Zurich and in the Evaluation section, we report on the results of a comprehensive performance evaluation with our prototype system. The last section concludes the chapter.

Towards an Unified Architecture for OLTP and OLAP

The overall goal is to achieve high scalability and performance for OLAP queries and to allow OLAP clients to access up-to-date data if they ask for it. In order to achieve this, we drop the strict distinction between operational databases and data warehouses. Instead of separating OLTP and OLAP workloads in space, we propose to deploy a middleware-based database cluster for both workloads simultaneously as illustrated in Figure 1. The ratio behind this unified architecture is to combine the scalability and performance of parallel database clusters with quality of service guarantees possible through a coordination middleware.

Database clusters are comprised of a cluster of commodity computers as hardware infrastructure and off-the-shelf database management systems as a transactional storage layer. Such a database cluster is an attractive platform for both OLTP and OLAP with regard to performance, scalability, fault tolerance, and cost/performance ratio. Several transactions can run in parallel on several nodes. When the workload

Copyright © 2007, Idea Group Inc. Copying or distributing in print or electronic forms without written permission of Idea Group Inc. is prohibited.

Figure 1. Unified OLTP/OLAP cluster architecture

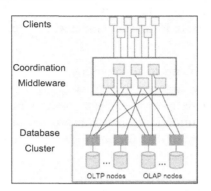

or the amount of data increases, one can "scale out" the cluster by simply adding new components (Gray, 1999). Finally, fault tolerance can be achieved using replication of either hardware or data. However, the challenge with a database cluster is to build it in a way that all these properties are present at the same time. To be able to give clients guarantees on both the consistency and the freshness of the data accessed, we need some sort of coordination between the OLTP and OLAP.

For this reason, we introduce a coordination middleware on top of the cluster that has complete knowledge about the system state. In particular, both OLTP and OLAP requests are passing through this coordination middleware: updates are executed immediately on one or more designated OLTP nodes and their effect is logged, while queries are routed to one of the OLAP nodes. The system can route queries to only one OLAP node because we assume that each cluster node holds its own copy of the database. Hence, we are able to execute several OLAP requests in parallel on different nodes without any internode communication or expensive distributed joins. The coordinator further allows those copies to have different freshness, that is, to represent different database snapshots. It uses those different database versions to serve OLAP clients faster that agree to access older database snapshots.

Example 1: OLAP with a Database Cluster. All client requests, that is both OLTP and OLAP workloads, are passing the coordination middleware. OLTP transactions are immediately forwarded to the OLTP nodes, and the effects and timestamps of successful updates are logged. OLAP queries are routed to one of the OLAP nodes depending on their data freshness requirements. The lower their requirements are, the higher is the probability that the coordinator finds a suitable OLAP node that (a) is fresh enough and (b) is free to execute another query. If such a node exists, the query will be immediately routed there and start executing.

Copyright © 2007, Idea Group Inc. Copying or distributing in print or electronic forms without written permission of Idea Group Inc. is prohibited.

Otherwise, the query has to wait while the coordinator first updates an OLAP node with previously logged updates to meet the reader's freshness requirements, before it can route the query there.

There are a number of problems to solve with such a setting, for example, which nodes to choose to evaluate an incoming OLAP query. But the central question is how to efficiently propagate updates into the cluster without sacrificing correctness or scalability. One solution is freshness-aware scheduling, which allows one to seamlessly trade freshness of data for query performance.

System Architecture

In the following, we give a more in-depth discussion of the system architecture as developed in the PowerDB project at ETH Zurich (Röhm, 2002; Schek et al., 2000). A database cluster consists of commodity PCs, each running an off-the-shelf commercial database system (DBMS) as a transactional storage layer. For the sake of simplicity let us assume that all cluster nodes are homogeneous, that is, they run the same DBMS with the same database schema. Each node holds a full copy of the database. We also refer to a database at the cluster nodes as a component DBMS. We distinguish between one or more dedicated master nodes and n secondary nodes.

There is a coordination middleware (also referred to as coordinator) that administers the cluster. It is responsible for scheduling, routing, and logging of the incoming requests. Except for this purpose-built coordinator, the cluster consists of off-the-shelf hardware and software components. The coordination middleware comprises an input queue, a scheduler with an input queue, a router, a refresher, and a logger (cf. Figure 2).

Figure 2. System architecture details (Röhm, 2002)

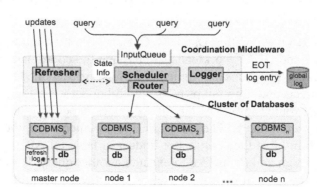

Copyright © 2007, Idea Group Inc. Copying or distributing in print or electronic forms without written permission of Idea Group Inc. is prohibited.

Clients submit read-only and update transactions to the middleware. The middleware schedules and routes updates and queries to cluster nodes. The scheduler generates a correct interleaved execution order. The master nodes serve as primary nodes where all updates will first be executed. In the following discussion, we consider only a single master node. However, the master node could actually be clustered itself. Its internal organisation is not of interest to the coordinator. It only needs to know the serialisation order and maintains a high-level log.

Queries arrive at an input queue. The input queue is not processed in a "first-in-first-out" manner. Instead, the scheduler decides in which order to process the incoming requests (a waiting time limit avoids starvation). In general, there can be several secondary nodes where a query of a read transaction may execute. The router chooses one of these nodes for each query. To do so, the coordination middleware maintains some global system state information, for example, the version of each node.

Transaction Model

With regard to transactions submitted by clients, that is, client transactions, we distinguish between read-only (OLAP) transactions and update transactions. A read-only transaction only consists of queries. An update transaction comprises at least one insert, delete, or update statement—shortly referred to as updates—next to arbitrarily many further SQL statements. In case of a read-only transaction, the client specifies an explicit freshness limit for the data accessed. Furthermore, decoupled refresh transactions propagate updates through the cluster.

Transaction management by the coordination middleware guarantees global correctness and consistency. We deploy a simplified two-layered open-nested transaction model (Weikum & Schek, 1992): The queries of read-only transactions as submitted by clients are executed and committed as separate subtransactions in the component DBMSs. The coordination middleware also contains a global logger. It keeps track of the update subtransactions on the master node and their decoupled refresh subtransactions on the secondary nodes. The latter are controlled by the refresher. This allows being globally correct without distributed commit processing as with, for example, two-phase-commit (2PC). Avoiding distributed commit processing is especially important for large clusters.

Physical Design Alternatives

A fundamental problem for OLAP with a database cluster is the physical organisation of data that yields good performance with regard to queries and updates. The two

Copyright © 2007, Idea Group Inc. Copying or distributing in print or electronic forms without written permission of Idea Group Inc. is prohibited.

primitives for physical design of individual relations that are specific to distribution are data partitioning and data replication. Partitioning, that is, data from a relation goes to different nodes, typically results in intraquery parallelism. Replication in turn leads to interquery parallelism, as different nodes can evaluate queries in parallel. Using these design primitives, we have the following basic alternatives for physical design in a database cluster:

- **Data partitioning:** The most common form of data partitioning in a parallel database environment is horizontal partitioning. With horizontal partitioning, the tuples of a relation are divided (or declustered) among many or all nodes of the cluster such that each tuple resides on only one node. There are several partitioning strategies possible in order to decide which tuple is stored at what node: round robin partitioning, hash partitioning, and range partitioning. Round robin partitioning is the only partitioning strategy, which is not based on the actual values of the data. Instead, assuming a cluster consisting of n nodes, the ith tuple is simply stored on the (i mod n)-th node. In contrast, with the other partitioning strategies one or more attributes from the given relational schema are designated as partitioning attributes. Hash partitioning hashes each tuple on the partitioning attributes using a hash function on the range $[1, \ldots, n]$. Range partitioning assigns value ranges of the partitioning attributes to certain cluster nodes. For efficiently evaluating queries that access or scan whole relations, round robin partitioning is best suited. However, if only a subset of a relation is accessed, hash or range partitioning are better than round robin partitioning because they allow accessing only the data needed (assuming that the tuples are partitioned on the same attributes used in the selection condition).

- **Data replication:** The other basic alternative is full replication, that is, each cluster node holds a copy of the whole database. Queries are served by a single cluster node; several queries can be evaluated in parallel on different nodes. A big advantage is that even for complex multijoin queries, no communication or data shipping between cluster nodes is needed; this might not be an issue with OLTP, but it is a massive problem with OLAP workloads (Röhm, 2000). However, full data replication limits the scalability with large datasets, as the whole dataset is stored several times. In spite of the capacity and the low costs of today's hard disks, this might not be a problem storagewise; but it provides no speedup for larger datasets, but rather for higher workloads, and it induces high maintenance costs (updates have to be executed on several copies instead of just once).

- **Hybrid designs:** Warehouse schemata are often of a regular form with a central fact table, which is connected to several dimension tables by foreign key relationships. Such a schema is also referred to as star or snowflake schema (Chaudhuri & Dayal, 1997). This observation motivates other alternatives,

Copyright © 2007, Idea Group Inc. Copying or distributing in print or electronic forms without written permission of Idea Group Inc. is prohibited.

subsequently called hybrid designs (Akal, Türker, Schek, Breitbart, Grabs, & Veen, 2005; Baru, Fecteau, Goyal, Hsiao, Jhingran, Padmanabhan, Copeland, & Wilson, 1995; Röhm, 2000). For example, in Röhm (2000), the fact relation is partitioned over all n nodes, and each node holds a copy of all the other relations. Previous work on physical organisation of individual relations showed that partitioning is of advantage as long as partitions do not become too small (Metha & DeWitt, 1997). In other words, one should partition the largest relation to obtain the optimal speedup. The other motivation is the heuristic that fact tables are subject to frequent updates. With this hybrid design, each update of the big relation goes to only one cluster node, as opposed to n cluster nodes in the case of full replication. Another hybrid design is to organise the cluster into subclusters, or node groups, with the whole database replicated at each subcluster, but using partial data partitioning within the subcluster (Akal et al., 2005).

- **Discussion:** Data partitioning is a very popular approach to the physical design for parallel databases. It provides a very good scalability with larger datasets, especially if the partitioning scheme is free of data skew, that is all partitions are about of the same size, and if all subqueries are evaluated locally on just one data partition. Otherwise, if for example two partitioned relations are joined on noncollocated join-attributes, large amounts of data must be shipped between the cluster nodes. This might not be an issue in an OLTP environment, but given the complex OLAP queries that typically access large parts of a database it is important to avoid any kind of noncollocated join processing.

The main advantage of replication over partitioning is that no distributed query processing is necessary at all. Instead of intraquery parallelism, it optimises interquery parallelism in that different queries can be evaluated in parallel and without interference on separate cluster nodes. The disadvantages of full replication are the limited scalability with the data size and the maintenance costs. Updates must be propagated to all replicas in the cluster, which gives rise to a number of problems with regard to correctness, update performance, and scalability. Hence, this is typically taken as "rule-out" argument for replication. We will discuss a possible solution to this update propagation problem in a later section of this chapter. The central idea is to allow and consciously make use of multiple (consistent) versions of the database at different cluster nodes.

The rationale behind hybrid designs is to combine the advantages of both data partitioning and data replication. Consider for example the approach to partition only the fact table while replicating the dimension tables (Röhm, 2000). With regard to query evaluation, there is a distinction between queries that refer to the partitioned relation and those that do not. In the first case, all cluster nodes process the original query, and the coordination middleware computes the overall result. If the query

Copyright © 2007, Idea Group Inc. Copying or distributing in print or electronic forms without written permission of Idea Group Inc. is prohibited.

does not contain aggregation, the overall result is simply the disjoint union of the intermediate results; computing the overall result in the other case is not difficult either. If the query does not refer to the partitioned relation, their evaluation is as with full replication.

While literature has proposed other schemes for physical organisation of databases as a whole, for example, collocated joins (Baru et al., 1995) or multiattribute declustering (Ghandeharizadeh, DeWitt, & Qureshi, 1992), one can see such techniques as refinements of the basic alternatives described previously. There are a variety of further physical design alternatives available for OLAP, for example, materialised views (Gupta & Mumick, 1995) or data cubes. However, such can be seen somewhat orthogonal to this discussion. The fundamental problems addressed here do not change. Of course, combining these techniques is natural and will lead to even better performance. But the general statements about the developed scheduling and routing techniques would not essentially differ.

Finally, researchers have proposed data compression schemes and approximative query-evaluation techniques (e.g., Chakrabarti, Garofalakis, Rastogi, & Shim, 2000), including techniques that allow to trade result quality for query-answering time. It should be noted that they are also orthogonal to our current concern, although they complement each other very well: different cluster nodes could hold different compressed versions of the database. The coordination middleware could then take into account that more sophisticated compression schemes typically induce higher maintenance costs. However, those combinations are beyond the scope of this chapter. So in the following we assume the physical design on all cluster nodes to be identical.

Query Routing

For the following section, we concentrate on a query-only environment, and to support the join-intensive OLAP queries, we assume full replication as physical design in a cluster of databases. As a consequence, there is no need for distributed query processing but instead each node of the cluster is capable of evaluating any OLAP query stand-alone and in parallel to other nodes. The decision on which node to actually use for query evaluation is called query routing.

The objectives of query routing are to balance the load of the cluster nodes and to reduce query response times. Effective query routing requires some knowledge about the current state of the cluster. In particular, this comprises the available nodes and the number of currently active transactions at each node. In the following, we refer to the latter as the load of a node, also known as current degree of multiprogramming (Weikum & Vossen, 2001).

Copyright © 2007, Idea Group Inc. Copying or distributing in print or electronic forms without written permission of Idea Group Inc. is prohibited.

A middleware-based approach has the advantage that global knowledge about the current system state can also be easily maintained if all clients issue their queries to the coordination middleware of the database cluster. In such a middleware-based architecture, query routing is actually twofold. Clients place their queries into the input queue of the cluster coordinator. In our terminology now, routing of a (single) query is the decision on which node of the cluster shall execute a query. Given this, routing of a set of queries consists of two steps: first, the scheduler decides in which order to route the queries in the input queue. Second, it routes the individual queries in this order.

Classification of Query Routing Strategies

We can classify query routing strategies alongside the following two dimensions:

- **Query-dependence:** As first classification, we can distinguish whether routing strategies make the routing decision query-dependent or -independent. Many conventional routing approaches are query-independent, which means that the query to be routed does not influence the routing decision. In contrast, more sophisticated approaches base the routing decision on the current query to be routed.
- **Previous knowledge:** Routing strategies can be further distinguished with regard to flexibility whether the routing decision is done dynamically at run-time or based on precomputed data. Standard affinity-based routing is a good example for a routing algorithm using precomputed affinity data. In contrast, cache approximation routing uses a completely dynamic approach.

In the following, we give an overview of existing query routing strategies and relate them to the presented classification scheme.

Conventional Routing Strategies

Traditionally, routing algorithms are published under the term transaction routing that can be considered equivalent to query routing as typically only read transactions are considered. Conventional, query-independent routing algorithms always route a set of queries in the same order as they arrive at the system. In other words, they process the input queue according to a first-come-first-served policy. A typical example is the FCFFS ("First-Come-First-Free-Server") strategy that assumes a multiprogramming level of one and routes each query to the first free server in a round-robin fashion.

Copyright © 2007, Idea Group Inc. Copying or distributing in print or electronic forms without written permission of Idea Group Inc. is prohibited.

Carey, Livny, and Lu (1985) and Carey and Lu (1986) addressed the problem of dynamically assigning queries to sites in a distributed (shared-nothing) database system with full replication. They presented two query-dependent algorithms that are based on a classification of queries according to their I/O and CPU demands: BNQRD ("Balance the Number of Queries by Resource Demands") routes queries to the site with the smallest number of queries of the same type (i.e., I/O-bound or CPU-bound), while LERT ("Least Estimated Response Time") uses the I/O and CPU demand information to route a query to the site with the least estimated response time. In a simulation study, BNQRD improved waiting times of queries by around 10% compared to a simple balancing strategy (BNQ—"Balance the Number of Queries"), while the LERT algorithm performed only a bit better than BNQRD in most cases.

Thomasian (1987) refined this approach. Queries are classified not only into CPU- or I/O-bound, but into a finite set of query types based on all their service demands (i.e., CPU, memory, different disks). Three routing algorithms have been compared in a simulation study. The results again showed that query-dependent routing based on query classification significantly improves the system performance. The article also concludes that an accurate response time prediction algorithm is quite complex and that the mapping of incoming queries into a fixed set of query types remains difficult to find and to achieve.

Affinity-Based Transaction Routing

The idea behind affinity-based routing is to assign queries that access the same data to the same component. These are typically query-dependent strategies. For example, Yu, Cornell, Dias, and Iyer (1987) presented an affinity-based approach to transaction routing that classified incoming transactions into affinity groups based on previous knowledge of the database call reference pattern. The reference pattern is retrieved from trace information of the transaction workload. The proposed routing scheme assigns a fixed destination system to each affinity group. In simulation study, the authors showed that affinity-based routing significantly reduced lock-contention and buffer I/O, and therefore clearly improved the response times of transactions.

An overview and framework for workload allocation in distributed database systems is presented in Rahm (1992). Approaches to affinity-based transaction routing typically concentrate on OLTP-like transactions. In particular, they only consider the data accessed by the queries to decide whether there is affinity between two given queries. The nature of the access is not taken into account, that is, "scan" vs. "random access." A strong disadvantage is that such approaches rely on precomputed data from low-level trace information of previous runs of the workload. This neglects the component-oriented nature of a database cluster.

Copyright © 2007, Idea Group Inc. Copying or distributing in print or electronic forms without written permission of Idea Group Inc. is prohibited.

Cache Approximation Query Routing

The objective of query routing is to reduce query response time. The execution times of queries—especially OLAP queries—are dominated by I/O costs. While caching plays a major role for performance of query evaluation, all previous mentioned routing algorithms do not take caching effects into consideration at all. In contrast, cache approximation routing estimates the benefit of a cache state for a query. The idea is that the execution time of a query is minimal at the cluster node whose cache contains the largest subset of data that will be accessed by the query (Röhm, Böhm, & Schek, 2001).

This also means that the scheduler no longer processes its input queue in a first-come-first-served manner. Instead, the scheduler reorders the queries in the input queue according to the estimated benefit values. The query for which the routing algorithm estimates the highest benefit is executed first. However, the scheduler has to ensure that all queries are still processed. That is, it must avoid starvation of queries with low benefit values. One approach is to tag queries with an age and reorder the input queue according to both benefit and age of the queries. Another one is to introduce a wait time threshold and to preferably route queries whose wait time exceeds this threshold.

A straightforward approach to approximate the set of tuples accessed by a query is to keep track of the relations accessed. This is simply achieved by analysing the FROM clause of the query. Such a "Cache Approximation by FROM Clause" (CAF) approximates the state of component caches by the set of relations accessed by the most recent n queries, and defines the benefit of the cache state of cluster node C for query Q by the size of the intersection of the cache state and the FROM clause of the query.

> **Example 2:** Cache Approximation Routing. Assume a small cluster of two nodes, N1 and N2, with the approximated cache states $CacheState_{N1}$ = {Region,Customer,LineItem} and $CacheState_{N2}$ = {Orders,LineItem,Suppliers}. Now the following query Qx has to be routed:
>
> SELECT   count(*)   FROM   Orders,   LineItem   WHERE   ...
>
> It accesses the two relations Orders and LineItem. The intersection with the approximated cache state of node N1 is {LineItem}, which is a caching benefit of 1; the intersection with the cache state of node N2 is {Orders, LineItem}, corresponding to a caching benefit of 2. Hence, CAF would route query Qx to node N2, because it expects there a higher caching benefit.

Copyright © 2007, Idea Group Inc. Copying or distributing in print or electronic forms without written permission of Idea Group Inc. is prohibited.

This approach relies on a very rough approximation of queried data. It does not take into account which portions of the relations are actually accessed by a query. These portions are described by each query predicate. However, quantifying the exact overlap of the sets of tuples specified by two different predicates having common attributes is difficult. In Röhm et al. (2001), an interesting refinement based on bit strings has been proposed. The authors proposed to further approximate the set of tuples specified by a predicate using bit string signatures. By doing so, one can reduce the calculation of benefits to bit string comparisons. This can be done efficiently.

Freshness-Aware Scheduling

The previous considerations have concentrated on a query-dominant environment. We have seen that replication is a key factor for query performance and how query routing can optimise its utilisation, for example, by approximating the state of the caches of the cluster nodes. Until now, we have left aside the problem field of updating our dataset. This might be state-of-the-art for data intensive applications like OLAP to strictly distinguish between query and update phases. However, a data warehouse offering data, which is a week old, will not be acceptable much longer. Rather, the intention should be to be able to run queries over up-to-date data if needed. And actually, a cluster-based approach to OLAP can provide this.

The simultaneous admission of queries and updates in the presence of replication necessitates a transaction management and replication control component. Transaction management is responsible for a correct interleaved execution of concurrent queries and updates, while replication management assures that updates eventually affect all copies of the data.

Replication and Correctness

A naïve approach to global correctness would use synchronous replication where each update immediately goes to all replicas, also referred to as eager replication. However, such approaches necessitate a distributed atomic commit protocol, which is not feasible for large number of nodes (Gray, Helland, O'Neil, & Shasha, 1996). This means that in a cluster environment, one has to propagate updates asynchronously without two-phase commit protocol.

An interesting approach is using group communication primitives (Kemme, 2000; Wu & Kemme, 2005): a client submits its update to one database server which then broadcasts the update to all other cluster nodes using an atomic broadcast protocol. The use of appropriate network primitives makes a concluding two phase commit

Copyright © 2007, Idea Group Inc. Copying or distributing in print or electronic forms without written permission of Idea Group Inc. is prohibited.

unnecessary, because those protocols guarantee the ordered delivery of the messages so that the global serialisation order can be determined locally by each node. However, group communication protocols must determine this global order first, and hence add a relatively high overhead. Approaches such as by Wu and Kemme (2005) furthermore require direct support by the database management system, which violates the component-oriented nature of a cluster of databases.

There are a variety of approaches to asynchronous replication. Most restrict transactions to access only a single node in order to be able to ensure serialisability for certain restricted cluster configurations (e.g., Breitbart, Komondoor, Rastogi, Seshadri, & Silberschatz, 1999). The latter alternative has also no control over the emerging serialisation order. It can only guarantee that the transactions of a client are serialised correctly between all other transactions, but not precisely in which order. However, if we do not want to sacrifice correctness—that is the system shall guarantee one-copy serialisability—this is not enough.

Hence, let us in the following look at an alternative approach to cluster replication control that combines the correctness and up-to-date guarantees of distributed transactions with the performance of asynchronous update propagation. It is using a primary-copy replication scheme with deferred refreshment: The coordination middleware executes updates first on the OLTP nodes (the number of update transactions that run in parallel on the OLTP node is not restricted). After an update transaction finishes, as soon as a refresh is activated, the refresher propagates the changes to the remaining replicas using decoupled refresh transactions.

In more detail, each of them refreshes one node and is activated separately. Each node guarantees locally sterilisable executions. In addition, we have to ensure read consistency: this means to propagate refresh transactions in a way that query-only transactions always see the same version during their lifetime. This has to be handled with care because as we discussed in the previous section, the router can send each query of a read-only transaction to a different OLAP node—routing of queries of the same transaction to different cluster nodes is beneficial because of caching effects.

Next to guaranteeing serialisability, OLAP systems aim foremost at improving query response time. The idea is to introduce freshness of data as a new quality-of-service parameter for transaction processing. This should allow for explicitly trading freshness of data accessed for query performance. OLAP clients specify a lower bound of freshness for the data accessed by queries of the current transaction t, denoted by f_t. The freshness limit is an additional constraint for query routing.

In the following, we introduce a freshness-of-data-driven approach to replication management in a database cluster: Freshness-aware scheduling (FAS). FAS comprises replication management and mechanisms of multiversion concurrency control. The notion of freshness of data is crucial in the context of FAS. We will presently discuss freshness metrics, before introducing FAS in more detail.

Copyright © 2007, Idea Group Inc. Copying or distributing in print or electronic forms without written permission of Idea Group Inc. is prohibited.

Freshness of Data

Freshness measures are closely related to the notion of coherency for which several ideas have been proposed in the literature (e.g., Alonso, Blott, Feßler, & Schek, 1997; Pacitti & Simon, 2000). Recently, those concepts have been revived under the terms freshness of data (Röhm, Böhm, Schek, & Schuldt, 2002) or currency (Guo, Larson, Ramakrishnan, & Goldstein, 2004). With those approaches, a so-called freshness index $f(d) \in [0, ..., 1]$ measures the freshness of some data d. This freshness index reflects how much the data has deviated from the up-to-date version. Intuitively, a freshness index of 1 means the data is up-to-date, while an index of 0 would characterise the data as "infinitely" outdated. One can distinguish three basic approaches to define the freshness index: delay freshness, version freshness, and data deviation.

- **Delay freshness:** A delay freshness index reflects how late a certain cluster node is as compared to the up-to-date OLTP node (Guo et al., 2004; Röhm et al., 2002). It is based on the period of time between the last propagated update and the most recent update on the up-to-date node. Let $\tau(c)$ denote the commit time of the last refresh subtransaction on an OLAP node c, and $\tau(c_0)$ the commit time of the most recent update subtransaction on the OLTP node. Then the delay freshness index is defined as $f(c) = \tau(c) / \tau(c_0)$. This implies that $f \in [0, 1]$.

- **Version freshness:** Alternatively, one can base the freshness definition on the version difference between a cluster node and the up-to-date node c_0. We define the version of a cluster node c as the number of committed update transactions, denoted by $v(c)$. Following Pacitti and Simon (2000), the version freshness index is then defined as $f(c) = v(c) / v(c_0)$; $f \in [0, 1]$. Note that a version can actually be seen as a kind of logical time.

- **Freshness index by data deviation:** For the sake of completeness, we also want to mention a definition of the freshness index based on data deviation (also known as arithmetic or numerical coherency condition) (Gallersdörfer & Nicola, 1995). However, such a freshness index definition is only meaningful for single numerical data items. Let $d(x,c)$ denote the data value of the replica x stored at some node c. Then the data deviation freshness index is defined as $f(x,c) := 1 - | (d(x,c) - d(x, c_0)) / d(x, c_0)|$.

For a middleware-based architecture pursuing a component-oriented approach, only the two first mentioned freshness indexes are feasible. The reason is that the coordinator follows a "black-box" principle when managing the cluster nodes, which means that it does not have direct access to the content of the nodes. Hence, it can-

Copyright © 2007, Idea Group Inc. Copying or distributing in print or electronic forms without written permission of Idea Group Inc. is prohibited.

not base its freshness definition on concrete data values. Delay freshness offers the most intuitive and workload-independent way of specifying the freshness needs of a client ("at most 10 minutes old" instead of "at most 1000 updates behind"). Hence we will assume delay freshness in the following discussion.

Overview of FAS

The basic mechanisms for ensuring serialisability and read consistency are as follows: FAS uses the primary-copy replication scheme with deferred refreshment as discussed before and executes updates first on the OLTP node. After an update subtransaction finishes, as soon as a refresh is activated, FAS propagates the changes to the remaining replicas using decoupled refresh subtransactions.

In more detail, some variant of multiversion concurrency control (MVCC) is used. Freshness-aware scheduling does not provide just any version to a client but a version which meets the given freshness limit. In other words, only cluster nodes with freshness above the given lower bound will be considered during query routing. Consequently, the higher the specified minimum freshness is, the smaller is the portion of the cluster to which the corresponding query may be routed. In the worst case, no node is available with the requested degree of freshness, and the coordination middleware must activate update propagation first. Hence, although FAS follows a lazy primary-copy replication approach with deferred updates, it nevertheless allows queries to access the most recent data.

> **Example 3:** Freshness-Aware Scheduling. Figure 3 shows three queries with different freshness limits (Röhm et al., 2002). The first query asks for data with a degree of freshness of at least 0.9. Only the first OLAP node has a freshness index that meets this limit and hence is the only possible target node. In contrast, Query 2 is asking only for data with a freshness of at least 0.5. This freshness limit is met by all cluster nodes.

Figure 3. Principle of freshness-aware scheduling

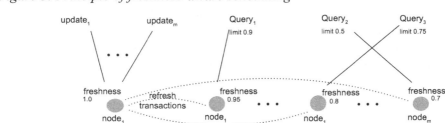

Copyright © 2007, Idea Group Inc. Copying or distributing in print or electronic forms without written permission of Idea Group Inc. is prohibited.

Hence, FAS is free to route Query 2 to any of the OLAP nodes. In Figure, the last node is chosen to serve the query. Note that it actually could have been evaluated by any node of the cluster. Query 2 sees indeed a cluster of size n, while for Query 1 only one node is usable.

The implications to correctness are that queries contended with stale data are serialised before update transactions which have already committed but have not been propagated to the query's target node so far. This requires that refresh and read-only transactions are interleaved correctly on the various nodes, and that read-only transactions access only one version of the data. To ensure this is the responsibility of the coordination middleware (Röhm et al., 2002).

Performance Evaluation

Let us finally have a short look at the performance characteristics of the presented query routing and update propagation algorithms. In the following, we report on results of an experimental evaluation of a prototype implementation as part of the PowerDB project at ETH Zurich using the TPC-R benchmark on a large cluster of 128 nodes (Röhm et al., 2002). We proceed as follows: First, we quantify the performance improvement one can achieve with different query routing algorithms. Then, we explore the overall performance and scalability of FAS. We are especially interested in the influence of different freshness requirements on the query and update performance in the cluster.

Evaluation Setup

The prototype comprises a database cluster, one designated OLTP node, the coordinator, and a client simulator. The evaluation has been conducted on a database cluster consisting of 128 PCs (1 GHz Pentium III, 256 MBytes RAM, and 2 SCSI hard disks) each running Microsoft SQL Server 2000 under Windows 2000 Advanced Server. We generated the databases according to the TPC-R benchmark with a scaling factor 1 (size including indexes about 2 GB). The master node, the global log, and the client simulator are Pentium II 400 MHz machines with the same software configuration. The coordinator runs on a separate PC with two 1 GHz Pentium III and 512 MB RAM. All nodes are interconnected by a switched 100 MBit Ethernet.

Copyright © 2007, Idea Group Inc. Copying or distributing in print or electronic forms without written permission of Idea Group Inc. is prohibited.

Comparison of Query Routing Algorithms

First, we are interested in the overall performance of the different query routing strategies as discussed earlier in this chapter for different cluster sizes, that is, their scalability. Therefore, we measured the performance of three different variants of a cache approximation router versus a conventional router for cluster sizes up to 24 nodes:

- **FCFFS:** Conventional first-come-first-free-server routing which is query in-dependent and not cache-aware. Its performance serves as an orientation point for the other strategies.
- **CAF:** Dynamic cache approximation routing based on the FROM clause of queries.
- **CAS:** Dynamic cache approximation routing based on predicate signatures.
- **CASweighted:** Like CAS, but with a refined benefit model using normalised benefits.

The results are shown in Figure 4 (Röhm et al., 2001).

Figure 4. Query routing performance and scalability: (a) throughput, (b) throughput scaled to FCFFS, (c) mean response time, and (d) MRT scaled to FCFFS

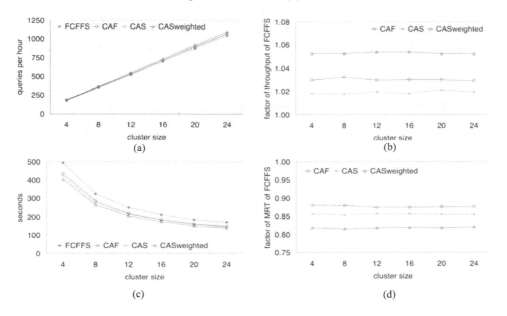

Copyright © 2007, Idea Group Inc. Copying or distributing in print or electronic forms without written permission of Idea Group Inc. is prohibited.

Although the throughput improves only by less than 10% with cache approximation routing as compared to FCFFS routing, the mean response time can be significantly shortened. The best results achieved CAS-weighted routing, which offers almost 20% faster mean response times over the whole cluster size. All four investigated routing strategies also showed a perfectly linear scalability over the cluster size. For example, the throughput with a 24-node cluster is 24 times higher than on a single node.

Performance of Freshness-Aware Scheduling

In the following, we are interested in the performance characteristics of FAS. We have used a dynamic workload of ten update streams concurrently executed with twice as many querying clients as there are nodes in the cluster. We further varied the mean freshness requested by read transactions from 0.6 up to 1. The results are shown in Figure 5 (Röhm et al., 2002).

The presented middleware-based cluster architecture proved to be very scalable and it also shows that freshness-aware scheduling effectively allows users to trade freshness of data for faster query response time. We see that the slowdown of queries by the concurrent update stream for FAS is around 10% up to 60% with regard to mean response time as compared to the no-update case. If clients issue queries with mean freshness limit 0.6 (which means at most 20 minutes old), they obtain the results about 30% faster, compared to a requested freshness of 1. This is exactly the effect freshness-aware scheduling is targeting on: trading data "up-to-dateness" for query performance. The results also nicely show that there is no slowdown with increasing cluster size, as it would be the case with synchronous updates: we were doubling the number of clients and the cluster size at the same time, and mean response time did not change, but query throughput doubled. This means that at least

Figure 5. Performance of FAS with varying freshness limits

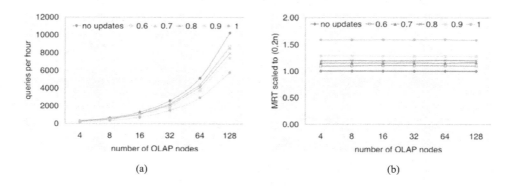

(a)   (b)

Copyright © 2007, Idea Group Inc. Copying or distributing in print or electronic forms without written permission of Idea Group Inc. is prohibited.

up to 128 nodes, freshness-aware scheduling scales linearly with increasing cluster size. At the same time, the throughput achieved by 10 concurrent update streams remains constant, even with a large OLAP cluster of up to 128 nodes (not shown in the graphs). Obviously, the coordination middleware can keep up with the updaters and the increasing OLAP workload (on 128 nodes, 256 query streams are active) without a slowdown for either queries or updates. At the same time, the CPU load of the scheduler with 128 nodes was only 30% on average. In other words, the coordination middleware is not becoming a bottleneck.

Summary

Online analytical processing must cope with huge volumes of data and at the same time allow for short response times to facilitate interactive usage—and the requirement that the data analysed should be up-to-date is becoming more and more important. This chapter has presented database clusters as a scalable infrastructure for interactive decision support systems that are capable of analysing up-to-date data. We discussed central architectural issues and performance aspects, such as several physical design alternatives, possible query routing algorithms, and innovative update propagation protocols.

Most data warehouses nowadays offer a compromise between freshness of data and maintenance costs. But recent developments such as FAS (freshness-aware scheduling) or relaxed currency constraints allow to explicitly trade freshness of data for query performance, while at the same time not sacrificing correctness:

1.   The requested freshness limit of queries is always met; and
2.   Data accessed within a transaction is consistent, independent of its freshness.

The presented middleware-based cluster architecture proved to be very scalable and it also shows that freshness-aware scheduling effectively allows users to trade freshness of data for faster query response time. It makes use of the different degrees of freshness of the OLAP nodes in the cluster in order to serve such queries, which agree to access less fresh data sooner than queries asking for the latest data. The proposed architecture has been implemented as part of the PowerDB project at ETH Zurich, and we conducted an extensive performance evaluation using the TPC-R benchmark. An important result is that the system scales linearly, even if providing clients access to up-to-date data in a database cluster with 128 nodes.

Copyright © 2007, Idea Group Inc. Copying or distributing in print or electronic forms without written permission of Idea Group Inc. is prohibited.

References

Akal, F., Türker, C., Schek, H.-J., Breitbart, Y., Grabs, T., & Veen, L. (2005). Fine-grained replication and scheduling with freshness and correctness guarantees. In *Proceedings of the 31st VLDB Conference on Very Large Databases, Trondheim,* Norway.

Alonso, G., Blott, S., Feßler, A., & Schek, H.-J. (1997, May 12-14). Correctness and parallelism of composite systems. In *Proceedings of the Sixteenth ACM SIGMOD Symposium on Principles of Database Systems (PODS)*, Tucson, Arizona (pp. 197-208). ACM Press.

Baru, C. K., Fecteau, G., Goyal, A., Hsiao, H., Jhingran, A., Padmanabhan, S., Copeland, G. P., & Wilson, W. G. (1995). DB2 parallel edition. *IBM Systems Journal, 34*(2), 292-322.

Breitbart, Y., Komondoor, R., Rastogi, R., Seshadri, S., & Silberschatz, A. (1999, June 1-3). Update propagation protocols for replicated databases. In *Proceedings of the 1999 ACM SIGMOD International Conference on Management of Data,* Philadelphia (pp. 97-108). ACM Press.

Carey, M. J., Livny, M., & Lu, H. (1985, May 13-17). Dynamic task allocation in a distributed database system. In *Proceedings of the Fifth International Conference on Distributed Computing Systems (ICDCS),* Denver, Colorado (pp. 282-291). IEEE Computer Society.

Carey, M. J., & Lu, H. (1986, May 28-30). Load balancing in a locally distributed database system. In *Proceedings of the 1986 ACM SIGMOD International Conference on Management of Data,* Washington, DC (pp. 108-119). ACM Press.

Chakrabarti, K., Garofalakis, M. N., Rastogi, R., & Shim, K. (2000, September 10-14). Approximate query processing using wavelets. In *Proceedings of the 26th International Conference on Very Large Data Bases (VLDB),* Cairo, Egypt (pp. 111-122). Morgan Kaufmann Publisher.

Chaudhuri, S., & Dayal, U. (1997). An overview of data warehousing and OLAP technology. *SIGMOD Record, 26*(1), 65-74.

Gallersdörfer, R., & Nicola, M. (1995, September 11-15). Improving performance in replicated databases through relaxed coherency. In *Proceedings of the 21st International Conference on Very Large Data Bases (VLDB),* Zurich, Switzerland (pp. 445-456). Morgan Kaufmann Publishers.

Ghandeharizadeh, S., DeWitt, D. J., & Qureshi, W. (1992, June 2-5). A performance analysis of alternative multi-attribute declustering strategies. In *Proceedings of the 1992 ACM SIGMOD International Conference on Management of Data,* San Diego (pp. 29-38). . ACM Press.

Copyright © 2007, Idea Group Inc. Copying or distributing in print or electronic forms without written permission of Idea Group Inc. is prohibited.

Gray, J. (1999). *How high is high performance transaction processing?* Paper presented at the 1999 Workshop on High Performance Transaction Processing Systems (HPTS), Asilomar, California.

Gray, J., Helland, P. , O'Neil, P. E., & Shasha, D. (1996, June 4-6). The dangers of replication and a solution. In *Proceedings of the 1996 ACM SIGMOD Conference*, Montreal, Quebec, Canada (pp. 173-182).

Guo, H., Larson, P., Ramakrishnan, R., & Goldstein, J. (2004, June 13-18). Relaxed currency and consistency: How to say, Good Enough' in SQL. In *Proceedings of the 2004 ACM SIGMOD Conference,* Paris.

Gupta, A., & Mumick, I. S. (1995). Maintenance of materialized views: Problems, techniques, and applications. *IEEE Database Engineering Bulletin, 18*(2), 3-18.

Kemme, B. (2000). *Database replication for clusters of workstations.* Doctoral dissertation ETH No. 13864, ETH Zurich, Departement of Computer Science.

Mehta, M., & DeWitt, D. J. (1997). Data placement in shared-nothing parallel database systems. *VLDB Journal, 6*(1), 53-72.

Pacitti, E., & Simon, E. (2000). Update propagation strategies to improve freshness in lazy master replicated databases. *VLDB Journal, 8*(3-4), 305-318.

Rahm, E. (1992). A framework for workload allocation in distributed transaction processing systems. *Systems Software Journal, 18,* 171-190.

Röhm, U. (2002). *Online Analytical Processing with a Cluster of Databases.* Doctoral thesis, DISDBIS 80, Aka Verlag, Berlin.

Röhm, U., Böhm, K., & Schek, H.-J. (2000, March 27-31). OLAP query routing and physical design in a database cluster. In Zaniolo et al. (Ed.), *Proceedings of the Sixth International Conference on Extending Database Technology* (LNCS 1777, pp. 254-268). Konstanz, Germany: Springer-Verlag.

Röhm, U., Böhm, K., & Schek, H.-J. (2001, April 2-6). Cache-aware query routing in a cluster of databases. In *Proceedings of the 17th International Conference on Data Engineering (ICDE)* (pp. 641-650). Heidelberg, Germany: IEEE Computer Society.

Röhm, U., Böhm, K., Schek, H.-J., & Schuldt, H. (2002, August 20-23). FAS: A freshness-sensitive coordination middleware for a cluster of OLAP components. In *Proceedings of the 28th International Conference on Very Large Data Bases (VLDB)* (pp. 754-765), Hong Kong, China: Morgan Kaufmann Publishers.

Schek, H.-J., Böhm, K., Grabs, T., Röhm, U., Schuldt, H., & Weber, R. (2000, June 19-21). Hyperdatabases. In *Proceedings of the First International Conference on Web Information System Engineering (WISE)* (pp. 14-25). Hong Kong, China: IEEE CS Press.

Copyright © 2007, Idea Group Inc. Copying or distributing in print or electronic forms without written permission of Idea Group Inc. is prohibited.

Thomasian, A. (1987, September). A performance study of dynamic load balancing in distributed systems. In *Proceedings of the Seventh International Conference on Distributed Computing Systems (ICDCS)* (pp. 178-184). Berlin, Germany. IEEE Computer Society.

Weikum, G., & Schek, H.-J. (1992). Concepts and applications of multilevel transactions and open nested transactions. In A. K. Elmagarmid (Ed.), *Database transaction models for advanced applications* (pp. 515-553). Morgan Kaufmann.

Weikum, G., & Vossen, G. (2001). *Transactional information systems: Theory, algorithms, and the practice of concurrency control and recovery.* Morgan Kaufmann Publishers.

Wu, S., & Kemme, B. (2005). Postgres-R(SI): Combining replica control with concurrency control based on snapshot isolation. In *Proceedings of the 21st International Conference on Data Engineering (ICDE),* Tokyo, Japan.

Yu, P. S., Cornell, D. W., Dias, D. M., & Iyer, B. R. (1987). Analysis of affinity based routing in multi-system data sharing. *Performance Evaluation, 7,* 87-109.

Copyright © 2007, Idea Group Inc. Copying or distributing in print or electronic forms without written permission of Idea Group Inc. is prohibited.

Chapter XI

Toward Integrating Data Warehousing with Data Mining Techniques

Rokia Missaoui
Université du Québec en Outaouais, Canada

Ganaël Jatteau
Université du Québec en Outaouais, Canada

Ameur Boujenoui
University of Ottawa, Canada

Sami Naouali
Université du Québec en Outaouais, Canada

Abstract

In this chapter, we present alternatives for coupling data warehousing and data mining techniques so that they can benefit from each other's advances for the ultimate objective of efficiently providing a flexible answer to data mining queries addressed either to a bidimensional (relational) or a multidimensional database. In particular, we investigate two techniques: (1) the first one exploits concept lattices for generating frequent closed itemsets, clusters and association rules from multidimensional data, and (2) the second one defines new operators similar in spirit to

Copyright © 2007, Idea Group Inc. Copying or distributing in print or electronic forms without written permission of Idea Group Inc. is prohibited.

online analytical processing (OLAP) techniques to allow "data mining on demand" (i.e., data mining according to user's needs and perspectives). The implementation of OLAP-like techniques relies on three operations on lattices, namely selection, projection and assembly. A detailed running example serves to illustrate the scope and benefits of the proposed techniques.

Introduction

Data mining (DM) is the process of discovering hidden knowledge (i.e., patterns and associations) from large data sets while data warehousing (DW) aims at integrating and aggregating data from multiple data sources for further analysis (Chaudhuri & Dayal, 1997; Han & Kamber, 2000). The two technologies present some common features such as (1) information/knowledge extraction from very large data sets, (2) support for decision making, (3) use of background knowledge for additional information (knowledge) extraction, and (4) need for a careful and generally time-consuming data preprocessing step.

There are many topics that have attracted researchers in the area of data warehousing: data warehouse design and multidimensional modeling, efficient cube computation, query optimization, discovery-driven exploration of cubes, data mining in cubes, and so on. In order to avoid computing a whole data cube, many studies have focused on iceberg cube calculation (Xin, Han, Li, & Wah, 2003), semantic summarization of cubes (Lakshmanan, Pei, & Zhao, 2002), and approximation of cube computation (Shanmugasundaram, Fayyad, & Bradley, 1999). Recently, there is an increasing interest for applying/adapting data mining techniques and advanced statistical analysis (e.g., cluster analysis, principal component analysis, log-linear modeling) for knowledge discovery (Ben Messaoud, Boussaïd, & Rabaséda, 2004; Lu, Feng, & Han, 2000; Sarawagi, Agrawal, & Megiddo, 1998) and data compression or query approximation purposes in data cubes (Babcock, Chaudhuri, & Das, 2003; Barbara & Wu, 2001).

The objective of this chapter is to propose techniques for reinforcing the collaboration and linkage between DW and DM techniques by using formal concept analysis and concept lattices (Ganter & Wille, 1999) as a sound and theoretical framework for data mining. More precisely, we first present our view of rule mining in data cubes. Then, we adapt the interactive exploratory mechanisms inherent to online analytical processing (OLAP) techniques to the framework of data mining tools and techniques in order to help the user select the appropriate subset of an already existing data mining output. To conduct the first task, we discuss association rule mining in multidimensional data and show how cube clustering using concept lattices and frequent closed itemsets can be exploited for generating meaningful association

Copyright © 2007, Idea Group Inc. Copying or distributing in print or electronic forms without written permission of Idea Group Inc. is prohibited.

rules. For the second task, we provide a formal definition and an interpretation of OLAP operations for exploratory data mining by redefining key OLAP operations in the framework of concept lattices using three operations: selection, projection, and assembly of lattices.

The chapter is organized as follows. First, an illustrative example about corporate governance quality in Canadian organizations is described in the next section and will serve to show the potential of the proposed solution. We then provide some background about data warehousing and data mining techniques and give an overview of related work. Our efforts towards the integration of the two technologies are described later, followed by a conclusion and further work.

A Running Example

The present running example will be used throughout this chapter to illustrate our solution towards the integration of DM and DW technologies. It is based on a study conducted on a sample of 216 Canadian companies listed on the Stock Market and aimed at establishing links between corporate governance practices and other variables such as the shareholding structure. In the context of this study, governance is defined as the means, practices and mechanisms put in place by organizations to ensure that managers are defending shareholders' interests. Governance practices include, but are not limited to, the size and the composition of the board of directors, the number of independent directors and women sitting on the board as well as the duality between the position of CEO and the position of board chairman.

The data used in this study were mainly derived from an article published in October 7, 2002 in the Canadian *Globe and Mail* newspaper, which discussed the quality of governance practices in a sample of companies. More precisely, the mentioned article provided a global evaluation of corporate governance practices in each company and assessed five governance practices: the composition of the board of directors, the shareholding system (or control structure which includes internal shareholders, blockholders and institutional investors), the compensation structure for managers, the shareholding rights and the information sharing system.

Data related to the types of shareholding systems, the associated percentage of voting rights and the total assets of each company were obtained from the "StockGuide 2002" database. Data related to the size of the board, the number of independent directors and women sitting on the board, as well as the duality between the position of CEO and the position of board chairman were extracted from the "Directory of Directors" of the Financial Post newspaper.

Based on the collected data, a data warehouse has been constructed with sixteen dimensions and an initial set of fact tables for data cube design and exploration.

Copyright © 2007, Idea Group Inc. Copying or distributing in print or electronic forms without written permission of Idea Group Inc. is prohibited.

Table 1. (a) Fact table with COUNT aggregate; (b) Fact table with AVG aggregate

Fact ID	Duality	Internal	Govern	NbEntr
1	0	1	2	23
2	0	1	3	20
3	0	2	1	1
4	0	2	2	50
5	0	2	3	23
6	0	3	2	16
7	0	3	3	3
8	1	1	2	4
9	1	1	3	4
10	1	2	1	1
11	1	2	2	32
12	1	2	3	3
13	1	3	1	2
14	1	3	2	30
15	1	3	3	4

(a)

Fact ID	Duality	Internal	Govern	AvgAsset
1	0	1	2	2
2	0	1	3	2
3	0	2	1	1
4	0	2	2	2
5	0	2	3	2
6	0	3	2	1
7	0	3	3	1
8	1	1	2	2
9	1	1	3	2
10	1	2	1	1
11	1	2	2	2
12	1	2	3	2
13	1	3	1	1
14	1	3	2	2
15	1	3	3	1

(b)

The left-hand side (LHS) of Table 1 is a fact table which provides the number of enterprises (*NbEntr*) according to three dimensions: *duality, internal,* and *govern,* while the right-hand side (RHS) gives *AvgAsset*, a codification of the average company asset according to the same set of dimensions. The value of *AvgAsset* is 1 when the average asset is less than 1,000K and 2 otherwise. When *Duality* is set to 1, this means that the CEO is also the board chairman. Dimension *Internal* represents the proportion of Top Management sitting on the board, and its possible values are 1 (proportion < 10%), 2 ($\geq$ 10 and < 25%), and 3 ($\geq$ 25%). *Govern* expresses the index of corporate governance quality (or simply quality index) and takes one of the following values (from bad to good quality): 1 (quality < 40%), 2 ($\geq$ 40 and < 70%), and 3 ($\geq$ 70%).

Background

In this section, we first provide some background on data warehousing and OLAP techniques. Then, we recall basic notions about the framework we use to identify

Copyright © 2007, Idea Group Inc. Copying or distributing in print or electronic forms without written permission of Idea Group Inc. is prohibited.

clusters (groupings) and mine association rules. Finally, some related studies about integrating DW with DM techniques will be presented.

Data Warehousing

A data warehouse is an integration of consolidated and non volatile data from multiple and possibly heterogeneous data sources for the purpose of decision support making. It contains a collection of data cubes which can be exploited via OLAP techniques such as drill-down and rollup in order to summarize, consolidate, and view data according to different dimensions (Chaudhuri & Dayal, 1997). In a multidimensional context with a set D of dimensions, a dimension (e.g., location of a company, time) is a descriptive axis for data presentation under several perspectives. A dimension hierarchy contains levels, which organize data into a logical structure (e.g., country, state and city for the location dimension). A fact table (see Table 1) contains numerical measures and keys relating facts to dimension tables. A cube $C=<D,M>$ is a visual representation of a fact table, where D is a set of dimensions of the cube (with associated hierarchies) and M its corresponding measures.

Data Mining

Data mining is a crucial step in the process of knowledge discovery in databases (KDD), which aims at discovering hidden patterns and relationships in a data collection for prediction and decision-making purposes. Major data mining functions include characterization, comparison, classification, association, prediction, cluster analysis, and time-series analysis (Han & Kamber, 2000). Association rule mining is by far the most frequently used DM technique.

As pointed out by Imielinski and Mannila (1996), a KDD system should offer two major functionalities: generating KDD objects (i.e., DM output) and retrieving the ones that were already extracted. This observation comes from the fact that in relational databases, the output of a query is a table that can be queried later like any basic table. We fully adhere to this opinion to apply the so-called closure principle to KDD systems, and we define a set of operations on data mining output.

Association Rule Mining

Mining association rules from a given database of transactions consists to generate all association rules that have user-specified minimum support and confidence (Agrawal & Srikant, 1994). Let $I=\{i_1, i_2,..., i_m\}$ be a set of m distinct items (e.g., milk, bread). A transaction T contains a set of items in I, and has an associated unique identifier

Copyright © 2007, Idea Group Inc. Copying or distributing in print or electronic forms without written permission of Idea Group Inc. is prohibited.

called *TID*. A subset *Y* of I where *k*=|*Y*| is referred to as a *k-itemset* (or simply an *itemset*), and *k* is called the length of *Y*. A transaction database T*D* is the whole set of transactions. A set $X \subseteq TD$ is called a *tidset* while the fraction of transactions in T*D* that contains an itemset *Y* is called the support of *Y* and is denoted by *supp*(*Y*). Thus, an itemset is frequent (or large) when *supp*(*Y*) reaches at least a user-specified minimum threshold called *minsupp*.

An association rule *r* is an implication of the form $Y_1 \Rightarrow Y_2$, where Y_1 and Y_2 are subsets of *I*, $Y_1 \cup Y_2$ is a frequent itemset, and $Y_1 \cap Y_2 = \varnothing$. The support of the rule *r* is equal to $supp(Y_1 \cup Y_2)$ while its confidence is computed as the ratio $supp(Y_1 \cup Y_2)/supp(Y_1)$.

In our running example, an association rule could be the following:

- *Female* = 1 and *Internal* = 1 $\Rightarrow$ *Govern* = 3 [10%, 52%]. The rule means that if there are females on the board and if the proportion of Top Management sitting on the board is less than 10% (i.e., *Internal* = 1), then the quality of governance is good (at least equal to 70%) with a confidence of 52%.

In APRIORI-like algorithms (Agrawal & Srikant, 1994), rule mining is conducted as follows. For every frequent itemset *Y*, all nonempty subsets of *Y* are extracted. Then, for every subset Y_1 of *Y*, a rule of the form $Y_1 \Rightarrow Y_2$ is generated if its confidence $\geq$ *minconf* (a user-defined threshold).

Since the introduction of APRIORI, a variety of approaches to the problem of association rule mining has been proposed. The main objective of most of them is to improve the efficiency of the basic method, while the key difficulty is the potentially large number of frequent itemsets (*FIs*). To reduce the size of the *FI* set, some studies were conducted on frequent *closed* itemsets *FCIs* (Pasquier, Taouil, Bastide, Stumme, & Lakhal, 2005; Wang & Karypis, 2003; Zaki & Hsiao, 2002). A frequent itemset *X* is *closed* if there exists no proper superset *Z* of *Y* with *supp*(*Y*)=*supp*(*Z*). In other words, any itemset has the same support (i.e., is frequent) as its closure. In a dual way, a *tidset X* is closed if there exists no proper superset *U* of *X* such that *U* and *X* have the same set of items.

In the closed itemset framework, some studies were concerned with the generation of nonredundant sets of association rules (Pasquier et al., 2005; Pfaltz & Taylor, 2002; Valtchev, 2002b) where Y_1 is a generator, that is, a minimal subset of *Y* such that its closure is equal to *Y*.

The following is a summary of the key results from concept lattice theory (Ganter & Wille, 1999), which provides the basis of our approach towards the generation of frequent closed itemsets and association rules as well as manipulation of DM output and visualization using a nested structure.

Copyright © 2007, Idea Group Inc. Copying or distributing in print or electronic forms without written permission of Idea Group Inc. is prohibited.

Concept Lattices

Let $K = (O, A, R)$ be a formal context (see Table 2), where O, A, and R are a set of objects (e.g., transactions), a set of attributes or properties (e.g., items in a transaction database), and a binary relation between O and A, respectively. Two functions f and g summarize the links between subsets of objects and subsets of attributes induced by R. Function f maps a set of objects into a set of common attributes, whereas g is the dual for attribute sets:

- $f : \mathscr{P}(O) \rightarrow \mathscr{P}(A), f(X) = X' = \{a \in A | \forall o \in X, oRa\}$, where $\mathscr{P}(O)$ is the power set of O.

- $g : \mathscr{P}(A) \rightarrow \mathscr{P}(O), g(Y) = Y' = \{o \in O | \forall a \in Y, oRa\}$.

Table 2 shows, for example, that $f(\{2, 6\}) = \{a, b\}$ and $g(\{a, c, d\}) = \{6, 7, 8\}$[1].

Furthermore, the compound operators $g.f(X)$ and $f.g(Y)$ (denoted by ") are *closure* operators over $\mathscr{P}(O)$ and $\mathscr{P}(A)$ respectively. This means, in particular, that $Z \subseteq Z''$ and $(Z'')'' = Z''$ for any $Z \in \mathscr{P}(A)$ or $Z \in \mathscr{P}(O)$.

A formal concept c is a pair of sets (X, Y) where $X \in \mathscr{P}(O)$, $Y \in \mathscr{P}(A)$, $X = Y'$ and $Y = X'$. X is called the extent of c (denoted by *Extent(c)*) and Y represents its intent (denoted by *Intent(c)*). The notion of concept is then nothing but a cluster since it consists of objects grouped together by proximity or similarity (here, according to a common intent). In the closed itemset mining framework (Pasquier et al., 2005; Valtchev et al., 2002b; Zaki et al., 2002), X and Y correspond to the notion of closed tidset and closed itemset respectively.

Table 2. Context K = (O={1, 2,...,8}, A={a, b,..., h, i}, R)

	A								
	A_1				A_2				
Tid	a	b	c	d	e	f	g	h	i
1	X	X					X		
2	X	X					X	X	
3	X	X	X				X	X	
4	X		X				X	X	X
5	X	X		X		X			
6	X	X	X	X		X			
7	X		X	X	X				
8	X		X	X		X			

Copyright © 2007, Idea Group Inc. Copying or distributing in print or electronic forms without written permission of Idea Group Inc. is prohibited.

Figure 1. The Hasse diagram of the lattice related to context K

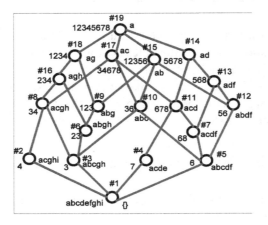

The set *G* of all concepts extracted from the context *K* is partially ordered by intent/extent inclusion:

$$(X_1, Y_1) \leq (X_2, Y_2) \Leftrightarrow X_1 \subseteq X_2, Y_2 \subseteq Y_1.$$

A concept (Galois) lattice associated with context *K* is then a complete lattice *L=B(O, A, R)* = ⟨ *G*, ≤⟩, where concepts in *G* are linked according to a partial order.

The Hasse diagram of the lattice *L* drawn from Table 2 is shown on Figure 1 where *tidsets* and *itemsets* are indicated on both sides of nodes. For example, node #11 represents the concept (678, *acd*) which means that the itemset *acd* is a closed itemset with three supporting objects: 6, 7, and 8.

A subset *B* of concepts in *G* is an *order filter* (*order ideal* respectively) if ∀*a* ∈ *G*, *b* ∈ *B*, *b* ≤ *a* ⇒ *a*∈*B* (*a* ≤ *b* ⇒ *a* ∈ *B* respectively). The smallest ideal that contains a given concept *b* in *G* is called a *principal ideal* and is given by ↓*b* = {*c* in *G* | *c* ≤ *b*}. Dually, ↑*b* denotes the principal filter for *b*. For example (see Figure 1), the principal ideal for concept #10 contains concepts labeled by #1, #3, #5, and #10, while its corresponding principal filter contains the set {#10, #15 , #17 , #19}.

Integrating DM with DW Techniques

Data warehousing and data mining have been greatly progressing in an independent way. However, many researchers and practitioners recognize the need for a deep integration of the two technologies (Han, 1998; Han & Kamber, 2000).

Copyright © 2007, Idea Group Inc. Copying or distributing in print or electronic forms without written permission of Idea Group Inc. is prohibited.

Some studies were conducted to either adapt multidimensional data so that classical data mining techniques can be used, or adapt data mining algorithms to the context of multidimensional data. The first solution consists for example to first flatten multidimensional data before applying DM techniques (Goil & Choudhary, 2001) or to first map multidimensional data onto data sequences (Pinto et al., 2001). The second solution aims to develop new solutions or revise existing ones to directly mine multidimensional data as in Dong, Han, Joyce, Pei, and Wang (2001) and Imielinski, Khachiyan, and Abdulghani (2002).

Substantial work has been conducted on data mining in data warehouses as reported in Han and Kamber (2000). This includes (but is not limited to) exception detection in dimensional datasets (Knorr, Ng, & Tucakov, 2000), cubegrade generation (Imielinski et al., 2002), constrained gradient analysis (Dong et al., 2001), and discovery-driven examination of cubes (Sarawagi et al., 1998). Cubegrades are association rules which express the impact of cube changes on a set of measures. In the context of the governance running example, cubegrades can help find (1) how the average asset held by enterprises is affected by the presence of females on the board, or (2) how the enterprises having a good governance index (70% and more) compare with enterprises with a lower governance index in terms of the average amount of assets. In Naouali and Missaoui (2005), an approach towards approximating the answer to OLAP queries and the identification of classification and characteristic rules is proposed using the rough set theory.

Data Mining Techniques for Data Warehousing

In this section we focus on association rule mining from data cubes.

Rule Mining from Cubes

Association rule mining (ARM) in data cubes is different from the classical ARM because measures in data cubes are aggregated values which depend intimately on the value taken by each one of the cube dimensions, while each item (respectively attribute) in transaction databases (resp. relational tables) exists (takes its value) in an independent way from the rest of items (attributes). Based on that fact, we revisit the notion of itemset and association rule by imposing additional constraints on them in order to make them more meaningful in a multidimensional context. Two cases will be considered:

Copyright © 2007, Idea Group Inc. Copying or distributing in print or electronic forms without written permission of Idea Group Inc. is prohibited.

- The cube $C=\langle D, M\rangle$ has a unique measure in M, which corresponds to a COUNT aggregate function

- The cube has at least a measure related to an aggregate function other than COUNT

In the first case, ARM from a given cube C whose dimensions are in D amounts to ARM from (a possibly subset of) the relational table T that generated C. However, support and confidence of rules need to rely on the support of each fact in C, that is, the number of individual records in T that support the fact. In the second case, we first need to impose constraints on the structure of frequent itemsets and rules so that the data mining output is meaningful. Then, a careful evaluation and interpretation of such output is needed because any reference to a given measure value must be expressed in terms of all the dimensions involved in the cube.

Frequent Closed Itemsets

Let $C=\langle D, M\rangle$ be a data cube, where D is a set of dimensions involved in C, and M a set of measures associated with D. When M is not limited to a count-based measure, we define a frequent (closed) itemset Y extracted from C as *meaningful* if the following conditions hold: (1) $Y \cap D \neq \varnothing$, and (2) $Y \cap M_1 \neq \varnothing$, where $M_1 \subset M$ is the set of non-count based measures. The two conditions impose the presence of at least one dimension and one non-count measure (e.g., MIN).

From Table 1(b), one can extract the frequent (support $= 41\%$) closed itemset $\{Duality = 0, AvgAsset=2, Govern = 2\}$ which is *meaningful* since the second item represents a range value of the measure related to the *average* company asset. Instead, $\{Internal = 3, Govern = 2\}$ is not a meaningful one.

Association Rules

Based on the observations made earlier in this section, we define two types of association rules: one which is computed from a data cube whose unique measure represents a COUNT aggregate function, and the other is computed from a data cube for which at least a measure represents an aggregate function other than COUNT (e.g, MIN, AVERAGE). The second one must be generated from *meaningful* frequent closed itemsets.

> **Definition 1:** Let Y_1 and Y_2 be two non-empty subsets of members in D, where D is a dimension set in cube $C = \langle D, M\rangle$ and $Y_1 \cap Y_2 = \varnothing$, and let X be the set of facts supporting $Y_1 \cup Y_2$. A COUNT-BASED MULTIDIMENSIONAL

Copyright © 2007, Idea Group Inc. Copying or distributing in print or electronic forms without written permission of Idea Group Inc. is prohibited.

association rule (CMAR) r drawn from C is an implication of the form $Y_1 \Rightarrow Y_2$. The support of rule r is:

$$supp(Y_1 \cup Y_2) = \frac{\sum_{f_j \in x} m_j}{\sum_{j=1}^{n} mj},$$

where n is the total number of facts, and m_j is a count value associated with fact f_j in X. The confidence of r is computed as the ratio $supp(Y_1 \cup Y_2)/supp(Y_1)$, where:

$$supp(Y_1) = \frac{\sum_{f_j \in Y1} m_j}{\sum_{j=1}^{n} mj} \text{ for all facts } f_j \text{ supporting } Y_1.$$

Definition 2: A NON-COUNT-BASED MULTIDIMENSIONAL association rule (NCMAR) r generated from a cube $C = <D, M>$ is an implication of the form $Y_1 \Rightarrow Y_2$, where $Y_1 \cup Y_2$ is a meaningful FCI and $Y_1 \cap Y_2 = \varnothing$, and $\exists\ m$ a non-count measure in M such that $m \in Y_1 \cup Y_2$. Let the set of facts supporting $Y_1 \cup Y_2$ be X. Then, the support of rule r is:

$$supp(Y_1 \cup Y_2) = \frac{\sum_{f_j \in x} m_j}{\sum_{j=1}^{n} mj},$$

where n is the total number of facts, and m_j is a count value associated with fact f_j in X. The confidence is computed as the ratio $supp(Y_1 \cup Y_2)/supp(Y_1)$, where:

$$supp(Y_1) = \frac{\sum_{f_j \in Y1} m_j}{\sum_{j=1}^{n} mj} \text{ for all facts } f_j \text{ supporting } Y_1.$$

It is important to note that in the case of NCMARs, the cube contains a non-count-based measure apart from a count-based one. The latter is used to compute the support of the rule.

As an illustration, the following rules (CMAR and NCMAR respectively) were extracted from the fact tables shown in Table 1 (left and right sides respectively) by first computing *FCI*s.

- **CMAR:** *Duality*=0 and *Internal*=2 $\Rightarrow$ *Govern*=2 [50/216, (50/216)/(74/216)]. This means that if the CEO does not act as a board chairman and if the proportion of Top Management on the board is between 10 and 25%, then the index

Copyright © 2007, Idea Group Inc. Copying or distributing in print or electronic forms without written permission of Idea Group Inc. is prohibited.

of corporate governance quality is between 40 and 70% with a support = 23% and a confidence = 67%.

- **NCMAR:** *Duality* = 0 and *Internal* = 1 $\Rightarrow$ *AvgAsset* = 2 [73/216, (73/216)/(74/216)]. This means that if the CEO does not act as a board chairman and if the proportion of top management on the board is less than 10%, then the average asset is over 1000K (according to the three defined dimensions) with a support = 34% and a confidence = 98%.

Data Warehousing Techniques for Data Mining

Many researchers recognize the need to have mechanisms for user exploration and guidance while mining from databases (Imielinski et al., 2002) or browsing through data cubes (Sarawagi et al., 1998).

Since the output of a data mining task can be very large even for a reasonably small dataset, our main objective here is to allow the user to explore an already computed DM output (a set of groupings/concepts in our case) in a discovery-driven manner similar to what is offered by OLAP techniques. The user can then go through coarser/finer levels of data abstraction (i.e., rollup vs. drill-down) when an attribute (or dimension) hierarchy is available (e.g., levels of company location are city, state, and country), see a DM output under different perspectives (one or many attributes), or use the dice operator to select some specific attributes (or attribute values) and/or a set of objects. As a preliminary illustration, a rollup on a DM output in our running example means either a reduction in the number of perspectives to consider (e.g., financial features) or a generalization upon one or many perspectives (e.g., company location).

Based on the background provided earlier, we define a set of operators inspired from OLAP techniques (e.g., drill-down, slice), which act like relational algebra by operating on concept lattices to get new ones.

Operations on Lattices

In this subsection, we formally define three main operations on lattices: projection, selection, and assembly. More details about theoretical results can be found in Ganter and Wille (1999) and Valtchev et al. (2002a).

The PROJECTION of $L = B(O, A, R)$ over $A_1 \subset A$ is given by the following mapping: $\varphi: L \rightarrow L_1 = B(O, A_1, R_1)$.

Copyright © 2007, Idea Group Inc. Copying or distributing in print or electronic forms without written permission of Idea Group Inc. is prohibited.

Figure 2. Projection of L on two distinct attribute subsets abcd and efghi to produce L_1 and L_2

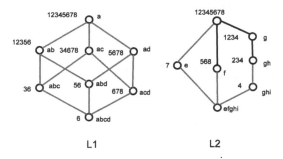

L1   L2

Function φ maps a concept (X, Y) from the lattice L into a concept of the resulting lattice L_1 by projecting its intent over the attribute set A_1: φ $((X,Y))=((Y∩A_1)'$, $Y∩A_1)$, where the operator ' upon an extent (respectively an intent) returns an intent (respectively an extent) in L_1.

When A_1 represents the intent of an existing concept c in L, then L_1 is nothing but the principal filter of c enriched with the partial order.

The ASSEMBLY of two lattices $L_1=B(O, A_1, R_1)$ and $L_2=B(O, A_2, R_2)$ according to a same set O of objects is a substructure of the direct product of L_1 and L_2 defined by:

$$ψ: L_1=B(O, A_1, R_1) × L_2=B(O, A_2, R_2) → L=B(O, A_1∪A_2, R_1∪R_2).$$

Function ψ maps a pair of concepts from L_1 and L_2 into a global concept by an intersection over their respective extents: ψ $((\langle (X_1,Y_1),(X_2,Y_2)\rangle) = (X_1∩X_2, (X_1∩X_2)')$.

The assembly of lattices can be used not only to "join" lattices, but also to define nested line diagrams as described in the Visualization Mechanisms section.

Figure 2 illustrates the projection of lattice L onto the subset *abcd* and *efghi* to get new lattices L_1 and L_2. The assembly of L_1 and L_2 produces lattice L.

The SELECTION operation, applied to a lattice $L=B(O, A, R)$, produces a new lattice in which a subset O_1 of O is considered. This operation is dual to the projection and is given by the mapping $ξ: L→L_3= B(O_1, A, R_3)$.

The function $ξ$ maps a concept (X, Y) from the lattice L into a concept of the resulting lattice L_3 by selecting a set O_1 of objects:

$$ξ((X,Y))=(X ∩ O_1, (X ∩ O_1)').$$

Copyright © 2007, Idea Group Inc. Copying or distributing in print or electronic forms without written permission of Idea Group Inc. is prohibited.

For example (see Figure 2), the selection on L_1 on the set $\{1, 2, 3, 4\}$ is a lattice that has the following concept set: $\{(1234, a), (123, ab), (34, ac), (3, abc), (\varnothing, abcd)\}$.

When O_1 represents the extent of an existing concept c in L, then L_3 is nothing but the principal ideal of c enriched with the partial order.

Operations on Data Mining Output

In the following, we show how known OLAP operations (drill-down, rollup, slice, and dice) can be translated in our data mining concept lattice framework as a combination of operations on lattices such as selection, projection, and assembly (noted respectively by σ, Π, and $\times$). As stated earlier in the section Integrating DM with DW Techniques, these operations can be assimilated to cubing for exploratory data mining.

The operations can be defined as follows:

- **Rollup:** go up the attribute hierarchy of one or many attributes (e.g., go from sector to sector category) or ignore a subset of attributes.
- **Drill-down:** go down the attribute hierarchy of one or many attributes or add a new attribute (e.g., introduce CEO's education).
- **Slice:** limit the analysis to a given attribute/property (e.g., proportion of internal shareholders on the board).
- **Dice:** focus on a subset of attributes and/or objects (e.g., features about board structure for firms working on some given industry sectors).

Additional exploratory operations can be defined (e.g, drill-through, nest-unnest, split).

In the sequel, we first provide a formal definition of the four key OLAP operations by borrowing the well-known notations used in relational algebra. Then, algorithms for implementing the projection and assembly are proposed and discussed.

Definition of OLAP Operations

In the following, we redefine four commonly known OLAP operations when they apply to a DM output that takes the form of a concept lattice.

Copyright © 2007, Idea Group Inc. Copying or distributing in print or electronic forms without written permission of Idea Group Inc. is prohibited.

Figure 3. Rollup of L₁ by replacing c and d with a more general value k

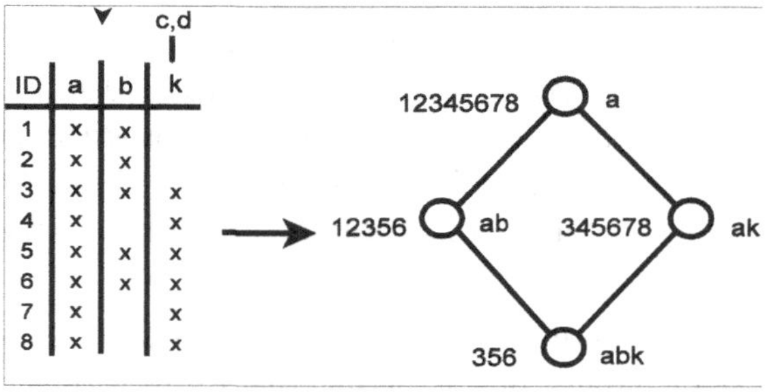

Rollup

Let $P \subseteq A$ be the attributes of a given relational (or fact) table on which the rollup will be conducted either by climbing up attribute hierarchies or by dropping attributes, and let $L=B(O, A, R)$ be a concept lattice. Assume that $AL=\{\langle A_1, l_{1i}\rangle,...,\langle A_j, l_{jm}\rangle, ...\}$ is a given pattern of the rollup (i.e., level climbing), where $\langle A_j, l_{jm}\rangle$ means the hierarchy attached to attribute j is to be climbed from the current level to a higher level l_{jm}. The size of AL represents the maximal number of attributes for which the attribute hierarchy needs to be explored bottom up, and hence $|AL| = |P|$. The operation $Rollup(L, P, AL)$ uses the lattice L as input to produce a new concept lattice in which the attributes in P are either replaced with more general ones or ignored. When $l_{jm} = \top$ for a given attribute Aj, this means that attribute Aj is temporarily discarded from analysis.

Like in data cubes, the rollup operation reduces the output set while the drill-down operation increases the size of the output. Therefore, the lattice resulting from a rollup is smaller than the initial one.

The algebraic representation of $Rollup(L, P, AL)$ using the projection and assembly is as follows:

$Rollup(L, P, AL) = \Pi_{A-P}(L) \times (L_1)$, where L and L_1 correspond to $B(O, A, R)$ and $B(O, A_1, R_1)$ respectively, and A_1 is the set of $|P|$ attributes generalized according to the pattern AL.

> **Example:** Figure 3 illustrates a rollup of lattice L_1 (see Figure 2) upon an attribute by climbing up the hierarchy from the level containing c and d to a higher level containing k.

Copyright © 2007, Idea Group Inc. Copying or distributing in print or electronic forms without written permission of Idea Group Inc. is prohibited.

Drill-Down

In a symmetric way, *Drill-down(L, P, AL)* can be defined, where l_{jm} in *AL* means that the attribute hierarchy attached to A_j is to be explored from the current level to a lower level $l_{jm'}$. Such operation uses *L* as input to produce a new concept lattice resulting from the context in which the attributes in *P* are replaced with more specific ones. When $l_{jm} = \perp$ for a given attribute A_j, this means that attribute A_j is a new attribute to be considered for data mining.

The algebraic representation of *Drill-down(L, P, AL)* is the same as the one for the rollup operation. The difference lies in the fact that for the drill-down operation, A_l is the set of P attributes specialized (through a move down in the attribute hierarchies) according to the pattern *AL*.

Slice

Slice(L, a_i) limits the analysis of a concept lattice *L* to a given attribute a_i in order to see its corresponding lattice. It is important to note that in data cubes, this operation consists in selecting a given value for one dimension. However, we generalize it to a given attribute (with its possible values) to allow the definition of new operations (e.g., nesting) based on the slice operation.

The algebraic representation of the slice operation is:

$$Slice(L, a_i) = \Pi_{ai}(L).$$

In our running example, *Slice(L, Internal)* will provide the lattice limited to the dimension (attribute) *Internal*.

Dice

Dice(L, P, Q) limits the analysis to an arbitrary subset *Q* of objects and/or a subset *P* of attributes. Here again, our definition of the dice operation in concept lattices has a meaning relatively distinct from the dice operation in data cubes.

The algebraic representation of the dice operation is:

$$Dice(L, P, Q) = \sigma_{o_i \in Q}(\Pi_P(L)) \text{ where } Q \subset O \text{ and/or } P \subset A.$$

Copyright © 2007, Idea Group Inc. Copying or distributing in print or electronic forms without written permission of Idea Group Inc. is prohibited.

For example, one would like to focus his/her analysis of the lattice L to companies 1, 2, and 3 using shareholding features only.

Algorithms

Now that the OLAP operations acting on DM output are formally defined using operations on lattices, we describe hereafter algorithms for the implementation of projection and assembly.

Algorithm 1 implements the projection and has two arguments: the attribute set P to be projected on, and the node n which is initially set to the infimum (i.e., the bottom of the lattice). It handles a traversal of the lattice in a recursive way from the bottom to the top (supremum). The ascending part of recursivity contributes to the production of concepts (nodes) while the descending part handles the partial order in the resulting lattice. Function $put(n')$ returns the node of the input lattice that corresponds to node n' in the output lattice. Function $get(n)$ conducts the opposite operation by returning the node in the output lattice that corresponds to node n. The function $parent\_pruning$ consists to check itemset inclusion to avoid the exploration of useless parent nodes in the lattice.

Algorithm 1: Projection

Input: Node n, P: a set of attributes

Output: Node n'

if n is already processed **then**

    return get(n)

Successors $\leftarrow \varnothing$ /* keep track of the successors of a given node */

$i_1 \leftarrow$ intent(n) $\cap P$

Parents $\leftarrow$ sort(Parents(n)) /* in a decreasing order of $|\text{intent}(p) \cap i_1|$ where $p \in$ *Parents* */

for each non visited parent p of *Parents* **do**

    $i_2 \leftarrow$ intent(p) $\cap i_1$

    if $i_2 \neq \varnothing$ and $i_1 \neq i_2$ **then**

        Successors $\leftarrow$ *Successors* $\cup$ *Projection*(p, P)

    else if $i_1 = i_2$ **then**

    Projection(p, P)

Mark n as a processed node

$n' \leftarrow$ (extent(n), i_2)

Link n' to *Successors*

Return n'

Copyright © 2007, Idea Group Inc. Copying or distributing in print or electronic forms without written permission of Idea Group Inc. is prohibited.

Table 3. Trace of the projection of lattice L (Figure 1) on abcd

n	il	Successors	Concept
1	abcd	5	no
5	abcd	7,10,12	yes
10	abc	15,17	yes
15	ab	19	yes
19	a	NIL	yes
17	ac	19	yes
7	acd	11	no
11	acd	14,17	yes
14	ad	19	yes
12	abd	13,15	yes
13	ad	14	no

Table 3 provides the trace of the projection algorithm applied to lattice L (depicted in Figure 1) and shows that the infimum of the output lattice is rapidly reached and the resulting lattice is quickly formed using heuristics for selecting the successors (parents) to explore.

The following algorithm exploits the properties defined in the section Operations on Lattices to perform the assembly of two lattices L_1 and L_2. A simplistic way to implement such operation is to compare each node in L_1 with each node in L_2. In order to rapidly get real concepts, each one of the two lattices is explored in a bottom-up way following a linear extension of the lattice order. The following procedure presents a simplified description of the implemented algorithm where E stores the intersection of two extents. If E is a new value, then it corresponds to the extent of a new concept c. In that case, concept c is then created and linked to its immediate predecessors (descendants). More details can be found in Valtchev et al. (2002a).

Algorithm 2: Assembly
Input: $L_1 = \langle G_1, \leq_{L1} \rangle,\ L_2 = \langle G_2, \leq_{L2} \rangle$
Output: $L = \langle G, \leq_L \rangle$

$L \leftarrow \emptyset$
Sort(G_1) according to a linear extension of $\leq_{L1}$;
Sort(G_2) according to a linear extension of $\leq_{L2}$;
for each c_i in G_1 **do**
  for each c_j in G_2 **do**
    $E \leftarrow extent(c_i) \cap extent(c_j)$

Copyright © 2007, Idea Group Inc. Copying or distributing in print or electronic forms without written permission of Idea Group Inc. is prohibited.

Figure 4. Projection on lattice vs. projection on context

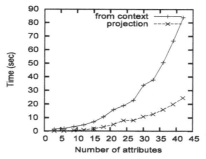

if *E* does not exist as an extent of a newly computed concept **then**

$c \leftarrow (E, intent(c_i) \cup intent(c_j))$

$L \leftarrow L \cup \{c\}$

Link *c* to its immediate predecessors

return *L*

Another way to implement the assembly operation consists to start with L_1 and iteratively conduct as many assembly operations as there are attributes in L_2.

Among the questions that we had to answer while exploring the projection and the assembly operations, we enumerate the following:

- Is it worthwhile to perform these operations on lattices rather than recomputing lattices from scratch based on the projection or the apposition (i.e., horizontal concatenation) of contexts?

- Are there other benefits of these operations on lattices?

To answer the first question, we have conducted an experimental study which showed that computing a projection on a lattice is generally more efficient than the lattice construction using the modified context. The gain increases significantly as the proportion of projection attributes augments. Figure 4 illustrates this fact for a context of 500 objects and 50 attributes.

Our work on lattice assembly (Valtchev et al., 2002a) shows that this operation has interesting empirical and theoretical performances. Furthermore, the other benefit of the two operations lies in the fact that they can be used to construct a lattice in a distributed or parallel environment, or construct a nested structure of the lattice, called *nested line diagram* (see Visualization Mechanisms section for more details).

Copyright © 2007, Idea Group Inc. Copying or distributing in print or electronic forms without written permission of Idea Group Inc. is prohibited.

Figure 5. Nested-line diagram from a subset of attributes in Table 1a

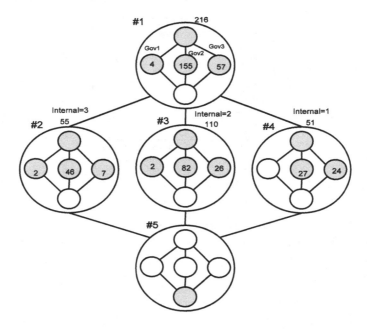

Visualization Mechanisms

In large and complex DM output, it is crucial to provide mechanisms to (1) select the mining space (i.e., input data), (2) limit the DM output to user's needs and perspectives, and (3) browse the DM results.

Our work about data visualization concerns mainly the implementation of projection and assembly of lattices to produce nested line diagrams and see the data mining output (drawn either from bidimensional or multidimensional data) under different perspectives.

Nested line diagrams (Ganter & Wille, 1999) are visualization aids which allow the construction of a lattice L as an assembly of two or many lattices $L_1,...,L_n$ by combining the respective Hasse diagrams of the n lattices L_i into a unique complex structure. However, neither the nodes of L nor their partial order are directly represented. Instead, the information about them is spread over the various levels of nesting. Figure 5 presents the nested line diagram (NLD) of the product lattice $L_{Internal, Govern}=L_{Internal} \times L_{Govern}$. As can be seen, the line diagram of the lattice *Internal* is used as an outer frame in which the diagram of *Govern* is embedded. The outer lattice shows the distribution of companies according to the dimension *Internal*. Each one of the three external nodes at the intermediate level focuses on a particular value of *Internal*. For example (see the node in the middle), 110 enterprises have

Copyright © 2007, Idea Group Inc. Copying or distributing in print or electronic forms without written permission of Idea Group Inc. is prohibited.

Internal = 2 (i.e., the top management represents a proportion of 10 to 25% of the board). A careful look at the inner lattice of the external LHS node allows to state that when *Internal* = 3, good quality of governance (i.e., *Govern* = 3) tends to be less frequent than in the case when *Internal* is equal to 1 or 2. In particular, a comparison between the inner diagrams related to the extreme nodes (LHS for *Internal* = 3 and RHS for *Internal* = 1) of the outer structure shows clearly that the quality of governance is overall higher for *Internal* = 1 than for *Internal* = 3 (e.g., 24 enterprises have *Govern* = 3 when *Internal* = 1 against 7 when *Internal* = 3).

The NLD in Figure 5 can be perceived as a rollup on the fact table depicted by Table 1a when the dimension *Duality* is ignored. However, the structure embeds multiple rollups since one can see at the same time aggregate values for one of the two dimensions or for a combination of the two dimensions. This fact is much more emphasized when the number of nesting levels is large. Therefore, the NLD structure offers a richer environment than OLAP operations for the exploration and navigation in aggregated data. To illustrate this fact, one can see that the inner diagram in the supremum of the outer lattice (node # 1) is a projection (rollup) of the lattice (produced from the fact table in Table 1(a)) on *Govern* while the immediate predecessors of that external node (i.e., nodes #2, #3, and #4) reflect a rollup limited to *Internal*. To get a rollup on the combination of *Internal* and *Govern*, we need to look at the inner lattices within outer nodes. For example, when *Internal* = 1 (see node #4), 51 enterprises have either *Govern* = 2 (27 cases) or *Govern* = 3 (24 cases), but no one of them has a bad quality of governance (i.e., *Govern* = 1) like in the case when *Internal* takes a value equal to 2 or 3 (internal structure in nodes #3 and #2) .

We have developed a set of tools for information and knowledge visualization: (1) the tool called CubeViz helps highlight the salient cells in a data cube as well as associations among cells, and (2) the module NLD allows a nested representation of lattices. The latter is built upon our DM platform called Galicia (2004).

Conclusion

In this chapter, we have presented our solution towards a mutual collaboration between data mining and data warehousing technologies with flexibility/interactivity and efficiency objectives in mind. It exploits the theoretical basis and attractive features of formal concept analysis and concept lattices to propose two techniques: (1) one which exploits lattice based mining algorithms for efficiently generating frequent closed itemsets from multidimensional data to further extract association rules and clusters, and (2) the second technique which defines new operators similar in spirit to OLAP techniques to allow "data mining on demand" by relying on operations like projection, selection, and assembly on concept lattices.

Copyright © 2007, Idea Group Inc. Copying or distributing in print or electronic forms without written permission of Idea Group Inc. is prohibited.

Our current work covers also statistical modeling in data warehouses in order to discover useful patterns in data (e.g., outliers), discard irrelevant dimensions and dimension members, and hide irrelevant cube cells. In particular, we are exploring the potential of log-linear modeling for data summarization and prediction of multi-dimensional data. Among the observed barriers, we note the difficulty to efficiently choose a parsimonious model (i.e., a reduced model that fits the data) from a possibly very large set of candidate models, and the applicability of log-linear models to high-dimension cubes.

Acknowledgments

We would like to thank the Natural Sciences and Engineering Research Council of Canada (NSERC) and *Le fonds québécois de la recherche sur la nature et les technologies* (FQRNT) for their financial support.

References

Agrawal, R., & Srikant, R. (1994). Fast algorithms for mining association rules. *Proceedings of the 20th International Conference on Very Large Data Bases,* Santiago de Chile (pp. 487-499). Morgan Kaufmann.

Babcock, B., Chaudhuri, S., & Das, G. (2003). *Dynamic sample selection for approximate query processing.* In *Proceedings of the 2003 ACM SIGMOD International Conference on Management of Data,* San Diego, CA (pp. 539-550). ACM Press.

Barbara, D., & Wu, X. (2001). *Loglinear-based quasi cubes. Journal of Intelligent Information Systems, 16*(3), 255-276.

Ben Messaoud, R., Boussaïd, O., & Rabaséda, S. (2004). A new OLAP aggregation based on the AHC technique. In *Proceedings of the 7th ACM International Workshop on Data Warehousing and OLAP,* New York (pp. 65-72). Washington, DC: ACM Press.

Chaudhuri, S., & Dayal, U. (1997). An overview of data warehousing and OLAP technology. *SIGMOD Record, 26*(1), 65-74.

Dong, G., Han, J., Joyce, M. W., Pei, J., & Wang, K. (2001). Mining multi-dimensional constrained gradients in data cubes. In *Proceedings of the 27th International Conference on Very Large Data Bases* (pp. 321-330). San Francisco: Morgan Kaufmann Publishers.

Copyright © 2007, Idea Group Inc. Copying or distributing in print or electronic forms without written permission of Idea Group Inc. is prohibited.

Galicia. (2004). *Galois Lattice Interactive Constructor. SourceForge project.* Retrieved June 14, 2006, from http://sourceforge.net/projects/galicia/

Ganter, B., & Wille, R. (1999). *Formal concept analysis: Mathematical foundations* (C. Franzke, Trans.). New York: Springer-Verlag.

Goil, S., & Choudhary, A. N. (2001). PARSIMONY: An infrastructure for parallel multidimensional analysis and data mining. *Journal of Parallel and Distributed Computing, 61*(3), 285-321.

Han, J. (1998). Towards on-line analytical mining in large databases. *SIGMOD Record, 27*(1), 97-107.

Han, J., & Kamber, M. (2000). *Data mining: Concepts and techniques.* San Francisco: Morgan Kaufmann Publishers Inc.

Imielinski, T., Khachiyan, L., & Abdulghani, A. (2002). Cubegrades: Generalizing association rules. *Data Mining and Knowledge Discovery, 6*(3), 219-257.

Imielinski, T., & Mannila, H. (1996). A database perspective on knowledge discovery. *Communications of the ACM, 39*(11), 58-64.

Knorr, E. M., Ng, R. T., & Tucakov, V. (2000). Distance-based outliers: Algorithms and applications. *The VLDB Journal, 8*(3-4), 237-253.

Lakshmanan, S., Pei, J., & Zhao, Y. (2002). Quotient cube: How to summarize the semantics of a data cube. In *Proceedings of the 28ᵗʰ International Conference on Very Large Databases,* Hong Kong (pp. 778-789). Morgan Kaufmann.

Lu, H., Feng, L., & Han, J. (2000). Beyond intratransaction association analysis: Mining multidimensional intertransaction association rules. *ACM Transactions on Information Systems, 18*(4), 423-454.

Naouali, S., & Missaoui, R. (2005). Flexible query answering in data cubes. In *Proceedings of the 7ᵗʰ International Conference on Data Warehousing and Knowledge Discovery* (pp. 221-232), Copenhagen, Denmark. Springer-Verlag.

Pasquier, N., Taouil, R., Bastide, Y., Stumme, G., & Lakhal, L. (2005). Generating a condensed representation for association rules. *Journal of Intelligent Information Systems, 24*(1), 29-60.

Pfaltz, J. L., & Taylor, C. M. (2002). Scientific discovery through iterative transformations of concept lattices. In *Proceedings of the 1ˢᵗ International Workshop on Discrete Mathematics and Data Mining,* Arlington, VA (pp. 65-74). SIAM.

Pinto, H., Han, J. Pei, J., Wang, K., Chen, Q., & Dayal, U. (2001). Multi-dimensional sequential pattern mining. *Proceedings of the 10th ACM International Conference on Information and Knowledge Manaagement,* Atlanta, GA (pp. 81-88). ACM Press.

Sarawagi, S., Agrawal, R., & Megiddo, N. (1998). Discovery-driven exploration of OLAP data cubes. In *Proceedings of the 6ᵗʰ International Conference on Extending Database Technology* (pp. 168-182). London: Springer-Verlag.

Copyright © 2007, Idea Group Inc. Copying or distributing in print or electronic forms without written permission of Idea Group Inc. is prohibited.

Shanmugasundaram, J., Fayyad, U., & Bradley, P. S. (1999). Compressed data cubes for olap aggregate query approximation on continuous dimensions. In *Proceedings of the Fifth ACM SIGKDD International Conference on Knowledge Discovery and Data Mining* (pp. 223-232). ACM Press.

Valtchev, P., Missaoui, R., Godin, R., & Meridji, M. (2002). Generating frequent itemsets incrementally: Two novel approaches based on Galois lattice theory. *Journal of Experimental and Theoretical Artificial Intelligence, 14*(2-3), 115-142.

Valtchev, P., Missaoui, R., & Lebrun, P. (2002). A partition-based approach towards constructing Galois (concept) lattices. *Discrete Mathematics, 256*(3), 801-829.

Wang, J., & Karypis, G. (2004). *Bamboo: Accelerating closed itemset mining by deeply pushing the length-decreasing support constraint.* In SDM.

Xin, D., Han, J., Li, X., & Wah, B. W. (2003). *Star-cubing: Computing iceberg cubes by top-down and bottom-up integration.* In VLDB.

Zaki, M. J., & Hsiao, C.-J. (2002). CHARM: An efficient algorithm for closed itemset mining. In R. Grossman, J. Han, V. Kumar, H. Mannila, & R. Motwani (Eds.), *Proceedings of the 2nd SIAM International Conference on Data Mining (ICDM'02).*

Endnote

[1]   We use a separator-free form for sets. For example, 167 stands for {1, 6, 7}, and bcd for {b, c, d}.

Copyright © 2007, Idea Group Inc. Copying or distributing in print or electronic forms without written permission of Idea Group Inc. is prohibited.

Chapter XII

Temporal Semistructured Data Models and Data Warehouses

Carlo Combi
University of Verona, Italy

Barbara Oliboni
University of Verona, Italy

Abstract

This chapter describes a graph-based approach to represent information stored in a data warehouse, by means of a temporal semistructured data model. We consider issues related to the representation of semistructured data warehouses, and discuss the set of constraints needed to manage in a correct way the warehouse time, that is the time dimension considered storing data in the data warehouse itself. We use a temporal semistructured data model because a data warehouse can contain data coming from different and heterogeneous data sources. This means that data stored in a data warehouse are semistructured in nature; that is, in different documents the same information can be represented in different ways, and the document schemata can be available or not. Moreover, information stored in a data warehouse is often time varying, thus as for semistructured data, also in the data warehouse context, it could be useful to consider time.

Copyright © 2007, Idea Group Inc. Copying or distributing in print or electronic forms without written permission of Idea Group Inc. is prohibited.

Introduction

In recent years the database community has proposed flexible data models to represent semistructured information. Semistructured data have no absolute schema fixed in advance. The structure may be irregular or incomplete (Abiteboul, 1997).

In the literature there are a number of approaches in which labeled graphs are used to represent semistructured data (Comai, Damiani, Posenato, & Tanca, 1998; Damiani, Oliboni, Tanca, & Veronese, 1999; Papakonstantinou, Garcia-Molina, & Widom, 1995). These models organize data in graphs where nodes denote objects or values, and edges represent relationships between them.

In the semistructured data context, the eXtensible Markup Language (XML) (World Wide Web Consortium, 1998) is spreading out as a standard for representing, exchanging, and publishing semistructured information (Abiteboul, Buneman, & Suciu, 2000), making information "self-describing," that is it is possible there is no separate description of the type or structure of data.

A data warehouse is a repository of data coming from different and heterogeneous data sources. This means that data stored in a data warehouse are semistructured in nature, because in different documents the same information can be represented in different ways, and moreover, the document schemata can be available or not. Furthermore, data warehouses can be used to store XML documents and WWW data. A data warehouse storing information represented by means of XML is called *XML data warehouse* (Marian, Abiteboul, Cobena, & Mignet, 2001), and a data warehouse collecting information from the Web is called *Web data warehouse* (Bhowmick, Madria, Ng, & Lim, 1998). In the literature are also considered *XML Web data warehouses* (Marian et al., 2001; Wang & Zaniolo, 2003).

A dynamic warehouse for XML data was proposed and implemented in the Xyleme project (Xyleme, 2001). The prototype was then turned into a product by a startup company also called Xyleme.

Information stored into a data warehouse is often time varying, thus as for semistructured data, also in the data warehouse context, it could be useful to consider time. The classical time dimensions, considered in the literature, are transaction time and valid time. The transaction time is the time when a fact is current in the database and may be retrieved, while the valid time is the time when a fact is true in the considered domain (Jensen, Dyreson, Bohlen, et al., 1998).

In the semistructured data context, graph-based data models have been extended to represent the time dimension of information, and issues related to the representation of transaction and valid times have been studied (Chawathe, Abiteboul, & Widom, 1998; Combi, Oliboni, & Quintarelli 2004; Oliboni, Quintarelli, & Tanca, 2001). In the data warehouse context, proposals in the literature focus on the representation

Copyright © 2007, Idea Group Inc. Copying or distributing in print or electronic forms without written permission of Idea Group Inc. is prohibited.

of successive versions of a document (Bębel, Eder, Koncilia, Morzy, & Wrembel, 2004; Marian et al., 2001).

In this chapter, we focus on the representation of semistructured warehouses, and consider issues related to their graph-based representations. In particular, we use a temporal semistructured data model, based on labeled graphs, to represent information stored in a data warehouse. Moreover, we discuss the set of constraints needed to manage in a correct way the warehouse time and the operations useful to handle the considered information. Topics related to the querying, the refreshment, and maintenance of semistructured data warehouses are not considered in this chapter.

The structure of the chapter is as follows: in the Background section we briefly describe the literature related to semistructured data, temporal semistructured data, and temporal data warehouses. In the Representing Semistructured Temporal Data Warehouses section we consider the main issues related to the management of temporal information in semistructured data warehouses, describe how to represent a data warehouse by means of a temporal graph-based data model, and define the set of constraint needed to manage time in the warehouse context. In the Future Trends section we describe the topics that are relevant in the semistructured data warehouse context and sketch possible lines for future works, while in the Conclusion section we summarize the chapter content.

Background

Semistructured Data

Semistructured data have irregular structure, and rapidly evolving or missing schema (Abiteboul, 1997). The classical example of semistructured data is related to data stored on the World Wide Web: at a typical Web site, data are varied and irregular, and the overall structure of the site changes often. Web data are integrated from multiple, heterogeneous data sources, where discrepancies among various data representations are likely.

In the semistructured data context, the database community has investigated flexible data models to represent in a uniform way this kind of information. The results of this research are a number of approaches in which labeled graphs are used to represent semistructured data. These models organize data in graphs where nodes denote objects or values, and edges represent relationships between them.

In this section, we briefly describe some semistructured data models based on labeled graphs (Damiani & Tanca, 1997; Papakonstantinou et al., 1995), and the eXtensible Markup Language (XML) (World Wide Web Consortium, 1998) which is spread-

Copyright © 2007, Idea Group Inc. Copying or distributing in print or electronic forms without written permission of Idea Group Inc. is prohibited.

ing out as a standard for representing, exchanging, and publishing semistructured information (Abiteboul et al., 2000).

In Papakonstantinou et al. (1995), the authors propose the object exchange model (OEM) which is a graph-structured data model where the basic idea is that each object has a label that describes its meaning.

An OEM label is a tuple (label;type;value;object-ID) where label denotes the kind of the object, type is a data type (atomic, composed, or reference), value denotes the actual value of the object, and object-ID represents a unique variable-length identifier for the object. The OEM label is used to extract information about objects that represent the underlying data. The OEM model represents semistructured data by means of graphs where nodes denote objects or values and edges represent relationships between objects; in particular an OEM graph is a directed labeled graph where the edge labels describe the pointed nodes. OEM does not actually represent the semantics of relationships between objects; that is, if an object pointed by an edge labeled as "Person" is connected by means of an edge labeled as "City" to another object, OEM allows one to represent only the fact that the object *City* is contained in the object *Person*, but does not express in which relationship they are. Thus, in this example it is impossible to understand if the person lives in the city or if the person works in the city. OEM uses edge labels to describe the pointed nodes, and thus edges represent only the containment relationship.

In Damiani and Tanca (1997), the authors propose a graph-oriented description and query language specifically designed for the needs of Web sites (WG-Log). WG-Log allows one to represent classical conceptual objects and standard hypermedia design notations, allowing the expression of model entities and relationships as well as navigational concepts. The WG-Log data model uses directed labeled graphs to represent schemata, instances, and queries. In WG-Log graphs, nodes represent objects, and edges indicate relationships between them. In particular, in WG-Log two main node types are defined: simple and complex nodes. Simple nodes represent simple objects (with an atomic, perceivable value as strings and numbers), while complex nodes represent abstract objects (whose properties are described by means of aggregates of simple objects). For example, a person is represented by means of a complex node *Person*, and the person's name by means of a simple node *Name* with a value. Moreover, there are other kinds of nodes to describe indexes and entry points, useful for the representation of the hypermedia structure. For example, the home page of a WWW site can be represented by means of an entry point. Graph edges can indicate both logical and navigational relationships. A logical edge has a label indicating the relationship name.

The eXtensible Markup Language (XML) (World Wide Web Consortium, 1998) is spreading out as a standard for representing, exchanging, and publishing semistructured information by means of a simple and flexible text format derived from the Standard Generalized Markup Language (World Wide Web Consortium, 1995).

Copyright © 2007, Idea Group Inc. Copying or distributing in print or electronic forms without written permission of Idea Group Inc. is prohibited.

XML is a markup language designed to describe data by means of a set of tags, which are not predefined. XML allows the author of the document to define the author's own tags and document structure.

XML documents can be easily represented as trees or graphs. For example the XPath Data Model (World Wide Web Consortium, 2005a) allows the representation of an XML document as a tree. XPath uses path expressions to address the nodes in the XML trees.

Temporal Semistructured Data

As in the classical context, also in the context of semistructured data it is interesting to take into account the dynamic aspects of data to represent their evolutions through time and eventually through consecutive updates.

In this section, we describe the different approaches proposed in the literature to represent time in the semistructured data context (Chawathe et al., 1998; Combi et al., 2004; Dyreson, Böhlen, & Jensen, 1999; Oliboni et al., 2001; Amagasa, Yoshi-kawa & Uemura, 2001).

In Chawathe et al. (1998), the authors propose the delta object exchange model (DOEM), a model based on the object exchange model (OEM) (Papakonstantinou et al., 1995). Change operations (i.e., node insertion, update of node values, addition and removal of labeled edges) are represented in DOEM by using *annotations* on the nodes and edges of an OEM graph. Intuitively, annotations are the representation of the history of nodes and edges. To implement the DOEM model the authors use a method that encodes DOEM databases as OEM databases. This proposal takes into account the transaction time dimension of a graph-based representation of semistructured data. As OEM graphs, DOEM graphs do not consider labeled relationships between two objects.

In Oliboni et al. (2001), the authors propose the temporal graphical model (TGM), which is a graphical model for representing semistructured data dynamics. A TGM graph is a directed labeled graph composed by two kinds of nodes (complex and simple nodes), and two kinds of edges (relational and temporal edges). Complex nodes are related to other complex nodes, and have a number of attributes (atomic nodes), whereas atomic nodes represent objects with an atomic value (i.e., a string, an integer, but also a text, an image, a sound) and do not exist independently of their parent complex node. This model represents the valid time dimension.

In Amagasa et al. (2001), the authors propose a logical data model for representing histories of XML documents. The proposed model is an extension of the XPath data model (World Wide Web Consortium, 2005a), with a label on edges expressing valid time. The result of a general XPath expression may be a selection of nodes from the input documents, or an atomic value, or more generally, any sequence allowed by

Copyright © 2007, Idea Group Inc. Copying or distributing in print or electronic forms without written permission of Idea Group Inc. is prohibited.

the data model. In the proposed extension, nodes can be selected also with respect to their valid time.

In Dyreson et al. (1999), the authors propose a graph-based model which uses labeled graphs to represent semistructured databases. In the defined graphs, each edge label is composed by a set of descriptive properties (e.g., name, transaction time, valid time, security properties of relationships): a property can be present in an edge and missing in another one. This proposal is very general and extensible: any property may be used and added to adapt the model to a specific context. In particular, the model allows one to represent temporal aspects and to consider only a temporal dimension or multiple temporal dimensions: to this regard, some examples of constraints which need to be suitably managed to correctly support semantics of the time-related properties are provided, both for querying and for manipulating graphs.

In Combi et al. (2004) the authors propose the Graphical sEmistructured teMporal data model (GEM), which is based on labeled graphs and allows one to represent in a uniform way semistructured data and their temporal aspects. In particular, they focus on transaction time. The GEM data model is based on rooted, connected, directed, labeled graphs. A GEM graph is composed by two kinds of nodes, complex and simple nodes, which are graphically represented in different ways. Complex nodes are depicted as rectangles and represent abstract entities, while simple nodes are depicted as ovals and represent primitive values. The transaction time of nodes and edges is represented by means of an interval. In this work, the authors define the set of constraints needed to manage in a correct way the transaction time dimension, and moreover describe the operations used to modify a GEM graph.

The GEM data model is general enough to represent both transaction and valid times.

In Figure 1, a GEM graph managing valid time is represented. In this example information about a group of restaurants is represented. The group of restaurants is represented as a complex node having label composed by the name *Group* and the valid time interval *[01/05/05,now]*. The name of the group (*"Red Horse"*) is represented by means of a simple node related to the complex node *Group*. This simple node has the label composed by the name *Name* and the valid time interval *[01/05/05,now]*. The node *Group* is the root of the graph, and is connected to its property by means of the edge with name *GroupName* and valid time interval *[01/05/05,now]*. The valid time interval *[01/05/05,now]* represents the fact that the group of restaurants is valid from June 1, 2005 until now.

Information about restaurants, addresses, and menu are represented respectively by means of the complex nodes *Restaurant, Address,* and *Menu.* Their properties are represented as simple nodes such as *Name, Position, Price, Street,* and *City.*

Data in Figure 1 are semistructured: the same information, such as the address of the restaurant, is represented in different ways, that is as a simple node for "Big Home,"

Copyright © 2007, Idea Group Inc. Copying or distributing in print or electronic forms without written permission of Idea Group Inc. is prohibited.

Figure 1. A GEM graph related to restaurant information

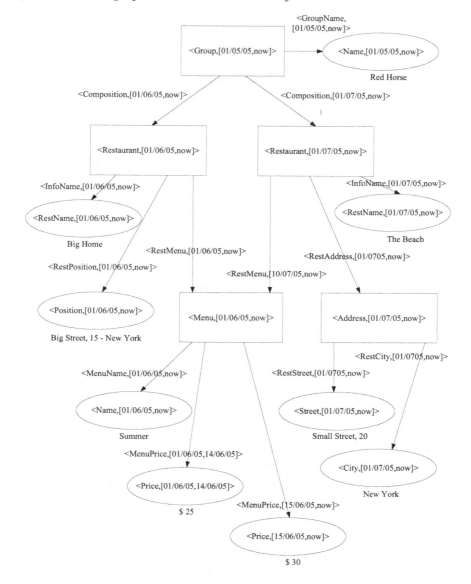

and as a complex node for "The Beach." The GEM data model allows the representation of data evolution, such as the increasing of a price. For example, in Figure 1, the price of the "Summer" menu increased from $25 to $30 on June 15, 2005. This evolution is represented, in a GEM graph managing valid time, by means of a new simple node with the same name ("*Price*"), with the new value ("*$30*") and valid time interval starting from "*15/06/05*" and ending "*now.*" The special value "*now*"

Copyright © 2007, Idea Group Inc. Copying or distributing in print or electronic forms without written permission of Idea Group Inc. is prohibited.

means that the considered node (edge) is currently valid (and will remain valid until a suitable update happens). The old price is represented in the GEM graph, but its valid time interval starts from "*01/06/05*" and ends "*14/06/05.*"

Temporal Data Warehouses

In the context of data warehouses it is very important to represent and consider time. Representing time in data warehouses means to allow one to compare data in different periods, that is, to consider the data evolution. The time dimension can be related either to the validity of information (valid time), or to the presence of information in the warehouse (transaction time). Moreover, the time dimension can be related to the evolution of data with respect to the time. In this case it is possible to store, in the data warehouse, successive versions of information.

In this section, we describe different approaches to consider and represent temporal information in a data warehouse (Eder & Koncilia, 2001; Eder, Koncilia & Morzy, 2001). Moreover, we focus on the representation of successive versions of a document (Bębel et al., 2004; Marian et al., 2001; Wang & Zaniolo, 2003; Wang, Zaniolo, Zhou, & Moon, 2005).

In Eder and Koncilia (2001), the authors propose an approach for representing changes in data dimensions of multidimensional data warehouses, by introducing temporal extension, structure versioning, and transformation functions. The proposed model is an extension of the multidimensional data model (Li & Wang, 1996; Vassiliadis & Sellis, 1999), and allows one to represent the valid time dimension by means of the time stamping of data. This approach considers the *structure version*, which is a view on a temporal data warehouse valid for a given time interval. The proposed system is able to represent successive versions of structures, and provides transformation functions to map data from a structure version to a different one.

In Eder et al. (2001), the authors propose an architecture for temporal data warehouse systems which allows the registration of temporal versions of dimension data, and the transfer of data between different temporal versions. In this work, the authors extend the model presented in Eder and Koncilia (2001) to represent also modifications at the schema level, such as the insertion of a new dimension level (e.g., the new dimension level *quarter* inserted between *month* and *year*).

In Marian et al. (2001), the authors present a change-centric method for managing versions in Web warehouses of XML data. These warehouses contain sequences of snapshots of XML documents coming from the Web. The approach is change-centric because the proposal focuses on changes (deltas). At each point in time, the last version of a document and the sequence of completed deltas (similar to logs of database systems) are stored. In this work, the time of a document version is

Copyright © 2007, Idea Group Inc. Copying or distributing in print or electronic forms without written permission of Idea Group Inc. is prohibited.

the time at which the system acquired this version, thus this proposal considers the transaction time dimension. The model introduced in Marian et al. (2001) is based on ordered trees, where all nodes have identifiers. The XML tree can be modified by means of basic operations such as *delete*, *insert*, *move*, and *update*, after the checking of consistency conditions.

In Wang and Zaniolo (2003), the authors propose XML-based techniques for managing a multiversion document as a unit, and representing successive versions by means of delta changes. In the XML document containing the successive versions of a document, each element has two attributes, *vstart* and *vend*, which represent the valid version interval of the element. The former attribute represents the moment at which the element is first added to the XML document (i.e., the initial version in which the element is valid), while the latter represents the moment at which the element is removed from the XML document (i.e., the last version in which the element is valid). The valid version interval can be represented by means of version numbers or timestamps. In the case of timestamps, the considered time dimension is the valid time.

To manage in a correct way the valid time dimension, the authors impose that the version interval of an ancestor node always contains those of its descendant nodes. The considered change operations are *delete*, *insert*, and *update*.

In Wang et al. (2005), the authors describe an approach to store and query the history of XML evolving document. In particular, they compute the difference between the successive versions of a document, and represent the history of the document by timestamping and temporally grouping the deltas. In this way, a multiversion document is managed as a unit and its successive versions are represented by the delta changes between versions. This approach makes it possible to support complex historical queries on the evolution of the document and its elements, by using Xquery (World Wide Web Consortium, 2005b), the standard query language of XML.

In Bębel et al. (2004), the authors propose a multiversion data warehouse that is capable of handling changes in the schema structure as well as simulating alternative business scenarios useful to predict trends by means of the *what-if* analysis. At this aim, the authors propose two different kinds of versions: real versions, which handle changes made to the external data sources, and alternative versions, which handle changes made by a user for the purpose of applying the *what-if* analysis. Several alternative versions can be created from a real version. Alternative versions can be created also to simulate changes in the structure of a data warehouse schema. Such a version is used for analyzing the system performances and the optimization of the data warehouse structure. The time dimension considered in this proposal is the valid time, which is represented by means of two timestamps: the beginning valid time and the ending valid time.

Copyright © 2007, Idea Group Inc. Copying or distributing in print or electronic forms without written permission of Idea Group Inc. is prohibited.

Representing Semistructured Temporal Data Warehouses

Data stored in a warehouse usually come from general heterogeneous data sources, and are semistructured in nature, thus a general and flexible data model to represent information stored in the data warehouse is needed. Moreover, data warehouses usually are used as a repository for time varying information. This means that, temporal aspects are a very important issue in this context.

In this section, we consider the main topics related to the management of time in semistructured data warehouses. In particular, we describe how to represent a data warehouse by means of a graph-based temporal semistructured data model, and propose the set of constraints needed to manage in the correct way the considered time dimension in the warehouse context.

In Figure 2 a GEM graph representing a portion of a data warehouse is reported. In this example information about products in a catalogue are stored. In particular, data in the graph represent a catalogue composed by two categories: *Clothes* and *SportProduct*. The complex node representing the catalogue is the root of the graph and has as label its name *Catalogue* and its valid time *[01/01/05,now]*. The valid interval *[01/01/05,now]* represents the fact that the catalogue is valid from January 1, 2005 until now. The *Clothes* and *SportProduct* categories are also represent by means of complex nodes with the same valid time intervals.

The former category has two products with their codes and prices, while the latter one is empty. In particular, the products included in the *Clothes* category are represented by means of two complex nodes with label *Product* and valid time interval *[01/01/05,now]*. The first product has a code equal to *"X1"* and a price equal to *"$10."* Both properties are represented as simple nodes. Each simple node has as label the name (*Code/Price*), and the valid time interval (*[01/01/2005]*), and the value of the property (*X1/$10*). The second product is structured as the first one, and represents a product having code equal to *"X2"* and a price equal to *"$20."* Each complex node is related to its children (complex or simple nodes) by means of edges having label composed by the name of the relation and the valid time of the relation itself. For example the complex node *Catalogue* is related to the category *Clothes* by means the edge with name *Category* and valid time interval *[01/01/2005,now]*.

The described information is valid since January 1, 2005; thus, the valid time interval of the objects in the data warehouse is *[01/01/05,now]*.

On March 1, 2005, the price of the product having code "X2" changes from "$20" to "$25." In Figure 3 this update is reported. In particular, the time interval of the simple node *Price* changes from *[01/01/05,now]* to *[01/01/05, 28/02/05]*, and the same for the time interval of the edge *ProdPrice* between the complex node *Prod-*

Copyright © 2007, Idea Group Inc. Copying or distributing in print or electronic forms without written permission of Idea Group Inc. is prohibited.

Figure 2. A GEM graph representing a data warehouse

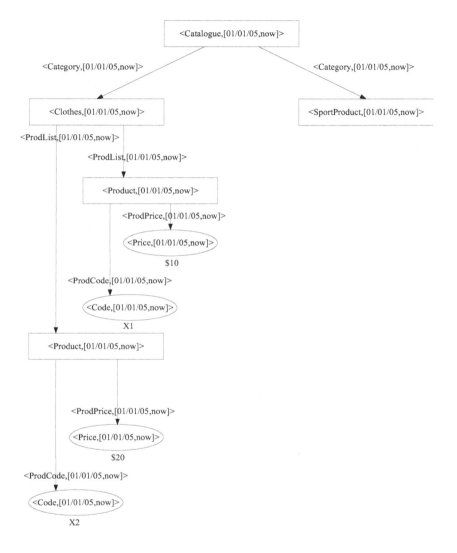

uct and the simple node *Price*. The interval *[01/01/05, 28/02/05]* means that the considered objects were valid from January 1, 2005 to February 28, 2005.

The new price is represented by means of the new simple node *Price* with value "$25" and valid time interval *[01/03/05,now]*, related to the complex node *Product*, representing the product having code "X2," by means of the edge *ProdPrice* with valid time interval *[01/03/05,now]*. The dashed region in Figure 3 contains the old and the new prices.

Copyright © 2007, Idea Group Inc. Copying or distributing in print or electronic forms without written permission of Idea Group Inc. is prohibited.

Figure 3. Changing the price

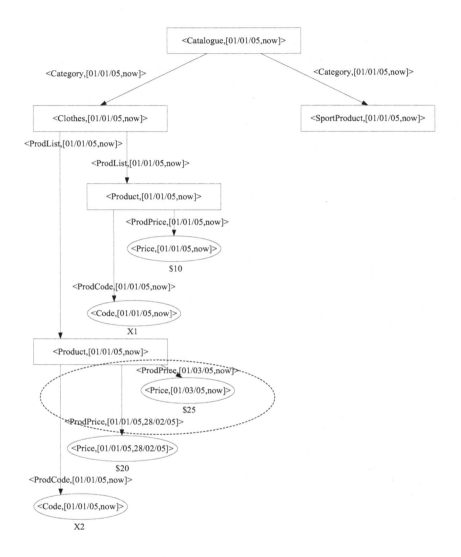

On April 1, 2005 a new product with code "Y1" and price "$50" is added to the cata-logue in the category *SporProduct*. The GEM graph after this insertion is reported in Figure 4. The dashed region contains the new product with its properties.

In particular, the new product is represented by means of the complex node *Product* with valid time interval *[01/04/05,now]*. The new product is related to *SportProduct* by means of the edge *ProdList* having the same time interval. Moreover, the new product has the simple node *Code* with value "*Y1*" and the simple node *Price*

Copyright © 2007, Idea Group Inc. Copying or distributing in print or electronic forms without written permission of Idea Group Inc. is prohibited.

Figure 4. Adding a new product

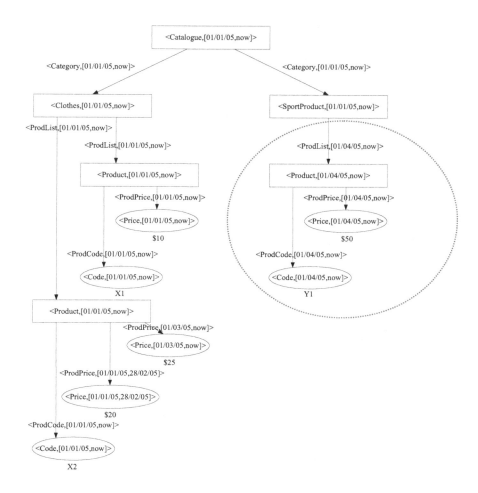

with value "*$50.*" These simple nodes have time interval *[01/04/05,now]*, as their ingoing edges.

On June 1, 2005 the *Clothes* category is replaced by the *KidClothes* and the *Adult-Clothes* categories. The GEM graph after this replacement is reported in Figure 5. The dashed region contains the new categories.

In particular, the time interval of the replaced *Clothes* category changes from *[01/01/05,now]* to *[01/01/05, 31/05/05]*, and the same for the time interval of the edge *Category* between the complex node *Catalogue* and the complex node *Clothes*. The new categories are represented by means of the complex nodes *KidClothes* and the *AdultClothes* with valid time interval *[01/06/05,now]*. The products included in

Copyright © 2007, Idea Group Inc. Copying or distributing in print or electronic forms without written permission of Idea Group Inc. is prohibited.

Figure 5. Replacing a category

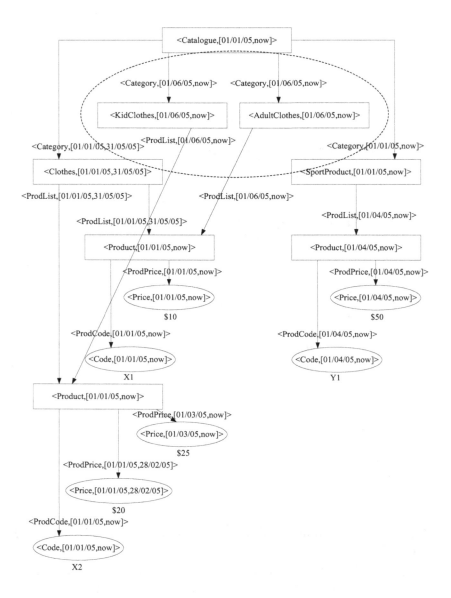

the replaced category are related to the new categories. In particular, the product with code "*X1*" is related to the *AdultClothes* category, while the product with code "*X2*" is related to the *KidClothes* category. This means that the valid time intervals between the *Clothes* category and the considered products changes from *[01/01/05,now]* to *[01/01/05, 31/05/05]*, and new edges between the new categories and the products are added. The new edges have valid time interval equal to *[01/06/05,now]*.

Copyright © 2007, Idea Group Inc. Copying or distributing in print or electronic forms without written permission of Idea Group Inc. is prohibited.

Figure 6. Adding a new subcategory

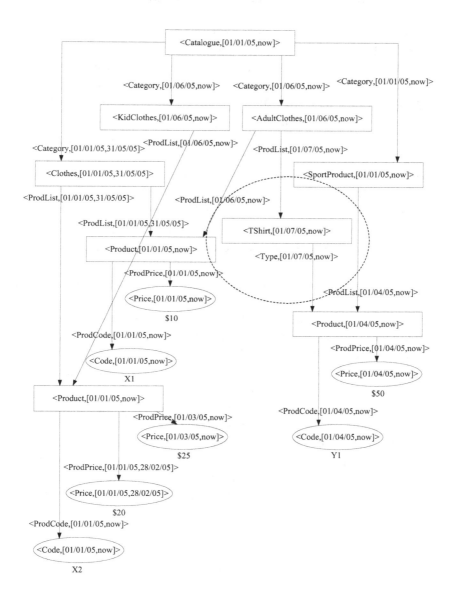

On July 1, 2005 the new *TShirt* subcategory is inserted under the *AdultClothes* category. The GEM graph after this insertion is reported in Figure 6. The dashed region contains the new subcategory.

As in the previous case, the new subcategory is represented by means of a new complex node. The valid time interval of the new objects (nodes/edges) is *[01/07/05,now]*.

Copyright © 2007, Idea Group Inc. Copying or distributing in print or electronic forms without written permission of Idea Group Inc. is prohibited.

Representing Constraints by Means of Graphs

In the context of temporal semistructured data, it is important to store the time dimension related to the represented information, and to manage in a correct way the considered time dimension. At this aim, a set of constraints must be defined. In this work, we consider the valid time dimension, thus the defined constraints must be able to guarantee that the history of the given application domain is consistent.

In our proposal, it is possible to define two different categories of constraints for valid time values of nodes and edges: *basic constraints* must be satisfied by every GEM graph; *domain-dependent constraints* are further constraints, which can be defined either for some specific nodes and edges or for the whole graph for a specific application domain. Domain-dependent constraints are strictly related to the semantics of the represented objects and relationships.

As an example of basic constraints, at a specific time instant, between two nodes it cannot exist more than one edge representing the same relation (Combi et al., 2004).

The graphical formalism used in the following constraints has been described in Damiani, Oliboni, Quintarelli, and Tanca (2003) and Oliboni (2003): a constraint is composed by a *graph*, which is used to identify the portions of a semistructured graph where the constraint has to be applied, and a set of *formulae*, which represent restrictions imposed on those subgraphs.

In Figure 7 a basic constraint is reported. In particular this constraint imposes that the time interval of an edge between a complex node and a simple node must be related to the time interval of the complex node. Intuitively, the relation between a complex node and a simple node cannot survive the complex node; thus, the time interval of the edge cannot start before and cannot end after the valid time of the complex node, as depicted in Figure 7. This is due to the fact that we suppose that a complex node is related to its properties (simple nodes) while it is valid. The edge-related time interval $[t_{js}, t_{je}]$ starts after and ends before the time interval $[t_{hs}, t_{he}]$ of the complex node.

Figure 7(a) identifies the subgraphs where the constraint has to be applied, and the set of formulae representing restrictions imposed on those subgraphs. Figure 7(b) shows an example of intervals satisfying the related constraint.

Figure 8 shows a domain-dependent constraint on the relation between a product and its categories. In particular this constraint imposes that a product must be related to a category; that is, a product can be inserted in the catalogue only if it is connected to at least one category.

Figure 8(a) identifies the subgraphs where the constraint has to be applied, and the formula representing restrictions imposed on those subgraphs. Figure 8(b) shows an example of intervals satisfying the related constraint.

Copyright © 2007, Idea Group Inc. Copying or distributing in print or electronic forms without written permission of Idea Group Inc. is prohibited.

Figure 7. A basic constraint

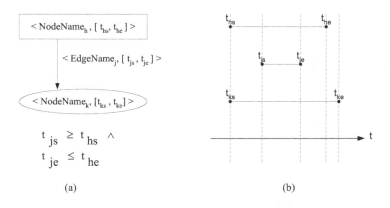

(a)   (b)

Figure 8. The constraint on the relation between a product and its categories

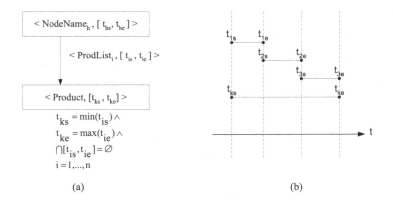

(a)   (b)

Future Trends

In the semistructured data warehouse context, the following issues are very relevant and interesting:

- **Querying of semistructured temporal data warehouse:** Starting from a graph-based representation of data stored in a data warehouse, it could be useful to study a temporal semistructured query language which allows one to impose temporal clauses, and retrieve information without knowing in advance the structure of data. In the semistructured data context, query languages use path

Copyright © 2007, Idea Group Inc. Copying or distributing in print or electronic forms without written permission of Idea Group Inc. is prohibited.

expressions to describe paths on the graph. In this context, the problems are related to the definition of a simple and intuitive syntax allowing the user to express complex temporal clauses, and to the definition of a query language which is general and flexible enough to overcome difficulties coming from the semistructured nature of data.

- **Data aggregation and materialization:** In the semistructured data context the same information can be structured in different ways, thus an interesting point is the study of suitable techniques to aggregate data having different structure, choosing a common graphical representation. Moreover, the result of data aggregation can be seen as a view on the data warehouse, and thus it could be interesting to materialize the view itself, and to study different possibilities to store data in the view, and to relate them to the original information.

- **Representation of versions:** In the XML data warehouse context, it could be useful to maintain the successive versions of an XML document stored in the data warehouse. A graphical representation of versions could be studied and proposed. The graph-based approach for representing successive versions would represent the valid time of data, and the valid (transaction) time of the document version. In this case the problem to consider is related to the best representation of different versions of the same document. This means to choose to represent either each version of the whole document or only the part of the new version which is different from the previous one, and to understand how to represent the time dimension related to the version time.

- **Querying successive versions of documents stored in a data warehouse:** In this context it could be useful to query by considering the valid time of information, or the valid version of a document, or a particular past version, or by considering both time dimensions. In this case the problems are related to the study of suitable temporal clauses allowing the user to express temporal conditions on different time dimensions, that is, version time dimension, document valid time. For example, the user could be interested in retrieving the evolution of a portion of the document, or in retrieving valid data. In the former case the user would query the successive versions of a document, while in the latter case the user would query the present (valid) version of the document. Moreover, the user would like to query a given past version of the document.

Conclusion

In this chapter we described a graph-based data model to represent semistructured data warehouse by considering the valid time dimension. This approach allows one

Copyright © 2007, Idea Group Inc. Copying or distributing in print or electronic forms without written permission of Idea Group Inc. is prohibited.

to represent data stored in a data warehouse by means of labeled graphs. Each object of the graph (node/edge) has a label composed by the description of the object itself (the name), and the valid time dimension (the valid time interval). In particular, we considered and represented the valid time dimension, and gave some examples of the constraints needed to manage in the correct way the considered time dimension.

References

Abiteboul, S. (1997, January 8-10). Querying semi-structured data. In *Proceedings of the International Conference on Database Theory,* Greece (LNCS 1186, pp. 262-275).

Abiteboul, S., & Buneman, P., & Suciu, D. (2000). *Data on the Web: From relations to semistructured data and XML.* Morgan Kaufman.

Amagasa, T., Yoshikawa, M., & Uemura, S. (2001, April 23-24). Realizing temporal XML repositories using temporal relational databases. In *Proceedings of the Third International Symposium on Cooperative Database Systems and Applications,* Beijing (pp. 63-68).

Bębel, B., Eder, J., Koncilia, C., Morzy, T., & Wrembel, R. (2004, March). Creation and management of versions in multiversion data warehouse. In *Proceedings of the 2004 ACM Symposium on Applied Computing,* Cyprus (pp. 717-723). ACM Press.

Bhowmick, S. S., Madria, S. K., Ng, W. K., & Lim, E. P. (1998). Web warehousing: Design and issues. In *Proceedings of International Workshop on Data Warehousing and Data Mining (in conjunction with International Conference on Conceptual Modelling,* Singapore (LNCS 1552, pp. 93-104).

Chawathe, S. S., Abiteboul, S., & Widom, J. (1998). Representing and querying changes in semistructured data. In *Proceedings of the Fourteenth International Conference on Data Engineering* (pp. 4-13). IEEE Computer Society.

Combi, C., Damiani, E., Posenoto, R., & Tanca, L. (1998, May 13-15). A scheme-based approach to modeling and querying WWW data. *Proceedings of Flexible Query Answering Systems* (LNCS 1495, pp. 110-125).

Combi, C., Oliboni, B., & Quintarelli, E. (2004). A graph-based data model to represent transaction time in semistructured data. In *Proceedings of the Database and Expert Systems Applications* (LNCS 3180, pp. 559-568).

Damiani, E., Oliboni, B., Quintarelli, E., & Tanca, L. (2003). Modeling semistructured data by using graph-based constraints. In *Proceedings of On The Move to Meaningful Internet Systems 2003: OTM 2003 Workshops* (LNCS 2889, pp. 20-21).

Copyright © 2007, Idea Group Inc. Copying or distributing in print or electronic forms without written permission of Idea Group Inc. is prohibited.

Damiani, E., & Tanca, L. (1997). Semantic approach to structuring and querying the Web sites. In *Proceedings of 7th IFIP Working Conference on Database Semantics* (pp. 21-49). Chapman & Hall.

Dyreson, C. E., Böhlen, M. H., & Jensen, C. S. (1999, September 7-10). Capturing and querying multiple aspects of semistructured data. In *Proceedings of 25th International Conference on Very Large Data Bases* (pp. 290-301). Morgan Kaufmann.

Eder, J., & Koncilia, C. (2001). Changes of dimension data in temporal data warehouses. In *Proceedings of the Third International Conference on Data Warehousing and Knowledge Discovery*, Munich, Germany (LNCS 2114, pp. 284-293). ACM.

Eder, J., Koncilia, C., & Morzy, T. (2001). A model for a temporal data warehouse. In *Proceedings of the OES-SEO Workshop* (pp. 48-54).

Jensen, C. S., Dyreson, C. E., Bohlen, M. H., et al. (1998). The consensus glossary of temporal database concepts (February 1998 Version). *Temporal Databases: Research and Practice,* Rockville, MD (LNCS 1399, pp. 367-405).

Li, C., & Wang, X. (1996, November 12-16). A data model for supporting on-line analytical processing. In *Proceedings of the Fifth International Conference on Information and Knowledge Management* (pp. 81-88). ACM Press.

Marian, A., Abiteboul, S., Cobena, G., & Mignet, L. (2001). Change-centric management of versions in an XML warehouse. In *Proceedings of the 27th International Conference on Very Large Data Bases* (pp. 581-590). Morgan Kaufmann Publishers Inc.

Oliboni, B. (2003). *Blind queries and constraints: Representing flexibility and time in semistructured data.* Doctoral thesis, Politecnico di Milano.

Oliboni, B., Quintarelli, E., & Tanca, L. (2001, June 14-16). Temporal aspects of semistructured data. In *Proceedings of the Eighth International Symposium on Temporal Representation and Reasoning* (pp. 119-127). IEEE Computer Society.

Papakonstantinou, Y., Garcia-Molina, H., & Widom, J. (1995). Object exchange across heterogeneous information sources. In *Proceedings of the Eleventh International Conference on Data Engineering,* Taipei, Taiwan (pp. 251-260). IEEE Computer Society.

Vassiliadis, P., & Sellis, T. (1999). A survey of logical models for OLAP databases. *SIGMOD Record 28,* 64-69.

Wang, F., & Zaniolo, C. (2003). Temporal queries in XML document archives and Web warehouses. In *Proceedings of the 10th International Symposium on Temporal Representation and Reasoning and Fourth International Conference on Temporal Logic* (pp. 47-55). IEEE Computer Society.

Copyright © 2007, Idea Group Inc. Copying or distributing in print or electronic forms without written permission of Idea Group Inc. is prohibited.

Wang, F., Zaniolo, C., Zhou, X., & Moon, H. J. (2005, July 8-10). Version management and historical queries in digital libraries. In *Proceedings of the 12th International Symposium on Temporal Representation and Reasoning* (pp. 207-209). IEEE Computer Society.

World Wide Web Consortium. (1995). Overview of Standard Generalized Markup Language (SGML) resources. Retrieved June 14, 2006, from http://www.w3.org/MarkUp/SGML/

World Wide Web Consortium. (1998). *Extensible Markup Language (XML) 1.0*. Retrieved June 14, 2006, from http://www.w3C.org/TR/REC-xml/

World Wide Web Consortium. (2005a). *XML Path Language (XPath) 2.0*. Retrieved June 14, 2006, from http://www.w3.org/TR/xpath20/

World Wide Web Consortium. (2005b). *XQuery 1.0: An XML query language*. Retrieved June 14, 2006, from http://www.w3.org/TR/xquery/

Xyleme, L. (2001, July 16-18). Xyleme: A dynamic warehouse for XML data of the Web. In *Proceedings of International Database Engineering & Applications Symposium, IDEAS '01* (pp. 3-7). IEEE Computer Society.

Copyright © 2007, Idea Group Inc. Copying or distributing in print or electronic forms without written permission of Idea Group Inc. is prohibited.

Chapter XIII

Spatial Online Analytical Processing (SOLAP):
Concepts, Architectures, and Solutions from a Geomatics Engineering Perspective

Yvan Bédard
Laval University, Canada

Sonia Rivest
Laval University, Canada

Marie-Josée Proulx
Laval University, CAnada

Abstract

It is recognized that 80% of data have a spatial component (e.g., street address, place name, geographic coordinates, map coordinates). Having the possibilities to display data on maps, to compare maps of different phenomena or epochs, and to combine maps with tables and statistical charts allows one to get more insights into spatial datasets. Furthermore, performing fast spatio-temporal analysis, interactively

Copyright © 2007, Idea Group Inc. Copying or distributing in print or electronic forms without written permission of Idea Group Inc. is prohibited.

exploring the data by drilling on maps similarly to drilling on tables and charts, and easily synchronizing such operations among these views is nowadays required by more and more users. This can be done by combining geographical information systems (GIS) with online analytical processing (OLAP), paving the way to "SO-LAP" (spatial OLAP). The present chapter focuses on the spatial characteristics of SOLAP from a geomatics engineering point of view: concepts, architectures, tools and remaining challenges.

Introduction

It is recognized that up to 80% of corporate data have spatial components such as street addresses, place names, geographic coordinates, or map coordinates. This fact, estimated by Franklin (1992), is still recognized today and it only starts to show its potential for the masses with recent commercial advances such as Google Maps and Google Earth. However, the true power of maps typically remains underused for geographic knowledge discovery unless one combines a geographic information system (GIS) to OLAP technology.

The Power of Maps

Map data are the raw material to produce the geographic information that leads to knowledge about the position, extent, and distribution of phenomena over our territories. Such phenomena are counted by thousands and include insect territorial expansions, environment-health correlations, land-use evolution, 911 vehicle tracking and watershed analysis, to name a few. Visualizing geographic phenomena on maps facilitates the extraction of insights that help to understand these phenomena. Such insights include spatial characteristics (position, shape, size, orientation, etc.), spatial relationships (adjacency, connectivity, inclusion, proximity, exclusion, overlay, etc.), and spatial distribution (concentrated, scattered, grouped, regular, etc.). When we visualize a map displaying different regions, we can compare. When we visualize different maps for a same region, we can discover correlations between phenomena. When we visualize the map of a region for different epochs, we can see the evolution of the phenomena. When we use maps, we often get a better understanding of the structures and relationships contained within spatial datasets than using simple tables and charts. When we combine maps with tables and statistical charts, we can relate these to make new discoveries. Maps are natural aids to the knowledge discovery process. In the context of spatial data exploration, maps do more than just make the data visible, they are active instruments to support the end user thinking process. Using maps for geographic knowledge discovery requires less

Copyright © 2007, Idea Group Inc. Copying or distributing in print or electronic forms without written permission of Idea Group Inc. is prohibited.

abstraction efforts for users, which in turn, increases their efficiency. Maps show information that would not be visible from nonspatial data for those phenomena having a spatial distribution that does not correspond to predefined boundaries (e.g., administrative boundaries). Numerous studies in cognitive sciences have shown the superiority of images over numbers and words to stimulate understanding and memory (Buzan & Buzan, 2003; Fortin & Rousseau, 1989; Standing, 1973), leading to a more efficient knowledge discovery process (more alert brain, better visual rhythm, more global perception).

Marrying OLAP with GIS

Geographic information systems (GIS) are very good at achieving the goal they have been developed for, that is, gathering, storing, manipulating and displaying spatial data (see Longley, Goodchild, Maguire, & Rhind, 2001). However, they are transaction-oriented systems and do not address summarized information, cross-referenced information, interactive exploration of data, and so forth. Furthermore, they are not suited for temporal data, they are very slow to aggregate data, they hardly deal with multiple levels of data granularity, and their user interface is too complex for most users. Similarly to database management systems (DBMS), GIS alone cannot fill the "analysis gap" between spatial data and geographic knowledge discovery. When one has to interactively dig into data, roll them up, and cross-reference them to get the information of interest, today's GIS interactivity and query interfaces are not appropriate in terms of functions, ease-of-use, or response times. Today's GIS do not support Newell's cognitive band of 10 seconds (Newell, 1990) when one needs to keep his train-of-thought while analyzing spatial data.

On the other hand, even though OLAP is well-suited for knowledge discovery, it is not adapted for the analysis of spatial data (Caron, 1998). In fact, OLAP treats spatial data like other data and spatial analysis is limited to predefined nominal locations (e.g., names of countries, states, regions, cities). Support for spatiotemporal analyses is seriously limited (no spatial visualization, practically no spatial analysis, no map-based exploration of data, etc.). Extraction, transformation, and load (ETL) processes cannot deal with most aspects of spatial data. Nevertheless, it is possible to achieve good results by marrying GIS with OLAP. Several projects in Canada, U.S., France, Portugal, and elsewhere have shown the superiority of this combination over stand-alone GIS or OLAP for interactive spatial data exploration.

Towards SOLAP

In most of those projects, GIS and OLAP are loosely coupled and the GIS serves as a map viewer of OLAP operations. In more tightly coupled cases, functions are

Copyright © 2007, Idea Group Inc. Copying or distributing in print or electronic forms without written permission of Idea Group Inc. is prohibited.

added to support cartographic drilling in the GIS and to maintain the synchronization between the GIS and OLAP displays. Sometimes, a common user interface is built over the GIS-OLAP combo to make the application appear as a unique system. Depending on the functions that are prioritized, the result is termed OLAP-centric, GIS-centric, or hybrid (LGS Group, 2000).

More recently, SOLAP software has reached the market, allowing even tighter integration between GIS and OLAP (data and functions). Bédard, Proulx, and Rivest (2005) make a clear distinction between "SOLAP applications" developed with any of the previously mentioned approaches and software, and "SOLAP software" which relies on a hybrid approach and is specifically meant to improve the development of SOLAP applications. In comparison to the loosely coupled GIS-OLAP, SOLAP software typically provides four major benefits: (1) important savings in development time (no programming required), (2) richer SOLAP applications (more advanced functions, better GIS-OLAP integration on complex issues), (3) tested user interfaces designed especially for SOLAP operations, and (4) easier editing of the multidimensional data structure (using a SOLAP administrator module). The first SOLAP software commercially available (JMap® Spatial OLAP) was developed by Bédard's team at Laval University. In spite of such advances, today's SOLAP implementations still face challenges to become more efficient. In fact, coupling GIS and OLAP is not enough, many hidden challenges must be overcome, resulting in important development efforts before obtaining an efficient solution.

The objective of the present chapter is to introduce the reader to the main advantages and challenges related to the use of spatial data and SOLAP. We begin with an overview of the particularities of spatial data to help readers to better assess the challenges that SOLAP development presents. After, we summarize the history of SOLAP applications and technologies as well as today's state-of-the-art. Then, we focus on the concepts, issues, challenges, and solutions related to SOLAP. In the last sections, we discuss future trends and present concluding remarks. This content is presented from a geomatics engineering perspective; it is written for computer scientists who know the fundamental concepts related to spatial datacubes and OLAP.

Background Information

With the recent evolution of geomatics sciences (geodesy, global positioning systems (GPS), photogrammetry, remote sensing, surveying, mapping, and GIS), we gather today terabytes of land-related data everyday at a cost that is much lower than a decade ago. Mainstream applications using spatial data are appearing everywhere. The benefits of using spatial data have been discussed previously in a general manner. In the particular case of SOLAP, the tight integration of GIS and

Copyright © 2007, Idea Group Inc. Copying or distributing in print or electronic forms without written permission of Idea Group Inc. is prohibited.

OLAP bring significant profits such as (1) offering the most intuitive user interface insofar to access cross-referenced spatial data, (2) offering the fastest solution to access aggregated spatial data, and (3) allowing the discovery of spatial patterns and clusters of phenomena that cannot be detected with OLAP solely (e.g., a phenomenon taking place in the forest stands located along a river gets unnoticed when the next aggregated level of OLAP spatial units are administrative regions made of thousands of stands). A tight GIS-OLAP integration is also needed when one requires a high level of interactivity between the maps and the tables or charts, a complete synchronization between the visual variables (semiology) of maps, tables, and charts, as well as a high level of flexibility into the display of information that relates to places or regions which may vary in time. This is the case for maps displaying simultaneously several dimensions and measures, for multimaps displaying a same phenomenon for categories of members, and for the sequential display of maps illustrating the evolution of a phenomenon over time, among others. For example, one may want to synchronize a first set of views where drilling into one of them triggers the others automatically (e.g., drilling on a national map of cancer ratio for men automatically triggers a drill operation into tabular national statistics and into a histogram), then to open a second set of views also synchronized among themselves (e.g., for women cancer) for comparison purposes, then to create a multimap displaying one map per year for the last 10 years (to see the evolution), then to add pie charts on top of each region of the map to see the distribution of cancers by category, then to synchronize with a second 10-year multimap displaying data from the National Inventory of Industrial Pollutants, to slice and dice into the first multimap to highlight a given type of cancers and into the second multimap to highlight a given type of pollutant, to visually look for clusters or spatial correlations that may take place regardless of region boundaries, to drill on a selection of three regions to see further details as well as the municipal boundaries, to overlay the hydrographic network and the sources for water distribution systems, to roll up rivers and sources per watershed, to get the total length of potentially contaminated rivers per municipality, to display and count the number of water sources per municipality for each of the 10 years, to show the municipalities with the highest ratio of cancers of a given type that overlay the rivers with a given type of pollutant and which happen to have their highest ratio of the given cancer within 5 years after this pollutant was released above a given threshold, to rollup for the entire country to check if this is a local or national pattern, to rollup for the last 25 years to see if this is an event-based phenomena or a general trend for this place, and so forth. Such flexibility to navigate into space as well as time to analyze a phenomenon requires a very efficient coupling between the GIS and the OLAP, in terms of interface, functions, and speed. We have encountered such needs in different experiments with university researchers (e.g., archaeologists, kinesiologists) and real-life projects at the Quebec National Institute of Public Health (users = epidemiologists), the Quebec Ministry of Transportation (users = civil engineers), Laval University

Copyright © 2007, Idea Group Inc. Copying or distributing in print or electronic forms without written permission of Idea Group Inc. is prohibited.

Executive Vice-Presidency (users = students recruitment team), Canada National Coast Guard (users = incident analysts), and so forth.

Typically, most transactional and analytical applications are simple from a geomatics point of view. They typically use spatial data obtained from a single source, they are out-of-date (one or more years old is the rule), they are incomplete and they show limited precision regarding the position of objects (in the order of tens of meters, and more). Although this is sufficient for most users (e.g., tourists, news, routing), other users have more complex needs that require frequent updates, integration of data from different sources, integration of data from different epochs, integration of field measurements, integration of real time data, and so on. Insofar, most research in SOLAP has been done with the needs of the former group in mind. We can say that today's research community is succeeding in bringing spatial data into the OLAP arena. However, major challenges remain for the next several years in order to satisfy the needs of more advanced users. We still need to bring OLAP capabilities into the geomatics engineering arena.

Particularities of Spatial Data

Computer displays are flat; however the Earth is not. Furthermore, it is not a simple sphere nor a simple ellipsoid flattened at the poles. Earth's true shape looks more like a nice potato and it is scientifically defined as the geoid. The geoid is an equipotential surface that corresponds to the mean sea level. This physical model is the mathematical figure of the Earth as defined by its irregular gravity field. It is the model used by national mapping agencies to produce topographic maps upon which most thematic maps are based. It is more irregular than the ellipsoid of revolution because of the irregularities of the Earth surface (19,000 meters from the top of Mount Everest to the bottom of Mariana Trench) and because of the different densities associated with different types of minerals. The difference between the ellipsoid and the geoid can be up to 100 meters but we project our measurements on the ellipsoid to simplify the mathematics and to remain more stable over time (the geoid changes over time). Since the force of gravity is everywhere perpendicular to the geoid (not to the ellipsoid), our measurements (land-based or satellite-based) are influenced by the geoid. A slight vertical deviation of the measuring instrument may create differences of hundreds of meters when reporting a position from the geoid to the ellipsoid. The geomatics science dealing with the geoid and the ellipsoid is called physical geodesy; it provides the basis for all measurements (see Hofmann-Wellenhof & Moritz, 2005).

Once we know the difference between the geoid and the ellipsoid, we must project the measured position to a flat surface such as a paper map or a computer display. This cannot be done without distortion, either of angles, areas, or more typically, of both at the same time. This has an immediate impact on the shapes of objects,

Copyright © 2007, Idea Group Inc. Copying or distributing in print or electronic forms without written permission of Idea Group Inc. is prohibited.

Figure 1. From one object measured on the Earth to different map representa-tions

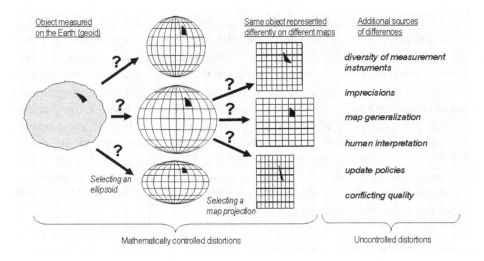

lengths, perimeters, areas, and positions, for example. To control these distortions, we use different map projections having different mathematical properties. Thus, from a unique position and shape on an ellipsoid, we may obtain different shapes and positions on different maps. These differences may be up to hundreds of meters in some cases. The geoid-ellipsoid-map transfer process is illustrated by Figure 1 (for details, see Iliffe, 2000).

In spite of the existence of a standard international ellipsoid, many mapping agencies prefer to use a national or continental ellipsoid that better fits the surface of their country. They also use different map projections that minimize the distortions for the geometry of their country. Furthermore, different projects or organizations within a same country often use different map projections over a same zone depending of the total area to be covered by their maps. Selecting the most appropriate ellipsoid and map projection allows them to minimize (for the entire zone covered by a map series) the distortion between map measurements and the measurements made on the Earth (i.e., with regard to the geoid).

Furthermore, there are different spatial referencing systems to determine the position of objects on maps. One may use a latitude-longitude-height international el-lipsoidal coordinate system, an x-y coordinate system based on a map projection, an x-y-z coordinate system from a 3D digital terrain model, a street address or street-intersection, a place name, a distance-direction to a landmark, a route-direc-tion-distance-offset linear referencing systems, and so on.

Copyright © 2007, Idea Group Inc. Copying or distributing in print or electronic forms without written permission of Idea Group Inc. is prohibited.

Figure 2. Example of spatial aggregation-generalization mismatch where aggregated data provide true data but unreadable map while generalized data produce readable map but inexact data

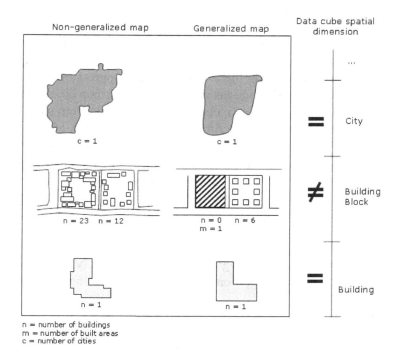

n = number of buildings
m = number of built areas
c = number of cities

The preceding differences can be controlled algorithmically and are currently handled by commercial software and interoperability standards. However, there remains other sources of distortion that cannot be controlled totally when dealing with multiple sources of data: diversity of measurement instruments, inherent imprecision of the measurement methods and tools used, data acquisition specifications that evolve over the years, limitations of the human interpretation of measured phenomena, independent data update policies, conflicting priorities over data quality, and so forth. The overall results are spatial data integration problems that cannot be avoided. Such problems happen, for example, when one integrates updates to an existing dataset (e.g., original maps can have been made from aerial photographs but updates may be coming from field surveys required by municipal bylaws). They also happen when one integrates data from two adjacent maps made by two municipalities. They also take place when integrating different data collected independently for different purposes such as land use maps and utilities maps. They also occur when using real-time GPS vehicle tracking over a road map made from satellite imagery. Many more examples could be presented to explain why spatial

Copyright © 2007, Idea Group Inc. Copying or distributing in print or electronic forms without written permission of Idea Group Inc. is prohibited.

data never fit together or with reality! This creates major challenges for SOLAP as explained later in this chapter.

In addition to the preceding issues, when one needs to have a more global carto-graphic view of a phenomenon, it is not possible to simply aggregate spatial data since the map or display becomes overcrowded and unreadable. One must rather use map generalization processes. According to Weibel and Dutton (1999, p. 126), "Map generalization is responsible for reducing complexity in a map in a scale reduction process, emphasizing the essential while suppressing the unimportant, maintaining logical and unambiguous relations between map objects, and preserv-ing aesthetic quality." Every map, including the map made from source data, uses some level of generalization. By definition, a map is a model of only a subset of the reality where unnecessary details are eliminated and useful data emphasized while maintaining the map readability. Going from a large map scale to a smaller map scale worsens the situation. Categories of objects as well as individual objects are eliminated, others are replaced by a symbol of larger or smaller size, some are displaced, their shape is simplified, topological relationships may change, groups such as "building blocks" replace individual buildings where the density is too high, and so on. In other words, the content of every map may lie, the measurements made on every map may lie, and a topological relationship on every map may lie. Taking this into account in a multiresolution spatial datacube goes beyond the traditional topological concepts.

Figure 2 shows an example of the impact of map generalization with regard to the spatial dimension of a datacube (a "spatial aggregation-generalization mismatch"). This introduces specific concerns for the interactive exploration of spatial data as seen later in this chapter.

From a geomatics point of view, spatial and temporal data are typically considered different from thematic data. Spatial and temporal data are reference data; they are used to locate phenomena in space and time rather than describing them. They are not intrinsic to a phenomenon like thematic data are. Since the human brain has built-in capabilities to use space and time, users intuitively rely on spatial and temporal data to integrate other data obtained from different sources. Such integration from different sources is typically performed without a priori planning since space and time are perceived by most to be universal reference systems. The preceding pages have shown that positioning objects in space is more complex than it appears, creat-ing unexpected problems when one develops more advanced SOLAP applications. Time shows similar problems but to a much lower level of difficulty since it can be perceived as a one-dimensional universe with 0D (instant) and 1D (interval) events, as compared to the 3D spatial universe having 0D (point), 1D (line), 2D (surface), and 3D (volume) objects. From a computer science point of view, recent techni-cal developments have reduced the need to maintain distinctions between spatial data and other data (Longley, Goodchild, Maguire, & Rhind, 1999). Nevertheless,

Copyright © 2007, Idea Group Inc. Copying or distributing in print or electronic forms without written permission of Idea Group Inc. is prohibited.

special care must always be taken when processing data from different maps and positioning technologies (e.g., GPS) as typically is the case when we build spatial data warehouses and spatial datacubes.

Evolution of SOLAP

In spite of a decade of research, testing, and experiments, it is only recently that SOLAP applications have been implemented into organizations for their daily decision making. Examples in very diverse fields exist in Canada, France, United States, and Portugal in particular. Furthermore, products supporting some SOLAP requirements have appeared on the market recently, either from key players such as SAS, ESRI, MapInfo, Business Objects, and Cognos, or from smaller innovative companies such as KHEOPS Technologies and ProClarity. These applications and technologies are still in their infancy but they already provide new services.

The term spatial OLAP, or SOLAP, was coined by Bédard (1997) in parallel to the term spatial databases. Several research projects aiming at combining analytical databases and spatial databases have been carried out since the mid-1990s. Pioneers from Simon Fraser University developed the GeoMiner prototype (Stefanovic, 1997) that included an efficient method for spatial datacube materialization (Han, Stefanovic, & Koperski, 1998; Stefanovic, Han, & Koperski, 2000). Other pioneers from Laval University (Bédard, 1997; Rivest, Bédard, & Marchand, 2001) experimented with varied combinations of GIS and OLAP technologies with external users in different fields of application (Bédard et al., 2005) before developing the first commercial hybrid solution: JMap® Spatial OLAP Extension (Bédard, 2005). They developed several concepts, including new OLAP functions, spatiotemporal topological dimensions (Marchand, 2004), the use of raster representations of space for evolving datacubes (Miquel, Bédard, & Brisebois, 2002), and integrating multiple representations in spatial datacubes (Bédard & Bernier, 2002; Bernier & Bédard, 2005), for instance. Many research projects have built bridges between OLAP and GIS to facilitate the development of hybrid systems similar to the most recent commercial releases, such as GOAL (Kouba, Matousek, & Miksovsky, 2000), SIGOLAP (Ferreira, Campos, & Tanaka, 2001), SOVAT (Scotch & Parmanto, 2005), GMLA Web Services (Silva, Times, Fidalgo & Barros, 2005), and CommonGIS (Hernandez, Voss, & Gohring, 2005). A team from the University of Minnesota developed MapCube, a data structure and visualization tool for spatial datacubes (Shekhar, Lu, Tan, Chawla, & Vatsavai, 2001). Another group from INSA-Lyon, in France, also developed a prototype of SOLAP application and is working on fundamental concepts (Tchonikine, Miquel, Laurini, Ahmed, Bimonte, & Baillot, 2005). In collaboration with the Laval University team, they worked on evolving dimensions (Body, Miquel, Bédard, & Tchounikine, 2002) and highly heterogeneous data (Miquel et al., 2002). Fidalgo, Times, Silva, and Souza (2004) have proposed a *GeoDWFrame* based on the star

Copyright © 2007, Idea Group Inc. Copying or distributing in print or electronic forms without written permission of Idea Group Inc. is prohibited.

schema to facilitate the design of spatial dimensional schemas. Several Italian researchers have been active in fundamental research related to SOLAP. Pourabbas, Rafanelli, Ferri, and others have published widely on PQL, a pictorial query language for spatial data using OLAP operators (Ferri, Pourabbas, & Rafanelli, 2002; Pourabbas, 2003; Pourabbas & Rafanelli, 2002). Pourabbas (2003) has presented the use of binding attributes to build a bridge while preserving the structure of both the spatial database and the OLAP datacube. Pestana is developing the concept of spatial dashboard based on SOLAP technology and collaborates with Laval team on conceptual modeling of spatial datacubes (Pestana, da Silva, & Bédard, 2005). Other projects aim at improving spatial indexation, spatial aggregation, or spatial operators (e.g., Gupta, Harinarayan, Rajaraman, & Ullman, 1997; Han et al., 1998; Papadias, Kalnis, Zhang, & Tao, 2001; Prasher & Zhou, 2004; Stefanovic et al., 2000; Wang, Pan, Ren, Cui, Ding, & Perrizo, 2003; Zhang, Li, Rao, Yu, Chen, & Liu, 2003; Zhou, Truffet, & Han, 1999).

In spite of all this research activity, commercial solutions efficiently coupling OLAP and GIS appeared on the market only very recently. These solutions, some OLAP-centric, some GIS-centric, some hybrid, present only a subset of the desirable functionalities of a spatial OLAP technology. Some are still limited to static map visualization of OLAP query results. Others require the storage of each potential individual map view on the server, thus affecting the update effectiveness of spatial data. These solutions present limitations with regard to interactive data manipulation and exploration through cartographic views. However, the main bottleneck still remains the building of spatial datacubes, especially when data come from different sources.

SOLAP Concepts

Spatial OLAP (SOLAP) can be defined as a type of software that allows rapid and easy navigation within spatial databases and that offers many levels of information granularity, many themes, many epochs, and many display modes synchronized or not: maps, tables, and diagrams. The key to SOLAP concepts is multiresolution spatial databases or data warehouses. Of particular interest is the 4-tier architecture for spatial data warehousing. The first tier represents the first data warehouse where integrated, homogeneous detailed data are stored. This first tier is very useful since the integration of spatial data from heterogeneous sources can be done automatically only for the simplest cases, that is, rarely. Current ETL technology does not handle spatial data while "spatial data integrators" and "interoperability standards" were not developed to support the aggregation of spatial data or the matching of map objects from different map scales. The second tier represents a second data warehouse where the results of the aggregation processes are stored. Since automatic

Copyright © 2007, Idea Group Inc. Copying or distributing in print or electronic forms without written permission of Idea Group Inc. is prohibited.

Figure 3. Three types of spatial dimensions: nongeometric, geometric, and mixed spatial dimensions (Modeled on Rivest, Bédard, Proulx, & Nadeau, 2003)

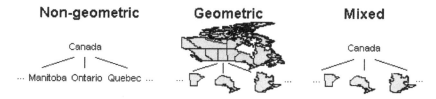

map generalization is not fully automated and requires important human intervention, this second tier is necessary to store the results. The third tier is comprised of the datamarts, which can be further processed and organized according to a vertical view of the data (e.g., within a range of map resolutions) or a horizontal view (e.g., within a region or a department). The fourth tier includes SOLAP clients that can add local information. Such architecture is useful when the fusion of detailed source data represents important efforts that cannot be fully automated. Bernier and Bédard (2005) describe the difficulties related to spatial data warehousing.

The SOLAP concepts support the multidimensional paradigm and enriched data exploration based on an explicit spatial reference represented on maps. This explicit spatial reference can relate to dimensions and measures as SOLAP supports "spatial" dimensions and "spatial" measures. Three types of spatial dimensions can be defined: the nongeometric spatial dimensions, the geometric spatial dimensions, and the mixed spatial dimensions (Bédard, Merrett, & Han, 2001). In the first type of spatial dimension, the spatial reference uses nominal data only (e.g., place names) as no geometry or cartographic representation is associated with the dimension members. It is the only type of spatial dimension supported by nonspatial OLAP. This type of spatial dimension is treated like other descriptive dimensions causing the spatiotemporal analysis to be potentially incomplete and the discovery of certain spatial relations or correlations between the phenomena under study to be missed by the analyst. The two other types of spatial dimensions aim at maximizing the potential to discover spatial relations and correlations that do not fit in predefined boundaries. The geometric spatial dimensions comprise, for all dimension members, at all levels of detail, geometric shapes (e.g., polygons to represent city boundaries) that are spatially referenced to allow their dimension members (e.g., New York) to be visualized and queried on maps. The mixed spatial dimensions comprise geometric shapes for a subset of the levels of details. The members of the geometric and mixed spatial dimensions can be displayed on maps using visual variables that relate to the values of the different measures contained in the datacube being analyzed. Figure 3 presents examples of the three types of spatial dimensions.

Two types of spatial measures can be defined (Bédard et al., 2001; Han et al., 1998; Rivest et al., 2001; Stefanovik, 1997; Tchounikine et al., 2005). A first type

Copyright © 2007, Idea Group Inc. Copying or distributing in print or electronic forms without written permission of Idea Group Inc. is prohibited.

Figure 4. The two types of spatial measures supported in SOLAP tools

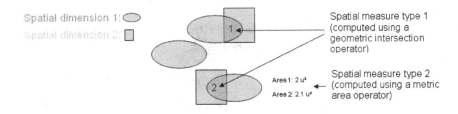

is geometric. It is the set of all the geometries representing the spatial objects corresponding to a particular combination of dimension members from one to many spatial dimensions. It consists of a set of coordinates, which requires computing geometric operations such as spatial union, spatial merge, or spatial intersection. A second type of spatial measure is numeric. It results from the computation of metric or topological spatial operators such as "surface," "distance," and "number of neighbors." Figure 4 presents the two types of spatial measures. A set of measures (spatial and nonspatial) organized according to a set of dimensions (spatial and nonspatial) form a spatial datacube.

In a SOLAP client interface, variants of the OLAP operators are used in order to take advantage of the spatial multidimensional data structure and of the different levels of detail of the spatial data. The general operators are drill-down, rollup (or drill-up), drill-across, swap (or pivot), and slice and dice. These operations are available in the different types of displays (maps, diagrams, or tables) and can be specialized according to the type of dimension they manipulate (Rivest, Bédard, Proulx, & Nadeau, 2003). *Thematic* operations allow the manipulation of thematic (or descriptive) dimensions, while keeping the same level of spatial and temporal granularities. *Temporal* operations allow the manipulation of temporal dimensions, while keeping the same level of thematic and spatial granularities. *Spatial* operations allow the manipulation of the spatial dimensions while keeping the same level of thematic and temporal granularities. Spatial operations can be executed directly by clicking on the elements (dimension members) shown on the maps.

SOLAP tools can support different types of views: tables, various types of diagrams and charts, and various types of maps. These include simple maps (i.e., single maps showing many geometric elements), multimaps (i.e., many maps, each related to a particular parameter, for example, one map per year), complex thematic maps (i.e., thematic maps composed of superimposed visual variables, e.g., color, pattern, shape of symbols, one per selected measure), and maps with superimposed diagrams (i.e., maps with little charts superimposed on the geometric elements of the map). The SOLAP views can support operator synchronization and graphical semiology synchronization. Figure 5 presents an example of a SOLAP display comprised of

Copyright © 2007, Idea Group Inc. Copying or distributing in print or electronic forms without written permission of Idea Group Inc. is prohibited.

Figure 5. An example of the use of semiology synchronization in a SOLAP between the map view (left), table view (centre), and chart view (right) spread over two contiguous computer displays (using JMap spatial OLAP)

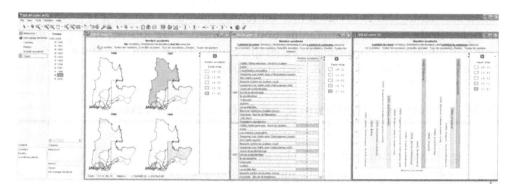

three views (map, table, chart) that use semiology synchronization (in a context of car accidents analysis).

The semiology synchronization helps to keep a visual homogeneity from one display to the other and from one navigation operation to the other. However, it involves taking care of potential collisions of graphical semiology rules since theoretically, the same rules do not always apply to all view types. Many more geographic visualization, or geovisualization, features can be incorporated. Geovisualization represents a research field of its own and can be defined as a private activity in which unknowns are revealed in a highly interactive environment. It is an active process in which an individual engages in sorting, highlighting, filtering, and otherwise transforming data in a search for patterns and relationships (MacEachren, 1994).

SOLAP tools may be used to implement a wide range of spatially referenced decision applications. For example, a road network management application may help to find, in seconds and without SQL queries, the effects of variations in the annual average daily traffic on the average road conditions, or calculating the intervention costs (Rivest et al., 2001). In a similar way, it is possible to analyze the number and the gravity of car accidents according to their position on the road network, the characteristics of the road, or the environment and the time period (Rivest, Gignac, Charron, & Bédard, 2004). Another example is an environmental health application that allows investigating the relationships between health and environmental phenomena, like the incidence of respiratory diseases according to air quality measurements (Bédard, Gosselin, Rivest, Proulx, Nadeau, Lebel, & Gagnon, 2003). Another example relates to the training of olympic-level speed skating athletes using GPS measurements, they use SOLAP to analyze their performances on various sections of a track according to various technical, mechanical, and meteorological

Copyright © 2007, Idea Group Inc. Copying or distributing in print or electronic forms without written permission of Idea Group Inc. is prohibited.

parameters (Veilleux, Lambert, Santerre, & Bédard, 2004). In forestry, a 3D SOLAP application has also been recently implemented (Brisebois, 2004) as well as one for archaeology (Rageul, 2004). These applications benefit from the three-dimensional aspect of space, that is, the volume of the phenomena being studied. For instance, when archaeological excavation lots are represented as volumes, it is possible to navigate in the various stratigraphic units to compare the lots according to their color, granulometry, consistency, geographic and stratigraphic positions, and the type of artifacts found (Fortin & Bédard, 2004).

SOLAP Issues, Challenges, and Recommendations

Although there remain computing challenges for SOLAP, our geomatics engineering perspective leads us to see the most crucial issues as the ones that relate to the management and processing of spatial referencing. We need to facilitate the flow of spatial data from the geospatial data sources to the datacubes. When compared to traditional GIS research, research in spatial data warehousing, spatial OLAP, and spatial datacubes requires to deal with more complex issues like:

- Integrating time (which is ubiquitous in datacubes) with space: Very few GIS databases are temporal, and when they are, they suffer from the same complexity issues as traditional DBMS (versionings, querying versions) but they must also deal with the evolution and tracing of the position of objects (e.g., a moving point representing a vehicle in real-time) as well as the evolution of their shape (e.g., a forest fire, a building which has been enlarged), and their mergings/splittings (e.g., many country boundaries have changed since the late 1980s). Furthermore, it is not rare to see spatial datacubes where the temporal resolution of the measures is finer (e.g., monthly values) than that of the available cartographic data (e.g., annual maps), creating new challenges especially with using the proper metadata and user warnings.

- Producing spatial data at different levels of granularity for a same display size: Today's SOLAP implementations sometimes lead to the display of "zoomed out" maps that become too crowded and inappropriate for the analysis of larger areas. Improperly applying on-the-fly automatic map generalization may lead to drilling deadends and incoherence between the map and the cube measures.

- Integrating spatial data from heterogeneous and spatially divergent sources, for instance (in spite of advances in interoperability, uncontrolled distortions cannot be resolved automatically): In particular, spatial aggregation and summarization often cannot be derived from detailed spatial data, requiring the use of smaller-scale maps from other sources and to automatically match corresponding spatial objects between different map scales (a step that is not yet

Copyright © 2007, Idea Group Inc. Copying or distributing in print or electronic forms without written permission of Idea Group Inc. is prohibited.

fully automatic). A similar challenge is to define and support spatial datacubes interoperability (e.g., extending ISO/TC211 and OGC standards).

- Improving the integration of spatiotemporal operators (topological and metric) in the measures and dimensions of spatial datacubes, and to feed the spatiotemporal facts

- Improving conceptual modeling of spatiotemporal datacubes (e.g., using multidimensional stereotypes in UML along with existing spatial and temporal stereotypes)

- Developing a SOLAP design method that helps users to discover earlier what they can do with SOLAP and how they can change their way of exploring their spatial data.

- Developing new graphical semiology rules simultaneously compatible with maps, charts, and tables to better support the cognitive process involved during the exploration of data

- Enriching the integrity constraints for combined spatial-temporal-aggregative constraints

- Developing methods that help to select the best sources and processes to feed the spatial datacube: In contrast to nonspatial datacubes, spatial data at the most aggregated levels do not necessarily come from the detailed maps. Moreover, there exist several potential sources of maps that are highly heterogeneous. Typically, every source of spatial data requires important work to make it fit the needs of the users. Considering the time and budget constraints along with the quality requirements of the users, selecting the best combinations of sources is a complex task that would benefit from a formal method.

- Developing explicit ways to assess and display the estimated quality of information, both internally (i.e., respect of data specifications) and externally (i.e., fitness for use)

- Improving the performance of spatial datacube building (spatiotemporal analysis, spatial aggregation, spatiotemporal indexing, etc.) and indexing (see for example the evolution of the R-Tree spatial indexing method in Manolopoulos et al., 2005)

- Improving existing technologies for enriched SOLAP and better integration into spatial data production workflows

Future Trends and Conclusion

Research related to spatial data warehousing and spatial OLAP has grown over a 10 year period from the first ideas developed in a small number of isolated university

Copyright © 2007, Idea Group Inc. Copying or distributing in print or electronic forms without written permission of Idea Group Inc. is prohibited.

laboratories to today's emergence of an R&D community. Researchers from several countries are addressing fundamental issues. Insofar, this community comes mainly from computer science departments. The geomatics community is only discovering the power of datacubes and OLAP. Rather, this community has looked into other directions such as geovisualization, advanced GIS, and expert systems to better support spatial decision making and geographic knowledge discovery. Looking at the issues of SOLAP from a geomatics engineering perspective is very promising. It brings a new level of challenges that relate to the very nature of spatial data and its use in multistakeholder environments. This enriches the concepts and technologies already available. In particular, it allows the integration of the early SOLAP solutions into the mainstream of spatial data production which is highly more complex than perceived at first sight. To further advance knowledge and to improve SOLAP applicability to complex interoperable environments, it is necessary to merge knowledge from the geomatics and the computer science communities. We expect that the most significant trends will emerge from this combination. From a scientific point of view, these trends would include the support of highly efficient building of spatial datacubes (i.e., without human intervention), real-time SOLAP, mobile SOLAP, spatial dashboards, and spatially constrained data mining. From a commercial point of view, trends are likely to follow the typical evolution from bridging separate technologies (OLAP-centric or GIS-centric) into more integrated solutions (bidirectional bridges with common user interface) into fully integrated technologies that interoperate via Web services and interoperate with spatial legacy systems. It is to contribute to these trends that we have put forward a major NSERC Industrial Research Chair and that we invite the interested readers to collaborate with us on the projects mentioned here.

Acknowledgments

We recognize the financial support of Canada NSERC Industrial Research Chair in Geospatial Databases for Decision-Support and its partners (http://mdspatialdb. chair.scg.ulaval.ca/).

References

Bédard, Y. (1997, November). *Spatial OLAP*. Paper presented at the Annual Forum on R&D, Geomatics VI, Canadian Institute of Geomatics, Montreal, Canada.

Copyright © 2007, Idea Group Inc. Copying or distributing in print or electronic forms without written permission of Idea Group Inc. is prohibited.

Bédard, Y. (2005, May). *Integrating GIS and OLAP: A new way to unlock geospatial data for decision-making*. Paper presented at the Location Technology and Business Intelligence Conference, Philadelphia.

Bédard, Y., & Bernier, E. (2002, July). *Supporting multiple representations with spatial view management and the concept of "VUEL"*. Paper presented at the Joint Workshop on Multi-Scale Representations of Spatial Data, International Society for Photogrammetry and Remote Sensing, Working Group IV/3, International Cartographic Association Communication on Map Generalization, Ottawa, Canada.

Bédard, Y., Gosselin, P., Rivest, S., Proulx, M. J., Nadeau M., Lebel, G. & Gagnon, M. F. (2003). Integrating GIS components with knowledge discovery technology for environmental health decision support. *International Journal of Medical Informatics, 70*(1), 79-94.

Bédard, Y., Merrett, T., & Han, J. (2001). Fundamentals of spatial data warehousing for geographic knowledge discovery. In H. Miller & J. Han (Eds.), *Geographic data mining and knowledge discovery* (pp. 53-73). London: Taylor & Francis.

Bédard, Y., Proulx, M. J., & Rivest, S. (2005). OLAP improvement for geographic analysis: Examples of realizations and technological solutions (Enrichissement du OLAP pour l'analyse géographique: Exemples de réalisations et différentes possibilités technologiques). *New Information Technologies Journal (Revue des nouvelles technologies de l'information), B-1*, 1-20.

Bernier, E., & Bédard, Y. (2005). Using a data warehousing architecture to combine automatic generalization and multiple representation for Web-based on-demand mapping. In A. Ruas & W. McKinnis (Eds.), *Challenges in the portrayal of geographic information: Issues of generalisation and multi scale representation*. (Forthcoming)

Body, M., Miquel, M., Bédard, Y., & Tchounikine, A. (2002). A multidimensional and multiversion structure for OLAP applications. In *Proceedings of the ACM Fifth International Workshop on Data Warehousing and OLAP* (pp. 1-6).

Brisebois, A. (2004). *Analysis of the potential of extension SOLAP concept for the investigation of the three-dimensional spatial data (Analyse du potentiel d'extension du concept SOLAP pour l'exploration des données spatiales 3D)*. Master's thesis, Laval University, Canada.

Buzan, T., & Buzan, B. (2003). *Mind map, drawing intelligence (Mind map, dessine-moi l'intelligence)*. Paris: Éd. l'Organisation.

Caron, P. Y. (1998). *Application of on-line analytical processing (OLAP) technologies in a spatio temporal context (Étude du potentiel OLAP pour supporter l'analyse spatio-temporelle)*. Master's thesis, Laval University, Canada.

Copyright © 2007, Idea Group Inc. Copying or distributing in print or electronic forms without written permission of Idea Group Inc. is prohibited.

Ferreira, A. C., Campos, M. L., & Tanaka, A. (2001). An architecture for spatial and dimen*sional analysis integration. In* Proceedings of SCI 2001, v.XIV CSE, Part II (pp. 392-395).

Ferri, F., Pourabbas, E., & Rafanelli, M. (2002). The syntactic and semantic correctness of pictorial configurations to query geographic databases by PQL. In *Proceedings of SAC 2002* (pp. 432-437).

Fidalgo, R. N., Times, V. C., Silva, J., & Souza, F. F. (2004). GeoDWFrame: A framework for guiding the design of geographical dimensional schemas. In *Proceedings of DaWaK 2004* (LNCS 3181, pp. 26-37).

Fortin, M., & Bédard, Y. (2004, October). *Development of geospatial data exploration application for spatio-temporal knowledge issue from archaeological excavation (Développement d'un système de découverte des connaissances spatio-temporelles issues d'un chantier de fouilles archéologiques).* Paper presented at Géomatique 2004, Canadian Institute of Geomatics, Montreal, Canada.

Fortin, C., & Rousseau, R. (1989). *Cognitive psychology: An information processing approach (Psychologie cognitive: Une approche de traitement de l'information).* Presses de l'Université du Québec.

Franklin, C. (1992, April). An introduction to geographic information systems: Linking maps to databases. *Database*, 13-21.

Gupta, H., Harinarayan, V., Rajaraman, A., & Ullman, J. D. (1997). Index selection for OLAP. In *Proceedings of the 13th International Conference on Data Engineering* (pp. 208-219).

Han, J., Stefanovic, N., & Koperski, K. (1998). Selective materialization: An efficient method for spatial data cube construction, research and development in knowledge discovery and data mining. In *Proceedings of the Second Pacific-Asia Conference, PAKDD'98* (pp. 144-158).

Hernandez, V., Voss, A., & Gohring, W. (2005). Sustainable decision support by the use of multi-level and multi-criteria spatial analysis on the Nicaragua Development Gateway, From pharaohs to geoinformatics. In *Proceedings of the Fédération Internationale des Géomètres Working Week 2005 and GSDI-8* (pp. 16-21).

Hofmann-Wellenhof, B., & Moritz, H. (2005). *Physical geodesy* (1st ed.). Springer.

Iliffe, J. C. (2000). *Datums and map projections*. London: Whittles Publishing.

KHEOPS. (2005). *JMAP spatial OLAP.* Retrieved June 14, 2006, from http://www.kheops-tech.com/en/jmap/solap.jsp

Kouba, Z., Matousek, K., & Miksovsky, P. (2000). On data warehouse and GIS integration. In *Proceedings of DEXA 2000* (LNCS 1873, pp. 604-613).

Copyright © 2007, Idea Group Inc. Copying or distributing in print or electronic forms without written permission of Idea Group Inc. is prohibited.

LGS Group Inc. (2000). *Analysis of health surveillance business intelligence tools and applications.* Final Draft.

Longley, P. A., Goodchild, M. F., Maguire, D. J., & Rhind, D. (Eds.). (1999). Introduction. In *Geographical information systems: Principles, techniques, applications and management* (2nd ed., p. 1296). Wiley.

Longley, P. A., Goodchild, M. F., Maguire, D. J., & Rhind, D. (2001). *Geographic information systems and science.* Wiley.

MacEachren, A. M. (1994). Visualization in modern cartography: Setting the agenda. In A. M. MacEachren & D. R. F. Taylor (Eds.), *Visualization in modern cartography, 28*(1), 1-12.

Manolopoulos, Y., Nanopoulos, A., Papadopoulos, A. N., & Theodoridis, Y. (2005). *Rtrees: Theory and applications* (Series in Advanced Information and Knowledge Processing). Springer.

Marchand, P. (2004). *The spatio-temporal topological operator dimension, a hyperstructure for multidimensional spatio-temporal exploration and analysis.* Doctoral thesis, Laval University, Canada.

Miquel, M., Bédard, Y., & Brisebois, A. (2002). Conception of a geospatial data warehouse from heterogeneous data sources, application example in foresty (Conception d'entrepôts de données géospatiales à partir de sources hétérogènes, exemple d'application en foresterie). *Engineering of Information Systems (Ingénierie des Systèmes d'information), 7*(3), 89-111.

Newell, A. (1990). *Unified theories of cognition.* Cambridge, MA: Harvard University Press.

Papadias, D., Kalnis, P., Zhang, J., & Tao, Y. (2001). Efficient OLAP operations in spatial data warehouses. *Proceedings of the 7th International Symposium on Spatial and Temporal Databases (SSTD)* (LNCS 2001, pp. 443-459). Springer Verlag.

Pestana, G., da Silva, M. M., & Bédard, Y. (2005). Spatial OLAP modeling: An overview based on spatial objects changing over time. In *Proceedings of the IEEE 3rd International Conference on Computational Cybernetics,* Mauritius.

Pourabbas, E. (2003). Cooperation with geographic databases. In M. Rafanelli (Ed.), *Multidimensional databases: Problems and solutions* (pp. 393-432). Hershey, PA: Idea Group Publishing.

Pourabbas, E., & Rafanelli, M. (2002). A pictorial query language for querying geographic databases using positional and OLAP operators. *SIGMOD Record, 31*(2), 22-27.

Prasher, S., & Zhou, X. (2004). Multiresolution amalgamation: Dynamic spatial data cube generation. In *Proceedings of the Fifteenth Conference on Australasian Databases, ACM International Conference Proceeding Series, 52,* 103-111.

Copyright © 2007, Idea Group Inc. Copying or distributing in print or electronic forms without written permission of Idea Group Inc. is prohibited.

Rageul, N. (2004). *Développement d'une application d'exploration de données géospatiales comme support à la fouille archéologique.* Undergraduate report, INSA-Strasbourg, France.

Rivest, S., Bédard, Y., & Marchand, P. (2001). Towards better support for spatial decision-making: Defining the characteristics of spatial on-line analytical processing. *Geomatica, 55*(4), 539-555.

Rivest, S., Bédard, Y., Proulx, M. J., & Nadeau, M. (2003, October). *SOLAP: A new type of user interface to support spatio-temporal multidimensional data exploration and analysis.* Paper presented at the ISPRS Joint Workshop of WG II/5, II/6, IV/1 and IV/2 on Spatial, Temporal and Multi-Dimensional Data Modelling and Analysis, Quebec, Canada.

Rivest, S., Gignac, P., Charron, J., & Bédard, Y. (2004, October). *Development of a spatio-temporal interactive data exploration system for the Information Data Bank of Ministry of Transportations, Quebec (Développement d'un système d'exploration spatio-temporelle interactive des données de la Banque d'information du ministère des Transports du Québec).* Paper presented at Géomatique 2004, Canadian Institute of Geomatics, Montreal, Canada.

Scotch, M., & Parmanto, B. (2005). SOVAT: Spatial OLAP visualization and analysis tool. In *Proceedings of the 38th Hawaii International Conference on System Sciences* (p. 142b).

Shekhar, S., Lu, C. T., Tan, X., Chawla, S., & Vatsavai, R. (2001). Map Cube: A visualization tool for spatial data warehouses. In H. Miller & J. Han (Eds.), *Geographic data mining and knowledge discovery* (pp. 74-109). London: Taylor & Francis.

Silva, J., Times, V., Fidalgo, R., & Barros, R. (2005). Providing geographic-multidimensional decision support over the Web. In *Proceedings of the APWeb 2005: 7th Asia-Pacific Web Conference* (LNCS 3399, pp. 477-488).

Standing, L. (1973). Learning 10000 pictures. *Quarterly Journal of Experimental Psychology, 25*(2), 207-222.

Stefanovic, N. (1997). *Design and implementation of on-line analytical processing (OLAP) of spatial data.* Master's thesis, Simon Fraser University, Canada.

Stefanovic, N., Han, J., & Koperski, K. (2000). Object-based selective materialization for efficient implementation of spatial data cubes. *IEEE Transactions on Knowledge Discovery and Data Engineering, 12*(6), 938-958.

Tchounikine, A., Miquel, M., Laurini, R., Ahmed, T., Bimonte, S., & Baillot, V. (2005). Overview of works about spatio-temporal data inetgration into hypercubes (Panorama de travaux autour de l'intégration de données spatio-temporelles dans les hypercubes). *New Information Technologies Journal (Revue des nouvelles technologies de l'information), B-1*, 21-33.

Copyright © 2007, Idea Group Inc. Copying or distributing in print or electronic forms without written permission of Idea Group Inc. is prohibited.

Veilleux, J. P., Lambert, M., Santerre, R., & Bédard, Y. (2004, October). *Uses of GPS and exploration and SOLAP analysis tools for the evaluation and analysis of outdoor sports (Utilisation du système de positionnement par satellites (GPS) et des outils d'exploration et d'analyse SOLAP pour l'évaluation et le suivi de sportifs de haut niveau)*. Paper presented at Géomatique 2004, Canadian Institute of Geomatics, Montreal, Canada.

Wang, B., Pan, F., Ren, D., Cui, Y., Ding, Q., & Perrizo, W. (2003). Efficient OLAP operations for spatial data using Peano trees. In *Proceedings of the 8th ACM SIGMOD Workshop on Research Issues in Data Mining and Knowledge Discovery* (pp. 28-34).

Weibel, R., & Dutton, G. (1999). Generalising spatial data and dealing with multiple representations. In P. Longley, M. Goodchild, D. Maguire, & D. Rhind (Eds.), *Geographical information systems: Principles and technical issues* (pp. 125-155). Wiley.

Zhang, L., Li, Y., Rao, F., Yu, X., Chen, C., & Liu, D. (2003). An approach to enabling spatial OLAP by aggregating on spatial hierarchy. In *Proceedings of DaWaK 2003* (pp. 35-44).

Zhou, X., Truffet, D., & Han, J. (1999). Efficient polygon amalgamation methods for spatial (OLAP) and spatial data mining. *Lecture Notes in Computer Sciences, 1651*, 167-187.

Copyright © 2007, Idea Group Inc. Copying or distributing in print or electronic forms without written permission of Idea Group Inc. is prohibited.

About the Editors

Robert Wrembel works as an assistant professor at the Poznań University of Technology, Poland. In 2001 he received a PhD in computer science (databases). In 1996-2006 he took part in four research projects on databases and four industrial projects in the field of information technologies. He has paid a number of visits to research and education centers, including the INRIA Paris-Rocquencourt (France), the Paris Dauphine University (France), the Klagenfurt University (Austria), and the Loyola University (USA). His research interests encompass mainly data warehouse technologies (temporal, multiversion, object-relational) and object-oriented systems (views, data access optimization). Robert Wrembel works also as a lecturer at Oracle Poland.

Christian Koncilia works as data warehouse consultant at Panoratio Database Images, Inc. in Munich, Germany. Prior to this position, he was lecturer at the Department of Informatics-Systems at the University of Klagenfurt, Austria. He holds a master's degree in information science, as well as a doctorate in applied computer science from the University of Klagenfurt. During his MS studies he worked as project manager for a large Carinthian company with more than 7,000 employees. Among other duties, he was responsible for the introduction of an OLAP system. His research interests include temporal databases, data warehousing, multidimensional databases, and data mining. He published several papers in international conference proceedings.

Copyright © 2007, Idea Group Inc. Copying or distributing in print or electronic forms without written permission of Idea Group Inc. is prohibited.

About the Authors

Jovanka Adzic received the political science degree in 1986 (University of Belgrade), then she received the computer science degree in 1996 (University of Turin) and a master's degree in the telecommunication field in 1998 (Politecnico of Turin). She joined TILAB in 1996 where she was involved in projects focused on evaluating database technologies (particularly OODBMS) for telecommunication needs, data analysis, and data warehouses solutions for traffic and customer data (fixed and mobile network). She has been involved as a technical expert and later as a project leader of the very innovative solution for the Fraud Detection & Analysis for mobile operator.

Yvan Bédard has been professor of GIS and spatial databases at Laval University Department of Geomatics Sciences, Canada since 1986. He was director of the Centre for Research in Geomatics for 7 years and is involved in the GEOIDE Network of Centers of Excellence. Dr. Bédard has participated to major projects with government agencies and private industries in Canada and abroad and has presented about 350 papers and conferences worldwide. Actually, Dr. Bédard is chair holder of the industrial research chair in geospatial database for decision support funded by National Science and Engineering Research Council of Canada.

Ameur Boujenoui holds bachelor's and master's degrees in engineering (applied mathematics) from INSEA (Morocco) and a PhD in management from HEC Montreal (Canada). He has more than 30 years experience in management and consulting. He is currently a teaching associate at the University of Ottawa. His research interests include business strategy and policy, corporate governance, and change management.

Copyright © 2007, Idea Group Inc. Copying or distributing in print or electronic forms without written permission of Idea Group Inc. is prohibited.

Carlo Combi received the master's degree in EE by the Politecnico of Milan. In 1993 he received the PhD in biomedical engineering. In 1994 and 1995 he was postdoctoral fellow at the Department of Biomedical Engineering of the Politecnico of Milan. From 1987 to 1996 he worked within the research group in medical informatics at the Politecnico of Milan. From April 1996 to October 2001, Carlo Combi was with the Department of Mathematics and Computer Science of the University of Udine as assistant professor. Since November 2001, he has been with the Department of Computer Science of the University of Verona: from November 2001 to February 2005, he was associate professor of computer science; since March 2005, he has been professor of computer science.

Karen C. Davis (karen.davis@uc.edu) is an associate professor of electrical and computer engineering and computer science at the University of Cincinnati, USA. She received an MS and a PhD in computer science from the University of Louisiana, Lafayette in 1987 and 1990, respectively. Her research interests include database design, query processing and optimization, and data warehousing. Dr. Davis has advised more than 20 graduate students and supervised more than 40 undergraduate senior design project students. She has been recognized for outstanding classroom instruction and curriculum innovation with five teaching awards. She is a senior member of IEEE and an ABET computer engineering program evaluator. She has served on program committees including DOLAP, DAWAK, ER, ICDE, and CIKM.

Valter Fiore joined TILAB in 1976. From the beginning of his work in TILAB, his research interest covered several aspects: software environments for advanced languages for telecommunications needs, operating systems, database technology, and architecture. Since 1996, he has been interested in ETL and data warehouse server-side problems with particular attention to the population aspects related to transformation and loading vast amounts of data into data warehouses. He has been technical leader in ideation and development of the infrastructure based ETL.

Pedro Furtado is an assistant professor of computer sciences at the University of Coimbra, Portugal where he teaches both undergraduate and postgraduate curricula, mostly in data management related areas. He is also an active researcher in the databases group of the CISUC research laboratory. His research interests include data warehousing, approximate query answering, parallel and distributed database systems, with a focus on performance and scalability and data management in distributed data intensive systems. He received a PhD in computer science from the University of Coimbra-Portugal in 2000.

Copyright © 2007, Idea Group Inc. Copying or distributing in print or electronic forms without written permission of Idea Group Inc. is prohibited.

Ashima Gupta obtained a BS in computer science in 1998 from Fergusson College, University of Pune, Pune, India. She earned an MS in computer science in 2002 from the University of Cincinnati. She worked for three years as a systems analyst in the Pediatric Informatics Department at Cincinnati Children's Hospital Research Foundation where she researched and implemented computational methods and applications to facilitate genome research (http://cismols.cchmc.org). Currently, she is based in Chicago and working with a nonprofit children's aid organization in an effort to provide basic rights of survival to underprivileged children.

Claudio Gutierrez is an associate professor at the Department of Computer Science, Universidad de Chile, Chile. He received his PhD from Wesleyan University in 1999. His research interests lie in the intersection of logic, databases and semantic Web. Currently he is associate researcher at the Center for Web Research where he works on semantic Web databases.

Carlos A. Hurtado is an assistant professor at the Department of Computer Science, Universidad de Chile, Chile. He received his PhD in computer science from the University of Toronto in 2002. His research areas include databases, semantic Web, data mining, OLAP, and data warehousing. Currently he is a researcher at the Center for Web Research and a visitor researcher at the School of Computer Science and Information Systems, Birkbeck College, University of London.

Ganaël Jatteau holds a bachelor's of engineering degree from ENSSAT (*École Nationale Supérieure de Sciences Appliquées et de Technologie*) and a master's in computer science from UQO. His research interests include data mining and association rule mining using concept lattices. He is currently working for PCI Geomatics (Gatineau, Canada).

Nikos Karayannidis received his degree in electrical and computer engineering in 1997 from the National Technical University of Athens. In 2003 he received the PhD from the same university. His thesis focused on the issues of physical organization and indexing of multidimensional data with hierarchies, as well as the processing of OLAP and data warehousing queries. Through his participation in several data warehousing and OLAP projects, Dr. Karayannidis has gained a useful experience in the field. He is currently working as the project manager and lead data modeler for the Data Warehouse implementation project for the Hellenic Telecommunications Organization (OTE S.A.). His research interests include indexing/storage structures for DW/OLAP systems, query processing for DW/OLAP systems, and processing of ETL procedures.

Copyright © 2007, Idea Group Inc. Copying or distributing in print or electronic forms without written permission of Idea Group Inc. is prohibited.

Rokia Missaoui has been a full professor in the Department of Computer Science and Engineering at UQO (Université du Québec en Outaouais) since August 2002. Before joining UQO, she was a professor at UQAM (Université du Québec à Montréal) between 1987 and 2002. She obtained her bachelor's (1971) and her master's in engineering (1978) in applied mathematics from INSEA (Morocco), and her PhD (1988) in computer science from Université de Montréal. Her research interests include knowledge discovery from databases, formal concept analysis, integration of data mining and data warehousing technologies, as well as content-based image retrieval and mining.

Tadeusz Morzy received his MSc, PhD, and Polish habilitation from the Technical University of Poznań, Poland. Currently, he is professor of computer science at the Institute of Computing Science of the Technical University of Poznań. He has held visiting positions at the Loyola University, New Orleans in the U.S., Klagenfurt University in Austria, University La Sapienza in Italy, Free University Amsterdam, and the Polish-Japanese Institute of Information Technology, Warsaw, Poland. He has authored and coauthored over 100 papers on databases, data mining, and data warehousing. He is a coauthor of the book *Concurrency Control in Distributed Database Systems* by North-Holland, and an editor and coauthor of *Handbook on Data Management* by Springer. He served as the general chair of the 2nd ADBIS Conference (1998), and has been a member of numerous program committees of international conferences and workshops. His research interests include data mining, data warehousing, transaction processing in database and data warehouse systems, access methods and query processing for databases, database optimization and performance evaluation.

Sami Naouali holds a PhD in computer science from Université de Nantes, and a master's degree in CS from Institut National Polytechnique (Grenoble, France). He was a postdoctoral fellow at UQO in 2005. His current research covers data warehousing and the integration of knowledge into data cubes.

Barbara Oliboni received the master's degree in computer science from the University of Verona with the thesis "Representing Semistructured Data by Means of WG-Log: Querying Lorel Data Sources." In 2003 she received the PhD in computer engineering from the Politecnico of Milan with the dissertation "Blind Queries and Constraints: Representing Flexibility and Time in Semistructured Data." Since 2004, she has been a postdoctoral fellow at the Department of Computer Science of the University of Verona.

Copyright © 2007, Idea Group Inc. Copying or distributing in print or electronic forms without written permission of Idea Group Inc. is prohibited.

Marie-Josée Proulx holds an MSc in geomatics sciences from Laval University, Canada. She actually works at the Centre for Research in Geomatics of Laval University as a research professional within the GIS and spatial databases team. She participates in the industrial research chair in geospatial databases for decision support. Her professional interests include spatial databases modeling, multidimensional modeling, spatial data warehouse, SOLAP, and metadata management.

Sonia Rivest holds a MSc in geomatics sciences from Laval University, Canada. She actually works at the Centre for Research in Geomatics of Laval University as a research professional with the GIS and spatial databases team. She is part of the industrial research chair in geospatial databases for decision support. Mrs. Rivest works in multidimensional databases, spatial data warehouses, and SOLAP.

Stefano Rizzi received his PhD in 1996 from the University of Bologna, Italy. Since 2005 he has been full professor at the University of Bologna, where he is the head of the Data Warehousing Laboratory. He has published about 60 papers in refereed journals and international conferences mainly in the fields of data warehousing, pattern recognition, and mobile robotics. He joined several research projects on the above areas and has been involved in the PANDA thematic network of the European Union concerning pattern-base management systems. His current research interests include all the aspects related to data warehouse design and business intelligence, in particular multidimensional modeling, data warehouse evolution, and what-if analysis.

Uwe Röhm obtained his master's degree in computer science from the University of Passau, Germany, in 1996. He received his PhD from ETH Zurich, Switzerland, in 2002 for his work on "Online Analytical Processing with a Cluster of Databases." This work was part of the PowerDB project at ETH Zurich that investigated large database clusters and that was partly sponsored by Microsoft. Uwe Röhm currently holds a position as lecturer in database systems at the School of Information Technologies at the University of Sydney, Australia. He has research interests in database clusters, freshness-aware caching, and database support for bioinformatics.

Timos Sellis received his degree in electrical engineering in 1982 from the National Technical University of Athens (NTUA), Greece. In 1983 he received the MSc from Harvard University and in 1986 the PhD from the University of California at Berkeley. In 1986, Professor Sellis joined the Department of Computer Science of the University of Maryland, College Park, and in 1992 the Computer Science Division of NTUA, where he is currently a full professor. His research interests include peer-to-peer database systems, data warehouses, the integration of Web and data-

Copyright © 2007, Idea Group Inc. Copying or distributing in print or electronic forms without written permission of Idea Group Inc. is prohibited.

bases, and spatial database systems. He has published over 120 articles in journals and conferences and has been an invited speaker in major international events.

Alkis Simitsis is a visiting lecturer at the University of Peloponnese. He received his PhD from the National Technical University of Athens (NTUA) in 2004. His research interests include extraction-transformation-loading (ETL) processes in data warehouses, query processing/optimization, and security issues. He has published more than 20 papers in refereed journals and international conferences in the above areas.

Luisella Sisto received the computer science degree in 1981 (University of Turin). She joined TILAB in 1982, where she was initially involved in projects in the artificial intelligence area, focusing on natural language understanding and expert systems for troubleshooting. Then she was involved in projects concerning use of constraints satisfaction techniques for workforce management, monitoring of telecommunication systems, services leveraging data analysis and data warehouse solutions, and identity management.

Spiros Skiadopoulos is an assistant professor at the University of Peloponnese, Greece. He received his diploma and PhD from the National Technical University of Athens and his MSc from UMIST. His research interests include spatial and temporal databases, constraint databases, query evaluation, and optimization and data warehouses. He has published more than 25 papers in international refereed journals and conferences.

Kurt Stockinger is a computer scientist with the Scientific Data Management Research Group of Berkeley Lab, Berkeley, California. His research interests include database access optimization, multidimensional indexing for large-scale data warehouses and performance optimization of parallel and distributed systems (data grids). Previously, Kurt was leading the Optimization Task of the European DataGrid Project managed by CERN. He was also a visiting researcher at the California Institute of Technology where he worked on object-oriented databases for high energy physics applications. Kurt studied computer science and business administration at the University of Vienna, Austria, and the Royal Holloway College, University of London, England. He received a PhD in computer science and business administration from the University of Vienna, Austria, under supervision of CERN's Database Group.

Aris Tsois received a diploma in electrical and computer engineering from the National Technical University of Athens (NTUA), Greece, in 1995 and a PhD in

Copyright © 2007, Idea Group Inc. Copying or distributing in print or electronic forms without written permission of Idea Group Inc. is prohibited.

computer science from the same university in 2005. In September 2005 he started working at the Joint Research Center in Italy on data warehousing and data mining projects. His research interests include on-line analytical processing technology, data warehouses, query optimization, and artificial intelligence. Dr. Tsois has worked in different projects related to data warehousing and OLAP and has published several articles in refereed international conferences and workshops.

Alejandro Vaisman was born in Buenos Aires, Argentina. He received a BA in civil engineering, a BA in computer science, and a PhD in computer science from the University of Buenos Aires. He has been a professor at the University of Buenos Aires since 1994. He was an invited professor at the Universidad Politecnica de Madrid in 1997. In 2001 he was appointed vice-dean of the School of Engineering and Information Technology at the University of Belgrano, in Argentina. He was a visiting researcher at the University of Toronto, University of Hasselt, and Universidad de Chile. His research interests are in the field of databases, particularly in OLAP, data warehousing, data mining, P2P databases, XML, and the semantic Web. He is currently with the University of Buenos Aires, lecturing several courses on database systems topics. In 2004 he was appointed vice-head of the Department of Computer Science, and chair of the graduate program in data mining.

Panos Vassiliadis is a lecturer at the University of Ioannina. He received his PhD from the National Technical University of Athens in 2000. His research interests include data warehousing, Web services, and database design and modeling. He has published more than 25 papers in refereed journals and international conferences in the above areas.

Kesheng Wu is a staff computer scientist with the Scientific Data Management Research Group of Berkeley Lab, Berkeley, California. His recent research interests focus on indexing large high-dimensional datasets and managing of distributed data warehouses. He is one of the principal contributors to the FastBit project which is developing a set of efficient bitmap indices and applying them to different applications. Previously, he had worked on a number of parallel computing projects and industrial software engineer projects. He received his PhD in computer science from the University of Minnesota in 1997.

Copyright © 2007, Idea Group Inc. Copying or distributing in print or electronic forms without written permission of Idea Group Inc. is prohibited.

Index

Copyright © 2007, Idea Group Inc. Copying or distributing in print or electronic forms without written permission of Idea Group Inc. is prohibited.

Copyright © 2007, Idea Group Inc. Copying or distributing in print or electronic forms without written permission
of Idea Group Inc. is prohibited.

Copyright © 2007, Idea Group Inc. Copying or distributing in print or electronic forms without written permission of
Idea Group Inc. is prohibited.

Copyright © 2007, Idea Group Inc. Copying or distributing in print or electronic forms without written permission of Idea Group Inc. is prohibited.

Copyright © 2007, Idea Group Inc. Copying or distributing in print or electronic forms without written permission of Idea Group Inc. is prohibited.